ANNUAL EDITIONS

Education

05/06

Thirty-Second Edition

EDITOR

Fred Schultz

University of Akron (Retired)

Fred Schultz, former professor of education at the University of Akron, attended Indiana University to earn a B.S. in social science education in 1962, an M.S. in the history and philosophy of education in 1966, and a Ph.D. in the history and philosophy of education and American studies in 1969. His B.A. in Spanish was conferred from the University of Akron in May 1985. He is actively involved in researching the development and history of American education with a primary focus on the history of ideas and social philosophy of education. He also likes to study languages.

McGraw-Hill/Dushkin

2460 Kerper Blvd., Dubuque, IA 52001

Visit us on the Internet
http://www.dushkin.com

Credits

1. **How Others See Us and How We See Ourselves**
   Unit photo—© Getty Images/Photodisc Collection.
2. **Rethinking and Changing the Educative Effort**
   Unit photo—© by PhotoDisc, Inc.
3. **Striving for Excellence: The Drive for Quality**
   Unit photo—© Getty Images/SW Productions.
4. **Morality and Values in Education**
   Unit photo—© Getty Images/Photodisc Collection.
5. **Managing Life in Classrooms**
   Unit photo—© CORBIS/Royalty-Free.
6. **Cultural Diversity and Schooling**
   Unit photo—© by PhotoDisc, Inc.
7. **Serving Special Needs and Concerns**
   Unit photo—© CORBIS/Royalty-Free.
8. **The Profession of Teaching Today**
   Unit photo—© by PhotoDisc, Inc.
9. **For Vision and Hope: Alternative Visions of Reality**
   Unit photo—© Getty Images/Ryan McVay.

Copyright

Cataloging in Publication Data
Main entry under title: Annual Editions: Education. 2005/2006.
1. Education—Periodicals. I. Schultz, Fred, *comp.* II. Title: Education.
ISBN 0–07–310220–2   658'.05   ISSN 0272–5010

© 2005 by McGraw-Hill/Dushkin, Dubuque, IA 52001, A Division of The McGraw-Hill Companies.

Copyright law prohibits the reproduction, storage, or transmission in any form by any means of any portion of this publication without the express written permission of McGraw-Hill/Dushkin, and of the copyright holder (if different) of the part of the publication to be reproduced. The Guidelines for Classroom Copying endorsed by Congress explicitly state that unauthorized copying may not be used to create, to replace, or to substitute for anthologies, compilations, or collective works. Inquiries concerning publishing rights to the articles herein can be directed to the Permission Department at Dushkin Publishing. 800.243.6532

Annual Editions® is a Registered Trademark of McGraw-Hill/Dushkin, A Division of The McGraw-Hill Companies.

Thirty-second Edition

Cover image © Photos.com and Mel Curtis/Getty Images
Printed in the United States of America   1234567890QPDQPD987654   Printed on Recycled Paper

Editors/Advisory Board

Members of the Advisory Board are instrumental in the final selection of articles for each edition of ANNUAL EDITIONS. Their review of articles for content, level, currentness, and appropriateness provides critical direction to the editor and staff. We think that you will find their careful consideration well reflected in this volume.

EDITOR

Fred Schultz
University of Akron (Retired)

ADVISORY BOARD

Timothy J. Bergen
University of South Carolina

Kenneth Bower
College of Charleston

Lynn M. Burlbaw
Texas A & M University

Robert C. Cienkus
Loyola University - Water Tower Campus

Anthony A. DeFalco
Long Island University

Lloyd Duck
George Mason University

Jennifer J. Endicott
University of Central Oklahoma

Stephanie Evans
California State University, Los Angeles

Robert E. Gates
Bloomsburg University of Pennsylvania

J. Merrell Hansen
Brigham Young University

Harvey R. Jahn
Radford University

Lawrence D. Klein
Central Connecticut State University

Douglas R. Knox
New Mexico Highlands University

Anne Meis Knupfer
Purdue University

Staff

EDITORIAL STAFF

Larry Loeppke, Managing Editor
Susan Brusch, Senior Developmental Editor
Jay Oberbroeckling, Developmental Editor
Lenny J. Behnke, Permissions Coordinator
Lori Church, Permissions Coordinator
Shirley Lanners, Permissions Coordinator
Bonnie Coakley, Editorial Assistant

TECHNOLOGY STAFF

Luke David, eContent Coordinator

PRODUCTION STAFF

Beth Kundert, Production Manager
Trish Mish, Production Assistant
Jade Benedict, Production Assistant
Kari Voss, Lead Typesetter
Jean Smith, Typesetter
Karen Spring, Typesetter
Sandy Wille, Typesetter
Tara McDermott, Designer

Preface

In publishing ANNUAL EDITIONS we recognize the enormous role played by the magazines, newspapers, and journals of the public press in providing current, first-rate educational information in a broad spectrum of interest areas. Many of these articles are appropriate for students, researchers, and professionals seeking accurate, current material to help bridge the gap between principles and theories and the real world. These articles, however, become more useful for study when those of lasting value are carefully collected, organized, and reproduced in a low-cost format, which provides easy and permanent access when the material is needed. That is the role played by ANNUAL EDITIONS.

We face a situation with reference to our educational policy priorities not unfamiliar in our history as a nation, divided and not easily resolved, the options which are open to us. On the one hand, we are to have "highly qualified teachers"; on the other hand, we leave it to state politicians and the local school authority as to what constitutes "highly qualified teachers." This is a typical enigmatic dilemma in the history of American education, and one we will soon regret. If we are not to leave any student behind, really and sincerely, can we come to grips with what it means to have a "highly qualified teacher?" We really need to deal with this. As has been the case throughout the history of American education, the politicians will decide what we will do with this situation. This is fine. We will deal with it as a profession, knowing full well that this is about as much as we can do.

Issues regarding the purposes of education as well as the appropriate methods of educating have been debated throughout all generations of literate human culture. This is because the meaning of the word "educated" shifts within ideological realms of thought and cultural belief systems. There will always be debates over the purposes and the ends of "education" as it is understood in any time or place. This is because each generation must continuously reconstruct the definition of "education" based upon its understanding of "justice," "fairness," and "equity" in human relations, and each generation must locate and position their understanding of social and personal reality.

In the twenty-first century, educators are presented with many new challenges caused by many forces at work in human society. We must decide really what knowledge is of most worth and what basic skills and information each child, of whatever heritage, needs to know. We must face this question once and for all. It is no longer a choice; it is a duty if we are disciplined persons interested in the well being of our children and adolescents. We have before us a great qualitative challenge, our response to which will determine the fate of future generations of our society.

The technological breakthroughs now developing in the information sciences will have an amazing impact on how people learn. The rates of change in how we learn and how we obtain information is already increasing at a very rapid pace that will assuredly continue.

The public conversation on the purposes and future directions of education is as lively as ever. Alternative visions and voices regarding the broad social aims of schools and the preparation of teachers continue to be presented. *Annual Editions: Education 05/06* attempts to reflect current mainstream as well as alternative visions as to what education ought to be. Equity issues regarding what constitutes equal treatment of students in the schools continue to be addressed. This year's edition contains articles on gender issues in the field and on the application of research in multicultural education to the areas of teacher preparation and the staff development of teachers already in the schools. The debate over whether all public monies for education should go to the public schools or whether these funds should follow the student into either public or private schools has again intensified.

Communities are deeply interested in local school politics and school funding issues. There continues to be healthy dialogue about and competition for the support of the various "publics" involved in public schooling. The articles reflect spirited critique of our public schools. There are competing and differing school reform agendas being discussed. All of this occurs as the United States continues to experience fundamentally important demographic shifts in its cultural makeup.

Compromise continues to be the order of the day. The many interest groups within the educational field reflect a broad spectrum of viewpoints ranging from various behaviorist and cognitive developmental perspectives to humanistic, postmodernist, and critical theoretical ones.

In assembling this volume, we make every effort to stay in touch with movements in educational studies and with the social forces at work in schools. Members of the advisory board contribute valuable insights, as do the production and editorial staffs at the publisher—McGraw-Hill/Dushkin—to coordinate our efforts. Through this process we collect a wide range of articles on a variety of topics relevant to education in North America.

The readings in *Annual Editions: Education 05/06* explore the social and academic goals of education, the current conditions of the nation's educational systems, the teaching profession, and the future of American education. In addition, these selections address the issues of change and the moral and ethical foundations of schooling. As always, we would like you to help us improve this volume. Please rate the material in this edition on the postage-paid *article rating form* provided at the back of this book. We care about what you think. Give us the public feedback that we need.

Fred Schultz Editor
Editor

Contents

Preface iv
Topic Guide xiv
Selected World Wide Web Sites xvii

UNIT 1
How Others See Us and How We See Ourselves

Unit Overview xx

1. **Public Schools; Public Will,** Arnold F. Fege, *The American School Board Journal,* May 2004
   The author raises the question as to whether the public is willing to support fair allocation of financial resources within the American public schools. He raises concerns that the schools are under constant pressure to privatize and that equitable distribution of available funds to all sectors of the public school system is in jeopardy. He proposes seven things the American public can do about this to improve the performance of public schools. 3

2. **Game Theory, Teen-Style,** Jason Meyers, *American Demographics,* May 2004
   The author synthesizes some of the changing demographics in how American teenagers are allocating their resources for electronic games and other telephonic online devices. 6

3. **Coming of Age in Consumerdom,** David G. Kennedy, *American Demographics,* April 2004
   The author summarizes the demographics of how "tweens," young Americans between the ages of 8 and 14 years, spend the estimated 38 billion dollars a year that is made available to them. 7

4. **Generational Pull,** William H. Frey, *American Demographics,* May 2004
   The author says that generations move in different directions. He looks at current career oriented "Gen-Xers" and their preferences in where they live, the places they prefer as well as the sorts of places they are going to and those sorts of places they tend to be leaving. Their demographic preferences are interesting. 9

5. **When I Was Young,** John Fetto, *American Demographics,* April 2003
   The author reports on extraordinarily important challenges reflecting **changes in American population statistics** between 1950 and the present. The author notes that more Americans are going to school and staying in school longer. The **demographic information** in this report is very informative regarding the current social contexts of American education. 11

The concepts in bold italics are developed in the article. For further expansion, please refer to the Topic Guide.

v

6. **Is America Raising Unhealthy Kids?,** Denise Willi, *Scholastic Instructor,* March 2003

    Current **health issues** affecting millions of American children and adolescents are reported in this article. There is valuable data reported on unhealthy dietary practices which are affecting the overall well-being of children in the United States. Other important health issues are also addressed. 13

7. **The 36th Annual Phi Delta Kappa/Gallup Poll of the Public Attitudes Toward the Public Schools,** Lowell C. Rose and Alec M. Gallup, *Phi Delta Kappan,* September 2004

    This annual poll of the public's attitude toward the public school system continues to be a very valuable source of information regarding the current state of publicly supported education. 17

UNIT 2
Rethinking and Changing the Educative Effort

Unit Overview 28

8. **No Child Left Behind: The Mathematics of Guaranteed Failure,** Lowell C. Rose, *Educational Horizons,* Winter 2004

    The author provides a critique of the possibilities of the federal No Child Left Behind legislation of 2002. The concepts underlying the rationale for the legislation are critically examined. The author argues that without important changes in this legislation it will fail to achieve its intended goals. 31

9. **Test Today, Privatize Tomorrow: Using Accountability to 'Reform' Public Schools to Death,** Alfie Kohn, *Phi Delta Kappan,* April 2004

    The author challenges the motivation of advocates of the No Child Left Behind (NCLB) legislation passed by Congress in 2002. He critiques current rhetoric regarding school reform. He examines motivation for attempts at the privatization of public schools and conservative rhetoric about "choice" and "freedom from public schools." 36

10. **Leadership That Sparks Learning,** J. Timothy Waters, Robert J. Marzano, and Brian McNulty, *Educational Leadership,* April 2004

    The authors raise the issue of whether, and if so how, school leaders (principals) make contributions to improving achievement of students in schools. They identify what their research shows regarding how improving the effectiveness of school leadership can lead to gains in student achievement. 44

11. **Meeting Challenges in Urban Schools,** Larry Cuban, *Educational Leadership,* April 2004

    The author argues that the situations of middle class or affluent school systems are very different from those of economically deprived school systems in urban areas, a fact that has been known for decades. He argues for high expectations for student achievement and challenging curricula in urban schools. He calls for moral leadership on the part of administrators and teachers in urban schools. 47

The concepts in bold italics are developed in the article. For further expansion, please refer to the Topic Guide.

12. **Transforming High Schools,** Pedro A. Noguera, *Educational Leadership,* May 2004

    The author explores possible reasons for the success or failure of efforts to improve student achievement in ten selected Massachusetts high schools. The reasons why the same structured reform efforts to be implemented in different schools resulted in higher student performance in some of these schools and no improvement in others are examined. The author did a comparative performance study of selected Boston high schools. 51

13. **Reinventing America's Schools,** Tony Wagner, *Phi Delta Kappan,* May 2003

    The author presents a very convincing case for responsible **reconception of how schooling should be perceived.** In doing this, he touches on the reality of life in classrooms, and he sends a message that all American public school administrators should be willing to hear. 55

UNIT 3
Striving for Excellence: The Drive for Quality

Unit Overview 58

14. **A Balanced School Accountability Model: An Alternative to High-Stakes Testing,** Ken Jones, *Phi Delta Kappan,* April 2004

    How to create alternative concepts of "accountability" in schooling is the topical focus of this essay. The author attempts to define and describe more balanced and comprehensive conceptions of accountability in schooling. He is attempting to create a new model of teaching and learning in schools. 61

15. **Turning Accountability on Its Head: Supporting Inspired Teaching in Today's Classrooms,** Kristin L. Droege, *Phi Delta Kappan,* April 2004

    The author argues that inspired teaching is essential to any model of "accountability" in schools and will thus result in improvements in student performance across the board. Not only test scores are important; educators must help students to achieve such broader goals as developing perserverance, cooperation, patience, and creativity, among others. 67

16. **Accountability with a Kicker: Observations on the Florida A+ Accountability Plan,** Dan Goldhaber and Jane Hannaway, *Phi Delta Kappan,* April 2004

    The authors review the state of Florida's school accountability program which provides students who meet state criteria to obtain educational vouchers for use in either public or private state qualified schools. Florida gives grades to schools based on their students' state mandated competency test scores. 69

The concepts in bold italics are developed in the article. For further expansion, please refer to the Topic Guide.

17. **No Flower Shall Wither; or, Horticulture in the Kingdom of the Frogs,** Gary K. Clabaugh, *Educational Horizons,* Winter 2004

The author provides a very creative metaphorical and satirical tale of "educational reform" and politically driven accountability in the mythical "King of the Frogs." This is good and interesting reading for all of those who follow the development to improve school accountability through high stakes competitive measures. 76

18. **The Power of Testing,** Matthew Gandal and Laura McGiffert, *Educational Leadership,* February 2003

The authors review currently developing challenges educators are facing as a result of state government mandated competency tests and the testing requirements of the federal No Child Left Behind act. The authors argue that standards of measurement must be clear in developing tests to measure levels of student achievement. 78

19. **Why Students Think They Understand—When They Don't,** Daniel T. Willingham, *American Educator,* Winter 2003/2004

The author discusses the possible contributions to students' academic development which cognitive science has to offer. Viewing how we learn and the ways in which we can know and problem solve is something cognitive scientists have to offer. 81

20. **The Homework Wars,** David Skinner, *Current,* February 2004

The author reviews the heated debate developing over increases in the amount of homework assignments being given to students. They cite the points of view of scholars who oppose the social impact of "homework" as well as noting the view of some of the supporters of homework who believe that it is academically beneficial to students. 86

21. **Studying Education: Classroom Research and Cargo Cults,** E.D. Hirsch Jr., *Policy Review,* October/November 2002

The author describes so-called "classroom research" in favor of more traditional methods of classroom research. He argues that it is difficult and undependable (unreliant) research. This is due to the many uncontrollable variables in classroom research. He argues as to how we learn. He offers a powerful critique to current standards of educational research. 91

UNIT 4
Morality and Values in Education

Unit Overview 100

22. **Practicing Democracy in High School,** Sheldon H. Berman, *Educational Leadership,* September 2003

The author describes a program whereby students learn what it means to become a just person working with others to construct a just society. Democratic values are placed in action by students and faculty at this high school. Students learn how to practice democratic values in school and in their community. 103

The concepts in bold italics are developed in the article. For further expansion, please refer to the Topic Guide.

viii

23. **Values: The Implicit Curriculum,** Linda Inlay, *Educational Leadership,* March 2003

The author attempts to determine how educators can help students to develop *personal and social responsibility* values such as mutual trust as well as how to foster *character education* in schools. 107

24. **The Missing Virtue: Lessons From Dodge Ball & Aristotle,** Gordon Marino, *Commonweal,* April 25, 2003

The author addresses the reality of several shifts in human values in recent years and the question of *which values should be taught,* if possible, *in schools.* He reminds us of Aristotle's admonition that we acquire *virtue* by practicing virtuous actions and developing a moral balance in our lives. He inquires as to how do we teach *courageous moral commitment.* 110

UNIT 5
Managing Life in Classrooms

Unit Overview 112

25. **Heading Off Disruptive Behavior,** Hill M. Walker, Elizabeth Ramsey, and Frank M. Gresham, *American Educator,* Winter 2003/2004

The authors discuss how teachers can either constructively deal with or, ideally, prevent anti-social behavior in students. How teachers can respond responsibly to prevent anti-social, disruptive behavior on the part of students is the major focus of this article. 115

26. **How Disruptive Students Escalate Hostility and Disorder—and How Teachers Can Avoid It,** Hill M. Walker, Elizabeth Ramsey, and Frank M. Gresham, *American Educator,* Winter 2003/2004

The authors present means by which teachers can avoid the escalation of hostility and disorder which can be caused by disruptive students. Their suggestions are clear and well considered. They describe the characteristics of "anti-social," "oppositional" students, and they suggest strategies teachers can use to deal with such students. 126

27. **Good Behavior Needs to Be Taught: How a Social Skills Curriculum Works,** Hill M. Walker, Elizabeth Ramsey, and Frank M. Gresham, *American Educator,* Winter 2003/2004

The authors provide suggestions as to how teachers can teach students skills in good behavior. They briefly describe a specific "second step" program that enables teachers to intervene constructively with students to teach them how to avoid conflict and disruption while they are taught principles of "good" behavior. 132

28. **True Blue,** M. Christine Mattise, *Teaching Tolerance,* Spring 2004

The author describes an "anti-bullying" program which she developed to help students feel safe in school and on school grounds. The program is creative; it involves teaching children what they can do when they are confronted by "bullying" behavior at school. It seems very workable. 134

The concepts in bold italics are developed in the article. For further expansion, please refer to the Topic Guide.

29. **A Profile of Bullying,** Dan Olweus, *Educational Leadership,* March 2003

Myths and realities concerning bullying behavior in schools are addressed here, with behavior patterns of both *victims* and *bullies* addressed. The Norwegian national program for *training teachers* to teach students how to manage bullying behavior in schools is described briefly. 136

UNIT 6
Cultural Diversity and Schooling

Unit Overview 142

30. **An Unfinished Journey: The Legacy of *Brown* and the Narrowing Of the Achievement Gap,** Ronald F. Ferguson and Jal Mehta, *Phi Delta Kappan,* May 2004

The authors provide a review of the historical significance of the decision from the Supreme Court of the United States on May 17, 1954, in the case of Brown v. Board of Education. They take the opportunity of the 50th anniversary of this Supreme Court decision to describe the history of the effort to desegregate American schools. They also describe the efforts since 1954 to put into practice the principles on which the Brown decision was based. 145

31. **Against the Tide: Desegregated High Schools and Their 1980 Graduates,** Amy Stuart Wells, Jennifer Jellison Holme, Anita Tijerina Revilla, and Awo Korantemaa Atanda, *Phi Delta Kappan,* May 2004

The authors celebrate the 50th anniversary of Brown v. Board of Education by reviewing efforts at the desegregation of American schools since 1980. They studied the graduates of six high schools and reviewed the problems of school desegregation efforts in the United States. 156

32. **Minding the Gap,** Jennifer L. Hochschild, *Harvard Magazine,* March/April 2004

The author addresses the problem of the academic achievement gaps among culturally diverse groups of students in American schools. This is a review of a book exploring reasons for what appear to be differences in learning achievement among students from cultural minority groups. 164

33. **Civic Education in Schools: The Right Time is Now,** Joyce Baldwin, *Carnegie Reporter,* Fall 2003

The author describes efforts to develop civic skills in students in schools across the United States. This is a really excellent effort to describe current efforts to conduct civic education in the United States. This article involves two case studies of innovative civic education efforts in two high schools, and it also puts a national focus on the topic. 167

The concepts in bold italics are developed in the article. For further expansion, please refer to the Topic Guide.

UNIT 7
Serving Special Needs and Concerns

Unit Overview 174

34. **Partnering with Families and Communities,** Joyce L. Epstein and Karen Clark Salinas, *Educational Leadership,* May 2004

    The authors describe efforts to create school learning communities where educators involve the families of students and community leaders in the planning and conduct of schools to create closer social and academic links in the life of school-community relations. They describe the work of the National Network of Partnership Schools at Johns Hopkins University. 177

35. **Popular Culture in the Classroom,** Dale Allender, *English Journal,* January 2004

    The author argues that popular culture has both affective and academic value. He describes how he integrates works in popular culture into the standard language arts curriculum at the high school level. He also gives his reasons why he believes this to be important. 182

36. **Living and Teaching on the Edge of a Pop Culture World,** Robert Gardner, *English Journal,* January 2004

    The author describes how it feels for a teacher to live "on the edge" of popular culture in the high school classroom. The author is not familiar with popular culture, but he does describe how his students introduce it in class as they attempt to relate to traditional literature in the curriculum. 184

37. **At the Crossroads of Expertise: The Risky Business of Teaching Popular Culture,** Meg Callahan and Bronwen E. Low, *English Journal,* January 2004

    The authors present an interesting argument as to how teachers can tap into students' expertise regarding current popular cultural phenomena in teaching mainstream language arts curricula at the secondary school level. They provide examples as to how this can be done. 186

38. **Healthier Students, Better Learners,** Beth Pateman, *Educational Leadership,* December 2003/January 2004

    The author addresses the links between student health and academic performance. She cites the efforts of the Council of Chief State School Officers and the Association of State and Territorial Health Officials to encourage development of state of the art education programs in the schools. She describes the Health Education Assessment Project. 191

39. **The Arithmetic Gap,** Tom Loveless and John Coughlan, *Educational Leadership,* February 2004

    The authors discuss somewhat comparatively the achievement gap in mathematical skills performance between American students and students from other countries. They compare American students' mathematics performance across recent decades based on the National Assessment of Educational Progress (NAEP). 195

The concepts in bold italics are developed in the article. For further expansion, please refer to the Topic Guide.

UNIT 8
The Profession of Teaching Today

Unit Overview 198

40. **The Search for Highly Qualified Teachers,** Barnett Berry, Mandy Hoke, and Eric Hirsch, *Phi Delta Kappan,* May 2004
The author synthesizes the current debate regarding how best to develop highly qualified teachers. They discuss how this debate relates to the federal No Child Left Behind (NCLB) legislation and the views of various advocacy groups on this issue. Specific policy recommendations for improving the quality of teachers are offered. 201

41. **The Other Side of Highly Qualified Teachers,** Wade A. Carpenter, *Educational Horizons,* Winter 2004
The author addresses the concerns over what it means to be "highly qualified" as a teacher. He points to developments under way in several states to create alternative certification programs as well as to the influence of state politicians in influencing the debate on what it means to be a "highly qualified teacher." 206

42. **The Marriage of Liberal Arts Departments and Schools of Education,** Sidney Trubowitz, *Educational Horizons,* Winter 2004
The author discusses possible ways in which departments or colleges of liberal arts might participate in teacher education along with departments or schools of education. He describes a case study regarding how one such cooperative effort between a liberal arts professor and a professor of education was done. 209

UNIT 9
For Vision and Hope: Alternative Visions of Reality

Unit Overview 212

43. **Building a Community of Hope,** Thomas J. Sergiovanni, *Educational Leadership,* May 2004
The author reviews what should be the elements at work in building communities of hope within school as well as cooperative community building efforts between school systems and their respective community environments. 215

44. **Mission and Vision in Education,** Edward G. Rozycki, *Educational Horizons,* Winter 2004
The author provides a creative, metaphorical essay on issues related to our visions for education and why some visions prevail and others fail. He offers suggestions for how we can assess our visions for education as they relate to our educational missions. 219

The concepts in bold italics are developed in the article. For further expansion, please refer to the Topic Guide.

45. **Education in America: The Next 25 Years,** Irving H. Buchen, *The Futurist,* January/February 2003

The author argues that within the next twenty-five years, the functions of educators will change to meet the needs for greater degrees of choice for parents and students. School-community relations will continue to evolve to meet the concerns of parents and students. He also argues that there will be major shifts in how educational success is measured. **222**

46. **An Emerging Culture,** Christopher Bamford and Eric Utne, *Utne Reader,* May/June 2003

The authors provide a ***worldwide vision*** of how the innovative alternative ***Waldorf School System*** has come about, which is part of the vision for a better human condition created by the social vision of ***Rudolf Steiner.*** Steiner's vision of a better human future has been played out in many different fields of human endeavor, education being one of them. **228**

Test Your Knowledge Form **234**
Article Rating Form **235**

Topic Guide

This topic guide suggests how the selections in this book relate to the subjects covered in your course. You may want to use the topics listed on these pages to search the Web more easily.

On the following pages a number of Web sites have been gathered specifically for this book. They are arranged to reflect the units of this *Annual Edition*. You can link to these sites by going to the DUSHKIN ONLINE support site at *http://www.dushkin.com/online/*.

ALL THE ARTICLES THAT RELATE TO EACH TOPIC ARE LISTED BELOW THE BOLD-FACED TERM.

Academic performance
- 8. No Child Left Behind: The Mathematics of Guaranteed Failure
- 9. Test Today, Privatize Tomorrow: Using Accountability to 'Reform' Public Schools to Death
- 11. Meeting Challenges in Urban Schools
- 12. Transforming High Schools
- 13. Reinventing America's Schools
- 17. No Flower Shall Wither; or, Horticulture in the Kingdom of the Frogs

Accountability
- 14. A Balanced School Accountability Model: An Alternative to High-Stakes Testing
- 15. Turning Accountability on Its Head: Supporting Inspired Teaching in Today's Classrooms
- 16. Accountability with a Kicker: Observations on the Florida A+ Accountability Plan
- 17. No Flower Shall Wither; or, Horticulture in the Kingdom of the Frogs
- 18. The Power of Testing

Achievement gap
- 10. Leadership That Sparks Learning
- 32. Minding the Gap
- 39. The Arithmetic Gap

Bullying
- 28. True Blue
- 29. A Profile of Bullying

Character education
- 22. Practicing Democracy in High School
- 33. Civic Education in Schools: The Right Time is Now

Civic education
- 22. Practicing Democracy in High School
- 33. Civic Education in Schools: The Right Time is Now

Classroom management
- 25. Heading Off Disruptive Behavior
- 26. How Disruptive Students Escalate Hostility and Disorder—and How Teachers Can Avoid It
- 27. Good Behavior Needs to Be Taught: How a Social Skills Curriculum Works
- 28. True Blue
- 29. A Profile of Bullying

Classroom research
- 21. Studying Education: Classroom Research and Cargo Cults

Cognitive science
- 19. Why Students Think They Understand—When They Don't

Communities of hope
- 34. Partnering with Families and Communities
- 43. Building a Community of Hope

Cultural diversity and schooling
- 30. An Unfinished Journey: The Legacy of *Brown* and the Narrowing Of the Achievement Gap
- 31. Against the Tide: Desegregated High Schools and Their 1980 Graduates
- 32. Minding the Gap
- 33. Civic Education in Schools: The Right Time is Now

Democracy and schooling
- 22. Practicing Democracy in High School
- 33. Civic Education in Schools: The Right Time is Now

Demographics in education
- 2. Game Theory, Teen-Style
- 3. Coming of Age in Consumerdom
- 4. Generational Pull
- 5. When I Was Young
- 6. Is America Raising Unhealthy Kids?

Disruptive students
- 25. Heading Off Disruptive Behavior
- 26. How Disruptive Students Escalate Hostility and Disorder—and How Teachers Can Avoid It
- 29. A Profile of Bullying

Excellence in education
- 14. A Balanced School Accountability Model: An Alternative to High-Stakes Testing
- 15. Turning Accountability on Its Head: Supporting Inspired Teaching in Today's Classrooms
- 16. Accountability with a Kicker: Observations on the Florida A+ Accountability Plan
- 17. No Flower Shall Wither; or, Horticulture in the Kingdom of the Frogs
- 18. The Power of Testing
- 19. Why Students Think They Understand—When They Don't
- 20. The Homework Wars
- 21. Studying Education: Classroom Research and Cargo Cults
- 30. An Unfinished Journey: The Legacy of *Brown* and the Narrowing Of the Achievement Gap
- 31. Against the Tide: Desegregated High Schools and Their 1980 Graduates
- 44. Mission and Vision in Education
- 46. An Emerging Culture

Good behavior
- 27. Good Behavior Needs to Be Taught: How a Social Skills Curriculum Works

Health Education Assessment Project (HEAP)
38. Healthier Students, Better Learners

High expectations of student achievement
11. Meeting Challenges in Urban Schools
12. Transforming High Schools

Highly qualified teachers
40. The Search for Highly Qualified Teachers
41. The Other Side of Highly Qualified Teachers

Homework
20. The Homework Wars

Integrity and civility
22. Practicing Democracy in High School
33. Civic Education in Schools: The Right Time is Now

Leadership
10. Leadership That Sparks Learning
44. Mission and Vision in Education

Liberal arts-schools of education
42. The Marriage of Liberal Arts Departments and Schools of Education

Math gap
28. True Blue
39. The Arithmetic Gap

Morality and values in education
22. Practicing Democracy in High School
23. Values: The Implicit Curriculum
24. The Missing Virtue: Lessons From Dodge Ball & Aristotle

National network of partnership schools
34. Partnering with Families and Communities

No Child Left Behind (NCLB)
8. No Child Left Behind: The Mathematics of Guaranteed Failure
9. Test Today, Privatize Tomorrow: Using Accountability to 'Reform' Public Schools to Death
18. The Power of Testing
40. The Search for Highly Qualified Teachers
41. The Other Side of Highly Qualified Teachers

Popular culture
35. Popular Culture in the Classroom
36. Living and Teaching on the Edge of a Pop Culture World
37. At the Crossroads of Expertise: The Risky Business of Teaching Popular Culture

Public perceptions of public schools
7. The 36th Annual Phi Delta Kappa/Gallup Poll of the Public Attitudes Toward the Public Schools

Quality of schooling
8. No Child Left Behind: The Mathematics of Guaranteed Failure
9. Test Today, Privatize Tomorrow: Using Accountability to 'Reform' Public Schools to Death
14. A Balanced School Accountability Model: An Alternative to High-Stakes Testing
15. Turning Accountability on Its Head: Supporting Inspired Teaching in Today's Classrooms
16. Accountability with a Kicker: Observations on the Florida A+ Accountability Plan
17. No Flower Shall Wither; or, Horticulture in the Kingdom of the Frogs
18. The Power of Testing
19. Why Students Think They Understand—When They Don't
21. Studying Education: Classroom Research and Cargo Cults
44. Mission and Vision in Education

Reform and education
8. No Child Left Behind: The Mathematics of Guaranteed Failure
9. Test Today, Privatize Tomorrow: Using Accountability to 'Reform' Public Schools to Death
10. Leadership That Sparks Learning
11. Meeting Challenges in Urban Schools
12. Transforming High Schools
13. Reinventing America's Schools
14. A Balanced School Accountability Model: An Alternative to High-Stakes Testing
15. Turning Accountability on Its Head: Supporting Inspired Teaching in Today's Classrooms
16. Accountability with a Kicker: Observations on the Florida A+ Accountability Plan
17. No Flower Shall Wither; or, Horticulture in the Kingdom of the Frogs

Rethinking the educational effort
8. No Child Left Behind: The Mathematics of Guaranteed Failure
9. Test Today, Privatize Tomorrow: Using Accountability to 'Reform' Public Schools to Death
10. Leadership That Sparks Learning
11. Meeting Challenges in Urban Schools
12. Transforming High Schools
13. Reinventing America's Schools

Rudolph Steiner
46. An Emerging Culture

School-community partnerships
33. Civic Education in Schools: The Right Time is Now
34. Partnering with Families and Communities
43. Building a Community of Hope

Social contexts of education
1. Public Schools; Public Will
2. Game Theory, Teen-Style
3. Coming of Age in Consumerdom
4. Generational Pull
5. When I Was Young
6. Is America Raising Unhealthy Kids?
7. The 36th Annual Phi Delta Kappa/Gallup Poll of the Public Attitudes Toward the Public Schools

Teaching
15. Turning Accountability on Its Head: Supporting Inspired Teaching in Today's Classrooms
40. The Search for Highly Qualified Teachers
41. The Other Side of Highly Qualified Teachers
42. The Marriage of Liberal Arts Departments and Schools of Education

Testing and assessment

9. Test Today, Privatize Tomorrow: Using Accountability to 'Reform' Public Schools to Death
14. A Balanced School Accountability Model: An Alternative to High-Stakes Testing
15. Turning Accountability on Its Head: Supporting Inspired Teaching in Today's Classrooms
16. Accountability with a Kicker: Observations on the Florida A+ Accountability Plan
17. No Flower Shall Wither; or, Horticulture in the Kingdom of the Frogs
18. The Power of Testing
19. Why Students Think They Understand—When They Don't

Urban schools

11. Meeting Challenges in Urban Schools
43. Building a Community of Hope

Values and education

22. Practicing Democracy in High School
23. Values: The Implicit Curriculum
24. The Missing Virtue: Lessons From Dodge Ball & Aristotle
33. Civic Education in Schools: The Right Time is Now

Vision and hopes

33. Civic Education in Schools: The Right Time is Now
43. Building a Community of Hope
45. Education in America: The Next 25 Years
46. An Emerging Culture

Waldorf schools

46. An Emerging Culture

World Wide Web Sites

The following World Wide Web sites have been carefully researched and selected to support the articles found in this reader. The easiest way to access these selected sites is to go to our DUSHKIN ONLINE support site at *http://www.dushkin.com/online/*.

AE: Education 05/06

The following sites were available at the time of publication. Visit our Web site—we update DUSHKIN ONLINE regularly to reflect any changes.

General Sources

Education Week on the Web
http://www.edweek.org
At this *Education Week* home page, you will be able to open its archives, read special reports on education, keep up on current events in education, look at job opportunities, and access articles relevant to educators today.

Educational Resources Information Center
http://www.eric.ed.gov
This invaluable site provides links to all ERIC sites: clearinghouses, support components, and publishers of ERIC materials. You can search the ERIC database, find out what is new, and ask questions about ERIC.

National Education Association
http://www.nea.org
Something about virtually every education-related topic can be accessed via this site of the 2.3-million-strong National Education Association.

National Parent Information Network/ERIC
http://npin.org
This is a clearinghouse of information on elementary and early childhood education as well as urban education. Browse through its links for information for parents and for people who work with parents.

U.S. Department of Education
http://www.ed.gov
Explore this government site for examination of institutional aspects of multicultural education. National goals, projects, grants, and other educational programs are listed here as well as many links to teacher services and resources.

UNIT 1: How Others See Us and How We See Ourselves

Charter Schools
http://www.edexcellence.net/topics/charters.html
Open this site for news about charter schools. It provides information about charter school research and issues, links to the U.S. Charter Schools Web site, and Best on the Web charter school sites.

Pathways to School Improvement
http://www.ncrel.org/sdrs/pathwayg.htm
This site of the North Central Regional Educational Laboratory leads to discussions and links about education, including the current state of education, reform issues, and goals and standards. Technology, professional development, and integrated services are a few of the subjects also discussed.

UNIT 2: Rethinking and Changing the Educative Effort

The Center for Innovation in Education
http://www.center.edu
The Center for Innovation in Education, self-described as a "not-for-profit, nonpartisan research organization" focuses on K–12 education reform strategies. Click on its links for information about and varying perspectives on school privatization and other reform initiatives.

Colorado Department of Education
http://www.cde.state.co.us/index_home.htm
This site's links will lead you to information about education-reform efforts, technology in education initiatives, and many documents of interest to educators, parents, and students.

National Council for Accreditation of Teacher Education
http://www.ncate.org
The NCATE is the professional accrediting organization for schools, colleges, and departments of education in the United States. Accessing this page will lead to information about teacher and school standards, state relations, and developmental projects.

Phi Delta Kappa International
http://www.pdkintl.org
This important organization publishes articles about all facets of education—from school vouchers and charter schools to "new dimensions" in learning.

UNIT 3: Striving for Excellence: The Drive for Quality

Awesome Library for Teachers
http://www.awesomelibrary.org
Open this page for links and access to teacher information on everything from educational assessment to general child development topics.

Education World
http://www.education-world.com
Education World provides a database of literally thousands of sites that can be searched by grade level, plus education news, lesson plans, and professional-development resources.

EdWeb/Andy Carvin
http://edwebproject.org
The purpose of EdWeb is to explore the worlds of educational reform and information technology. Access educational resources around the world, learn about trends in education policy and information infrastructure development, examine success stories of computers in the classroom, and much more.

Kathy Schrock's Guide for Educators
http://www.discoveryschool.com/schrockguide/
This is a classified list of sites on the Internet found to be useful for enhancing curriculum and teacher professional growth. It is updated daily.

www.dushkin.com/online/

Teacher's Guide to the U.S. Department of Education
http://www.ed.gov/pubs/TeachersGuide/
Government goals, projects, grants, and other educational programs are listed here as well as many links to teacher services and resources.

UNIT 4: Morality and Values in Education

Association for Moral Education
http://www.amenetwork.org/
AME is dedicated to fostering communication, cooperation, training, curriculum development, and research that links moral theory with educational practices. From here it is possible to connect to several sites on ethics, character building, and moral development.

Child Welfare League of America
http://www.cwla.org
The CWLA is the United States' oldest and largest organization devoted entirely to the well-being of vulnerable children and their families. This site provides links to information about issues related to morality and values in education.

Ethics Updates/Lawrence Hinman
http://ethics.acusd.edu
This site provides both simple concept definition and complex analysis of ethics, original treatises, and sophisticated search engine capability. Subject matter covers the gamut from ethical theory to applied ethical venues. There are many opportunities for user input.

The National Academy for Child Development
http://www.nacd.org
This international organization is dedicated to helping children and adults reach their full potential. Its home page presents links to various programs, research, and resources into such topics as ADD.

UNIT 5: Managing Life in Classrooms

Classroom Connect
http://www.classroom.com
This is a major Web site for K–12 teachers and students, with links to schools, teachers, and resources online. It includes discussion of the use of technology in the classroom.

Global SchoolNet Foundation
http://www.gsn.org
Access this site for multicultural educational information. The site includes news for teachers, students, and parents, as well as chat rooms, links to educational resources, programs, and contests and competitions.

Teacher Talk Forum
http://education.indiana.edu/cas/tt/tthmpg.html
Visit this site for access to a variety of articles discussing life in the classroom. Clicking on the various links will lead you to electronic lesson plans covering a variety of topic areas from Indiana University's Center for Adolescent Studies.

UNIT 6: Cultural Diversity and Schooling

American Scientist
http://www.amsci.org/amsci/amsci.html
Investigate this site to access a variety of articles and to explore issues and concepts related to race and gender.

American Studies Web
http://www.georgetown.edu/crossroads/asw/
This site provides links to a wealth of resources on the Internet related to American studies, from gender studies to race and ethnicity. It is of great help when doing research in demography and population studies.

Multicultural Publishing and Education Council
http://www.mpec.org
This is the home page of the MPEC, a networking and support organization for independent publishers, authors, educators, and librarians fostering authentic multicultural books and materials. It has excellent links to a vast array of resources related to multicultural education.

National Institute on the Education of At-Risk Students
http://www.ed.gov/offices/OERI/At-Risk/
The At-Risk Institute supports research and development activities designed to improve the education of students at risk of educational failure due to limited English proficiency, race, geographic location, or economic disadvantage.

Prospects: The Congressionally Mandated Study of Educational Growth and Opportunity
http://www.ed.gov/pubs/Prospects/index.html
This report analyzes cross-sectional data on language-minority and LEP students in the United States and outlines what actions are needed to improve their educational performance. Family and economic situations are addressed. Information on related reports and sites is provided.

UNIT 7: Serving Special Needs and Concerns

Constructivism: From Philosophy to Practice
http://www.stemnet.nf.ca/~elmurphy/emurphy/cle.html
Here is a thorough description of the history, philosophy, and practice of constructivism, including quotations from Socrates and others, epistemology, learning theory, characteristics, and a checklist.

National Association for Gifted Children
http://www.nagc.org/home00.htm
NAGC, a national nonprofit organization for gifted children, is dedicated to developing their high potential.

National Information Center for Children and Youth With Disabilities (NICHCY)
http://www.nichcy.org/index.html
NICHCY provides information and makes referrals in areas related to specific disabilities, early intervention, special education and related services, individualized education programs, and much more. The site also connects to a listing of Parent's Guides to resources for children and youth with disabilities.

UNIT 8: The Profession of Teaching Today

Canada's SchoolNet Staff Room
http://www.schoolnet.ca/home/e/
Here is a resource and link site for anyone involved in education, including special-needs educators, teachers, parents, volunteers, and administrators.

Teachers Helping Teachers
http://www.pacificnet.net/~mandel/
This site provides basic teaching tips, new teaching methodology ideas, and forums for teachers to share their experiences. Download software and participate in chat sessions. It features educational resources on the Web, and new ones are added each week.

www.dushkin.com/online/

The Teachers' Network
http://www.teachers.net
Bulletin boards, classroom projects, online forums, and Web mentors are featured on this site, as well as the book *Teachers' Guide to Cyberspace* and an online, 4-week course on how to use the Internet.

Teaching with Electronic Technology
http://www.wam.umd.edu/~mlhall/teaching.html
Michael Hall's Web site leads to many resources of value to those contemplating the future of education, particularly regarding the role of technology in the classroom and beyond.

UNIT 9: For Vision and Hope: Alternative Visions of Reality

Goals 2000: A Progress Report
http://www.ed.gov/pubs/goals/progrpt/index.html
Open this site to survey a progress report by the U.S. Department of Education on the Goals 2000 reform initiative. It provides a sense of what goals educators are reaching for as they look toward the future.

Mighty Media
http://www.mightymedia.com
The mission of this privately funded consortium is to empower youth, teachers, and organizations through the use of interactive communications technology. The site provides links to teacher talk forums, educator resources, networks for students, and more.

Online Internet Institute
http://www.oii.org
A collaborative project among Internet-using educators, proponents of systemic reform, content-area experts, and teachers who desire professional growth, this site provides a learning environment for integrating the Internet into educators' individual teaching styles.

We highly recommend that you review our Web site for expanded information and our other product lines. We are continually updating and adding links to our Web site in order to offer you the most usable and useful information that will support and expand the value of your Annual Editions. You can reach us at: *http://www.dushkin.com/annualeditions/*.

UNIT 1

How Others See Us and How We See Ourselves

Unit Selections

1. **Public Schools; Public Will**, Arnold F. Fege
2. **Game Theory, Teen-Style**, Jason Meyers
3. **Coming of Age in Consumerdom**, David G. Kennedy
4. **Generational Pull**, William H. Frey
5. **When I Was Young**, John Fetto
6. **Is America Raising Unhealthy Kids?**, Denise Willi
7. **The 36th Annual Phi Delta Kappa/Gallup Poll of the Public Attitudes Toward the Public Schools**, Lowell C. Rose and Alec M. Gallup

Key Points to Consider

- Describe the change in American population statistics between 1950 and the present. How have these changes affected education?

- What can teachers do about the unhealthy dietary practices of children and adolescents?

- How can we most accurately assess public perceptions of the educational system?

- What is the fundamental effect of public opinion on national public policy regarding educational development?

 **Links: www.dushkin.com/online/**
These sites are annotated in the World Wide Web pages.

Charter Schools
http://www.edexcellence.net/topics/charters.html

Pathways to School Improvement
http://www.ncrel.org/sdrs/pathwayg.htm

There are many ways in which children and youth are educated. The social, racial, and cultural landscape in the United States is becoming more and more diverse and multifaceted. How youth respond to current issues is a reflection of their perceptions as to how older citizens respond to social reality. How to improve the quality of educational services remains a concern of the general public. Public perceptions of the nation's efforts in the education of its youth are of great importance to those who work with children and youth. We must be attentive to the peoples' concerns; we cannot ignore them.

How the people served by a nation's schools perceive the quality of the education they received is of great interest, because public perceptions can translate into either increased or decreased levels of support for a nation's educational system. Achieving a public consensus as to what the aims or purposes of education ought to be can be difficult. Americans debate what the purposes of education should be in every generation. Many different sorts of schools exist at both the elementary and the secondary levels. Many different forms of "charter" schools are attracting the interest of parents; some of these charter schools are within public school systems and some are private ones. Parents wish to have choices as to the types of schools their children attend.

Schools need to be places where students and teachers feel safe, places that provide hope and that instill confidence in the prospects for a happier and better future for all. The safety of students and teachers in schools is a matter of concern to many persons due to tragic events in the recent past. Schools also need to be places where students can dream and hope and work to inform themselves in the process of building their futures. Schools need to help students learn to be inquiring persons.

There are several major policy issues regarding the content and form of schooling that are being debated. We are anticipating greater ranges of choice in the types and forms of schooling that will become available to our children and youth. The United States has great interest in policy issues related to increased accountability to the public for what goes on in schools. Also, we are possibly the most culturally pluralistic nation in the world, and we are becoming even more diverse.

We may be approaching a historic moment in our national history regarding the public funding of education and the options parents might be given for the education of their children. Some of these options and the lines of reasoning for them are explored in this volume. Financial as well as qualitative options are being debated. Scholars in many fields of study as well as journalists and legislators are asking how we can make our nation's schools more effective as well as how we might optimize parents' sense of control over how their children are to be educated.

Young people "read" certain adult behaviors well; they see it as hypocrisy when the adult community wants certain standards and values to be taught in schools but rewards other, often opposite behaviors in society. Dialogue regarding what it means to speak of "literacy" in democratic communities continues. Our students read much from our daily activities and our many information sources, and they form their own shrewd analyses of what social values actually do prevail in society. How to help young people develop their intellectual potential and become perceptive students of and participants in democratic traditions are major public concerns.

There is serious business yet to be attended to by the social service and educational agencies that try to serve youth. People are impatient to see some fundamental efforts made to meet the basic educational needs of young people. The problems are the greatest in major cities and in more isolated rural areas. Public perceptions of the schools are affected by high levels of economic deprivation among large sectors of the population and by the economic pressures that our interdependent world economy produces as a result of international competition for the world's markets.

Studies conducted in the past few years, particularly the Carnegie Corporation's studies of adolescents in the United States, document the plight of millions of young persons. Some authors point out that although there was much talk about educational change in the 1990s, those changes were only marginal and cosmetic at best. States responded by demanding more course work and tougher exit standards from schools. With still more than 25 percent of school children in the United States living at or below the poverty level, and almost a third of them in more economically and socially vulnerable nontraditional family settings, the overall social situation for many young people continues to be difficult. The public wants more effective responses to public needs.

So, in the face of major demographic shifts and of the persistence of many long-term social problems, the public watches how schools respond to new as well as old challenges. In recent years, these challenges have aggravated rather than allayed much public concern about the efficacy of public schooling. Various political, cultural, corporate, and philanthropic interests continue to articulate alternative educational agendas. At the same time the incumbents in the system respond with their own educational agendas, which reflect their views from the inside.

PUBLIC SCHOOLS PUBLIC WILL

It's not just whether we have enough funding for education—it's whether we have the political will to allocate the money fairly

BY ARNOLD F. FEGE

At the core of the budget crisis facing local districts is nothing less than the public's ownership of its schools—and its responsibility to demand high-quality public education for every child. Democracy is inextricably related to the equitable, adequate, and fair allocation of our nation's abundant resources. Implicit in the allocation and distribution of educational resources in a school district is the distribution of quality. We are challenged not only to make the right cuts, but to make the right expenditures. Which students get the high-quality teachers and principals, the new facilities, the state-of-the-art technology? Who wins and who loses? What is the impact of class and race on our major policy and allocation decisions? Are our communities meaningfully engaged in those decisions?

Balancing the budget these days requires that we ask not only how to comply with No Child Left Behind, but how we can comply cost-effectively to improve achievement and quality, as well as equality. It is easy to lose sight of these issues when we are enticed by alternative funding mechanisms, such as private capital for public schools, nonprofit fund-raising arms, private school scholarship programs, marketing contracts and naming rights, and private school vouchers paid for from the public purse.

As we seek alternative funding sources, we need to keep important policy considerations in mind. How can we ensure equity in the distribution of resources so that schools do not compete with each other for scarce additional resources? How can we ensure that we adopt initiatives that will help children with the highest need rather than initiatives that are based on the highest bidder? And as we rely more and more on funding sources other than tax revenue, how long will it be before the private donors begin to ask for a larger chunk of school decision making?

The post office effect

Never has there been a time in public education when the expectations and demands for accountability have been so far out of alignment with the resources necessary to accomplish the task.

We are witnessing in education what's called the post office effect. There was a time when the post office did what it was supposed to do—deliver the mail, at low cost, and deliver it dependably. Whether the mail got to you on time was immaterial—it got to you. But the expectations of the public began to change. People wanted the mail delivered more quickly, and the post office was not able to adapt. Congress allowed the private sector to handle parcel post, thus creating choice for postal customers. But like school vouchers, the new postal choice did not serve all communities—only those that were profitable, and only those customers who could afford it. The post office was then made quasi-private, then privatized, and now delivers primarily junk mail. The quality of the post office did not diminish, but expectations changed. The same is happening with public schools, and I fear the schools will continually be pushed to privatize, all in the name of accountability.

No Child Left Behind is a laudable and critical next step in realizing the efforts initiated by Title I of the original Elementary and Secondary Education Act. Under NCLB, children who need help will be on the public radar screen for all to see. The next step is to translate the NCLB commitment into reality for every child so that the 14 million poor children and the 12 million children who lack health insurance and the millions more who face violence and neglect get the high-quality schools and the after-school and preschool services they need.

LOCAL EDUCATION FUNDS

First conceived and funded by the Ford Foundation in 1983 following the release of *A Nation At Risk*, local education funds (LEFs) were designed primarily to promote public engagement by providing outright financial assistance to urban school districts. The first LEFs were in San Francisco, Pittsburgh, Philadelphia, and Oakland, Calif. There are now more than 80 such funds, represented by the Public Education Network and located in large and middle-sized school districts.

Since 1983, LEFs have gone from educating the public about the public schools to taking on the larger task of building political will. Unlike school foundations, which focus on individual giving, LEFs focus on the public's responsibility to take ownership of its public schools.

Currently, many LEFs are becoming proficient in building knowledge and expertise in how communities work and change, leveraging public action, building community partnerships, leading bond and millage campaigns, and measuring results and accountability. They practice public school advocacy by collecting and disseminating data, working with the community to understand the data, and working with the community to act on the data.

Alabama's Mobile Education Fund, for example, has undertaken an extensive community engagement project funded by the Annenberg Foundation and coordinated by the Public Education Network. The fund conducted 48 public meetings involving more than 1,400 citizens. In the second phase of the project, 50 grassroots leaders formed a Citizen Advisory Team and went into neighborhoods, schools, churches, and businesses to talk not just about increased funding, but also about community accountability and sustained mobilization for public schools and policy change.

Another example is Oregon's Portland Education Partnership, which played a major role in leading the state tax increase referendum for public education. Working with other community partners, the partnership formed a political campaign to push the tax hike and endorse candidates for school board. Although the referendum failed at the state level, the partnership won a tax increase for six countries. —A.F.F

This is not a question of money; it is a question of values. The United States has a $10 trillion economy. The challenge is not whether we can get rid of poverty and illiteracy, or whether we can eradicate the tremendous resource inequalities between schools and states—it is whether we have the will to do so.

Meanwhile, when we don't have resources, we become slaves to those who do. We are often obliged to offer ourselves up to the highest bidder, to reach for the newest financial carrot. And high-poverty schools and districts are the most vulnerable to the enticing quick-fix solution—the advertisements masquerading as curriculum materials, the soda contract come-ons, the marketing promotions that "help save taxes" by subsidizing school programs through the corporate route.

The loss of the common

We are dealing with competing visions of the American dream, a clash that pits the goals of private individuals and a romanticized view of the market against the expanding needs of our children and the public interest. Every special interest now requires a boutique charter school or voucher program, and public schools are increasingly regarded as little more than a functional means for attaining private ends.

When it is impossible to recognize what we hold in common, then we have indeed lost our common sense. It is, after all, what is shared by all of us—what must be maintained and cared for by all of us—that is the defining mark of an excellent public education. When our sense of the common deteriorates, we can be persuaded that a failing educational system is an acceptable price to pay to accommodate ideological clichés and bumper-sticker causes.

To realize the dream of our nation's beginnings, we must take on the hard work of restoring the sense of what we hold in common, fashioning new and more compelling images of community and public education ownership, and bridging the traditional gap between private interests and public responsibilities. We must configure the idea of commonness within the public space of our schools and thereby build the capacity to create the conditions for genuine plurality and diversity.

We cannot do this in a business-as-usual mode. Nor can we do it alone. The work of providing high-quality education for all children, building a constituency for public schools, and restructuring tax and finance systems will take partners. It will take a model of participation that goes way beyond the traditional parent involvement of reading to students or the lip-service public engagement that only asks citizens to vote for the next bond issue.

The new model must involve building public will and sustained responsibility for public schools. One such model is represented by local education funds, which constitute an intermediary nonprofit organization, independent of the school district, but closely aligned with harnessing the civic strength of the community through use of mobilization and campaign strategies.

A call to action

Making a difference for all children will take seven not-so-simple steps:

1. Be outspoken in calling the national question about closing the achievement gap. It is time to hold Congress and the White House responsible for providing the necessary funding for education, their share of the accountability cost. We cannot let state and national officials off the hook. On the other hand, we cannot afford to let No Child Left Behind unravel. The political consequences for poor and disadvantaged children would be too great. We need to recommend revisions and amendments to NCLB that will make it even stronger and shift its focus from high-stakes tests for kids to high-stakes accountability for adults.

2. Take the lead in the next phase of education accountability. NCLB is just the first phase of the current accountability movement. In the next phase, it will be critical to make the case for additional resources in more and different ways. Parents and community members are hungry for performance data about their schools. They want data that make sense, in language they can understand—not only related to their children, but also to their school and community.

We need to use data not punitively, but for diagnostic and planning purposes. We also need to link performance data to productivity to prove to the public at large that investing in education will make a difference. But instead of simply asking for more money, we need to tie that money more closely to well defined goals and vision.

3. Build partnerships with local education funds and other community-based organizations. Data alone will not create political action and may even create misunderstanding if we do not have in place the community base to receive, interpret, and act on the data. Many of the issues we face go beyond the schools themselves; that is, we can fix the schools, but we still might not fix the kids. School leaders must have conversations with local public health directors, juvenile justice officials, social service personnel, civic organizations, churches, and civil rights organizations.

I once taught in a Michigan school district that was in crisis. Fully half the students were reading two or more years below grade level by fourth grade, and the percentage was even higher in upper grades. Today, 50 percent or more of those children are still reading two or more years below grade level-despite heavy infusions of money, a plethora of reforms, turnover of leadership, and committed teachers and principals. What is missing is a powerful, committed intermediary organization with the legitimacy, authority, and skill to hold the community and its elected officials accountable. In successful school districts, these organizations share power and responsibility with their school boards in educating the public and building a constituency for public education.

4. Work with children comprehensively. Working collaboratively with other agencies can be difficult. Frequently, representatives of the various agencies get together and decide how to divvy up the child more efficiently and more effectively. What is supportive of the child is not necessarily supportive of the school as it is currently configured or of organizations that exist to serve their own old needs and interests. The old territorial and organizational prerogatives need to give way to the new needs of schools.

We need to boil down the many different messages that various child advocacy organizations send and work together to consolidate and make changes. The objective is not to add another voice—the objective is to speak with one voice, and the route to this goes directly through politics, not around it.

5. Make a commitment to the major transformation of our schools. The factory model of schooling, which is based on efficiency, cannot provide the effectiveness that the standards movement requires. Additional revenue and resources will be based on our vision of redesign and transformation, not tinkering and patching. Many school districts are experiencing "systems crash," because the factory-model school is irreconcilable with the expectation that every child will achieve at a given level of performance. Standards-based reform cannot succeed without major transformation of schools; on the other hand, a new model cannot be built without additional resources.

6. Build public will. It's not that we don't have the knowledge to get the job done. We know how to get children reading; we know how to ensure that every child has preschool supports and comes to school healthy and nourished. We know how to provide modern school buildings, how to ensure that the most challenged schools have qualified teachers, and how to develop programs based on research. But without the public will to do these things, they will not be done.

7. Plan for the long haul. Survival dictates that we devote energy to finding supplemental dollars, but in the long run, an overhaul of school financing will be required, along with state and federal policy changes to provide needed resources.

Among these changes might be tax restructuring; levying taxes on entertainment or on Information Age technology, such as Internet products and cell phones; pushing states to settle adequacy cases; and getting IDEA fully funded.

As we try to figure out the proper funding alchemy and the proper roles of government, philanthropy, nonprofits, and the private sector, we must respond to the information needs of these four sectors but, at the same time, maintain local control and democratic processes. If we don't, we will lose one of the most important aspects of public education: citizen ownership and responsibility for public schools.

Arnold F. Fege (*arnie@publiceeducation.org*) is director of public engagement and advocacy for the Public Education Network, Washington, D.C. This article is adapted from a presentation to the National School Boards Association's Council of Urban Boards of Education in June 2003.

GAME THEORY, TEEN-STYLE

BY JASON MEYERS

Given the unforeseen and seemingly overnight successes of mobile services like ring tone downloads and picture messaging, the U.S. wireless industry's ongoing campaign to decipher the mobility habits of the highly coveted teen market could be fairly labeled a futile effort. Still, the ever-vigilant and never-satisfied wireless sector persists in trying to pry open the minds of teens and calculate what services might finally warrant the elusive designation of killer app.

A recent example is a report released in March by Telephia, a San Francisco-based provider of market research and network performance statistics to the wireless industry. The firm surveyed 1,500 mobile teens in the 35 largest U.S. markets and found that two-thirds of them already use some form of mobile data services. The study also identified mobile online gaming as the one application best poised to usurp camera phones and Jay-Z ring tones as the next must-have for teenagers.

According to Alex von Krogh, senior research editor for Telephia, 41 percent of teens surveyed expressed interest in having online gaming capabilities on their next wireless device. The ones who do are also already more lucrative customers for both wireless service providers and mobile handset manufacturers: The average mobile online gamer used 811 monthly minutes of use, nearly double that of teens who don't use the apps. Telephia also found that gamers paid $94 on average for their devices and reported a 65 percent satisfaction rating with their phones, while non-gamers paid an average of $71 and were less satisfied (50 percent).

"There's a pretty big upside," von Krogh says. "Gaming represents a high-growth application and an opportunity to drive adoption and boost ARPU."

Telephia's hypothesis looks strong, if the recent Wireless 2004 trade show held in Atlanta by the Cellular Telecommunications & Internet Association is any indication. For the first time ever, network technology—and even the health of the high-tech industry—took a backseat and entertainment applications, content usage and handsets priced and designed for younger users dominated both the exhibitions and buzz on the show floor.

Telephia's study is part of the firm's new focus on the teen market. Its Mobile Teen Report, based on a dedicated survey of those 1,500 mobile teens and 1,100 parents of mobile teens, will be produced semi-annually, and track growth metrics like average revenue, penetration, churn and quality of service, von Krogh says.

EARLY ADOPTION

Teens account for double-digit subscriber percentage rates for four of the top six carriers in the nation.

Carrier	Youth Subs as Percent of Total Subs
AT&T Wireless	12.5%
Cingular Wireless	13.0%
Nextel Communications	5.6%
Sprint PCS (includes Virgin)	16.7%
Verizon Wireless	8.9%
T-Mobile	14.4%

Source: Adventis

TEEN TELEPHONY

Teens who play mobile online games were notably less likely to list price as a key factor in choosing a handset, indicating they are less concerned about price.

Teen Attitudes and Behavior	Teens Who Play Mobile Online Games	Teens Who Do Not Play Online Games
Pay for all or some of their wireless bill	33%	14%
Price a key factor in handset selection*	29%	46%

*Percent who listed price as one of top 3 reasons they chose current handset (asked of teens who chose own handset)

Source: Telephia Mobile Teen Report

From *American Demographics*, May 2004, p. 10. Copyright © 2004 Primedia Business Magazines and Media, Inc. All rights reserved. Reprinted by permission.

Article 3

COMING OF AGE IN CONSUMERDOM

Psychologically, 'tweens may have neither the innocence of children nor the power of adults. What they do have is money—and time to spend it just how they want.

BY DAVID G. KENNEDY

They watch cable channels designed just for them, they cruise the Net with ease, they know what they want and often times get it. Today's pre- and early adolescents draw from the last birth years of Generation Y and from the start of the Millennials crop. They are America's 'tweens (ages 8 to 14), a population 29 million strong according to the 2000 census, and one desperately sought by marketers. With attitudes, access to information and sophistication well beyond their years and purchasing power to match, these young consumers will spend an average of $1,294 in 2004, estimates MarketResearch.com, for an aggregate total of $38 billion. Add to this the nearly $126 billion parents will spend on their 'tweens by year-end, a number expected to balloon to $150 billion by 2007, and one grasps the importance and potential of the market.

"Intuitively, these kids are more savvy" than people give them credit for, says Carol Fitzgerald, president of New York-based Buzzback Market Research. Overwhelmingly, 'tweens recognize television commercials for what they are (92 percent), according to Buzzback's fourth-quarter 2003 survey of 524 'tweens. About three-quarters regard billboards and radio spots as paid advertising, and about half recognize promotional mediums such as product placements on television shows.

Just because 'tweens get the business motive behind ads, however, doesn't mean they are averse to them. Of the 'tweens surveyed, 43 percent think advertising is "funny," 39 percent find it "informative," and around 35 percent believe it "entertaining" or "interesting." Despite this generally positive attitude toward advertising, 'tweens are discerning. In fact,

---

YOUNG AND HUNGRY

Food purchases account for almost 50 percent of total spending in households with a 'tween.

ANNUAL FAMILY EXPENDITURES ON FOOD, CLOTHING, PERSONAL-CARE ITEMS, ENTERTAINMENT, AND READING MATERIALS FOR 8- TO 14- YEAR-OLDS. BY PERCENT OF TOTAL FOR EACH AGE GROUP, 2001 ($ VALUES IN MILLIONS)

AGE GROUP	FOOD AMOUNT	% OF TOTAL	CLOTHING AMOUNT	% OF TOTAL	PERSONAL-CARE ITEMS, ENTERTAINMENT AND READING MATERIALS AMOUNT	% OF TOTAL	TOTAL AMOUNT	% OF TOTAL
8-11	$33,605	27%	$9,916	8%	$23,661	19%	$67,182	53%
12-14	$26,728	21%	$12,248	10%	$19,660	16%	$58,636	47%
Total	$60,333	48%	$22,164	18%	$43,321	35%	$125,818	100%

Note: Food expenses include food and nonalchoholic beverages purchased at grocery, convenience and specialty stores, including purchases with food stamps; dining at restaurants; and household expenditures on school meals. Clothing expenditures include children's apparel such as shirts, pants, dresses and suits, foot wear; and clothing services such as dry cleaning, alterations and repair, and storage.

Source: U.S. Department of Agriculture, Expenditures on Children by Families. 2001 Annual Report: Packaged Facts, a publishing division of MarketResearch.com

a majority of the 'tweens surveyed (52 percent) said they tune-out during television commercials, mainly because the commercials are repeats or are "boring."

Harnessing the power of celebrity through product placements in television shows and movies seems to succeed where television ads fail. Three-quarters of the 'tweens said that they notice brands used on their favorite shows, while 72 percent admit that seeing a favorite character using a certain brand makes them want to use that brand at least some of the time.

For a specific look at product placement Buzzback asked 'tweens about Fox's perennially powerful reality show *American Idol*, the results of which highlight the efficacy of placing products in the hands of the popular. About half of the surveyed 'tweens had watched *American Idol*, and of that number 56 percent recalled watching the music videos and skits in which the crooning contestants used branded products. What's more, even as three-quarters of the group considered the videos advertising, 92 percent stayed to watch them—a retention rate far better than the 48 percent television commercials can claim. Nearly half of the viewers thought the singers actually used the endorsed products; of those who didn't, 95 percent said the endorsements had no negative effect on their impression of the singers or the products.

SPENDERS IN TRAINING

The $38 billion that 'tweens control puts a twinkle in the eyes of marketers.

BUYING POWER OF 8- TO 14- YEAR-OLDS BY AGE GROUP, 2002

AGE GROUP	PER CAPITA	AGGREGATE (MILLIONS)	% OF TOTAL
12-14	$1,972	$24,975	66%
8-11	$780	$13,027	34%
Total	$1,294	$38,002	100%

Source: Packaged Facts, a publishing divison of MarketResearch.com

---

From *American Demographics*, April 2004, pp. 14. Copyright © 2004 Primedia Business Magazines and Media, Inc. All rights reserved. Reprinted by permission.

Article 4

GENERATIONAL PULL

A weather eye on Gen X gains and losses indicates hot "post-cool" areas.

BY WILLIAM H. FREY

Generations move in different directions. Gen Xers—building careers and "settling down" to the extent that this notoriously independent generation will ever be tied to one place—are blazing new migration trails. The news is that pricey, glitzy, lifestyle-only cities are not cutting it with Gen X, according to the maze of migration flows across state and metro destinations, recently released from the 2000 census for the 1995–2000 period.

Other generations provide a backdrop. Baby Boomers are largely settled in long-term residences, befitting their middle-aged status—although there is some "to-ing" and "fro-ing" among those who have one eye on retirement. For the pre-Boomer generations, born before 1945, retirement is a primary migration consideration. Those under 25 years old, who tend to make transitory, discretionary moves, head to and from college, to new jobs and often to places where the social life is attractive to young singles.

Yet, to get the truest picture of where the nation's economic opportunities are emerging, follow the recent migration leads of Gen X. In the 25-to-39 age range, they are running out their string of "discretionary" moves. Focused more on career and family, long-term employment opportunities and amenities factor into their destinations. Gen X moves differ from the more Sun Belt, Florida and Arizona-oriented retirees and older Baby Boomers, and from the "cool city" destinations of the youngest adults.

GENERATIONAL MAGNETS

Between 1995 and 2000, more Gen Xers moved to Atlanta than any other U.S. metro area.

GREATEST GEN X METROPILITAN MIGRATION GAINERS* (NET DOMESTIC MIGRATION GAINS, 1995–2000)

Atlanta, GA MSA	98,019
Dallas, TX PMSA	58,774
Phoenix/Mesa, AZ MSA	55,774
Denver, CO PMSA	53,795
Las Vegas, NV/AZ MSA	47,824
Charlotte/Gastonia/Rock Hill, NC/SC MSA	37,363
Portland/Vancouver, OR/WA PMSA	34,696
Minneapolis/ST. Paul, MN/WI MSA	34,204
Washington, DC/MD/VA/WV PMSA	29,597
Seattle/Bellevue/Everett, WA PMSA	27,201

GREATEST GEN X METROPOLITAN MIGRATION LOSERS* (NET DOMESTIC MIGRATION GAINS, 1995–2000)

Los Angeles/Long Beach, CA PMSA	-83,013
New York, NY PMSA	-63,659
Miami, FL PMSA	-35,120
Honolulu, HI MSA	-23,316
San Diego, CA MSA	-22,105
Norfolk/Virginia Beach/Newport News, VA/NC MSA	-16,725
Pittsburgh, PA MSA	-15,109
Buffalo/Niagara Falls, NY MSA	-14,891
Boston, MA/NH PMSA	-14,791
Nassau/Suffolk, NY PMSA	-14,440

*among metropolitan areas greater than 500,000 population it looks at the highlights of the changes in people's spending habits.

Source: William H. Frey analysis

Rather, Gen Xers select a mix of interior and coastal states with metro areas known for their New Economy, knowledge jobs and general employment growth, without the sting of high housing costs. In contrast to retirement magnets like Florida, Arizona, Nevada and North Carolina, which are attracting large numbers of their elders, the dominant destination states for Gen Xers are Georgia, Texas and Colorado.

Atlanta, Dallas and Denver are among the top four metro magnets (along with Phoenix) for this group. Also attractive are the "techie" centers, Minneapolis-St. Paul and Seattle, as well as growing, yet affordable places, such as Las Vegas, Charlotte, N.C., Portland, Ore. and Kansas City. Back when they were this age, the more audacious Baby Boomers were prone to select pricey, cosmopolitan coastal areas. Two of these, Washington, D.C., and San Francisco, are also on the list of gaining destinations for Gen Xers, though low in ranking (No. 9 and No. 24, respectively)

Late Boomers (35 to 44 years old) share Atlanta as their No. 1 destination, but other Xer top choices, Denver and Dallas, are further down their list. Post-Xer generation young adults (15- to 24-year-olds), share Phoenix, Atlanta and Las Vegas with Xers, on their top 10 list (ranked Nos. 3, 5 and 7). But they tend to be more Sun Belt and "fun city"-oriented. Austin, Texas and San Diego lead with greatest migration gains, on a list that also contains attractive college towns both large (Boston) and small (Ann Arbor, Mich.).

Among college grad Gen Xers, coastal locations tend to be more attractive than for the generation as a whole. Aside from sharing a penchant for Colorado, and to a lesser extent, Minnesota, college grad Gen Xers head for the prosperous coasts, including their No. 1. destination, California. African American Gen Xers are partial to the South, following a general black migration return to this region. In contrast, destinations among white Gen Xers are more balanced between the South and the West.

The greatest exodus of Gen Xers occurs from places with high housing costs or with stagnating economies. New York state has both, and leads all others in their loss of 154,000 Gen Xers in the last half of the 1990s. Downsizing upstate New York locales, Buffalo, Syracuse, Rochester and Albany, together lost 40,000 Gen Xers; as well, the pricey New York metro region lost over 63,000. Among the other attractive but expensive metros losing large numbers of Xers were Los Angeles, Miami, Honolulu and San Diego.

William H. Frey is a demographer at the Brookings Institution and Research Professor at the University of Michigan Population Studies Center. His Web site is www.frey-demographer.org

---

From *American Demographics,* May 2004, pp. 18-19. Copyright © 2004 Primedia Business Magazines and Media, Inc. All rights reserved. Reprinted by permission.

Article 5

READER REQUEST: YOUR QUESTIONS ANSWERED

WHEN I WAS YOUNG...

Not only are Americans going to school in record numbers,
they're also staying in school longer.

BY JOHN FETTO

To the Editors of *American Demographics:*
Politicians continue to attack our K–12 system of public education, proffering some vague notion that if we could just have teachers and schools as good as those we had when we were growing up, everything would be better. I argue that things weren't better 40 or 50 years ago. In fact, I believe they were worse. However, I'm unable to locate comparable education statistics from the 1950s or 1960s that could be measured against today's figures. Are statistics regarding high school completion, college attendance, teen drug usage, teen pregnancy and the like available for such a comparison?
Rick DeGraw
Maricopa Community Colleges
Tempe, Ariz.

Dear Rick:
There are actually quite a few surveys, dating as far back as the mid-1800s, that continually collect data on school-age children and education. Of course, there are certain aspects of the lives of young Americans, including their use of alcohol and drugs, for which continuous data collection has only recently begun.

Some of the oldest studies on education can be found in the annually published *Digest of Education Statistics*, from the National Center for Education Statistics (NCES). According to the latest edition of the digest, released in February 2002, there were 46.5 million students enrolled in the nation's public and private elementary and secondary schools as of the 1998–1999 school year (the latest complete year for which data is available), or 91 percent of those between the ages of 5 and 17—the highest percent of any year on record. A half century earlier (1949–1950), the number of enrolled pupils was just 25.1 million, or 83 percent of all young people. The data reveals that the student-to-teacher ratio today is markedly lower than it was "back then." In 1949, there were 26.1 students per instructional staff member (which, in addition to teachers, includes principals, supervisors, librarians, etc.); by the fall of 1998, there were 12.6 students per staff member.

Statistics from the U.S. Census Bureau show that Americans are not just going to school in record numbers, they're also staying there longer. In 1940, barely a quarter of Americans age 25 and older (18 million adults) had completed high school. By 1960, 41 percent of the population (41 million adults) had at least a high school diploma. Today, 84 percent of all adults age 25 and older (147 million individuals) have completed secondary school, and many of them have gone on to college: The percentage of Americans with a four-year college degree is now 26 percent, up from just 5 percent in 1940.

NEW KIDS, SAME OLD PROBLEMS
In Gallup polls sponsored by Phi Beta Kappa that have been conducted every year since 1970, Americans continue to cite "lack of discipline" and "lack of financial support" as major problems facing the nation's public schools. In more recent years, concerns about overcrowding and school violence have cropped up, while concerns over racial segregation have gone by the wayside.

ITEMS MOST FREQUENTLY CITED BY THE GENERAL PUBLIC AS A MAJOR PROBLEM FACING PUBLIC SCHOOLS:

	1970	1985	2002
Lack of discipline	18%	25%	17%
Lack of financial support	17%	9%	23%
Fighting/violence/gangs	—	—	9%
Use of drugs	11%	18%	13%
Large schools/overcrowding	—	5%	17%
Getting good teachers	12%	10%	8%
Integration/segregation/racial discrimination	17%	4%	—

—Not identified as a major problem

Source: Gallup/Phi Beta Kappa

YOU EARNED IT

The percent of Americans with a college diploma has increased dramatically during the past half century, especially among black men and women.

PERCENT OF ADULTS AGE 25+ WHO HAVE COMPLETED 4 YEARS OF COLLEGE OR MORE:

	1950	1962*	1970	1980	1990	2000
All adults	6%	9%	11%	17%	21%	26%
Whites	NA	10%	12%	18%	22%	28%
Men	NA	12%	15%	22%	25%	31%
Women	NA	7%	9%	14%	19%	26%
Blacks	2%	4%	5%	8%	11%	17%
Men	2%	4%	5%	8%	12%	16%
Women	2%	4%	4%	8%	11%	17%
Hispanics	NA	NA	NA	8%	9%	11%
Men	NA	NA	NA	10%	10%	11%
Women	NA	NA	NA	6%	9%	11%

*Detailed data for 1960 is not available; data from 1962 has been used instead.
NA: Data not available.

Source: U.S. Census Bureau

As educational attainment rises, so do employers' demands from the work force. In 1973, for example, only 28 percent of prime-age workers (defined as those between the ages of 30 and 59) had attended a postsecondary institution, according to a report published by the U.S. Department of Education. By 2000, 59 percent of prime-age workers said they had continued their education after completing high school. Money is also drawing more Americans to get a college degree. In 2000, men and women with a bachelor's degree earned 79 percent more each year than their peers who had just a high school diploma.

Women these days are freer to continue their education without having to care for a baby. According to the National Center for Health Statistics, there were just 45.9 births per 1,000 women ages 15 to 19 in 2001, the lowest number ever recorded. In fact, the teen birth rate has been falling fairly consistently since the height of the Baby Boom years in 1957, when there was a record 96.3 births for every 1,000 teenage girls.

Drug use, however, has not seen a similar decline. According to a study on drug use of high school seniors, conducted each year since 1975 by the University of Michigan, 55 percent of students in the class of 1975 had tried at least one illicit drug. By 2002, 53 percent of students had tried drugs—hardly a significant reduction. Drug use is actually higher among high school seniors today than it was during the late '80s and early '90s.

Another problem that has captured the attention of parents and educators more recently is school violence. While hard numbers on the topic can be found dating back only to the early '90s, it appears that the situation is already improving. According to "Indicators of School Crime and Safety," a report published by the NCES and the Bureau of Justice Statistics, the number of nonfatal crimes against students ages 12 through 18, occurring either at school or on the way to or from school, fell to 1.9 million in 2000 (the latest year for which data is available) from a high of 3.8 million reported in 1994. That's a 50 percent reduction.

Although you didn't ask about suicide information specifically, you might find it sobering that the rate which young people (ages 15 to 24) take their own lives has risen significantly over the years. In 1950, the NCES reported that there were 4.5 suicides for every 100,000 individuals ages 15 to 24; in 2000, there were 10.4 suicides. Among certain subgroups, the rate is even higher. For white males between 15 and 24 years of age, for instance, the suicide rate today is 18.2, up from 6.6 in 1950. That's something to think about when celebrating advances in other areas.

HOW TO REACH US:

John Fetto
Fax: (212) 716-8472
E-mail: jfetto@mediacentral.com
Address: 261 Madison Avenue, 9th floor, New York, NY 10016

From *American Demographics*, April 2003, pp. 8-9. © 2003 by PRIMEDIA Business Magazines & Media Inc. All rights reserved.

Article 6

SPECIAL REPORT: KIDS' HEALTH

IS AMERICA RAISING Unhealthy KIDS?

YES, BUT TEACHERS CAN DO SOMETHING ABOUT IT

Children across the U.S. are failing to make the grade when it comes to fitness and nutrition. Some experts say kids' lack of exercise, and the excess of junk food in their diets, may negatively affect their academic performance....

By Denise Willi

Couch Potato Crisis

Diabetes, obesity, little physical exercise... the news is bleak for the health of America's children

Nine million American children aged 6 to 19 are overweight. That is triple the number of 20 years ago, according to the Centers for Disease Control and Prevention. Between video games, computers, and TV, children have become more sedentary than ever before. One study found that 33 percent of children watched three hours or more of television daily. Much of that time involves kids watching about 10,000 commercials for junk food a year, according to researchers at Yale University. Throw in the fact that only two percent of American kids eat the recommended daily requirements for all five major food groups, and it's no wonder that we're in danger of raising a generation of super-sized youth.

"The kids aren't the problem, it's what we're modeling for them that's the problem," says Dr. Mary Story, a professor of Public Health Nutrition at the University of Minnesota. "Americans are eating more on the run. They're serving less fruits and vegetables at home and eating more at fast food restaurants. They're having fewer family meals and eating more convenience foods."

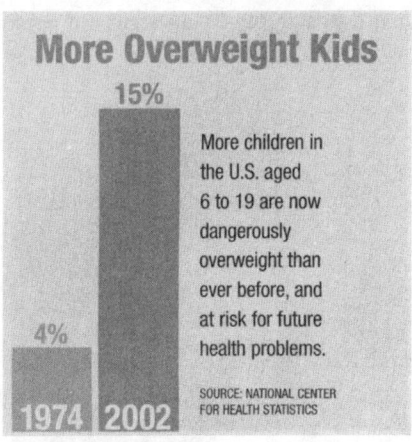

More children in the U.S. aged 6 to 19 are now dangerously overweight than ever before, and at risk for future health problems.

SOURCE: NATIONAL CENTER FOR HEALTH STATISTICS

Schools are also playing a role in the health and fitness crisis facing children. Many have installed vending and soda machines to help close their budget gaps. While school lunches are generally healthier than before, many children head straight for the calorie-laden food items or snack machines. The problem is

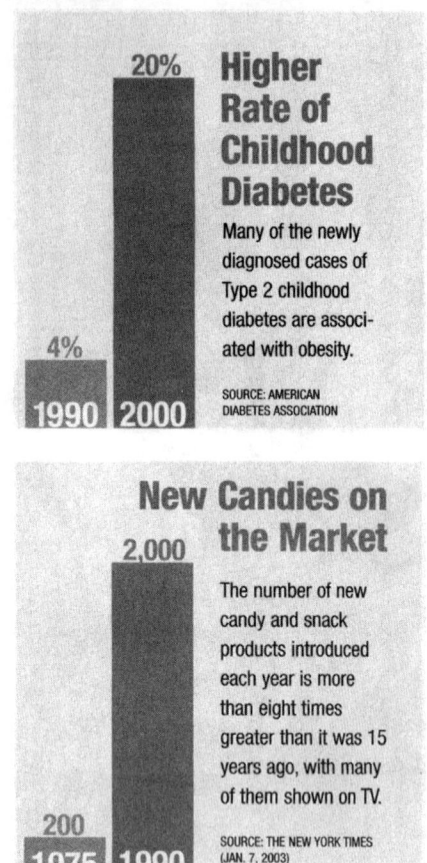

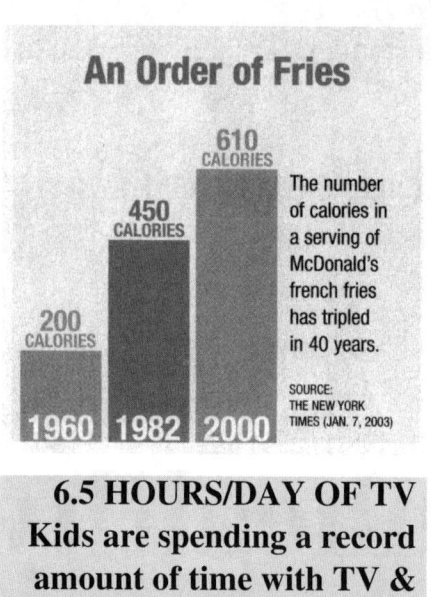

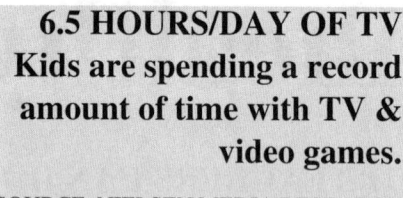

exacerbated by schools increasingly cutting back on physical education and recess time in favor of academics.

"Everywhere in the nation, we're feeling the pressure of testing, testing, testing," says Beverly Samek, director of School Coordinated Health Programs for District 60 in Boulder, Colorado. "We've lost the connection to the whole child and what they need to be a successful person—not just academics, but social skills, emotional skills, and health and fitness as well."

Studies show that children who are less active and eat poorly underachieve in the classroom. "Cutting recess time will not get the kind of academic results schools might be hoping for," says Dr. Vincent Ferrandino, Executive Director of the National Association of Elementary School Principals. "In fact, the opposite may occur."

Calling rising childhood obesity rates a "silent epidemic," former U.S. Surgeon General David Satcher chaired the Healthy Schools Summit in Washington, D.C., last fall, which focused on improving kids' health and educational performance. More than 500 educators, doctors, and nutritionists met to help develop statewide plans to address the issue through legislation and curricula to enhance nutrition, and fitness education.

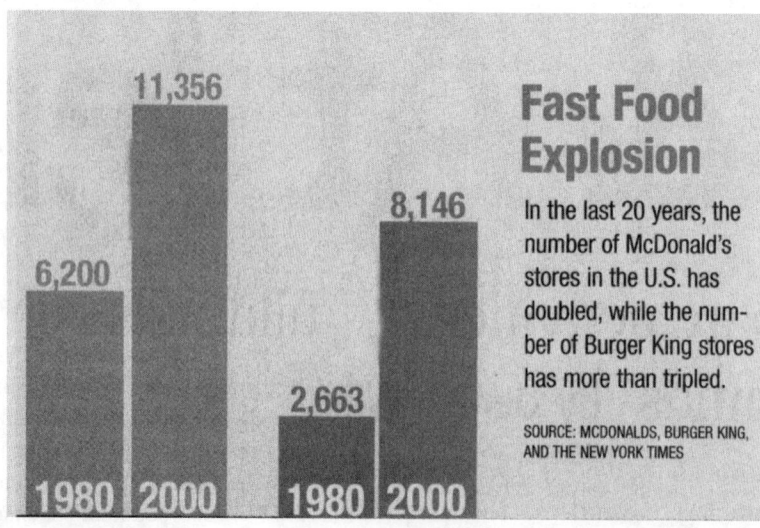

Up & At 'em

Teachers share activities to build kids' bodies & minds

Darla Perry knows an active body means an active mind. So when her third-grade students have been sitting in their chairs too long, Perry gives their bodies—and their brains—a boost. She weaves 10 minutes of movement into her curriculum. When they're done, her students feel recharged and refreshed. Here are some creative ways other teachers are incorporating physical activity and nutrition into the classroom day. They all help to improve kids' exercise and healthy eating habits.

1 Ready, Set, Spell!

This game uses movement to stimulate the brain and motivates students to remember their spelling words. To do this activity, you'll need clipboards, crayons, and room for your students to walk briskly. First, create a worksheet for each child. Down the side of the worksheets write the names of six to ten colors. Have the children line up at a start line. Each child should have crayons that represent the colors listed on the worksheet. Place the clipboards with the worksheets about 15 to 25 yards away. Then, call out a color, announce a spelling word from that week's vocabulary list, and say "Go!" Have students walk briskly to their clipboards, spell the word on the correct space on their worksheets in the color you have called out, and return to the start line. Repeat this activity, each time with a different color and vocabulary word, until students have completed their worksheets. When students are finished, have them grab their clipboards and head back to the start!

—*Carol Goodrow, Grade Two, Parker Memorial School, Tolland, CT*

2 Quick-Feet Math

Running and/or brisk walking lends itself to an unlimited number of lessons that reinforce math concepts. Whether you run or walk as a class, tell students to set a goal at the beginning of the year of how many miles or laps around the schoolyard they will complete each week. Have students keep a calendar to record their laps or miles as they try to reach that goal. Then have them use those calendars to add their total laps, convert the laps to miles, get the class total for the week, and average their daily, weekly, and monthly totals. You can even use brisk walking or running to teach the metric system, converting meters into miles.

—*Peter Saccone, Grade Five, Meridian Elementary School, El Cajon, CA*

3 Healthy-Body Salad

This lesson is a great way to teach young children about how healthy eating benefits the heart and mind. You can do it to celebrate a great week of student work, or as the culmination of a thematic unit about My Amazing Heart/Body. Tell students you will have a "heart-friendly party" with healthy foods that are fun to prepare and tasty to eat. Ask each child to bring in a healthy ingredient to make a salad—such as green-leaf lettuce (rather than iceberg, which has low nutritional value), carrots, black olives, low-fat cheese, or fat-free dressing. As each child adds his or her ingredient into a large bowl, describe how the ingredient is a heart-smart food. Then toss the salad and enjoy! For added fun, serve angel food cake with fresh strawberries.

—*Cammie Breedlove, Grade One, Grove Hill Elementary, Grove Hill, AL*

4 Animated Food Chain

When students incorporate movement into a unit about the food chain, they're more likely to remember what they've learned. To help them, have students choose a plant that is a producer—either a fruit or vegetable—that they will act out during an imaginary growing period. Tell students not to reveal their choice and remain silent. Then have them make their bodies as low to the ground as they can, as if they were simulating the shape of a plant that has yet to grow. Tell students they will grow based on the sound and rhythms of a hand drum. Then play the drum very softly when they are seedlings in the ground, medium loud when they are half way to maturation, and very loud when they are fully mature and ready to be harvested. Walk around and gently tap each student to signal that they can reveal what plant they have grown into. You might also ask students to tell what they know about the plant or describe its nutritional value.

—*Patty Aronofsky, Grade Four, Beulah Heights Elementary, Pueblo, CO*

5 Heart-Thumping Science

This cross-curricular lesson will show students the benefits of being physically active by teaching them what a healthy heart rate should be. As part of a science respiratory system unit, have students create a three-column chart with the following headings: date, pulse at rest, pulse after activity. Teach students how to find their pulse on their wrists or necks. Have them count their pulse rates for 15 seconds and multiply that number by four to get a pulse rate per minute. Set aside 15 minutes a day for the following: First, have each student record his or her pulse at rest on the chart. Then have kids do a vigorous activity indoors or out—a fast walk, jog, or jumping jacks—for five minutes. After five minutes call "time," and count down 4, 3, 2, 1. Have students record their pulse after the activity. At the end of two weeks, have students use their data to find mean, median, mode, and range of resting versus active pulse. Use the statistics to build double-line graphs with both pulses. Then have students write an essay or paragraph comparing and contrasting the two and telling what they learned.

—*Suzanne Bechina, Grade Five, Ben Franklin Elementary School, Pueblo, CO*

6 Roundabout Writing

This active, story-writing lesson helps build students' cardiovascular strength while getting their creative juices flowing. First, tell students to take out paper and pencil and to stand at their desks. Give them a topic to write about (e.g., You've just landed on an unexplored planet. Describe life on that planet). Then give students two minutes to start their stories. After two minutes, call "time" and tell students to walk briskly around the perimeter of the classroom and find another paper to stop at without sitting down. Give students four minutes to read what's on the paper and add to it. After four minutes, call time. Repeat the process three more times. Students must stop when time is called, even if it's mid-sentence. The next student can pick up from that exact spot. Tell students to go back to their own paper, read what others wrote, and then add their own ending to the story. Then have students share their stories with the class.

—*Julie Fischer, Grade Six, Spann Elementary School, Pueblo, CO*

7 The Great Plot Race

This lively activity helps students hone sequencing skills for the major events of a story. First, prepare a list of the main events of a story the class is reading. Using a 36- or 48-point font, type one event per page. Print out the events and laminate them as cards. Collate the cards into sets of four or more, then mix up each set so the cards are not in sequential order. Put each set into a folder. Then divide the class into groups of four, giving each member a number from one to four. Designate sections of the classroom wall as "hanging" areas, where students will tape or tack the events in order. Give each group a folder with a set of cards containing the event cards. At the sound of a starting whistle, the group arranges the events in sequential order. As soon as the group has all of the events in order, Runner 1 hangs the first event in that team's area of the room. When Runner 1 returns and is seated, Runner 2 hangs the second event. Continue until all the events are hung.

—*Susan Van Zile, Grade Six, Eagle View Middle School, Mechanicsburg, PA*

Visit **www.scholastic.com/instructor** for a full and rich array of kids' books on health, nutrition, and exercise.

Denise Willi is a freelance writer based in Sleepy Hollow, New York. She has written and edited for *The Washington Post* and *Reader's Digest*.

From *Scholastic Instructor*, March 2003, pp. 19-22, 24, 76. © 2003 by Scholastic Inc. Reprinted by permission.

Article 7

The 36th Annual
Phi Delta Kappa/Gallup Poll
of the Public's Attitudes Toward the Public Schools

By Lowell C. Rose and Alec M. Gallup

THE 36TH ANNUAL Phi Delta Kappa/Gallup Poll of the Public's Attitudes Toward the Public Schools continues the previous poll's focus on the No Child Left Behind (NCLB) Act because of that act's potential for improving student achievement and because of last year's finding that the strategies employed by NCLB at that time lacked the public support necessary to bring success. While some critics may question the appropriateness of the expanded federal presence in the area of K–12 education and others may believe that the federal mandate of NCLB is inadequately funded, this poll focuses on whether the public supports the strategies used in NCLB, strategies that are crucial to its primary goals of improving student achievement and simultaneously closing a minority achievement gap that has plagued our society for years. Without public support for these strategies, the goals of NCLB are not likely to be accomplished.

Executive Summary

The public's attitudes toward the public schools shape the initiatives and strategies that can be brought to bear to improve those schools so that they can meet the changing needs of our society. As this poll has evolved over 35 years, its primary purpose has become that of tracing and interpreting the public's view of its schools. This, the 36th poll in the series, continues that effort. However, readers are encouraged to do their own take on the data, to measure the authors' interpretations of the data against their own, and to draw their own conclusions. If the information provided here advances the discussion of the issues, the poll's purpose will have been served.

The federal No Child Left Behind Act dominates the public education scene. It is inextricably linked to the effort to improve overall student achievement while simultaneously moving to close the achievement gap. Closely tied to this effort is the debate over the appropriate role of standardized testing. The poll addresses these issues against the background of the public's assessment of the public schools. It then turns to questions about the appropriate venue for pursuing change and how the public views selected proposals for change. Finally, the poll explores the public's opinion of the two political parties' relationship to public education and how that thinking is likely to affect the November election.

We begin this report with 16 conclusions that the authors believe capture the poll's most significant findings. Rationales are provided, and the tables containing the data on which the conclusions are based are referenced by number.

1. The trend line showing that the public in general gives reasonably high marks to the public schools continues. Those marks go higher when parents do the rating and even higher when parents rate the school their oldest child attends. This year 47% of all respondents give the schools in their community an A or a B; 61% of parents give the schools in their community an A or a B; and 70% of parents give the school attended by their oldest child an A or a B. (See Tables 1 and 3.)

2. It is important to distinguish between the schools in the community and the schools nationally, since the marks vary greatly. It is the latter schools that traditionally receive low grades. Schools nationally receive a total of 26% A's and B's in this year's poll. (See Table 2.) Respondents have no direct knowledge of these schools, and it would seem that public policy should be based on judgments of schools that are familiar to those doing the assessing.

3. Lack of financial support is now firmly established in the public's mind as the major problem facing the public schools. Issues related to discipline and drugs dominated the poll as the major concern until 2000, when lack of financial support rose to the top. In 2001, it was tied for first place; in each subsequent year it has stood alone at the top. Twenty-one percent in this year's poll mention finance as the number-one problem. (See Table 4.) No other problem exceeds 10%.

ANNUAL EDITIONS

4. As it has indicated in every poll since 1999, the public expects change in the public schools to come through reforming the existing system, not through seeking an alternative. Given the choice of reforming the existing system or finding an alternative system, 66% choose reform of the existing system while 26% point to seeking an alternative. (See Table 5.)

5. The public lacks the information it believes it would need to form an opinion about NCLB.

- Last year, 76% of respondents said they knew little or nothing about NCLB; this year, that figure is 68%. (See Table 6.)
- Last year, 78% of public school parents said they knew little or nothing about NCLB; this year, that figure is 62%. (See Table 6.)
- Last year, 69% of respondents said they did not know enough about NCLB to say whether their view was favorable or unfavorable; this year, that figure is 55%. (See Table 7.)

6. The public disagrees with the major strategies NCLB uses to determine whether a school is or is not in need of improvement. Unless these strategies are modified, there is little reason to change last year's conclusion that greater familiarity with NCLB is unlikely to bring approval.

- Sixty-seven percent say the performance of a school's students on a single test is not sufficient for judging whether the school is in need of improvement. (See Table 8.)
- Eighty-three percent say testing in English and math only will not yield a fair picture of a school. (See Table 9.)
- Seventy-three percent say it is not possible to judge a student's proficiency in English and math on the basis of a single test. (See Table 10.)
- Eighty-one percent are concerned that basing decisions about schools on students' performance in English and math only will mean less emphasis on art, music, history, and other subjects. (See Table 11.)
- If a school is found to be in need of improvement, 80% would favor keeping students in that school and making additional efforts to help them, while 16% would favor permitting students to transfer to a school not in need of improvement. (See Table 12.)
- If a school is found to be in need of improvement, 55% would prefer to have students tutored by teachers in that school as compared to 40% who would prefer tutoring to be provided by an outside agency. (See Table 13.)

7. At this time the public does not support the separate reporting of test data mandated by NCLB and does not support the inclusion of special education students on the same basis as all other students. Fifty-two percent of respondents oppose separating test scores by race and ethnicity, disabled status, English-speaking ability, and poverty level; 61% oppose requiring special education students to meet the same standards as other students; 57% oppose including special education scores in determining whether a school is in need of improvement; and 56% oppose designating a school as in need of improvement based on special education scores alone. (See Tables 14–17.)

8. There is still time to make the changes that must be made in NCLB if it is to improve student achievement while contributing to closing the achievement gap. Despite the problems NCLB has encountered, 56% of respondents believe the goal of having a highly qualified teacher in every classroom by the end of 2005-06 is likely to be met, and 51% believe the act will improve student achievement in their local schools. (See Tables 18 and 19.)

9. Despite the controversy that has accompanied the increasing use of standardized tests for high-stakes purposes, there is majority support for at least the current level of testing. Forty percent say there is about the right amount of emphasis on standardized tests, 32% say there is too much emphasis, and 22% say there is too little emphasis. The percentage saying there is too much emphasis is up 12% since 1997. (See Table 20.)

10. The public is divided regarding the use of standardized tests for high-stakes purposes. This poll queried respondents about the use of standardized tests for deciding whether to grant a high school diploma and for judging the quality of teachers and principals.

- Fifty-one percent of respondents favor using a single standardized test as the basis for awarding a diploma; 47% oppose. (See Table 21.)
- Forty-nine percent say students' performance on standardized tests should be one of the measures used in judging teacher quality; 47% say student test scores should not be used. (See Table 22.)
- As to judging principals, 47% say standardized test scores of students in the school should be one measure of quality; 50% say test scores should not be used for this purpose. (See Table 23.)

11. The public believes strongly that the achievement gaps that separate white students from black and other minority students must be closed. Though respondents do not attribute the gap to schools, they believe the schools must close it. Eighty-eight percent say that it is important that the achievement gap be closed. Although 74% attribute the gap to factors other than schooling, 56% say it is the responsibility of the schools to close it. (See Tables 24–26.)

12. The public gives strong support to a variety of measures mentioned as possibilities for closing the gap. Six strategies that are among those frequently mentioned as possibilities for closing the gap all draw strong support. Strategies supported by more than 90% of respondents include encouraging more parent involvement, providing more instructional time for low-performing students, and strengthening remedial programs for low-performing students. (See Table 27.)

13. The idea of allowing parents to choose a private school for their child to attend at public expense continues to lack majority support. Fifty-four percent of respondents oppose this choice option, as compared to 42% who favor it. (See Table 30.) The other choice-related questions suggest that religious reasons would be the major factor in causing people to use a voucher to attend a nonpublic school. This conclusion applies whether the voucher covers all or half of the tuition. (See Tables 31 and 32.)

14. The public supports adding rigor to the high school curriculum and supports mandatory attendance until age 18. Seventy-eight percent of respondents favor requiring students to complete four years of English, math, and science in order to receive a diploma, and 66% would increase the mandatory attendance age to 18. (See Tables 34 and 35.)

15. While a plurality of respondents believe the Democratic Party is more interested in improving public education, the Republican Party continues to narrow the gap. Forty-two percent of respondents identify the Democratic Party as more interested in education, while 35% identify the Republican Party. The gap narrowed by 5 percentage points from 1996 to 2000 and by 5 percentage points from 2000 to 2004. (See Table 38.)

16. A dead heat results when respondents are asked which of the Presidential candidates they would support if they were voting solely on education issues. John Kerry and George Bush each draw support from 41% of respondents. (See Table 39.)

Assessment, Problems, and Change

Grading the Public Schools

Tables 1, 2, and 3 report the trend questions used to track the public's assessment of the public schools. Adding this year's 33% of respondents who give the schools a C to the 47% who give the schools an A or a B brings the total to 80%. For public school parents, the percentage who assign the top three grades is 85%.

TABLE 1. Students are often given the grades of A, B, C, D, and FAIL to denote the quality of their work. Suppose the public schools themselves, in your community, were graded in the same way. What grade would you give the public schools here—A, B, C, D, or FAIL?

	National Totals '04 %	National Totals '03 %	No Children In School '04 %	No Children In School '03 %	Public School Parents '04 %	Public School Parents '03 %
A & B	47	48	42	45	61	55
A	13	11	11	8	17	17
B	34	37	31	37	44	38
C	33	31	37	30	24	31
D	10	10	9	10	10	10
FAIL	4	5	3	7	5	3
Don't know	6	6	9	8	*	1

*Less than one-half of 1%.

TABLE 2. How about the public schools in the nation as a whole? What grade would you give the public schools nationally—A, B, C, D, or FAIL?

	National Totals '04 %	National Totals '03 %	No Children In School '04 %	No Children In School '03 %	Public School Parents '04 %	Public School Parents '03 %
A & B	26	26	28	26	22	26
A	2	2	2	1	3	5
B	24	24	26	25	19	21
C	45	52	45	52	44	49
D	13	12	13	11	13	13
FAIL	4	3	3	4	6	2
Don't know	12	7	11	7	15	10

TABLE 3. Using the A, B, C, D, FAIL scale again, what grade would you give the school your oldest child attends?

	Public School Parents '04 %	Public School Parents '03 %
A & B	70	68
A	24	29
B	46	39
C	16	20
D	8	8
FAIL	4	4
Don't know	2	*

* Less than one-half of 1%.

The Biggest Problem

Table 4 provides responses to an open-ended question for which the public initiates the answers. The question is also the only one to have appeared in all 35 previous polls. The major problem has varied with the times and has included discipline, use of drugs, lack of financial support, and gangs and violence. For the moment, the public is firmly settled on lack of financial support as the biggest problem.

TABLE 4. What do you think are the biggest problems the public schools of your community must deal with?

	National Totals '04 %	National Totals '03 %	National Totals '02 %	No Children In School '04 %	No Children In School '03 %	No Children In School '02 %	Public School Parents '04 %	Public School Parents '03 %	Public School Parents '02 %
Lack of financial support/ funding/money	21	25	23	22	26	23	20	24	23
Lack of discipline, more control	10	16	17	10	17	18	8	13	13
Overcrowded schools	10	14	17	9	12	14	13	16	23
Use of drugs/dope	7	9	13	7	10	14	7	7	11
Fighting/ violence/gangs	6	4	9	6	3	9	6	5	9

The Means of Improving Public Education

Starting in 2000, the poll began to ask the public how it expected improvement in schooling to come about. The choices offered were reforming the existing system or finding an alternative system. The public has consistently opted for improving the existing system.

19

TABLE 5. In order to improve public education in America, some people think the focus should be on reforming the existing public school system. Others believe the focus should be on finding an alternative to the existing public school system. Which approach do you think is preferable—reforming the existing public school system or finding an alternative to the existing public school system?

	National Totals '04 %	'03 %	'02 %	'01 %	'00 %	No Children In School '04 %	'03 %	'02 %	'01 %	'00 %	Public School Parents '04 %	'03 %	'02 %	'01 %	'00 %
Reforming existing system	66	73	69	72	59	63	73	69	73	59	72	73	69	73	60
Finding alternative system	26	25	27	24	34	28	24	26	23	34	21	25	27	25	34
Don't know	8	2	4	4	7	9	3	5	4	7	7	2	4	2	6

No Child Left Behind Act

Information and Attitudes

More than two years after the passage of NCLB and despite the publicity it has received, the public continues to regard itself as insufficiently informed to comment on the law. The data in Table 6 indicate that public school parents have gained the most knowledge in the past year: the percentage saying they know very little or nothing at all about NCLB has dropped from 78% to 62%. Table 7, which reports on attitudes toward NCLB, summarizes separately the results for those saying they know "a great deal" or "a fair amount" about the law and those saying they know "very little" or "nothing at all" about it. In the groups claiming knowledge, a greater number of respondents indicate a favorable attitude toward NCLB, while a somewhat smaller number indicate an unfavorable attitude. The division between favorable and unfavorable opinions is smaller among those saying they know "very little" or "nothing at all." Note, however, that a large percentage of those in this group do not feel they know enough to express an opinion.

TABLE 6. Now, here are a few questions about the No Child Left Behind Act. How much, if anything, would you say you know about the No Child Left Behind Act—the federal education bill that was passed by Congress in 2001—a great deal, a fair amount, very little, or nothing at all?

	National Totals '04 %	'03 %	No Children In School '04 %	'03 %	Public School Parents '04 %	'03 %
Great deal + fair amount	31	24	28	25	37	22
A great deal	7	6	6	5	8	7
A fair amount	24	18	22	20	29	15
Very little	40	40	41	37	38	44
Nothing at all	28	36	30	38	24	34
Don't know	1	*	1	*	1	*
Very little + nothing at all	68	76	71	75	62	78

* Less than one-half of 1%.

TABLE 7. From what you know or have heard or read about the No Child Left Behind Act, do you have a very favorable, somewhat favorable, somewhat unfavorable, or very unfavorable opinion of the act—or don't you know enough about it to say?

	National Totals '04 %	'03 %	Those Knowing Great Deal '04 %	Those Knowing Fair Amount '04 %	Those Knowing Very Little '04 %	Those Knowing Nothing At All '04 %
Very favorable + somewhat favorable	24	18	50	47	19	5
Very favorable	7	5	27	9	5	2
Somewhat favorable	17	13	23	38	14	3
Somewhat unfavorable	12	7	10	26	11	1
Very unfavorable	8	6	31	11	6	3
Don't know enough to say	55	69	8	14	64	89
Don't know	1	*	1	2	*	2
Somewhat unfavorable + very unfavorable	20	13	41	37	17	4

* Less than one-half of 1%.

Reaction to NCLB Strategies

Tables 8 through 13 focus on specific NCLB strategies, some of which are used to determine if a school is in need of improvement and others that come into play after such a determination has been made. In Table 8 respondents reject the use of a single statewide test for determining a school's status. In Table 9 they reject basing that decision on English and math only. In Table 10 they reject using a single test as the basis for judging student proficiency in English and math. Table 11 data reflect the public's concern over the negative impact the emphasis on English and math will have on other subjects. The data in Table 12 show that parents prefer helping students in the school over allowing students to transfer out. Table 13 indicates that parents prefer tutoring by teachers in their child's school over tutoring by an outside agency. And those claiming knowledge of NCLB are as critical of its strategies as those claiming little knowledge and in some cases more critical.

Article 7. The 36th Annual Phi Delta Kappa/Gallup Poll of the Public's Attitudes Toward the Public Schools

TABLE 8. According to the NCLB Act, determining whether a public school is or is not in need of improvement will be based on the performance of its students on a single statewide test. In your opinion, will a single test provide a fair picture of whether or not a school needs improvement?

	National Totals '04 %	National Totals '03 %	No Children In School '04 %	No Children In School '03 %	Public School Parents '04 %	Public School Parents '03 %	Those Knowing Great Deal/Fair Amount '04 %	Those Knowing Very Little/Nothing At All '04 %
Yes	31	32	33	32	28	31	28	32
No	67	66	64	67	70	66	71	65
Don't know	2	2	3	1	2	3	1	3

TABLE 9. According to the NCLB Act, the statewide tests of students' performance will be devoted to English and math only. Do you think a test covering only English and math would provide a fair picture of whether a school in your community is or is not in need of improvement, or should the test be based on other subjects also?

	National Totals '04 %	National Totals '03 %	No Children In School '04 %	No Children In School '03 %	Public School Parents '04 %	Public School Parents '03 %	Those Knowing Great Deal/Fair Amount '04 %	Those Knowing Very Little/Nothing At All '04 %
Test covering only English and math would provide a fair picture of whether a school is in need of improvement	16	15	15	14	18	18	20	14
Test should be based on other subjects also	83	83	84	84	81	81	79	85
Don't know	1	2	1	2	1	1	1	1

TABLE 10. In your opinion, is it possible or not possible to accurately judge a student's proficiency in English and math on the basis of a single test?

	National Totals '04 %	National Totals '03 %	No Children In School '04 %	No Children In School '03 %	Public School Parents '04 %	Public School Parents '03 %	Those Knowing Great Deal/Fair Amount '04 %	Those Knowing Very Little/Nothing At All '04 %
Yes, possible	25	26	26	27	24	22	27	24
No, not possible	73	72	72	71	75	77	72	74
Don't know	2	2	2	2	1	1	1	2

TABLE 11. How much, if at all, are you concerned that relying on testing for English and math only to judge a school's performance will mean less emphasis on art, music, history, and other subjects? Would you say you are concerned a great deal, a fair amount, not much, or not at all?

	National Totals '04 %	National Totals '03 %	No Children In School '04 %	No Children In School '03 %	Public School Parents '04 %	Public School Parents '03 %	Those Knowing Great Deal/Fair Amount '04 %	Those Knowing Very Little/Nothing At All '04 %
A great deal + a fair amount	81	80	81	80	85	82	84	81
A great deal	37	40	35	38	43	45	42	35
A fair amount	44	40	46	42	42	37	42	46
Not much	13	14	13	13	11	15	10	14
Not at all	4	6	4	7	3	3	4	5
Don't know	2	*	2	*	1	*	2	0

* Less than one-half of 1%.

TABLE 12. Assume you had a child attending a school identified as in need of improvement by the NCLB Act. Which would you prefer, to transfer your child to a school identified as NOT in need of improvement or to have additional efforts made in your child's present school to help him or her achieve?

	National Totals '04 %	National Totals '03 %	No Children In School '04 %	No Children In School '03 %	Public School Parents '04 %	Public School Parents '03 %	Those Knowing Great Deal/Fair Amount '04 %	Those Knowing Very Little/Nothing At All '04 %
To transfer child to school identified as not in need of improvement	16	25	16	24	14	25	18	15
To have additional efforts made in child's present school	80	74	79	75	85	74	81	80
Don't know	4	1	5	1	1	1	1	5

TABLE 13. Now, let's assume that your child was failing in his or her school. Which kind of tutoring would you prefer—tutoring provided by teachers in your child's school or tutoring provided by an outside agency that you would select from a state-approved list?

	National Totals '04 %	National Totals '03 %	No Children In School '04 %	No Children In School '03 %	Public School Parents '04 %	Public School Parents '03 %	Those Knowing Great Deal/Fair Amount '04 %	Those Knowing Very Little/Nothing At All '04 %
Tutoring provided by teachers in child's school	55	52	53	52	60	54	53	56
Tutoring provided by outside agency	40	45	42	46	34	42	41	39
Don't know	5	3	5	2	6	4	6	5

Reaction to NCLB's Separate Reporting of Data

The findings in Table 14 are the most surprising and should be of most concern for the supporters of NCLB. The separate reporting of test data would appear to have brought much-needed attention to the existing achievement gap. Nonetheless, Table 14 data indicate that a divided public rejects this strategy. The data in Tables 15 through 17 may be part of the problem, since they indicate that the public rejects holding special education students to the same grade-level standards as other students, rejects their inclusion in the base for determining if a school is in need of improvement, and rejects deciding a school's status on the basis of special education students' performance alone. This issue may prove difficult to resolve, since many in the special education community believe special education students should be included and judged according to the same standards as all other students.

ANNUAL EDITIONS

TABLE 14. The No Child Left Behind Act requires that test scores be reported separately by students' race and ethnicity, disability status, English-speaking ability, and poverty level. Do you favor or oppose reporting test scores in this way in your community?

	National Totals %	No Children In School %	Public School Parents %	Those Knowing Great Deal/ Fair Amount %	Those Knowing Very Little/ Nothing At All %
Favor	42	41	45	47	41
Oppose	52	53	53	51	53
Don't know	6	6	2	2	6

TABLE 15. In your opinion, should students enrolled in special education be required to meet the same standards as all other students in the school?

	National Totals '04 %	National Totals '03 %	No Children In School '04 %	No Children In School '03 %	Public School Parents '04 %	Public School Parents '03 %
Yes, should	36	31	37	31	35	31
No, should not	61	67	59	66	63	68
Don't know	3	2	4	3	2	1

TABLE 16. In your opinion, should the standardized test scores of special education students be included with the test scores of all other students in determining whether a school is in need of improvement under NCLB or not?

	National Totals %	No Children In School %	Public School Parents %
Yes, should	39	40	40
No, should not	57	56	57
Don't know	4	4	3

TABLE 17. In your opinion, should a school be designated in need of improvement if the special education students are the only group in that school that fails to make state goals or not?

	National Totals %	No Children In School %	Public School Parents %
Yes, should	39	40	39
No, should not	56	54	58
Don't know	5	6	3

Some Good News About NCLB

The findings in Table 18 indicate that a majority of respondents believe that the NCLB goal of having a highly qualified teacher in every classroom by the end of the 2005–06 school year is likely to be achieved. The findings in Table 19 show that 51% believe NCLB is likely to improve achievement in schools in the community, while 32% believe it will not. Given the fact that so many have not made up their minds about NCLB, these findings suggest that there is still time to deal with the strategy issues that appear, at this time, to be hampering NCLB.

TABLE 18. NCLB requires that there be a highly qualified teacher in each classroom by the end of the 2005–06 school year. What do you think is the likelihood of this happening in the public schools in your community by that time?

	National Totals %	No Children in School %	Public School Parents %	Those Knowing Great Deal/Fair Amount %	Those Knowing Very Little/ Nothing At All %
Very likely	19	17	24	26	17
Somewhat likely	37	36	41	37	37
Not very likely	31	33	25	25	34
Not at all likely	11	11	10	12	10
Don't know	2	3	*	*	2

* Less than one-half of 1%.

TABLE 19. From what you have seen or heard about the No Child Left Behind Act, how much do you think it will help to improve student achievement in the public schools in your community?

	National Totals %	No Children in School %	Public School Parents %	Those Knowing Great Deal/ Fair Amount %	Those Knowing Very Little/ Nothing At All %
Great deal + fair amount	51	49	57	53	51
A great deal	21	19	25	20	21
A fair amount	30	30	32	33	30
Not very much	23	23	21	32	19
Not at all	9	11	7	13	8
Don't know	17	17	15	2	22
Not very much + not at all	32	34	28	45	27

Appropriate Uses of Standardized Tests

How Much and for What Purpose

Standardized tests have become a flash point as they are used more frequently to support high-stakes decisions related to efforts to improve achievement and close the achievement gap. The data in Table 20 indicate that, while a good majority continue to believe that the amount of testing is about right or not enough, the percentage saying "too much" has gone up 12% since 1997. Tables 21 through 23 may help to explain this since they show a public that is divided regarding the use of standardized tests to make high-stakes decisions related to graduation and the quality of educators.

Article 7. The 36th Annual Phi Delta Kappa/Gallup Poll of the Public's Attitudes Toward the Public Schools

TABLE 20. Now, here are some questions about testing. In your opinion, is there too much emphasis on achievement testing in the public schools in this community, not enough emphasis on testing, or about the right amount?

	National Totals '04 %	'02 %	'01 %	'00 %	'97 %	No Children In School '04 %	'02 %	'01 %	'00 %	'97 %	Public School Parents '04 %	'02 %	'01 %	'00 %	'97 %
Too much	32	31	31	30	20	30	30	29	28	20	36	32	36	34	19
Not enough	22	19	22	23	28	23	20	22	26	28	20	14	20	19	26
About the right amount	40	47	44	43	48	40	46	45	41	46	43	54	43	46	54
Don't know	6	3	3	4	4	7	4	4	5	6	1	*	1	1	1

* Less than one-half of 1%.

TABLE 21. Do you favor or oppose using a single standardized test in the public schools in your community to determine whether a student should receive a high school diploma?

	National Totals %	No Children In School %	Public School Parents %
Favor	51	50	52
Oppose	47	47	45
Don't know	2	3	3

TABLE 22. In your opinion, should one of the measurements of a teacher's ability be based on how well his or her students perform on standardized tests or not?

	National Totals %	No Children In School %	Public School Parents %
Yes, should	49	50	49
No, should not	47	45	49
Don't know	4	5	2

TABLE 23. How about school principals? In your opinion, should one of the measurements of a principal's quality be based on how well the students in his or her school perform on standardized tests or not?

	National Totals %	No Children In School %	Public School Parents %
Yes, should	47	47	48
No, should not	50	50	51
Don't know	3	3	1

The Achievement Gap

Closing the Achievement Gap

The data in Table 24 indicate that the public has consistently given high priority to closing the achievement gap between white students and minority students. The public is equally consistent, as indicated in Table 25, in its belief that the gap results from factors other than schooling. In last year's poll, respondents indicated that the three most important factors in creating the gap were lack of parent involvement, home life and upbringing, and lack of interest on the part of the students themselves. Although the public does not believe that the gap is related to schooling, the data in Table 26 indicate that the public believes the schools must close it. The data in Table 27 reflect strong public support for six strategies for closing the gap. A 1978 question found 80% expressing the view that educational opportunities for whites and minorities were the same. The data in Table 28 indicate that this view is unchanged. The data in Table 29 suggest that the public places the responsibility for how well students learn primarily on parents. This view is in line with last year's finding that a lack of parent involvement is crucial to creating the gap.

TABLE 24. Black and Hispanic students generally score lower on standardized tests than white students. In your opinion, how important do you think it is to close this academic achievement gap between these groups of students?

	National Totals '04 %	'03 %	'02 %	'01 %	No Children In School '04 %	'03 %	'02 %	'01 %	Public School Parents '04 %	'03 %	'02 %	'01 %
Very + somewhat important	88	90	94	88	89	91	93	89	89	88	96	87
Very important	64	71	80	66	65	70	80	66	63	73	80	67
Somewhat important	24	19	14	22	24	21	13	23	26	15	16	20
Not too important	5	5	2	5	4	5	2	5	3	4	2	5
Not at all important	5	4	3	5	5	3	4	4	7	7	1	6
Don't know	2	1	1	2	2	1	1	2	1	1	1	2

TABLE 25. In your opinion, is the achievement gap between white students and black and Hispanic students mostly related to the quality of schooling received or mostly related to other factors?

	National Totals '04 %	'03 %	'02 %	'01 %	No Children In School '04 %	'03 %	'02 %	'01 %	Public School Parents '04 %	'03 %	'02 %	'01 %
Mostly related to quality of schooling received	19	16	29	21	19	15	31	20	20	18	22	22
Mostly related to other factors	74	80	66	73	73	80	64	72	76	80	75	74
Don't know	7	4	5	6	8	5	5	8	4	2	3	4

TABLE 26. In your opinion, is it the responsibility of the public schools to close the achievement gap between white students and black and Hispanic students or not?

	National Totals '04 %	National Totals '01 %	No Children In School '04 %	No Children In School '01 %	Public School Parents '04 %	Public School Parents '01 %
Yes, it is	56	55	56	56	56	53
No, it is not	40	41	39	39	41	45
Don't know	4	4	5	5	3	2

TABLE 27. Numerous proposals have been suggested as ways to close the achievement gap between white, black, and Hispanic students. As I mention some of these proposals, one at a time, would you tell me whether you would favor or oppose it as a way to close the achievement gap.

	Favor %	Oppose %	Don't Know %
Encourage more parent involvement	97	2	1
Provide more instructional time for low-performing students	94	5	1
Strengthen remedial programs for low-performing students	92	6	2
Provide free breakfast and free lunch programs as needed	84	15	1
Provide state-funded preschool programs	80	18	2
Provide in-school health clinics	76	21	3

TABLE 28. In your opinion, do black children and other minority children in your community have the same educational opportunities as white children?

	National Totals '04 %	National Totals '01 %	National Totals '78 %	No Children In School '04 %	No Children In School '01 %	No Children In School '78 %	Public School Parents '04 %	Public School Parents '01 %	Public School Parents '78 %
Yes, the same	78	79	80	76	78	78	82	80	86
No, not the same	20	18	14	22	17	15	16	18	11
Don't know	2	3	6	2	5	7	2	2	3

TABLE 29. In your opinion, who is most important in determining how well or how poorly students perform in school—the students themselves, the students' teachers, or the students' parents?

	National Totals %	No Children In School %	Public School Parents %
Students themselves	22	23	21
Students' teachers	30	31	29
Students' parents	45	42	48
Don't know	3	4	2

Vouchers and Other Proposals

We have already noted that the public expects improvement in the public schools to come through reforming the existing public school system. That does not preclude the consideration of alternatives such as vouchers. The following tables provide an update regarding public opinion on vouchers and other proposals for change.

The Public View of Vouchers

Support for vouchers ranged from 41% to 44% in the late 1990s but dropped to 39% in 2000 and 34% in 2001. Fluctuations in support are now the norm, with a jump of 12% between 2001 and 2002, followed by a decline of 8% in 2003 and an increase of 4% this year.

TABLE 30. Do you favor or oppose allowing students and parents to choose a private school to attend at public expense?

	'04 %	'03 %	'02 %	'01 %	'00 %	'99 %	'98 %	'97 %
Favor	42	38	46	34	39	41	44	44
Oppose	54	60	52	62	56	55	50	52
Don't know	4	2	2	4	5	4	6	4

TABLE 31. Suppose you had a school-age child and were given a voucher covering full tuition that would permit you to send that child to any public, private, or church-related school of your choice. Which kind of school do you think you would choose?

	National Totals '04 %	National Totals '03 %	No Children In School '04 %	No Children In School '03 %	Public School Parents '04 %	Public School Parents '03 %
A public school	37	35	38	35	38	39
A church-related private school	36	38	33	37	40	38
A non-church-related private school	20	24	22	25	17	21
Don't know	7	3	7	3	5	2

TABLE 32. What if the voucher covered only half of the tuition, which do you think you would choose?

	National Totals '04 %	National Totals '03 %	No Children In School '04 %	No Children In School '03 %	Public School Parents '04 %	Public School Parents '03 %
A public school	46	47	46	45	50	55
A church-related private school	32	34	29	34	34	29
A non-church-related private school	16	17	18	19	11	15
Don't know	6	2	7	2	5	1

Other Proposals for Change

The next four tables report public opinion on a variety of suggestions for change that have surfaced at the state level this year. The data in Table 33 show that the public believes that an increased emphasis on English, math, and science will benefit a great many students. The data in Table 34 document strong support for requiring students to complete four years of English, math, and science in order to graduate from high school. The data in Table 35 show strong support for increasing the mandatory attendance age to 18. As reported in Table 36, the idea of eliminating the senior year of high school is soundly rejected. (This idea surfaced in a state facing a financial crisis.) Finally, Table 37 reports respondents' views on criteria that might be used to determine whether teachers should receive extra pay.

TABLE 33. Some states are now requiring the public schools to place greater emphasis at all grade levels on English, math, and science. Thinking about the needs of the public school students in your community, do you think this increased emphasis will serve all, most, some, or only a few of these students' needs?

	National Totals %	No Children In School %	Public School Parents %
All	29	28	29
Most	32	30	37
Some	28	30	25
Only a few	9	10	6
Don't know	2	2	3

TABLE 34. Some states are now requiring that high school students complete four years of English, math, and science in order to graduate from high school. Would you favor or oppose this requirement in the public schools in your community?

	National Totals %	No Children In School %	Public School Parents %
Favor	78	79	76
Oppose	20	20	22
Don't know	2	1	2

TABLE 35. Some people have proposed increasing the mandatory attendance age to 18 as a way to deal with the school dropout problem. Would you favor or oppose increasing the mandatory attendance age to 18 in your state?

	National Totals %	No Children In School %	Public School Parents %
Favor	66	66	68
Oppose	30	31	28
Don't know	4	3	4

TABLE 36. Some people have proposed eliminating the senior year of high school so that students could get an earlier start on getting a college education or on entering the work force. Would you favor or oppose using this plan in the high schools in your community?

	National Totals %	No Children In School %	Public School Parents %
Favor	24	23	25
Oppose	74	75	73
Don't know	2	2	2

TABLE 37. I am going to mention some possible reasons for awarding extra pay to a public school teacher. As I read each reason, would you tell me whether you think it should be used to determine whether or not a teacher receives extra pay?

	Should Be Used %	Should Not Be Used %	Don't Know %
Having an advanced degree such as a master's or a Ph.D.	76	23	1
High evaluations of the teacher by his or her principal and other administrators	70	28	2
Length of his or her teaching experience	71	28	1
High evaluations by other teachers in the teacher's school district	65	33	2
High evaluations by his or her students	64	34	2
High opinions from the parents of his or her students	59	39	2

The Political Component

Election-Year Issues

K–12 education has moved close to the top of the political agenda at both the state and federal levels, thereby adding importance to the political questions that this poll reserves for Presidential election years. The data in Table 38 show that the Republican Party has made progress in closing a gap that had Democrats enjoying a 17% advantage in 1996 as the party more interested in improving public education. The gap is now 7%. Table 39 shows John Kerry and George Bush in a dead heat when voters are asked to choose between them based on education issues alone. Four years ago, Al Gore and George Bush were also in a dead heat in this poll. Table 40 tends to verify the conventional wisdom regarding policies that the two major parties would be inclined to support. And Tables 41 and 42 suggest that supporting vouchers would give a slight edge to candidates nationally, while supporting NCLB would be a major plus.

TABLE 38. In your opinion, which of the two major political parties is more interested in improving public education in this country—the Democratic Party or the Republican Party?

	National Totals			No Children In School			Public School Parents		
	'04 %	'00 %	'96 %	'04 %	'00 %	'96 %	'04 %	'00 %	'96 %
Democratic Party	42	41	44	45	41	45	37	41	41
Republican Party	35	29	27	35	29	26	34	28	29
No difference volunteered	*	*	15	*	*	15	*	*	14
Don't know	23	30	14	20	30	14	29	31	16

* Less than one-half of 1%.

TABLE 39. Suppose you were voting solely on the basis of a desire to strengthen the public schools. Who would you vote for in the Presidential election this November—John Kerry or George W. Bush?

	National Totals %	No Children In School %	Public School Parents %
John Kerry	41	42	37
George W. Bush	41	41	41
Don't know	18	17	22

TABLE 40. I am going to mention several policies pertaining to the public schools in this country. As I mention each policy, would you tell me which political party—the Democratic Party or the Republican Party—you feel would be more sympathetic to that policy?

	Democratic Party %	Republican Party %	Don't Know %
Providing financial support for private or church-related schools	31	55	14
Privatizing such school services as transportation, food, maintenance, etc.	34	50	16
Improving student achievement in the nation's public schools	45	39	16
Closing the achievement gap between white students and black and Hispanic students	55	30	15

TABLE 41. Would knowing that a candidate for national office supports vouchers for parents to use to pay for private schools make you more likely or less likely to vote for that candidate?

	National Totals		No Children In School		Public School Parents	
	'04 %	'00 %	'04 %	'00 %	'04 %	'00 %
More likely	43	41	43	41	43	40
Less likely	37	44	37	45	36	44
Makes no difference	15	12	15	11	15	12
Don't know	5	3	5	3	6	4

TABLE 42. Would knowing that a candidate for national office supports the No Child Left Behind Act make you more or less likely to vote for that candidate?

	National Totals %	No Children In School %	Public School Parents %
More likely	53	53	53
Less likely	25	26	23
Makes no difference	15	15	14
Don't know	7	6	10

Closing Statement

Polling is now a high-stakes component in the effort to improve the public schools. The issues explored herein are shaping the daily decisions made in K–12 schools. Poll findings have taken on added importance, and, given the inexact nature of data analysis, it is not surprising that this report and the interpretations we provide are always subject to a critical review. That is as it should be. The poll is intended to contribute to the ongoing debate regarding the public schools, and disagreement fuels that debate. The public does, however, have a way of getting it right with issues that are both complex and puzzling. And, right or wrong, public attitudes determine, over the long haul, how those issues can be addressed.

Research Procedure

The Sample. The sample used in this survey embraced a total of 1,003 adults (18 years of age and older). A description of the sample and methodology can be found at the end of this report.

Time of Interviewing. The fieldwork for this study was conducted during the period of 28 May to 18 June 2004.

Due allowance must be made for statistical variation, especially in the case of findings for groups consisting of relatively few respondents.

The findings of this report apply only to the U.S. as a whole and not to individual communities. Local surveys, using the same questions, can be conducted to determine how local areas compare with the national norm.

Sampling Tolerances

In interpreting survey results, it should be borne in mind that all sample surveys are subject to sampling error, i.e., the extent to which the results may differ from what would be obtained if the whole population surveyed had been interviewed. The size of such sampling error depends largely on the number of interviews. For details and tables showing the confidence intervals for the data cited in this poll, please visit the Phi Delta Kappa website at http://www.pdkintl.org/kappan/kpoll0409sample.htm.

Design of the Sample

For the 2004 survey the Gallup Organization used its standard national telephone sample, i.e., an unclustered, directory-assisted, random-digit telephone sample, based on a proportionate stratified sampling design.

The random-digit aspect of the sample was used to avoid "listing" bias. Numerous studies have shown that households with unlisted telephone numbers are different in important ways from listed households. "Unlistedness" is due to household mobility or to customer requests to prevent publication of the telephone number.

To avoid this source of bias, a random-digit procedure designed to provide representation of both listed and unlisted (including not-yet-listed) numbers was used.

Telephone numbers for the continental United States were stratified into four regions of the country and, within each region, further stratified into three size-of-community strata.

Only working banks of telephone numbers were selected. Eliminating nonworking banks from the sample increased the likelihood that any sample telephone number would be associated with a residence.

The sample of telephone numbers produced by the described method is representative of all telephone households within the continental United States.

Within each contacted household, an interview was sought with the household member who had the most recent birthday. This frequently used method of respondent selection provides an excellent approximation of statistical randomness in that it gives all members of the household an opportunity to be selected.

Up to three calls were made to each selected telephone number to complete an interview. The time of day and the day of the week for callbacks were varied so as to maximize the chances of finding a respondent at home. All interviews were conducted on weekends or weekday evenings in order to contact potential respondents among the working population.

The final sample was weighted so that the distribution of the sample matched current estimates derived from the U.S. Census Bureau's Current Population Survey (CPS) for the adult population living in telephone households in the continental U.S.

Composition of the Sample

Adults	%
No children in school	67
Public school parents	29
Nonpublic school parents	4

Gender	%
Men	45
Women	55

Race	
White	81
Nonwhite	15
Black	11
Undesignated	3

Age	
18–29 years	20
30–49 years	40
50 and over	38
Undesignated	2

Education	%
Total college	57
College graduate	24
College incomplete	33
Total high school	42
High school graduate	35
High school incomplete	7

Income	
$50,000 and over	34
$40,000–$49,000	10
$30,000–$39,000	12
$20,000–$29,000	12
Under $20,000	17
Undesignated	15

Region	
East	22
Midwest	24
South	32
West	22

Community Size	
Urban	27
Suburban	47
Rural	26

Conducting Your Own Poll

The Phi Delta Kappa Center for Professional Development and Services makes available PACE (Polling Attitudes of Community on Education) materials to enable nonspecialists to conduct scientific polls of attitude and opinion on education. The PACE manual provides detailed information on constructing questionnaires, sampling, interviewing, and analyzing data. It also includes updated census figures and new material on conducting a telephone survey. The price is $60. For information about using PACE materials, write or phone Jeanne Storm at Phi Delta Kappa International, P.O. Box 789, Bloomington, IN 47402-0789. Ph. 800/766-1156.

Lowell C. Rose is executive director emeritus of Phi Delta Kappa International. ALEC M. GALLUP is co-chairman, with George Gallup, Jr., of the Gallup Organization, Princeton, NJ.

From *Phi Delta Kappan*, September 2004. Copyright © 2004 by Phi Delta Kappa International. www.pdkintl.org Reprinted by permission.

UNIT 2
Rethinking and Changing the Educative Effort

Unit Selections

8. **No Child Left Behind: The Mathematics of Guaranteed Failure**, Lowell C. Rose
9. **Test Today, Privatize Tomorrow: Using Accountability to 'Reform' Public Schools to Death**, Alfie Kohn
10. **Leadership That Sparks Learning**, J. Timothy Waters, Robert J. Marzano, and Brian McNulty
11. **Meeting Challenges in Urban Schools**, Larry Cuban
12. **Transforming High Schools**, Pedro A. Noguera
13. **Reinventing America's Schools**, Tony Wagner

Key Points to Consider

- What are some issues in the debate regarding educational reform?

- Should the focus of educational reform be on changing the ways educators are prepared, on the changing needs of students, or on both of these concerns? Defend your answer.

- Compare American concepts about alternative schooling and the uses of public funds to the views of other countries on school choice issues.

Links: www.dushkin.com/online/
These sites are annotated in the World Wide Web pages.

The Center for Innovation in Education
http://www.center.edu

Colorado Department of Education
http://www.cde.state.co.us/index_home.htm

National Council for Accreditation of Teacher Education
http://www.ncate.org

Phi Delta Kappa International
http://www.pdkintl.org

The "No Child Left Behind" (NCLB) legislation has sparked a major debate among the educational community in the United States. What constitutes a "highly qualified teacher?" How many of them do we have? Which students get them? The questions roll on and on. We are left to decide the equity issues involved in all of this. We are also left to decide the most fundamental questions of all: What constitutes a "highly qualified teacher?" What educational background should the person have? What are the motivations to do this? How are we to assess this person's ability to take this role? All of these questions need to be addressed plus the question as to how "highly qualified teachers" are to be permitted to play their professional roles in the classrooms assigned to them. We are a democratic society committed to the free education of all of our citizens.

Rethinking and re-directing the educational system of a nation requires intensive reflective and analytical effort. How to best restructure educational services is a question which requires considerable contemplation and forethought as to the consequences of our decision-making processes. The dialogical processes involved among citizens as they engage in this decision-making process will shape the forms of our educational futures.

American educators could have a much better sense of their own past as a profession, and the public could better understand the history of public education. In the United States, a fundamental cycle of similar ideas and practices reappears in school curricula every so many years. The decades of the 1970s and 1980s witnessed the rise of "behavioral objectives" and "management by objectives," and the 1990s brought us "outcome-based education" and "benchmarking" in educational discourse within the public school system's leadership. These are related behavioral concepts focusing on measurable ways to pinpoint and evaluate the results of educational efforts. Why do we seem to "reinvent the wheel" of educational thought and practice every so many decades? This is an important question worth addressing. Many of our ideas about change and reform in educational practice have been wrongheaded. There is a focus on more qualitative, as opposed to empirical, means of assessing the outcomes of our educative efforts; yet many state departments of education still insist on objective assessments and verifications of students' mastery of academic skills. How does this affect the development of imaginative teaching in schools? All of us in the education system are concerned, and many of us believe that there really are some new and generative ideas to help students learn basic intellectual skills and content.

Our current realities in the field of education reflect differing conceptions of how schooling ought to change. It is difficult to generalize regarding school quality across decades because of several factors; high schools, for instance, were more selective in 1900 when only 7 percent of American youths graduated from them. Today we encourage as many students as possible to graduate. The social purposes of schooling have been broadened; now we want all youths to complete some form of higher education.

We have to consider the social and ideological differences among those representing opposing school reform agendas for change. The differences over how and in what directions change is to occur in our educational systems rest on which educational values are to prevail. These values form the bases for differing conceptions of the purposes of schooling. Thus the differing agendas for change in American education have to be positioned within the context of the different ideological value systems that underpin each alternative agenda for change.

There are several currently contending (and frequently conceptually conflicting) strategies for restructuring life in schools as well as options open to parents in choosing the schools that they want their children to attend. On the one hand, we have to find ways to empower students and teachers to improve the quality of academic life in classrooms. On the other hand, there appear to be powerful forces contending over whether control of educational services should be even more centralized or more decentralized (site-based). Those who favor greater parental and teacher control of schools support greater decentralized site management and community control conceptions of school governance. Yet the ratio of teachers to nonteaching personnel (administrators, counselors, school psychologists, and others) continues to decline as public school system bureaucracies become more and more "top heavy."

In this unit, we consider the efforts to reconceive, redefine, and reconstruct existing patterns of curriculum and instruction at the elementary and secondary levels of schooling and compare them with the efforts to reconceive existing conflicting patterns of teacher education. A broad spectrum of dialogue is developing in North America, the British Commonwealth, Russia, Central Eurasia, and other areas of the world about the redirecting of learning opportunities for all citizens.

Prospective teachers here are being encouraged to question their own individual educational experiences as part of this process. We must acknowledge that our values affect our ideas about curriculum content and the purpose of educating others. This is perceived as vitally important in the developing dialogue over liberating all students' capacities to function as independent inquirers. The dramatic economic and demographic changes in our society necessitate a fundamental reconceptualization of how schools ought to respond to the many social contexts in which they are located. This effort to reassess and reconceive the education of persons is a vital part of broader reform efforts in society as well as a dynamic dialectic in its own right. How can schools, for instance, better reflect the varied communities of interest that they serve? What must they do to become better perceived as just and equitable places in which all young people can seek to achieve learning and self-fulfillment?

Each of the essays in this unit relates to the tension involved in reconceiving how educational development should proceed in response to all the dramatic social and economic changes in society.

Article 8

NCLB: Failed Schools—or Failed Law?

No Child Left Behind: The Mathematics of Guaranteed Failure

Lowell C. Rose

I. History and Background of NCLB

The signing of the No Child Left Behind Act on January 8, 2002, moved the federal effort to influence K–12 schooling to a new and higher level—more aggressive, focused, and directive. The act requires that school districts and schools demonstrate adequate yearly progress (AYP) toward a particular goal: universal student achievement of standards established by each state. Each year, school districts and schools that do not achieve AYP will be labeled "Did Not Make AYP," and after two such years they may suffer sanctions that include loss of federal funding, termination of staff, and dissolving the school district.

The new law was accompanied by promises of higher funding, both to enhance the prospects of success and to serve as an incentive for compliance. However, two years after NCLB was signed amid bipartisan euphoria and more than one year into implementation, its chances of success and prospects for increased funding are, at best, uncertain. In Indiana, for example, Title I funding has increased only 11 percent over the year before NCLB was signed; virtually all of that amount funds new programs mandated by NCLB; and members of the state's congressional delegation say that there is little prospect of increased funding in future years. Many educators suspect that NCLB may join special education as a major unfunded mandate.

The fanfare that accompanied NCLB seemed to herald a new federal initiative. Technically, however, NCLB is but the latest reauthorization of the 1965 Elementary and Secondary Education Act. During the past thirty-seven years, it became the practice to assign each reauthorization a distinctive title: hence, 2001's "No Child Left Behind Act." Each version of the ESEA has sought in particular to improve the achievement of low-performing students. Over the years an increasing emphasis on outcomes culminated in the 1994 reauthorization (dubbed "Goals 2000"), which emphasized higher standards, testing based on those standards, and demands for accountability. Also along the way, federal frustration over a perceived lack of progress began to grow.

That was the background against which the provisions of the 2001 NCLB reauthorization were framed. Both presidential candidates in 2000 had promised change and improvement in education. Upon taking office, the new Bush administration garnered support by focusing on the seductive promise that no child would be left behind. Those heady days of bipartisanship in education were symbolized by pictures of the president and a partisan archrival, Sen. Edward Kennedy, dining at the White House to discuss the future of K–12 education.

II. The Problem with NCLB

So just what is wrong with NCLB? To understand the answer, it's important to understand one of the act's major requirements (and greatest strengths): breaking out test scores by demographic groups—black, Hispanic, Native American, Asian, special education, LEP (limited English proficient), economically disadvantaged, and white. The act requires demographic breakouts in order to avoid a classic anomaly in education data: satisfactory overall group performance that simultaneously obscures poor performance by subgroups. Unreported subgroup performance is one reason U.S. society and policymakers have tolerated achievement gaps between certain subgroups—students living in poverty, blacks, Hispanics—and other groups, usually white or more advantaged students.

The strength of NCLB is in forcing educators to confront disparate student achievement. That strength is, however, negated by the act's single numerical goal for all groups and its requirement that each group reach 100 percent proficiency in twelve years, no matter the achievement level at which it began. NCLB's single goal for all breakout groups, applied without concern for where a group starts or how much improvement it demonstrates, virtually guarantees immediate failure for school districts and schools that enroll high percentages of the most challenged students. (See Part IV, "Calculating Your District's AYP.")

The single-goal approach also guarantees that students who have had the greatest difficulty achieving must demonstrate the greatest progress. Virtually all the research on aspiration and student achievement has found, however, that improvement must be measured against the point at which the student begins; that it is hard work; that it comes unevenly, with significant gains accompanied by plateaus and temporary setbacks; and that improvement requires ongoing effort and commitment. The literature as well as direct professional experience and common sense tell us that both effort levels and chances of success are enhanced by goals that force stretching but are nonetheless, given enough effort and commitment, within reach.

Unreported subgroup performance is one reason U.S. society and policymakers have tolerated achievement gaps between certain subgroups—students living in poverty, blacks, Hispanics—and other groups.

The NCLB scheme, ignoring the research consensus, assumes that improvement is continuous and consistent and that goals can be reached in a fixed time, regardless of the distance to be traveled. It says, simply, that we use 2001–2002 as the base year and progress in equal annual steps for twelve years, when 100 percent proficiency will be achieved. At the risk of oversimplifying, *measuring improvement from the point at which the school district, school, or breakout performance begins, using measures based on same-student performance*, would avert the NCLB's harshest consequences almost immediately. The school-improvement plans of Indiana and several other states already employ such an improvement focus.

However, even with realistic performance goals and measurements based on improvement by same-student cohorts, the issue of what constitutes realistic achievement will have to be addressed. This writer has yet to encounter a single person who believes that 100 percent proficiency for all students is a realistic or reachable goal.

III. Applying NCLB to Indiana: A Hypothetical

A good place to examine the potential impact of NCLB is in my home state of Indiana, one of the earliest states to embrace the accountability movement. Structured efforts to improve student achievement in Indiana began in the mid- to late 1980s. Indiana became one of seventeen states that complied fully with the provisions of the 1994 initiative, Goals 2000; when NCLB was signed in 2002, Indiana had already been measuring its own AYP benchmarks for four years. In addition, Indiana's Public Law 221, passed in 1999, places schools in categories based on improvement shown, with the first such placements to be made after the fall 2005 testing. Under P.L. 221, student progress for grades 3 to 10 will be assessed through same-student comparisons that use year-to-year test scores. In 2000, a graduation-qualifying exam at grade 10 was implemented, with few of the problems encountered in other states.

The passage of NCLB provided good news immediately for Indiana's budgetary woes: the funding needed to support the planned expansion of ISTEP (Indiana Statewide Testing for Educational Progress) testing. The Indiana Department of Education (IDOE) accepted the challenge of NCLB and began planning to implement NCLB. The IDOE planning effort involved all those interested in K–12 schools (including the author, as a consultant to the Indiana Urban Schools Association [IUSA]). As a result, Indiana became one of five states placed on the fast track for federal approval.

As familiarity with the demands of NCLB grew, however, the law's ultimate feasibility came into question in many quarters. During that period, I developed and made several presentations on implementing NCLB in Indiana. In the process I used the results of the ISTEP tests given in September 2001 to calculate AYP for the participating schools (at that point, Indiana's AYP determinations for the NCLB base year, 2001-2002, were not yet made). I planned to use the figures to provide specific examples of the way AYP data could be used to focus instruction. Soon, however, I realized that NCLB's AYP calculations doomed the vast majority of schools and virtually every school district in Indiana to failure, with the schools that serve the highest percentage of challenged students achieving failure first.

In general, I concluded that applying NCLB to Indiana using 2001 data without mitigating measures would produce drastic and unexpected results. Here are the projections I made for Indiana school districts and schools based on the 2001 test data:

- Two hundred sixty-nine of the state's 293 school districts would have failed to achieve AYP.
- The twenty-four school districts that would have achieved AYP had an average enrollment of 770 students and an average minority enrollment of 1.7 percent.
- Each of the thirty school districts in the Indiana Urban Schools Association would have failed to make AYP. (The thirty-four IUSA school districts tested 93.8 percent of the state's black students, 68.2 percent of the Hispanic students, and 56.4 percent of the free- or reduced-lunch students.)

- Sixty-eight percent of the schools in the IUSA would have failed to achieve AYP.
- The failing schools in the IUSA would have included 95 percent of the high schools, 92 percent of the middle schools, and 57 percent of the elementary schools.

Those results reflect a particularly pernicious consequence of the way AYP is to be calculated. As mentioned earlier, larger schools test more students, which means more breakouts and a greater chance of failure to achieve AYP. Larger numbers tested also mean that less relief will be gained from applying the test of statistical significance, a test used to guarantee that differences are real. In addition, NCLB applies a single goal without concern for where a group starts or how much improvement it demonstrates. Therefore, when diversity adds more students who start far from the goal, the odds of achieving AYP diminish. At the school district level, achieving AYP in Indiana is almost beyond reach.

To see why it is vital to take into account both the starting point and the ability of the students in a breakout group, let's examine how the act would treat Indiana's special education students. The data for special education students in Indiana measured in the 2001 ISTEP testing showed that 252 of the 256 breakout groups would have failed to achieve AYP. (Communities with high socioeconomic levels furnished the four breakout groups that would have achieved AYP, which leads me to speculate that the basis of their special education placement was something other than cognitive ability.)

Most of Indiana's special education breakouts in 2001 would have missed NCLB targets by twenty to forty percentage points. Even taking into account NCLB's alternative assessments for some special education students, it appears that, regardless of the effort put forth, most special education breakout groups will not meet NCLB's standards. Special education groups will bear the brunt of the failure of school districts and schools to make AYP. It is difficult to believe that such a result is good for either special education or the school-improvement effort.

Given such projections, the logical question becomes: "Will any purpose be served by giving the schools that enroll a high percentage of disadvantaged and minority students a label that will be equated with 'failing'?" After all, Indiana's recent scores on the National Assessment of Educational Progress (NAEP) and other external measures suggest that the state's students have performed well in comparison to students in other states and consistently improved in recent years.

I realized that NCLB's AYP calculations doomed the vast majority of schools and virtually every school district in Indiana to failure.

But beyond that, if the "retro" exercise in applying NCLB to Indiana's 2001 numbers proves anywhere close to accurate, NCLB's methodology guarantees that matters will progressively worsen. For reasons related to the state of technology, more grades will be added to the testing pool each year, so "Did Not Make AYP"—which will be understood by everyone to mean "This school district or school is a failure"—will occur more often each year. The handful of school districts and schools left standing in 2005 will then be further challenged when, in compliance with NCLB, the goals will jump by 25 percent of the difference between the initial goals and 100 percent proficiency.

Due in part to abbreviated media coverage, few people realize that AYP determinations and the possibility of improvement and corrective action status apply not only to schools but to school districts. AYP and NCLB sanctions may, in fact, prove most severe and immediate at the school district level. A district that fails to achieve AYP for two consecutive years will move to "school improvement" status. It must, at that point, work with the state to develop a plan for achieving AYP. A school district failing to make AYP for the fourth consecutive year moves to "corrective action" status, which under NCLB authorizes the state to exercise one of seven options:

- Reduce programmatic or administrative funds.
- Replace the curriculum.
- Terminate personnel relevant to the failure.
- Move some schools from the jurisdiction and provide alternative governance.
- Appoint a receiver to replace the superintendent and the board.
- Abolish and restructure the school district.
- Provide choice for school district students to attend successful neighboring school districts.

How does Indiana plan to proceed in relation to the seven options? The indication to date has been that none is permissible under Indiana law and that virtually all the state will be able to do is consult with school districts on how they spend their money. Given the federal government's supremacy in distributing money, that statement is of little comfort. In early 2003 I spoke to twenty relatively small school districts. Six of those districts will undoubtedly fail to make AYP—even though every school in them will achieve AYP. Think of that in terms of the purposes for which the school district exists!

IV. Calculating Your District's AYP

Judge NCLB and its AYP system not in the abstract or based on what others say. To really understand AYP, familiarize yourself with the process. Take actual data for school districts and schools with which you are familiar, and calculate AYP. I have calculated AYP several thousand times for school districts and schools with large enrollments, small enrollments, great diversity, and little or no diversity. That hands-on experience has led me to conclude that the NCLB's AYP system will prove useless for improving student achievement. AYP targets not individual students but school districts and schools, and it effectively guarantees that virtually all of them will be labeled failures. That inevitability derives from the mandated mechanics of AYP.

The mechanics of AYP. The overall group and each breakout group in a school district or school are required to meet goals specifying the percentage of students who must pass the state tests on English and math. The goals are fixed by the state using a formula prescribed in NCLB. The goal is the same for all groups.

To determine if your school achieved AYP, you start with the overall group and ask, "Did the group make the goal in English?" If the answer is yes, you ask the same question for math. If the answer again is yes, you have two yeses. Now move to the first breakout group. A breakout group is any group—say, students with disabilities—for which the number of students tested in the school district or school is greater than the threshold number (the "N") stated in the state plan. In Indiana and most other states the N is 30. Ask the same two questions for the first breakout and then repeat the process for each of the other breakouts. The first "no" answer means that the school district or school did not make AYP.

> *A predominantly white elementary school with an enrollment of 250 or less will seldom miss achieving AYP because it won't contain groups large enough.*

The typical urban school district in Indiana includes between four and seven breakout groups. The more breakouts, the more difficult it becomes to make AYP. In a school district or school with every one of the eight breakout groups, it will be necessary to answer "yes" eighteen times (twice for the eight breakout groups, and twice more for the overall group) to meet AYP based on test data alone. But for those with all yeses on the questions related to test data, there are still hurdles to jump. To protect against the possibility that school districts or schools might hold low-achieving students out of the testing, NCLB's authors included a requirement that 95 percent of the overall group and 95 percent of all students in each breakout group must be tested in English and 95 percent in math. The N required for a breakout differs from state to state. In Indiana, it is thirty students tested. Apply that standard next. That adds two more required yeses for the overall group and two for each breakout group, bringing the number to thirty-six for a school district or school with the full complement of breakouts.

NCLB also requires at least one secondary indicator for each school. At the high school level, it must be the graduation rate. For other schools, the secondary indicator is determined by the state. Indiana's goal is a graduation rate of 95 percent for its high schools and 95 percent average daily attendance for all other schools. The secondary indicator, at least in Indiana, applies only to the overall group, thereby bringing the possible number of yeses required to thirty-seven.

It is plain to see how small schools with little diversity can achieve AYP. White breakouts achieve AYP. A predominantly white elementary school with an enrollment of 250 or less will seldom miss achieving AYP because it won't contain groups large enough. Given the N of 30 used in most states, it will have few, if any, breakouts. Case in point: the principal of an elementary school studied the data, realized his 600-plus-student elementary school would not make AYP, and called me to say, "If we split this school into three schools in the same building, we wouldn't have any breakouts and all three would make AYP."

Extend the game as long as you can. It is an interesting, albeit perverse, exercise to see how far any school or district can "drill down" into its breakout groups before it fails. The first rule in extending the game is to avoid beginning with the special education breakout. Most school districts and large schools have such breakouts and few will make AYP. As already noted, using the 2001 data, 256 of Indiana's 293 school districts would have had special education breakouts in the 2001 testing, and all but three would have failed to achieve AYP. I used the more-recent 2002 ISTEP data to calculate AYP for the thirty-four school districts in the Indiana Urban Schools Association. Had I started with the special education breakouts, I would have identified each of the school districts as "Did Not Make AYP." The game would have been over.

> *Absent significant change, NCLB will at minimum fail to improve schooling and do nothing to aid low-performing students.*

To extend the game one must carefully choose the order in which the breakout groups are taken. If Indiana is a typical state, the breakout for Asians is a good place to start. That group is likely to score highest in terms of the goals. The white breakout also will earn two yeses in most schools. From that point on, the prospects of making AYP are iffy; nonetheless, there is much to be learned from extending the game. For example, free/reduced-lunch, Hispanic, black, Native American, and LEP groups are among the least likely to make AYP. The finding should not be surprising given what we know about the achievement gap.

Drilling down further, however, you will quickly conclude from the free/reduced-lunch percentages that there is legal poverty and then there is real poverty. Free/reduced-lunch groups in urban areas are unlikely to achieve AYP, while their counterparts outside the urban areas sometimes outperform the paid-lunch group.

Therefore, Hispanic and black students in school districts with high socioeconomic levels are far more likely to achieve AYP than their counterparts in school districts serving students from lower socioeconomic levels.

As you drill down into your own data, you gradually become aware of a paradox: as the information you acquire about the correlates of student performance in your own schools becomes more textured and valuable, the notion of measuring school performance with the types of tests mandated by NCLB becomes less plausible. That realization made it easier for me to accept the overall conclusions of my analysis. Even without including special education, thirty-two of the thirty-four Indiana Urban Schools Association school districts were ultimately identified as "Did Not Make Adequate Yearly Progress." The special education breakouts made it unanimous.

Safe harbor or Russian roulette? To be fair, it must be noted that NCLB includes a "safe harbor" provision that schools can use to make AYP. Safe harbor is reached if the actual percentage of students failing a given test is reduced by 10 percent. Note that the percentage itself must be reduced, not the number of students. To maintain rigor where safe harbor is used to make AYP, NCLB requires that any group using AYP to reach safe harbor must also satisfy the secondary indicator. It is the only time that secondary indicators come into play for breakout groups.

At best safe harbor is a Russian roulette kind of process because, in different years, the students will be different, the "N's" may be different, and the demographics of those tested may change. However, that is not why I downplay the safe-harbor provision here. I do so because urban school districts and schools in Indiana and most other states will miss AYP in multiple instances, leaving moot the issue of safe harbor in relation to a specific percentage.

V. Where Do We Go from Here?

Looking back, it is easy to see that my initial positive reaction to NCLB was based on general support for the act's goals and incomplete understanding of the specifics of implementation. One early warning sign of NCLB's deficiencies was its goal of 100 percent proficiency; nonetheless, many supporters, including this writer, generally withheld comment, confident that the matter could be addressed later. *[Congress may consider changes in NCLB beginning in 2007, when the act comes up for reauthorization.—Ed.]* One hopes that such thinking does not prove wishful.

We have a saying in Indiana: "That dog won't hunt." Putting it bluntly, the current No Child Left Behind Act merits that description. Absent significant change, NCLB will at minimum fail to improve schooling and do nothing to aid low-performing students. In the worst-case scenario, NCLB could do serious damage to the school-improvement effort nationally and to the promising efforts already under way in states such as Indiana. The students most in need of help would be the biggest losers.

Where, then, do NCLB and AYP leave us? There is much in NCLB to like and embrace. The focus on "leaving no child behind"—systematically identifying and then addressing the needs of low-achieving students —is still a worthy if distant goal. Analyzing test scores, especially those of subgroups, is so basic to improving achievement that it is difficult to understand why its implementation required a federal mandate.

The prospects for change depend on many factors, among them political will; the willingness to face the fact that changes are needed; the staying power of those promoting change; and the true motives of those responsible for NCLB—whether they were good intentions marred by haste, disappointment over the results of past legislation, or even a desire to create a stalking-horse for vouchers. If the provisions of NCLB as they stand at this writing are not changed, the greatest consolation for the education community and all concerned may be that the results of NCLB will so lack credibility that they will be not be taken seriously. In that event, NCLB will go down as one of the greatest missed opportunities in the history of American education.

Notes

1. In calculating AYP, consider the compound probabilities alone: if every group has a 99 percent chance of making AYP—nearly ideal conditions that are rarely seen—the odds that all thirty-seven groups will achieve AYP are equal to .99 to the 37th power, which is 0.689, or only slightly more than two out of three. Thus, despite the fact that our hypothetical school is nearly ideal, there is a nearly one in three chance that it will not achieve AYP. If each breakout has an 80 percent chance of making AYP—probably not bad in the real world—the chances that all thirty-seven will achieve AYP are fewer than 3 in 10,000. If one does not consider that situation impossible, factor in that the reason for defining a breakout group in the first place is usually to focus on students who have historically underachieved.—Ed.

Lowell C. Rose, Ph.D., is a past executive director of Phi Delta Kappa International. Among other posts, he has also served as executive director of the Indiana School Boards Association and of the Indiana Urban Schools Association. Currently he is a consultant to school corporations on Indiana's school improvement legislation and an adjunct professor at Indiana University.

From *Educational Horizons*, Winter 2004, pp. 121-129. Copyright © 2004 by Lowell C. Rose. Reprinted by permission of the author.

Article 9

Test Today, Privatize Tomorrow
Using Accountability to 'Reform' Public Schools to Death

Under the guise of improving public education, No Child Left Behind is paving the way for the Right to achieve its goal of undermining it, Mr. Kohn warns.

By Alfie Kohn

I just about fell off my desk chair the other day when I came across my own name in an essay by a conservative economist who specializes in educational issues. The reason for my astonishment is that I was described as being "dead set against any fundamental changes in the nation's schools." Now having been accused with some regularity of arguing for too damn many fundamental changes in the nation's schools, I found this new criticism more than a bit puzzling. But then I remembered that, during a TV interview a couple of years ago, another author from a different right-wing think tank had labeled me a "defender of the educational status quo."

In an earlier age, I might have suggested pistols at dawn as the only fitting response to these calumnies. But of course there's a lot more going on here than the fact that one writer has had his radical credentials unjustly called into question. The point is that the mantle of school reform has been appropriated by those who oppose the whole idea of public schooling. Their aim is to paint themselves as bold challengers to the current system and to claim that defenders of public education lack the vision or courage to endorse meaningful change. This rhetorical assault seemed to come out of nowhere, as though a memo had been circulated one day among those on the Right: "Attention. Effective immediately, all of our efforts to privatize the schools will be known as 'reform,' and any opposition to those efforts will be known as 'anti-reform.' That is all."

Those who hunt for silver-linings may note that this strategy pays a backhanded compliment to the very idea of change. It implicitly acknowledges the inadequacy of conservatism, at least in the original sense of that word. These days everyone insists there's a problem with the way things are. (On one level, this posture is familiar: polemicists across the political spectrum frequently try to describe whatever position they're about to criticize as "fashionable." The implication is that only the bravest soul—that is, the writer—dares to support an unfashionable view.) But the word *reform* is particularly slippery and tendentious. The *Associated Press Guide to Newswriting* urges journalists to exercise caution about using it, pointing out that "one group's reform can be another group's calamity."[1]

Making schools resemble businesses often results in a kind of pedagogy that's not merely conservative but reactionary, turning back the clock on the few changes that have managed to infiltrate and improve classrooms.

Yet at the same time, conservative politicians are being exhorted (for example, by a like-minded *New York Times* columnist) to embrace the word. "For my money," David Brooks wrote earlier this year, "the best organizing principle for Republicans centers on the word 'reform'"—which can give the impression that they want to "promote change, while Democrats remain the churlish defenders of the status quo."[2]

Of course, this begs the question of what kind of change is actually being promoted, but begging the question is really the whole point, isn't it? The "reform" of environmental laws has often meant diluting them or simply washing them away. And just ask someone who depends on public assistance what "welfare reform" really implies. The privatizers and deregulators have gone after health care, prisons, banks, airlines, and electric utilities (say, *that's* been going well, hasn't it?). Now they're setting their sights on Social Security. I was recently reading about the added misery experienced by desperately poor families in various parts of the world as a result of the privatization of local water supplies. The clarity of language be damned: they come to bury a given institution rather than to improve it, but they describe their mission as "reform." As Lily Tomlin once remarked, "No matter how cynical you become, it's never enough to keep up."[3]

THE NATURE OF 'SCHOOL REFORM'

But back to education. People with an animus against public schooling typically set the stage for their demolition plans by proclaiming that there isn't much there worth saving. Meanwhile, those who object are portrayed as apologists for every policy in every school. It's a very clever gambit, you have to admit. Either you're in favor of privatization or else you are inexplicably satisfied with mediocrity.

Let's state what should be obvious, then. First, a defense of public education is wholly consistent with a desire for excellence. Second, by most conventional criteria, public schools have done surprisingly well in managing with limited resources to educate an increasingly diverse student population.[4] Third, notwithstanding that assessment, there's plenty of room for dissatisfaction with the current state of our schools. An awful lot is wrong with them: the way conformity is valued over curiosity and enforced with rewards and punishments, the way children are compelled to compete against one another, the way curriculum so often privileges skills over meaning, the way students are prevented from designing their own learning, the way instruction and assessment are increasingly standardized, the way different avenues of study are rarely integrated, the way educators are systematically deskilled. . . . And I'm just getting warmed up.

Notice, however, that these criticisms are quite different from—in fact, often the exact opposite of—the particulars cited by most proponents of vouchers and similar "reforms." To that extent, even if privatization worked exactly the way it was supposed to, we shouldn't expect any of the defects I've just listed to be corrected. If anything, the micro-level impact (on teaching and learning) of such a system-level shift is likely to exacerbate such problems at the level of teaching and learning. Making schools resemble businesses often results in a kind of pedagogy that's not merely conservative but reactionary, turning back the clock on the few changes that have managed to infiltrate and improve classrooms. Consider the stultifyingly scripted lessons and dictatorial discipline that pervade for-profit charter schools. Or have a look at some research from England showing that "when schools have to compete for students, they tend to adopt 'safe,' conventional and teacher-centered methods, to stay close to the prescribed curriculum, and to tailor teaching closely to test-taking."[5] (Here we have just one more example of the destructive effects of competition.)

This is a point worth emphasizing to the handful of progressive-minded individuals who have made common cause with those on the Right by attacking public education. John Taylor Gatto is an example here. In a recent *Harper's* magazine essay entitled "Against School," he asserts that the goal of "mandatory public education in this country" is "a population deliberately dumbed down," with children turned "into servants."[6]

In support of this sweeping charge, Gatto names some important men who managed to become well-educated without setting foot in a classroom. (However, he fails to name any defenders of public education who have ever claimed that it's impossible for people to learn outside of school or to prosper without a degree.) He also cites a few "school as factory" comments from long-dead policymakers, and observes that many of our educational practices originated in Prussia. Here he's right. Our school system is indeed rooted in efforts to control. But the same indictment could be leveled, with equal justification, at other institutions. The history of newspapers, for example, and the intent of many powerful people associated with them, has much to do with manufacturing consent, marginalizing dissent, and distracting readers. But is that an argument for no newspapers or for better newspapers?

Ideally, public schools can enrich lives, nourish curiosity, and introduce students to new ways of formulating questions and finding answers. Their existence also has the power to strengthen a democratic society, in part by extending those benefits to vast numbers of people who didn't fare nearly as well before the great experiment of free public education began.

Granted, "ideally" is a hell of a qualifier. But an attack on schooling as we know it is generally grounded in politics rather than pedagogy, and is most energetically advanced by those who despise not just public schools but all public institutions. The marketplace, which would likely inherit the task of educating our children if Gatto got his way, is (to put it gently) unlikely to honor the ideals that inform his critique. Some folks will benefit from that kind of "reform," but they certainly won't be kids.[7]

People who want to strike a blow for individual liberty understandably lash out against the government—and these days they don't want for examples of undue interference from Washington and state capitals. But in education, as in other arenas of contemporary American life, there is an equal or greater danger from concentrating power in *private* hands, which is to say in enterprises that aren't accountable to anyone (save their own stockholders) or for anything (save making a profit).

Worst of all is a situation where public entities remake themselves in the image of private entities, where politicians pass laws to codify corporate ideology and impose it on our schools.[8] Perhaps the two most destructive forces in education these days are the tendency to view children as "investments" (whose ultimate beneficiary is business) and a market-driven credentialism in which discrete individuals struggle for competitive distinctions. To attack the institution of public education is like hollering at the shadows on the wall. The source of the problem is behind you, and it grows larger as you train your rage on the flickering images in front.

'FREEDOM' FROM PUBLIC EDUCATION

I try to imagine myself as a privatizer. How would I proceed? If my objective were to dismantle public schools, I would begin by trying to discredit them. I would probably refer to them as "government" schools, hoping to tap into a vein of libertarian resentment. I would never miss an opportunity to sneer at researchers and teacher educators as out-of-touch "educationists." Recognizing that it's politically unwise to attack teachers, I would do so obliquely, bashing the unions to which most of them belong. Most important, if I had the power, I would ratchet up the number and difficulty of standardized tests that students had to take, in order that I could then point to the predictably pitiful results. I would then defy my opponents to defend the schools that had produced students who did so poorly.

How closely does my thought experiment match reality? One way to ascertain the actual motivation behind the widespread use of testing is to watch what happens in the real world when a lot of students manage to do well on a given test. Are schools credited and teachers congratulated? Hardly. The response, from New Jersey to New Mexico, is instead to make the test harder, with the result that many more students subsequently fail. Consider this item from the *Boston Globe*:

> As the first senior class required to pass the MCAS exam prepares for graduation, state education officials are considering raising the passing grade for the exam. State Education Commissioner David Driscoll and Board of Education chairman James Peyser said the passing grade needs to be raised to keep the test challenging, given that a high proportion of students are passing it on the first try.... Peyser said as students continue to meet the standard, the state is challenged to make the exam meaningful.[9]

You have to admire the sheer Orwellian chutzpah represented by that last word. By definition, a test is "meaningful" only if large numbers of students (and, by implication, schools) fare poorly on it. What at first seems purely perverse—a mindless acceptance of the premise that harder is always better—reveals itself instead as a strategic move in the service of a very specific objective. Peyser, you see, served for eight years as executive director of the conservative Pioneer Institute, a Boston-based think tank devoted to "the application of free market principles to state and local policy" (in the words of the organization's website). The man charged with overseeing public education in Massachusetts is critical of the very idea of public education. And how does he choose to pursue his privatizing agenda? By raising the bar until alarming failure[10] is assured.

Of course, tougher standards are usually justified in the name of excellence—or, even more audaciously (given the demographics of most of the victims), equity. One doesn't expect to hear people like Peyser casually concede that the real point of this whole standards-and-testing business is to make the schools look bad, the better to justify a free-market alternative. Now and then, however, a revealing comment does slip out. For example, when the *School Choice Advocate*, the newsletter of the Milton and Rose Friedman Foundation, approvingly described Colorado's policy of publishing schools' test scores, a senior education advisor to Republican Gov. Bill Owens remarked that the motive behind reporting these results was to "greatly enhance and build pressure for school choice."[11]

An op-ed by by William Bennett and Chester Finn, published in the *Wall Street Journal* just before Christmas, underscored the integral relationship between the push for high-stakes testing (which they call "standards") and the effort to undermine public schooling (which they call "feedom"). The latter bit of spin is interesting in its own right: vouchers, having been decisively rejected by voters on several occasions, were promptly reintroduced as "school choice" to make them sound more palatable.[12] But apparently an even more blatant appeal to emotionally charged values is now called for. In any case, the article notes (correctly, I fear) that "our two political parties ... can find common ground on testing and accountability" but then goes on to announce that "what Republicans have going for them in education is freedom." They understand this value "because of their business ties." Unlike Democrats, they are "not afraid of freedom."

Even in an era distinguished by unpleasantly adversarial discourse, Bennett and Finn plumb its lower depths with the charge that freedom is a "domain that few Democrats dare to visit." (Their evidence for this charge is that most Democrats exclude private schools from choice plans.) But this nasty little essay, headlined "No Standards Without Freedom," serves primarily to remind us that the most vocal proponents of accountability—defined, as it usually is these days, in terms of top-down standards and coercive pressure to raise scores on an endless series of standardized tests—have absolutely no interest in improving the schools that struggle to fulfill these requirements. Public education in their view is not something to be made better; it is something from which we need to be freed.

MANY CHILDREN LEFT BEHIND

None of this is exactly new. "Standards" have been used to promote "freedom" for some time. But if that picture has been slowly coming into focus as education policies are enacted at the state level, it now attains digital clarity as a result of federal involvement—in particular, the law that some have rechristened No Child Left Untested (or No Corporation Left Behind, or No Child's Behind Left). Even those observers who missed—or dismissed—the causal relationship up until now are coming to realize that you don't have to be a conspiracy nut to understand the real purpose of this new law. Indeed, you have to be vision-impaired *not* to see it.

Jamie McKenzie, a former superintendent, put it this way on his website, (nochildleft.com): "Misrepresented as a reform effort, NCLB is actually a cynical effort to shift public school funding to a host of private schools, religious schools and free-market diploma mills or corporate experiments in education." The same point has been made by Gerald Bracey, Stan Karp, and a number of others. Lately, even some prominent politicians are catching on. Sen. Jim Jeffords (I-Vt.), who chaired the Senate committee that oversees education from 1997 to 2001, has described the law as a back-door maneuver "that will let the private sector take over public education, something the Republicans have wanted for years."[13] Former Sen. Carol Moseley Braun recently made the same point.

So what is it about NCLB in particular that has led a growing number of people to view it as a stalking horse for privatization? While any test can be, and many tests have been, rigged to create the impression of public school failure, nothing has ever come close to NCLB in this regard. Put aside for a moment the rather important point that higher scores on standardized tests do not necessarily reflect meaningful improvement in teaching or learning—and may even indicate the opposite.[14] Let's assume for the sake of the argument that better performance on these tests *was* a good sign. This law's criteria for being judged successful—how fast the scores must rise, and how high, and for how many subgroups of students—are nothing short of ludicrous. NCLB requires every single student to score at or above the proficient level by 2014, something that has never been done before and that few unmedicated observers believe is possible.[15]

As Monty Neill of FairTest explained in these pages not long ago, even the criteria for making "adequate yearly progress" toward that goal are such that "virtually no schools serving large numbers of low-income children will clear these arbitrary hurdles." Consequently, he adds, "many successful schools will be declared 'failing' and may be forced to drop practices that work well. Already, highly regarded schools have been put on the 'failing' list."[16] Schools that do manage to jump through these hoops, which include a 95-percent participation rate in the testing, must then contend with comparable hurdles involving the qualifications of its teachers.

The party line, of course, is that all these requirements are meant to make public schools improve, and that forcing every state to test every student every year (from third through eighth grades and then again in high school) is intended to identify troubled schools in order to "determine who needs extra help," as President Bush recently put it.[17] To anyone who makes this claim with a straight face, we might respond by asking three questions.

- How many schools will NCLB-required testing reveal to be troubled that were not previously identified as such? For the last year or so, I have challenged defenders of the law to name a single school anywhere in the country whose inadequacy was a secret until yet another wave of standardized test results was released. So far I have had no takers.
- Of the many schools and districts that are obviously struggling, how many have received the resources they need, at least without a court order? If conservatives are sincere in saying they want more testing in order to determine where help is needed, what has their track record been in providing that help? The answer is painfully obvious, of course. Many of the same people who justify more standardized tests for information-gathering purposes have also claimed that more money doesn't produce improvement. The Bush administration's proposed budgets have fallen far short of what states would need just to implement NCLB itself, and those who point this out are dismissed as malcontents. (Thus Bennett and Finn: "Democrats are now saying that Republicans are not spending enough. But that is what they always say—enough is never sufficient for them when it comes to education spending.")
- What have the results been of high-stakes testing to this point? To the best of my knowledge, no positive effects have ever been demonstrated, unless you count higher scores on these same tests. More low-income and minority students are dropping out, more teachers (often the best ones) are leaving the profession, and more mind-numbing test preparation is displacing genuine instruction. Why should anyone believe that annual do-or-die testing mandated by the federal government will lead to anything different? Moreover, the engine of this legislation is punishment. NCLB is designed to humiliate and hurt the schools that, according to its own warped standards, most need help. Families whose children attend those schools are given a green light to abandon them—and, specifically, to transfer to other schools that don't want them and probably can't handle them. This, it quickly becomes clear, is an excellent way to sandbag the "successful" schools, too.

So who will be left undisturbed and sitting pretty? Private schools and companies hoping to take over public schools. In the meantime, various corporations are already benefiting. The day after Bennett and Finn's rousing defense of freedom appeared on its op-ed page, the *Wall Street Journal* published a news story that began as follows: "Teachers, parents, and principals may have their doubts about No Child Left Behind (NCLB). But business loves it." Apart from the obvious bonanza for the giant companies that design and score standardized tests, "hundreds of 'supplemental service providers' have already lined up to offer tutoring, including Sylvan, Kaplan Inc., and Princeton Review Inc.... Kaplan says revenue for its elementary- and secondary-school division has doubled since No Child Left Behind passed."[18]

THE ACCOUNTABILITY/PRIVATIZATION CONNECTION

Ultimately, any attempt to demonstrate the commitment to privatization lurking behind NCLB doesn't require judgments about the probability that its requirements can be fulfilled, or speculation about the significance of which companies find it profitable. That commitment is a matter of public record. As originally proposed by the Bush Administration, the legislation would have used federal funds to provide private school vouchers to students in Title I schools with lagging test results. This provision was dropped only when it threatened to torpedo the whole bill; instead, the stick used to beat schools into raising their scores was limited to the threat that students could transfer to other public schools.

Since then, Bush's Department of Education has taken other steps to pursue its agenda, such as allocating money hand over fist to private groups that share its agenda. A few months ago, People for the American Way reported that the administration has funneled more than $75 million in taxpayer funds to pro-voucher groups and miscellaneous for-profit entities. Among them is William Bennett's latest gamble, known as K12—a company specializing in on-line education for home-schoolers. (Finn sits on the board of directors.) "Standards" plus "freedom" may eventually add up to considerable revenue, then. Meanwhile, the Department of Education is happy to ease the transition: a school choice pilot program in Arkansas received $11.5 million to buy a curriculum from Bennett's outfit, and a virtual charter school in Pennsylvania affiliated with K12 got $2.5 million.[19]

At the center of the conservative network receiving public funds to pursue what is arguably an antipublic agenda is the Education Leaders Council (ELC), which was created in 1995 as a more conservative alternative to the Council of Chief State School Officers (which is not all that progressive itself). One of its founders was Eugene Hickok, formerly secretary of education in Pennsylvania and now the second-ranking official in the U.S. Department of Education. Hickok brushes off the charge that the Education Department is promoting and funding privatization. If there's any favoritism reflected in these grants, he says, it's only in that "we support those organizations that support No Child Left Behind."[20]

But that's exactly the point. A hefty proportion of those who support vouchers also support NCLB, in large part because the latter is a means to the former. Take Lisa Graham Keegan, who was Arizona's school chief and is now ELC's executive director. She was a bit more forthcoming about the grants than Hickok, telling a reporter that it's only natural for the Bush administration to want to correct a "liberal bias" in American education by giving grants to groups that share its philosophy. "It is necessary to be ideological in education these days if you want to promote academic standards, school choice, and new routes to certifying teachers."[21] Notice again the juxtaposition of "standards" and "choice," this time joined by another element of the conservatives' agenda: an initiative, undertaken jointly by the ELC and a group set up by Finn's Thomas B. Fordham Foundation—and, again, publicly funded thanks to the U.S. Department of Education—to create a new quasi-private route to teacher credentialing.

For that matter, take Secretary of Education Rod Paige, who appeared at an ELC conference to assure its members that they were "doing God's work" and has been quoted as saying that "the worst thing that can happen to urban and minority kids is that they are not tested."[22] Indeed, Paige spent his years as superintendent in Houston doing anything and everything to raise test scores (or, rather, as it turns out, to give the *appearance* of raising test scores). At the same time, his "tenure as superintendent was marked by efforts to privatize or contract out not only custodial, payroll, and food services, but also educational services like 'alternative schools' for students with 'discipline problems.'"[23]

Just this past January, Paige made his way around the perimeter of the U.S. Capitol to speak at the conservative Heritage Foundation, whose headquarters stand about a dozen blocks from the Department of Education. His purpose was twofold: to laud NCLB for injecting "competition into the public school system" and to point out that vouchers—which he called "opportunity scholarships"—are the next logical step in offering "educational emancipation" from "the chains of bureaucracy."

Paige was particulaly enthusiastic about the legislation that earmarks $14 million in public funds—for the first time—for religious and private schools in Washington, D.C., which he hoped would turn out to be "a model program for the nation."

The arguments and rhetoric his speechwriters employed on that occasion are instructive. For example, he explained that the way we improve education is "one child at a time"—a phrase both more substantive and more dangerous than it may seem at first hearing. And he demanded to know how anyone could oppose vouchers in light of the fact that the GI Bill was "the greatest voucher program in history." Paige was particularly enthusiastic about the newly passed legislation that earmarks $14 million in public funds—federal funds, for the first time—for religious and private schools in Washington, D.C., which he hoped would turn out to be "a model program for the nation." (However, "this isn't a covert plan to finance private, especially Catholic, schools," he assured his audience. The proof? "Many of the students in Catholic schools are not Catholic.")

Paige couldn't restrain himself from gloating over how the passage of this law represented a triumph over "special interests"—that is, those who just "ask for more money" and want "to keep children in schools in need of improvement." These critics are "the real enemies of public schools." In fact, they put him in mind of France's determined opposition to the Bush Administration's efforts to secure UN approval for an invasion of Iraq.[24]

Notice that Paige chose to deliver these remarks at the Heritage Foundation, which publishes "No Excuses" apologias for high-stakes testing while simultaneously pushing vouchers and "a competitive market" for education. (Among its other reports: "Why More Money Will Not Solve America's Education Crisis.") Nina Shokraii Rees, a key education analyst at Heritage who helped draft the blueprint for NCLB and pressed for it to include annual high-stakes testing, is now working for Paige, implementing the plans that she and her group helped to formulate. So it goes for the Hoover Institution in California, the Manhattan Institute in New York, the Center for Education Reform in Washington, and other right-wing think tanks. All of them demand higher standards and more testing, and all of them look for ways to turn education over to the marketplace where it will be beyond the reach of democratic control. Over and over, accountability and privatization appear as conjoined twins.

To point out this correlation is not to deny that there are exceptions to it. To be sure, some proponents of public schooling have, with varying degrees of enthusiasm, hitched a ride on the Accountability Express. In fact, I've even heard one or two people argue that testing requirements in general—and NCLB in particular—represent our last chance to *save* public education, to redeem schools in the public's mind by insisting that they be held to high standards.

But the idea that we should scramble to feed the accountability beast is based on the rather desperate hope that we can satisfy its appetite by providing sufficient evidence of excellence. This is a fool's errand. It overlooks the fact that the whole movement is rooted in a top-down, ideologically driven contempt for public institutions, not in a grassroots loss of faith in neighborhood schools. The demand for accountability didn't start in living rooms; it started in places like the Heritage Foundation. After a time, it's true, even parents who think their own children's school is just fine may swallow the rhetoric they've been fed about the inadequacy of public education in general. But do we really think that the people who have cultivated this distrust, who bellow that we need more testing, who brush off structural barriers like poverty and racism as mere "excuses" for failure, will be satisfied once we agree to let them turn our schools into test-prep factories?

COLLATERAL DAMAGE

In any event, if we did so we'd be destroying the village in order to save it. No, scratch the conditional tense there: The devastation is already underway. Every few days there is fresh evidence of how teaching is being narrowed and dumbed down, standardized and scripted—with poor and minority students getting the worst of the deal as usual. I have an overstuffed file of evidence detailing what we're sacrificing on the altar of accountability, from developmentally appropriate education for little children to rich, project-based learning for older ones, from music to field trips to class discussions.[25]

Lately, it has become clear that piling NCLB on top of the state testing that was already assuming nightmarish proportions is producing still other sorts of collateral damage. For example, there is now increasing pressure to:

- *segregate schools by ethnicity.* A new California study confirms what other scholars had predicted: NCLB contains a "diversity penalty" such that the more subgroups of students that attend a given school, the lower the chance that it will be able to satisfy all the federally imposed requirements for adequate progress.[26]
- *segregate classes by ability.* While there are no hard data yet, it appears that schools may be doing more grouping and tracking in order to maximize the efficiency of test-preparation.[27] All children lose out from less heterogeneity, but none more than those at the bottom—yet another example of how vulnerable students suffer the most from the shrill demands for accountability.
- *segregate classes by age.* Multi-age education is reportedly becoming less common now—not because its benefits haven't been supported by research and experience (they have), but because of "grade-by-grade academic standards and the consequences tied to not meeting those targets as measured by state tests."[28]
- *criminalize misbehavior.* "In cities and suburbs around the country, schools are increasingly sending students into the juvenile justice systems for the sort of adolescent misbehavior that used to be handled by school administrators."[29] There are many explanations for this deeply disturbing trend, including the loss of school-based mental health services due to budget cuts. But Augustina Reyes of the University of Houston observes, "If teachers are told, 'Your scores go down, you lose your job,' all of a sudden your values shift very quickly. Teachers think, 'With bad kids in my class, I'll have lower achievement on my tests, so I'll use discretion and remove that kid.'"[30] Moreover, attempts to deal with the kinds of problems for which children are now being hauled off by the police—programs to promote conflict resolution and to address bullying and other sorts of violence—are being eliminated because educators and students are themselves being bullied into focusing on test scores to the exclusion of everything else.[31]
- *retain students in grade.* The same get-tough sensibility that has loosed an avalanche of testing has led to a self-congratulatory war on "social promotion" that consists of forcing students to repeat a grade. The preponderance of evidence indicates that this is just about the worst course of action to take with struggling children in terms of both its academic and social-psychological effects. And the evidence *uniformly* demonstrates that retention increases the chance that a student will leave school; in fact, it's an even stronger predictor of dropping out than is socioeconomic status.[32]

If flunking kids is a terrible idea, flunking them solely on the basis of their standardized test scores is even worse. But that's precisely what Chicago, Baltimore, and now the state of Florida are doing, harming tens of thousands of elementary-school children in each case. And even that isn't the whole story. Some students are being forced to repeat a grade not because this is believed (however inaccurately) to be in their best interest, but because pressure for schools to show improved test results induces administrators to hold back potentially low-scoring children the year before a key exam is administered. That way, students in, say, tenth grade will be a year older, with another year of test prep under their belts, before they sit down to start bubbling in ovals.

Across the U.S., according to calculations by Walt Haney and his colleagues at Boston College, there were 13% more students in ninth grade in 2000 than there were in eighth grade in 1999.[33] Retention rates are particularly high in states like Texas and North Carolina, which helps to explain their apparently impressive scores on the National Assessment of Educational Progress. The impact on the students involved, most of whom end up dropping out, is incalculable, but it makes schools and states look good in an age where accountability trumps all other considerations. Moreover, Haney predicts, "senseless provisions of NCLB likely will lead to a further increase of 5% or more in grade nine retention. And of those who are flunked," he adds, "70% to 75% will not persist to high school graduation."[34]

THE DANGERS OF COMPLYING WITH NCLB

Take a step back and consider these examples of what I'm calling collateral damage from high-stakes testing: a more traditional, back-to-basics curriculum; more homogeneity; a retreat from innovations like multi-age classrooms; more tracking and retention and harsher discipline. What's striking about these ostensibly accidental by-products of policies designed to ensure accountability is that, they, themselves, are on the wish list of many of the same people who push for more testing—and, often, for vouchers.

In fact, we can add one more gift to the Right. By virtue of its definition of a qualified teacher, NCLB helps to cement the idea that education consists of pouring knowledge into empty receptacles. We don't need people who know how to help students become proficient learners (a skill that they might be helped to acquire in a school of education); we just need people who know a lot of stuff (a distinction that might simply be certified by a quasi-private entity—using, naturally, a standardized test). Or, as Bennett and Finn explain things to the readers of the *Wall Street Journal*, "A principal choosing teachers will make better-informed decisions if she has access to comparable information about how much history or math or science each candidate knows." This nicely rounds out the "reform" agenda, by locking into place a model that not only deprofessionalizes teachers but confuses teaching with the transmission of facts.

The upshot of all this is that the Right has constructed a single puzzle of interlocking parts. They are hoping that some people outside their circle will be persuaded to endorse some of those parts (specific, uniform curriculum standards, for example, or annual testing) without understanding how they are integrally connected to the others (for example, the incremental dissolution of public schooling and the diminution of the very idea that education is a public good).

They are succeeding largely because decent educators are playing into their hands. That's why we must quit confining our complaints about NCLB to peripheral problems of implementation or funding. Too many people give the impression that there would be nothing to object to if only their own school had been certified as making adequate yearly progress or if only Washington were more generous in paying for this assault on local autonomy. We have got to stop prefacing our objections by saying that, while the execution of this legislation is faulty, we agree with its laudable objectives.

No. What we agree with is some of the rhetoric used to *sell* it, invocations of ideals like excellence and fairness. NCLB is not a step in the right direction. It is a deeply damaging, mostly ill-intentioned law, and no one genuinely committed to improving public schools (or to advancing the interests of those who have suffered from decades of neglect and oppression) would want to have anything to do with it.

Ultimately, we must decide whether we will obediently play our assigned role in helping to punish children and teachers. Every inservice training session, every article, every memo from the central office that offers what amounts to an instruction manual for capitulation slides us further in the wrong direction until finally we become a nation at risk of abandoning public education altogether. Rather than scrambling to comply with its provisions, our obligation is to figure out how best to resist.

NOTES

1. Cited in Jan Freeman, "Reform School," *Boston Globe*, January 11, 2004, p. L-3.
2. David Brooks, "Running on Reform," *New York Times*, January 3, 2004, p. 15.
3. To be precise, those who decry these semantic misrepresentations should be described as "skeptical" or "critical." It's those responsible for them who are more accurately described as cynical. And while we're being precise, the line I've quoted, like much of Tomlin's material, was actually written by Jane Wagner.
4. See David C. Berliner and Bruce J. Biddle, *The Manufactured Crisis: Myths, Fraud, and the Attack on America's Public Schools* (Reading, MA: Addison-Wesley, 1995); Richard Rothstein, *The Way We Were?: The Myths and Realities of America's Student Achievement* (New York: Century Foundation Press, 1998); and the collected works of Gerald Bracey.
5. Kari Delhi, "Shopping for Schools," *Orbit* Ontario Institute for Studies in Education vol. 25, no. 1, 1998, p. 32. The author cites three studies from the UK in support of this conclusion.
6. John Taylor Gatto, "Against School," *Harper's*, September 2003, pp. 33–38.
7. After I made some of these points in a letter to the editor that appeared in *Harper's*, Gatto wrote to tell me I had missed the point of his essay because he actually doesn't support "the elimination of public education." However, he does "hope to undermine centralized institutional schooling which uses the police power of the state to impose habits, attitudes, etc." I can only assume that he is using the word *public* in a way I don't understand. In any case, his furious attack on "mandatory" education—on universal schooling that is supported by the public treasury and administered by elected authorities—is one that has been warmly received by those on the right. Indeed, Gatto was one of the first endorsers of the Alliance for the Separation of School and State, which repudiates the idea of a "common school" and calls for "the end of federal, state, and local involvement with schooling." (A conference sponsored by the Alliance "featured a wide variety of conservative speakers, including John Taylor Gatto," according to a newsletter of Phyllis Schlafly's Eagle Forum.) Elsewhere, Gatto has written that he is "deeply depressed by Jonathan Kozol's contention that money would improve the schools of the poor. It would not."
8. For more, see my article "The 500-Pound Gorilla," *Phi Delta Kappan*, October 2002, pp. 113–19; and various chapters in the anthology that I edited with Patrick Shannon: *Education, Inc.: Turning Learning into a Business*, rev. ed. (Portsmouth, NH: Heinemann, 2002).
9. C. Kalimah Redd, "Raising of MCAS Bar Is Weighed," *Boston Globe*, April 30, 2003, p. B-2.
10. Alarming failure, not universal failure. As education policy makers across the country have learned, there are political costs to having too many students flunk the tests, particularly if an unseemly number of them are white and relatively affluent. At that point, politically potent parents—and, eventually, even education reporters—may begin to ask inconvenient questions about the test itself. Fortunately, by tinkering with the construction of items on the exam and adjusting the cut score, it is possible to ensure virtually any outcome long before the tests are scored or even administered. For the officials in charge, the enterprise of standardized testing is reminiscent of shooting an arrow into a wall and then drawing the target around it.
11. "In the Spotlight: Colorado," *The School Choice Advocate*, December 2001, p. 7. Available at: www.friedmanfoundation.org/resources/publications/advocate/dec2001_1.pdf.

12. For an account of the carefully coordinated decision to stop using the V word, see Darcia Harris Bowman, "Republicans Prefer to Back Vouchers by Any Other Name," *Education Week*, 31 January 2001.
13. The McKenzie quotation is from "The NCLB Wrecking Ball," an essay first posted on www.nochildleft.com in November 2003. The Jeffords quotation is from Sally West Johnson, "Mathis Rips Feds Over School Act," *Rutland* [Vermont] *Herald*, 5 February 2003.
14. See, for example, my book *The Case Against Standardized Testing: Raising the Scores, Ruining the Schools* (Portsmouth, N.H.: Heinemann, 2000).
15. See, for example, Robert L. Linn, "Accountability: Responsibility and Reasonable Expectations," the 2003 Presidential Address to the American Educational Research Association available at www.aera.net/pubs/er/pdf/vol32_07/AERA320701.pdf.
16. Monty Neill, "Leaving Children Behind: How No Child Left Behind Will Fail Our Children," *Phi Delta Kappan*, November 2003, pp. 225–26.
17. Bush is quoted in Eric W. Robelen, "Bush Marks School Law's 2nd Anniversary," *Education Week*, 14 January 2004, p. 20.
18. June Kronholz, "Education Companies See Dollars in Bush School-Boost Law," *Wall Street Journal*, 24 December 2003, p. B-1.
19. The report by People for the American Way, entitled "Funding a Movement," is available at www.pfaw.org/pfaw/dfiles/file_259.pdf.
20. Michael Dobbs, "Critics Say Education Dept. Is Favoring Political Right," *Washington Post*, 2 January 2004, p. A-19.
21. Ibid.
22. The ELC quote is from Joetta L. Sack, "ELC Receives Grant to Craft Tests to Evaluate Teachers," *Education Week*, 10 October 2001. The testing quote is from Robert C. Johnston, "Urban Leaders See Paige as 'Our Own,'" *Education Week*, 7 February 2001.
23. Stan Karp, "Paige Leads Dubious Cast of Education Advisors," *Rethinking Schools*, Spring 2001, p. 4.
24. Paige's 28 January 2004 speech, "A Time for Choice," is available at www.ed.gov/news/speeches/2004/01/01282004.html.
25. Among many other sources, see M. Gail Jones, Brett D. Jones, and Tracy Hargrove, *The Unintended Consequences of High-Stakes Testing* (Lanham, Md.: Rowman & Littlefield, 2003); and the examples cited at www.susanohanian.org.
26. See John R. Novak and Bruce Fuller, *Penalizing Diverse Schools* (University of California at Berkeley and Stanford University, Policy Analysis for California Education, December 2003). Available at: http://pace.berkeley.edu/policy_brief_03-4_Pen.Div.pdf.
27. See Laura Pappano, "Grouping Students Undergoes Revival," *Boston Globe*, 14 December 2003.
28. Linda Jacobson, "Once-Popular 'Multiage Grouping' Loses Steam," *Education Week*, 10 September 2003, pp. 1, 15.
29. Sara Rimer, "Unruly Students Facing Arrest, Not Detention," *New York Times*, 4 January 2004, p. 1.
30. That explanation also makes sense to Mark Soler of the Youth Law Center, a public interest group that protects at-risk children: "Now zero tolerance is fed less by fear of crime and more by high-stakes testing. Principals want to get rid of kids they perceive as trouble." Both Reyes and Soler are quoted in Annette Fuentes, "Discipline and Punish," *The Nation*, 15 December 2003, pp. 17–20.
31. Scott Poland, a school psychologist and expert in crisis intervention, writes: "School principals have told me that they would like to devote curriculum time to topics such as managing anger, violence prevention and learning to get along with others regardless of race and ethnicity, but ... [they are] under tremendous pressure to raise academic scores on the state accountability test." (See "The Non-Hardware Side of School Safety," *NASP* [National Association of School Psychologists] *Communique*, vol. 28, no. 6, March 2000.) Poland made the same point while testifying at a Congressional hearing on school violence in March 1999—a month before the shootings at Columbine.
32. See, for example, the studies cited in Jay P. Heubert, "First, Do No Harm," *Educational Leadership*, December 2002 / January 2003, p. 27.
33. That's triple the rate for the disparity between ninth and eighth grade during the 1970s. See Walt Haney et al., *The Education Pipeline in the United States, 1970–2000*. Boston: National Board on Educational Testing and Public Policy, January 2004. Available at: www.bc.edu/research/nbetpp/statements/nbr3.pdf.
34. Walt Haney, personal communication, January 15, 2004. Haney's study also found that there was a substantial drop in high school graduation rates, beginning, as a reporter noticed, "just as President Bill Clinton and Congress ushered in the school accountability measures [that were later] strengthened in the No Child Left Behind Act." Haney is quoted in that same article as saying, "The benign explanation is that this whole standards and reform movement was implemented in an ill-conceived manner." (See Diana Jean Schemo, "As Testing Rises, 9th Grade Becomes Pivotal," *New York Times*, 18 January 2004, p. 23.) This, of course, invites us to consider explanations that are less benign.

ALFIE KOHN is the author of nine books, including The Schools Our Children Deserve *and* The Case Against Standardized Testing. *The beginning of this article was adapted from the introduction to his newest book,* What Does It Mean to Be Well Educated? And More Essays on Standards, Grading, and Other Follies *(Beacon Press, 2004). Orders may be placed at www.beacon.org. Kohn's previous Kappan articles are available at www.alfiekohn.org © 2004, Alfie Kohn.*

Copyright © 2004 by Alfie Kohn. Reprinted from *Phi Delta Kappan*, April 2004, pp. 569–577. Reprinted by permission of the author, Alfie Kohn. For more information: www.ALFIEKOHN.org

Article 10

Leadership That Sparks Learning

Research shows that effective school leadership can substantially boost student achievement.

J. Timothy Waters, Robert J. Marzano, and Brian McNulty

Educators have long known that some principals are more effective leaders than others. Yet what exactly characterizes effective principals? For many years, principals have been told that they must be *instructional leaders*. This term, however, has remained a vague concept, supported by anecdotal evidence at best. Similarly, we have struggled to define the specific training that principals need to become effective leaders. Most educators can think of principals who graduated from the same programs or received the same professional development yet achieved different levels of success in their respective schools. Likewise, we can point to principals who tried to replicate others' successful strategies in their own schools with only minimal—or worse, negative—consequences.

Does leadership really make a difference in schools, and is it science or art? After examining quantitative research on school leadership spanning more than 25 years, Mid-continent Research for Education and Learning (McREL) has begun to answer these questions and establish a science of leadership.

McREL's study, *School Leadership That Works*, is the third in a series of meta-analytic studies of classroom, school, and leadership practices that are highly correlated with student achievement. This study addressed two important questions: Do the focus and quality of leadership have a significant relationship to student achievement? What specific leadership responsibilities and practices have the greatest impact?

For this analysis, we reviewed more than 5,000 studies that purported to examine the effect of leadership on student achievement. Of these 5,000 studies, we found only 70 published since 1978 that reported standardized, objective, and quantitative measures of student achievement, such as those provided by state-adopted norm-referenced tests, with achievement as the dependent variable and perceptions of leadership as the independent variable. Instead of relying on principals' self-assessments, these studies asked teachers to rate their principals' leadership qualities. The 70 studies created a sample size of 2,894 schools, 14,000 teachers, and more than 1.1 million students.

From the resulting data, we reached the following conclusions:
- *Leadership matters*. McREL found a significant, positive correlation between effective school leadership and student achievement.
- *We can empirically define effective leadership*. McREL identified 21 key areas of leadership responsibility that are significantly correlated with student achievement.
- *Effective leaders not only know what to do, but how, when, and why to do it.* McREL researchers concluded that effective leaders understand which school changes are most likely to improve student achievement, what these changes imply for both staff and community, and how to tailor their leadership practices accordingly.

Leadership Matters

The data from our meta-analysis demonstrate a substantial relationship between leadership and student achievement. We found that the average effect size (expressed as a correlation) between leadership and student achievement is .25, which means that as leadership improves, so does student achievement.

To interpret this correlation more precisely, consider two schools (school A and school B) with similar student and teacher populations. Both demonstrate student achievement on a standardized, norm-referenced test at the 50th percentile. Principals in both schools also are average—that is, their abilities in key leadership responsibilities rank at the 50th percentile. Now assume that the principal of school B improves his or her demonstrated abilities in all key responsibilities by exactly one standard deviation, meaning that these abilities now fall in the 84th percentile of all principals rather than in the 50th percentile.

Effective leaders establish strong lines of communication with teachers and students.

Our research findings indicate that this increase in leadership ability would translate into an expected mean student achievement at school B that is 10 percentile points higher than mean achievement at school A. Expressed differently, the studies taken as a whole suggest that improving principals' leadership abilities by one standard deviation, from the 50th to the 84th percentile, would lead to an increase in average student achievement from the 50th to the 60th percentile—a substantial improvement.

Leadership Defined

So what is effective leadership? Our analysis of the 70 studies found that effective leadership comprises 21 key areas of responsibility, all of which are positively correlated with higher levels of student achievement. Although these responsibilities are interrelated, they have unique defining characteristics, and we report them as distinct responsibilities.

- *Culture:* fosters shared beliefs and a sense of community and cooperation.
- *Order:* establishes a set of standard operating procedures and routines.
- *Discipline:* protects teachers from issues and influences that would detract from their teaching time or focus.
- *Resources:* provides teachers with the materials and professional development necessary for the successful execution of their jobs.
- *Curriculum, instruction, and assessment:* is directly involved in the design and implementation of curriculum, instruction, and assessment practices.
- *Knowledge of curriculum, instruction, and assessment:* is knowledgeable about current practices.
- *Focus:* establishes clear goals and keeps these goals at the forefront of the school's attention.
- *Visibility:* has high-quality contact and interactions with teachers and students.
- *Contingent rewards:* recognizes and rewards individual accomplishments.
- *Communication:* establishes strong lines of communication with teachers and students.
- *Outreach:* is an advocate and spokesperson for the school to all stakeholders.
- *Input:* involves teachers in the design and implementation of important decisions and policies.
- *Affirmation:* recognizes and celebrates school accomplishments and acknowledges failures.
- *Relationship:* demonstrates empathy with teachers and staff on a personal level.
- *Change agent role:* is willing and prepared to actively challenge the status quo.
- *Optimizer role:* inspires and leads new and challenging innovations.
- *Ideals and beliefs:* communicates and operates from strong ideals and beliefs about schooling.
- *Monitoring and evaluation:* monitors the effectiveness of school practices and their impact on student learning.
- *Flexibility:* adapts his or her leadership behavior to the needs of the current situation and is comfortable with dissent.
- *Situational awareness:* is aware of the details and undercurrents in the running of the school and uses this information to address current and potential problems.
- *Intellectual stimulation:* ensures that faculty and staff are aware of the most current theories and practices in education and makes the discussion of these practices integral to the school's culture.

The Differential Impact of Leadership

The correlation of .25 represents the average correlation between leadership and student achievement for all of the 70 studies that we examined. These studies reported a range of correlations, however; some were stronger and some much weaker. More specifically, some studies reported the effect size for leadership and achievement as high as .50, which translates mathematically into a one-standard-deviation difference in demonstrated leadership ability correlating with a 19 percentile point increase in student achievement.

Other studies, however, reported that leaders who displayed the very same leadership qualities had only a marginal—or worse, a *negative*—impact on student achievement. Specifically, some studies reported correlations as low as -.02. This indicates that a one-standard-deviation improvement in leadership practices was correlated with a 1 percentile point *decrease* in student achievement.

On the basis of extensive professional wisdom and a review of theoretical literature on leadership, we interpret this data to mean that two primary variables determine whether leadership will have a positive or a negative impact on student achievement. The first is the *focus of change*—whether or not leaders properly identify the correct focus for school and classroom improvement efforts, those that are most likely to have a positive impact on student achievement in their schools. The second variable is whether or not leaders properly understand the magnitude or order of change that they are leading and adjust their leadership practices accordingly.

The Focus of Change

Harvard scholar Richard Elmore has noted that "knowing the right thing to do is the central problem of school improvement" (2003, p. 9). Leaders can act like effective leaders, but if they fail to guide their schools toward making the correct changes, these changes are likely to have a diminished or negative impact on student achievement. We believe that the school and classroom practices we identified in our two previous meta-analytic studies are, in fact, the "right things to do" in school improvement.

At the school level, these practices encompass a guaranteed and viable curriculum, challenging goals and effective feedback, parent and community involvement, a safe and orderly environment, and collegiality and professionalism. At the teacher level, they entail effective instructional strategies, classroom management, and classroom curriculum design. At the student level, they entail a positive home environment, learned intelligence and background knowledge, and motivation.

The Order of Change

Many educators can point to examples of leaders who knew the right things to do in one setting or with one initiative but who were unable to replicate their successes in other settings or with other initiatives. The theoretical literature on leadership, change, and the adoption of new ideas provides some insights into why this may occur.

Many theorists (Beckard & Pritchard, 1992; Bridges, 1991; Fullan, 1993; Heifetz, 1994; Hesslebein & Johnston, 2002; Nadler, Shaw, Walton, & Associates, 1994; Rogers, 1995) have made the case that not all changes are of the same magnitude. Some changes have greater implications than others for staff members, students, parents, and other stakeholders. Different labels have been used to differentiate between magnitudes of change: technical versus adaptive, incremental versus fundamental, and continuous versus discontinuous, for example. We use the terms *first-order changes and second-order changes* to make this distinction.

First-order changes build on past and existing models. They are consistent with stakeholders' prevailing values and norms and can be implemented largely with existing knowledge and skills—and with help from outside experts. In short, they merely tinker at the edges and don't seek to change the core values, beliefs, or structures of the school.

Second-order changes, on the other hand, dramatically break with the past and challenge existing models, norms, and values. As a result, they cannot be implemented by outside experts. Stakeholders must find their way through the changes together, acquiring along the way new sets of knowledge, skills, ways of thinking, and, often, values.

Order of change has less to do with the change itself than with how stakeholders view the change. They may find the change consistent with existing values and norms, be able to implement the change with existing knowledge and resources, and agree on the changes needed and the procedure for implementing them. These are first-order changes. In an education context, these might be new classroom instruction practices, curricular programs, or data collection and reporting systems that build on established patterns and use existing knowledge.

Reporting these data and demonstrating ways in which schools have *not* adequately served all students could challenge some stakeholders' deeply held norms and values.

The same changes, however, may represent different orders of change for different individuals or stakeholder groups. What some will experience as a first-order change others may experience as a second-order change. For example, some educators, policymakers, and parents may view the implementations of standards, high-stakes testing, and accountability measures as first-order changes, as an appropriate response—consistent with their prevailing values and norms—to problems in schools. Others see these changes as dramatic and undesirable breaks with the past. For these individuals, the "solution" of standards, testing, and accountability is, in fact, a problem. Thus, for these stakeholders, such changes are second-order.

If leaders fail to understand or acknowledge that some changes are second-order for some or all of their stakeholders, they may struggle to get support for the successful implementation of these changes. As a result, their initiatives may fail to improve student achievement.

To more clearly illustrate second-order changes, imagine a school implementing some of the changes required by the No Child Left Behind Act. One key provision of the law requires schools to disaggregate their data by student subgroups and find ways to ensure that all subgroups demonstrate proficiency on the state test. At first blush, simply reporting disaggregated data may seem to be a rather incremental change, a minor modification to existing assessment systems. Yet this seemingly simple change could cause tremendous ripples among school staff and community members. Reporting these data and demonstrating ways in which schools have *not* adequately served all students could challenge some stakeholders' deeply held norms and values. Some teachers and parents may hold a sink-or-swim philosophy of schooling that sees the main purpose of schools as sorting and selecting students according to ability. These individuals may question why the school is devoting additional resources to help struggling students improve achievement—or question whether doing so will have any real impact.

Achieving the goals of the No Child Left Behind Act will undoubtedly require schools to undertake numerous changes, many of which may challenge prevailing norms and values and require educators to acquire new knowledge and skills. Successfully implementing these second-order changes requires effective leadership.

It has been said that if you want to change the world, start by looking in the mirror. Given the strong correlation that we have found between leadership and student achievement, the same notion may apply to leaders who want to change their schools. Our research on school leadership, with its quantitative data defining the traits of effective leaders, may be just the mirror that leaders need.

References

Beckard, R., & Pritchard, W. (1992). *Changing the essence: The art of creating and leading fundamental change in organizations.* San Francisco: Jossey-Bass.

Bridges, W. (1991). *Managing transitions: Making the most of change.* Reading, MA: Addison-Wesley.

Elmore, R. (2003). *Knowing the right thing to do: School improvement and performance-based accountability.* Washington, DC: NGA Center for Best Practices.

Fullan, M. G. (1993). *Change forces: Probing the depths of educational reform.* Bristol, PA: Falmer Press.

Heifetz, R. (1994). *Leadership without easy answers.* Cambridge, MA: Belknap Press.

Hesselbein, F., & Johnston, R. (Eds.). (2002). *On leading change: A leader to leader guide.* San Francisco: Jossey-Bass.

Nadler, D. A., Shaw, R. B., Walton, A. E., & Associates. (1994). *Discontinuous change.* San Francisco: Jossey-Bass.

Rogers, E. (1995). *Diffusion of innovations.* New York: The Free Press.

J. Timothy Waters (twaters@mcrel.org) is Executive Director, **Robert J. Marzano** (rmarzano@mcrel.org) is Senior Scholar, and **Brian McNulty** (bmcnulty@mcrel.org) is Vice President of Field Services at Mid-continent Research for Education and Learning in Aurora, Colorado.

From *Educational Leadership*, April 2004, pp. 48-51. Reprinted by permission of the Association for Supervision and Curriculum Development. Copyright © 2004 by ASCD. All rights reserved. The Association for Supervision and Curriculum Development is a worldwide community of educators advocating sound policies and sharing best practices to achieve the success of each learner. To learn more, visit ASCD at www.ascd.org

Article 11

Meeting Challenges in Urban Schools

Rhetoric about leadership often obscures the fact that school leadership is rooted in the realities of place, roles, and resources.

By Larry Cuban

President George W. Bush steps out of a plane onto the flight deck of the USS *Abraham Lincoln* in May 2003 to declare the end of the war in Iraq. It's a 100-octane image of can-do leadership. Yet such media-hyped images do not show how real leadership emerges—within a given context and role, and often constrained by limited resources. Teachers, principals, and superintendents in urban, largely minority districts lack the photo ops that presidents can command. They find ways to lead nevertheless, in settings that differ dramatically from those of their affluent suburban counterparts.

Films, magazines, and books have portrayed a number of urban teachers, principals, and superintendents as heroic leaders: Los Angeles math teacher Jaime Escalante, who helped underachieving Latino students at Garfield High School pass the advanced placement calculus test; Joe Clark of bullhorn and baseball bat fame, who as principal famously turned around New Jersey's Eastside High School; and New York school chancellor Rudy Crew, who tangled with Mayor Rudolph Giuliani on education issues. They were instructional, managerial, and political leaders in their classrooms, schools, and districts; the media caught their glow and made them famous for longer than their allotted 15 minutes.

But when Escalante, Clark, and Crew moved on to other posts, their high-profile leadership slipped away. How come?

It has to do with the settings in which these leaders worked, the varied and complex ways they exerted authority in their roles, and the resources they commanded. All come into play in understanding not only the stiff challenges facing urban schools but also how those challenges can produce effective urban leaders.

Settings

In middle-class and affluent suburbs, students generally attend adequately funded schools in safe communities. These students usually have an ample network of home support—parental guidance, sufficient food, and access to books and computers, for example. Students also benefit from the services of professionals, such as tutors, optometrists, dentists, and therapists, as the need arises.

Not so for low-income students in rural and urban schools. Teachers, principals, and superintendents working in low-income schools and districts face different challenges than those of their peers working in middle-class and affluent areas. Although parents in low-income communities want the same opportunities for their children as middle- and upper-income parents do, they live in places that threaten their safety and lack the resources to support their aspirations. Moreover, schools in these areas seldom provide the minimum services that middle-class families and districts take for granted.

Refusing to Accept Low Expectations

Take Locke High School in Los Angeles, California, for example. Three thousand students attend the school, which has an average class size of 37 students. More than half of the school's 120 teachers have fewer than two years of teaching experience. The 9th grade class of 1,200 students shrinks to approximately 250 students by senior year. Textbooks for specific classes are apt to be unavailable.

This school's setting—characterized by unwieldy class sizes, inexperienced teachers, large numbers of at-risk students, low expectations for its student body, and lack of resources—differs enormously from the settings of more-affluent schools. But new principal Gail Garrett decisively and thoughtfully worked to change Locke's conditions. Ninth graders have been divided into groups and are taught by teams of teachers. Garrett has made sure that textbooks are available. And every morning, she announces over the loudspeaker, "Welcome to Locke

High School, where each and every one of our students is expected to go to college." Locke's small gains in test scores may be linked to such improvements. But how different the situation is just a few miles away in Beverly Hills and Santa Monica, where the high school principals don't have to worry about textbook availability, large class size, poorly trained teachers, or students who won't make it to college (Winerup, 2003).

Insisting on a Challenging Curriculum

Most affluent schools wouldn't debate the necessity for a rigorous curriculum. But consider veteran teacher Rafe Esquith's experience at Hobart Boulevard Elementary School in Los Angeles. The school has more than 2,100 students. In Esquith's English class, 32 low-income Latino and Asian 5th and 6th graders read Shakespeare, Dickens, Salinger, and Steinbeck; in math, he starts his students on algebra. These highly motivated students—who begin school at 6:30 a.m. and finish at 5:00 p.m.—work together and help one another. Those who lag behind receive tutoring to bring them up to speed. The students perform classroom jobs and receive scrip for their work, which they can then redeem for prizes. Parents vie to get their children into Esquith's class knowing how hard their sons and daughters will work. Esquith also schedules class trips so that his students can perform Shakespearean plays for other schools in California.

After battling with district supervisors over his challenging curriculum, the plays that his students performed, and his high expectations for student achievement, Esquith became an entrepreneur in raising the necessary funds and support for his ambitious program. Compared to other students in schools with similar demographics, his students have scored high on state-mandated tests as a result of his efforts (Mathews, 2003).

Focusing on Instructional Excellence

Discouraged teachers and wary parents are also common features of the urban school landscape. Consider Betty Belt, who presided over Oakridge Elementary School in urban Arlington, Virginia, in the 1970s and 1980s. In a community deeply worried about sharp increases in minority students and declining district test scores, Belt knew exactly what to do to satisfy administrators, teachers, students, and parents.

Popping in and out of the 30-plus classrooms and occasionally taking over a class or tutoring a student, Belt knew the names of most of Oakridge's 500 students. Her goal was straightforward: to make Oakridge the number-one school in the district.

To achieve that goal, Belt tirelessly focused on classroom instruction and student achievement. She asked teachers to give her samples of student writing to read so she could write comments to the authors. Every nine weeks, she reviewed report cards—both grades and teacher appraisals—before the assessments were sent home. She kept student reading and math records in her office, monitoring them periodically for sudden changes in performance. Teachers assigned to Oakridge soon realized that the school was no place for tired practitioners to hide. For both teachers and students, Belt set a high bar for performance and outcomes.

Teachers and administrators must provide moral leadership to build proud, engaged, and humane young men and women of high moral stature.

When it came to parents, Belt responded quickly to their concerns and kept them up-to-date on school and district policies. She knew that parents were powerful political allies and that they could help her reach her goals. Making Oakridge the highest-performing school in Arlington depended, however, on several factors: experienced teachers, parent volunteers, fund raising, Belt's expertise as a leader and educator, her negotiating skills with the superintendent, and her regular presence at school board meetings to lobby for the school. As Oakridge steadily improved, parents increasingly sought to transfer their children there.

Rallying Broad Support

Turning an entire urban school district around requires a special set of skills. The Seattle, Washington, school board chose John Stanford to become its superintendent in 1995. Stanford, a former U.S. Army general and county executive in Georgia, had no experience as either a teacher or a principal. Failed tax levies, declining public support for the schools, and fractious relations between teachers and the school board and between blacks and whites over the quality of schooling had convinced Seattle civic and business leaders to seek out a different kind of superintendent (Yee & McCloud, 2003).

Within three years, Stanford's focus on student learning produced content standards for every grade that were consistent with state requirements. He shifted more authority to the school site, made principals into veritable CEOs by making them accountable, and signed an agreement with the teachers union that pulled all parties together to work on improving teaching and learning. He launched a new student assignment plan that ended mandatory busing. He devised a new formula for student funding that provided additional money for teachers, all-day kindergartens, and other support services to schools that took in students from low-income families. In concert with an intense media campaign that asked all Seattle citizens to work together on behalf of all students, Stanford went into schools daily to speak with teachers and students, attended all parent meetings in the schools, and worked closely with the city's civic and business elite. Stanford's political and managerial know-how resulted in organizational changes and a climate of strong support for public schools.

Roles and Authority

If setting matters in leadership, so does organizational position. The authority vested in teachers, principals, and superintendents sets up the expectation that each will lead. Authority can be a valuable resource for taking initiative and providing moral leadership.

Esquith was a successful school leader because—unlike many colleagues who settle for less—he took risks in revising the curriculum, fought supervisors who challenged his brand of teaching, created a climate for learning, and built close relationships with his students. He succeeded because he persisted and because he had the political know-how to use the strong performance of his students to persuade parents and his superiors that his approach was worthwhile.

Belt used her authority as principal to enhance instruction and motivate both students and teachers to learn. Stanford used his formal position as superintendent to reach out to the larger Seattle community. He created a moral climate of support for students and learning as he prodded a creaky, problem-filled system toward higher achievement.

Teachers, principals, and superintendents such as these perform three crucial roles in instruction, management, and politics. These roles are the grist of leadership, cutting across classrooms, principal offices, and district headquarters.

Instructional Role

Instruction is the central task that teachers are expected to perform. In urban schools where low expectations reign, teachers have a special obligation to push students academically. Flamboyant Rafe Esquith chose his classroom content and methodology; his students learned as much about character and duty as they learned about algebra and Shakespeare. School principals like Betty Belt instruct students, teachers, and parents with the moral example they set; the practices they implement in their schools; the teacher workshops they lead; and the written documents they produce, such as memos, daily bulletins, and articles for professional journals. For superintendents like John Stanford, the instructional stage is larger, taking in students, teachers, principals, and the community at large, and the instructional goal is raising academic achievement.

Managerial Role

Teachers face the basic task of establishing class rules—often proxies for moral values. Like their suburban counterparts, urban teachers must deal with mountains of paperwork, arbitrate classroom squabbles, keep conflicts to a minimum, oversee homework, regularly grade students, and hold parent-teacher conferences. But in urban schools, where multiple languages, cultures, and values come into play, teachers need exquisitely fine-tuned skills for managing the inevitable rush of conflicts.

Think about Rafe Esquith in that Los Angeles 5th and 6th grade classroom. His conflict management skills ensured that the various classroom activities proceeded smoothly. For principal Betty Belt and superintendent John Stanford, the managerial role not only meant channeling paper flow, delegating tasks to the right people, and keeping the school and district on an even keel. It also meant keeping a firm hold on the tiller to steer the ship in the right direction as political squabbles and crises inevitably brewed and threatened a change in course.

Political Role

Deciding what is important and how to achieve organizational and personal goals falls in the purview of the political role. Of course, teachers and administrators who find little value in the press for higher standardized test scores or in the idea of identifying schools as underperforming when scores dip one year will seldom publicly argue against district, state, or federal laws, such as No Child Left Behind. They are expected to exercise their technical and organizational skills in implementing the decisions of school boards, governors, state legislatures, and the U.S. Congress.

But this does not mean that teachers and administrators do not engage in politics. They do, both inside and outside the organization. John Stanford negotiated with school board members, principals, unions, parent groups, and city officials. Betty Belt bargained with her superintendent and lobbied parents and school board members. Rafe Esquith made unspoken deals with his 5th and 6th graders that if they worked hard in and out of school, they would have a splendid time learning about themselves and the world in which they lived. These urban teachers and administrators found ways to achieve their priorities by building political coalitions in and out of their classrooms, schools, and districts.

For urban teachers and administrators to make political choices, they must make moral ones as well. Teachers give gold stars to 2nd graders who score highest on an arithmetic test; a middle school principal permits an English teacher to show an anti-abortion film to present a balanced view of a controversial issue; a superintendent angered by the unfunded and flawed No Child Left Behind Act nevertheless signs an open letter to legislators to keep the law because it prods districts to raise expectations that all minority students can learn. These are political and moral actions aimed at achieving specific priorities.

Urban teachers and administrators enact their intertwined instructional, managerial, and political core roles daily to create unique melds of leadership that are contingent on the setting and their levels of authority. If ex-Chancellor Rudy Crew became superintendent in affluent Chappaqua, New York, there would be no guarantee that he would flourish as top administrator. In affluent suburban districts, superintendents must often focus on soothing highly educated parents who are concerned for their children's futures. Urban leaders, however, are often driven by a concern for social justice. They focus on raising student achievement for the students in the lowest percentiles.

If Rafe Esquith left Hobart Boulevard Elementary School and drove 20 miles to teach 5th graders in a Beverly Hills school, he would not necessarily receive a standing ovation from the principal and parents who want their 11-year-olds to get into Stanford, Yale, and Duke. For students at Hobart, doing algebra, performing Shakespeare, and taking field trips open up brand-new experiences. In Beverly Hills, parents might well yawn.

Smart teachers, principals, and superintendents can certainly transfer their sharp problem-solving skills and experience to different settings and leave their mark on students and adults. But enduring leadership comes from a subtly woven match among setting, roles, and resources that too often eludes policy makers eager to see quick, deep improvements in schools and districts.

The Threshold of Adequate Resources

Implementing standards-based reforms, increased testing, and strict accountability as solutions to urban education's woes demands that teachers and administrators take on new responsibilities for which no manuals have been written or resources allocated. Teachers and administrators must provide moral leadership to raise students' academic performance, reduce the achievement gap, and build proud, engaged, and humane young men and women of high moral stature.

Is this too much to expect of urban teachers, principals, and superintendents who work with mostly low-income minority students and their families? Yes. Too often, the call for leadership is a less-than-subtle call to educators to do more with less.

Private school tuition in most big cities ranges from $15,000 to $20,000, an amount that seldom covers the full cost of educating the student (National Association of Independent Schools, 2002-2003). Even after equity financing court decisions, suburban schools still outspend urban schools, a fact that seldom tarnishes the glowing words about education leadership. Instead of giving underfunded urban institutions and neglected communities the resources they need—competent professionals, time, and money, for example—both political parties, many governors, and the past four U.S. presidents have offered only promises and flamboyant rhetoric, not line items in federal and state budgets. Recent cuts in state education budgets and the federally funded No Child Left Behind legislation graphically demonstrate the gap between words and deeds. As class sizes increase, as teacher professional development shrinks, and as experienced teachers and administrators flee urban districts, leadership in urban settings becomes little more than salvaging those students who can succeed. These are realities that no amount of eloquent rhetoric about leadership can hide.

> **Most urban teachers and administrators are well-intentioned mortals, not heroic figures.**

Photo ops don't make leaders. Neither do front-page newspaper stories, television programs, or Hollywood films. Contexts, authority and its three interrelated roles, and the availability of resources give rise to leadership in urban classrooms, schools, and districts. Depending on such selfless educators as Jaime Escalante and Rudy Crew for urban leadership obscures the fact that most urban teachers and administrators are well-intentioned mortals, not heroic figures. And they need more to succeed than just inspiring rhetoric.

References

Mathews, J. (2003, Oct. 14). Pursuing happiness through hard work. *Washington Post,* p. A13.

National Association of Independent Schools. (2002-2003). *Statistical Indicators, 2002-2003.*

Winerup, M. (2003, Nov. 5). A test for Schwarzenegger: Adding muscle to bare bone. *New York Times,* p. A21.

Yee, G., & McCloud, B. (2003). A vision of hope: A case study of Seattle's two non-traditional superintendents. In L. Cuban & M. Usdan (Eds.), *Powerful reforms with shallow roots* (pp. 54-76). New York: Teachers College Press.

Larry Cuban (cuban@stanford.edu) is Professor Emeritus of Education at the School of Education, Stanford University, and author of the forthcoming book, *The Blackboard and the Bottom Line: Why Can't Schools Be Like Businesses?* (Harvard University Press).

From *Educational Leadership,* April 2004, pp. 64-67, 69. Reprinted by permission of the Association for Supervision and Curriculum Development. Copyright © 2004 by ASCD. All rights reserved. The Association for Supervision and Curriculum Development is a worldwide community of educators advocating sound policies and sharing best practices to achieve the success of each learner. To learn more, visit ASCD at] www.ascd.org

Article 12

Transforming High Schools

A study of 10 high schools finds that some schools just go through the motions, whereas other schools listen to teachers, parents, and students and make sure stakeholders understand the purpose of reforms.

By Pedro A. Noguera

As educators grapple with various strategies for raising student achievement, it is becoming increasingly clear that we face our biggest challenge in improving high schools. Steeped in tradition and dependent on practices that have long outlived their usefulness, high schools are in dire need of reform. We can find many examples of elementary schools that have been turned around, but relatively few examples of high schools that have undergone a similar transformation.

Although the problems confronting high schools do show up in affluent suburbs and rural areas, these problems most acutely affect high-poverty urban neighborhoods. Especially among African Americans and Latinos, dropout rates in many urban districts are high—often above 50 percent (Education Trust, 2002; National Education Association, 2001). In addition, many high schools are plagued by violence and bullying, vandalism and gang activity, poor attendance, low teacher morale, and an inability to attract and retain strong principals. These problems are not limited to high schools, but available evidence indicates that they are more common there (Cohen, 2001).

During the last 10 years, several national studies have attempted to diagnose the causes of the problems that beset so many U.S. high schools in the hope of devising strategies for reform. The findings from this research reveal that

- High schools suffer from organizational flaws, including fragmentation, insufficient attention to quality control in programs and services, and a lack of coherence in mission (Annenberg Foundation, 2003).
- The school curriculum typically offers a broad but disconnected variety of courses that lack depth and intellectual rigor (Hill & Celio, 1998).
- Teachers tend to rely on a lecture format and emphasize delivery of content without looking for evidence of learning or mastery of knowledge and skills (Cohen, 2001).
- Pervasive student alienation, boredom, strained relationships between adults and students, and anti-intellectual peer cultures undermine efforts to raise academic achievement (Bryk & Schneider, 2002; Steinberg, 1996).
- Many schools are too large and overcrowded to provide students with the support and attention they need (Ayers & Klonsky, 2000).

Responding to the growing evidence that something has to be done to overhaul U.S. high schools, several public and private organizations—including the Gates, Carnegie, Brode, and Annenberg Foundations—have funded costly and far-reaching reform efforts. To date, the effectiveness of these initiatives remains largely unknown.

The Pathways for Student Success Study

Aware of the challenges and the failure of past reform efforts, I decided to study the reform process itself to learn why high schools had proven so difficult to change and improve. When I began this exploration in 10 Boston, Massachusetts, high schools, the Boston Public Schools had already spent several years and a substantial sum of money on efforts aimed at high school improvement. These efforts had produced a mixed track record. At several of the most troubled schools, the district's initiatives were clearly not working.

Like many urban districts across the United States, Boston Public Schools had experimented with a variety of reform strategies. In the early 1990s, the district established several pilot schools that functioned with the flexibility of charter schools. At the same time, several charter schools sprang up in the district. Although many of the pilot and charter schools successfully raised student achievement for their own students, the schools did not fulfill their intended role as models for innovative practice. The district's traditional schools resented the pilot and charter schools' special status, and little communication occurred among leaders from different types of schools.

In consultation with superintendent Tom Payzant and other Boston school administrators, I devised a plan to conduct a comparative study of high schools and their reforms, which were at various stages of implementation. We launched the Pathways for Student Success research project in fall 2001 with funding from the National Science Foundation, the Nellie Mae Foundation, and the Schott Family Foundation. Ten schools representing the different types of high schools operating in the city participated in the study: four comprehensive schools, three pilot schools, two charter schools, and one exam school (an academic magnet school for which students must qualify). At all 10 schools, most students came from minority and low-income homes.

At each school, we recruited approximately 15 10th grade students—five high achievers, five midlevel achievers, and five low achievers. We worked with site leaders to select a sample of students that represented the overall school population in terms of race, gender, and native language. We collected a variety of data on the students by observing them inside and outside the classroom, interviewing their teachers and parents, and examining their school records. By studying the students' experiences as closely as possible, we hoped to gain insights into the ways various reforms affected students' academic performance and social development.

High-Stakes Testing

The most significant and far-reaching reform being implemented when we carried out this research was standards-based accountability. The graduating class of 2003 was the first in which students were required to pass the Massachusetts Comprehensive Assessment System (MCAS) exams to graduate. Each of the 10th graders in our sample was required to take the exam in the spring. Threatened with the prospect of large numbers of their students failing to receive diplomas, all of the schools in the study were under intense pressure to find ways to prepare their students for the exam. Given these high stakes, what we learned about how schools were preparing their students was surprising and troubling.

On the surface, the schools appeared to be doing all they could to ensure that their students were ready for the state exam. For example, at several schools, students who had failed the exam once or more were enrolled in double-period test preparation courses modeled after the Princeton Review courses used to help students study for the SAT. Close examination of these courses, however, revealed that most of the schools lacked a system of quality control. In many of the classes we visited, the courses were disorganized, poorly managed, and taught by unskilled teachers. For example, in one language arts course for students who had failed the exam twice, students informed us that for three months they had been taught by a substitute teacher who took attendance and then spent most of his time reading the newspaper. When we informed the principal of this situation, she indicated that she knew about the problem but could do nothing about it until the regular teacher returned from maternity leave.

> **What set the successful schools apart was not what they did, but how they did it.**

Student records revealed that several of the students in our sample who had failed the math portion of the MCAS had failed algebra and had not taken any higher-level math courses. To be fully prepared for the math portion of the MCAS, a student should have taken three years of college prep math: Algebra I, Geometry, and Algebra II. Many of the schools in our study offered only a limited number of sections of advanced math, and few if any 10th graders had completed this course sequence. Moreover, several principals admitted that they did not have enough teachers who could teach the material covered on the exam.

Clearly, many of the schools hoped to raise student scores without actually improving instruction or aligning the curriculum with the standards. Recognizing that efforts to improve the quality of teaching would take years to bear fruit, the schools most commonly responded to high-stakes testing by teaching test-taking skills to students who were behind academically. This strategy was clearly ineffective: At some of the schools, nearly half of all seniors failed the MCAS and therefore did not receive a diploma.

Attempts to Personalize Schooling

Several schools were also experimenting with other reforms that had the common goal of providing students with a more personalized learning environment, thereby leading to improved student-teacher relationships and higher achievement levels. These reforms included developing Small Learning Communities (or schools-within-schools), new systems for advising students, and block scheduling to implement a more integrated curriculum.

The rationale behind these changes seemed to make sense. Research indicates that student alienation and lack of engagement contribute to low achievement and that these reforms can help (Newman, 1992; Wasley et al., 2000). As we looked closely, however, we once again saw a tremendous gap between the intent of the reforms and their implementation.

Amazingly, at several of the schools, the administrators responsible for running the Small Learning Communities were the only people who even knew that they were in such a community. Most of the Small Learning Communities had been in operation for three years or less, and they had not yet found a way to create a sense of connection or common identity for students or teachers. Students said that aside from changing the courses they took, the Small Learning Communities had done very little to transform their school experience.

The schools' attempts to personalize schooling through an advisory system, in which teachers served as student counselors through an extended homeroom period held once each week, seemed equally ineffective. We sat in on several advisory classes where no advising was occurring. The teachers obviously had no idea of how to use the allotted time, and most lacked experience in counseling.

Considering the gap between idea and implementation, it is hardly surprising that Small Learning Communities and advisory groups had not improved teacher-student relationships, academic engagement, or student achievement. At all of the schools we asked students, Is there an adult at your school to whom you would turn if you were experiencing a serious personal problem? With the exception of two of the schools, described later, more than 80 percent of the students at each school replied "No." We also asked students if they believed their teachers were concerned about how well they did in school. Disturbingly, 56 percent of the students said they did not believe that their teachers really cared.

It was also clear that at most of the schools, adopting new structures had not changed the quality of instruction that students received. Even in schools that had instituted longer periods as part of a new block schedule, we typically found the traditional approach to teaching: heavy reliance on lecture and passive learning. We observed several classrooms in which students were sleeping, putting on makeup, or watching films that were unrelated to the course content.

During a visit to one of the schools, a student complained to us that if we observed in his class, his teacher would not allow the students to play cards as they normally did. To our surprise and dismay, the student's fears were unfounded: Even with two researchers seated in the back of the classroom, most of the students played cards for the entire class period while the teacher presented an assignment to a small group of students seated at the front of the room.

Reasons for the Implementation Gap

What could explain the poor implementation of these reforms and the lack of alignment between the administrators' intentions and the students' experiences? The newness of the reforms and the inordinate pressures of budget cuts and high-stakes testing were no doubt partly to blame. But our research at the 10 schools provided scant encouragement that the situation would improve over time. Some school staffs expressed a willingness to use findings generated from the research to modify their reform plans. At the most troubled schools, however, administrators were more likely to claim that they could not use the information because they were under too much pressure.

Sadly, the pressure on these principals is unlikely to decrease. And without a commitment to quality control in program delivery, we have little reason to believe that their schools will improve.

Administrators' limited ability to institute reforms that have an impact on teaching and learning in the classroom is disturbing. Many administrators continue to assume that changes in the organizational structure of schools—block scheduling, advisories, Small Learning Communities—will result in changes in the classroom. Research on school reform has shown that such change rarely occurs (Fullan & Miles, 1992), and that lasting improvements in teaching and learning can only come from a strategy focused on improving instruction (Elmore, 1996).

A laserlike focus on teaching and learning is precisely what we saw at the two schools in the study that were experiencing the greatest success. These exceptional schools provide lessons that can help guide other districts' efforts to improve their high schools.

Learning from Success

At two of the schools in the Pathways study—one a pilot school, the other a charter school—reform efforts appeared to be producing higher levels of student achievement. Both schools were relatively small—the pilot school had 330 students and the charter school had 226—and both had specific requirements for admission, intended not to screen out students but to let them know that they would have to meet high standards and expectations. Although some other schools in the study were also small and selective, these two schools combined these features with others to shape a positive school culture.

For example, students at both schools were required to work harder—and in some cases, longer—than students in traditional schools. The charter school had a longer school day (9:00 a.m. to 4:30 p.m.) and an extended school year that went through the first week of July. The pilot school required a portfolio assessment and a junior and senior project in addition to the state exit exam.

Both schools had also gone to great lengths to develop their own school cultures. The charter school was organized around an Asian theme and required students to study Mandarin Chinese and martial arts. Although relatively small, the pilot school was divided into three Small Learning Communities, and students spent significant amounts of time in community-based internships. Both schools provided on-site, year-round professional development designed around teachers' needs. Finally, both schools required a high level of parent involvement and provided students with college counseling beginning in 9th grade.

Student achievement data and student responses to our interview questions indicated that these practices and the schools' other reform efforts were effective. These two schools were the only ones in the study in which all seniors passed the MCAS. Even more encouraging, at both schools the average student scored at the proficient level, and several students achieved the highest level on the state exam. In contrast to most students at the other schools, who reported that there were no adults to whom they would speak about a personal problem, 93 percent of the students at the charter school and 100 percent of the students at the pilot school said that they did have access to such adults. Similarly, when asked whether or not they felt encouraged to do well at school, students at both schools responded affirmatively. One 11th grader put it this way:

> At school, you have no choice but to work hard. They're on you from the time you first get here. If you don't do your homework, they call home, and then they make you do it. You can't

get away with nothing here, and after a while you start to realize that everybody's working, and it starts to feel good to know that everyone is going to make it. They make sure that we're all going to college at this school.

Students Want Meaningful Reform

The two high-performing schools in the Pathways study had no secret strategies or special resources that were not available to the other schools. In fact, many of the reforms they pursued were also being implemented at the other schools. What set these schools apart was not what they did, but how they did it.

Rather than simply introduce a reform and hope for the best, these schools took the time to make sure that teachers, parents, and students understood the purpose behind a given reform strategy. Equally important, they looked for evidence that the reform was achieving its goals.

In contrast, at most of the other schools the adults responsible for implementing reforms were oblivious to how the changes affected students. These schools had no systematic process to evaluate their reforms, nor did they seem to recognize the value of seeking input from students.

Listening to students is, in fact, a radical departure from the way schools typically run. The Pathways study purposely focused on students, gathering various data to show how high school reforms were affecting students' school experiences. At the suggestion of the students from one of the schools in the study, we decided to supplement the in-school observations by asking students directly what their schools should do to make learning more meaningful.

> **Steeped in tradition and dependent on practices that have long outlived their usefulness, high schools are in dire need of reform.**

We brought all 150 students together at Harvard University for a retreat one Saturday. We divided them into small groups and asked several questions: If you were to attend a school where you would be excited to learn and study, how would that school be organized? How would you be taught? What would you learn? For two hours, the students brainstormed responses to these questions. As they reported to the whole group, some consistent themes emerged: Students wanted a more interactive teaching style, a more relevant curriculum, school rules that were responsive to their living circumstances, and schools that gave them a role and a voice in their own education.

Too often we assume that if the adults do things right, the kids will fall into line. If we were more willing to listen and solicit their opinions, we might find ways to engage students more deeply in their own education. The students may not have the answers to the problems confronting high schools, but perhaps if we engage them in discussions about how to make school less alienating and more meaningful, together we might find ways to move past superficial reforms and break the cycle of failure.

References

Annenberg Foundation. (2003). *Rethinking accountability: Voices in urban education.* Providence, RI: Author.

Ayers, W., & Klonsky, M. (2000). *A simple justice.* New York: Teachers College Press.

Bryk, A. S., & Schneider, B. L. (2002). *Trust in schools: A core resource for improvement.* New York: Russell Sage Foundation.

Cohen, M. (2001). *Transforming the American high school.* Washington, DC: Aspen Institute.

Education Trust. (2002). *Dispelling the myth: Lessons from high-performing schools.* Washington, DC: Author.

Elmore, R. (1996). *Restructuring in the classroom.* San Francisco: Jossey-Bass.

Fullan, M., & Miles, M. (1992, June). Getting reform right: What works and what doesn't. *Phi Delta Kappan,* 745-752.

Hill, P., & Celio, M. B. (1998). *Fixing urban schools.* Washington, DC: Brookings Institution Press.

National Education Association. (2001). *School dropouts in the United States: A policy discussion.* Washington, DC: Author.

Newman, F. (Ed.). (1992). *Student engagement and achievement in American secondary schools.* New York: Teachers College Press.

Steinberg, L. (1996). *Beyond the classroom.* New York: Simon & Schuster.

Wasley, P., Fine, M., Gladden, M., Holland, N., King, S., Mosak, E., & Powell, L. (2000). *Small schools, great strides: A study of small schools in Chicago.* New York: Bank Street College of Education.

Pedro A. Noguera is Professor, Steinhart School of Education, New York University; pedro.noguera@nyu.edu.

From *Educational Leadership,* May 2004, pp. 26-31. Reprinted by permission of the Association for Supervision and Curriculum Development. Copyright © 2004 by ASCD. All rights reserved. The Association for Supervision and Curriculum Development is a worldwide community of educators advocating sound policies and sharing best practices to achieve the success of each learner. To learn more, visit ASCD at www.ascd.org

Article 13

SCHOOL REFORM THAT WORKS

Reinventing America's Schools

Mr. Wagner presents evidence that the theory that high-stakes testing will improve performance is fatally flawed. To create better accountability systems, he argues that we need policy makers who truly understand the realities of schools and can work more collaboratively with educators. He also cites some important lessons from another country, where education systems have been reinvented through such a collaborative process.

BY TONY WAGNER

SINCE THE PASSAGE of the No Child Left Behind (NCLB) Act and now that many new state tests have been put in place, a great deal—and nothing at all—has changed in the universe of public education. What has changed is the frequency of standardized testing in schools and the consequences for educators and students of not performing well on these tests. What has not changed is the daily reality of teaching and learning for the overwhelming majority of students in America. To better understand how these two realities coexist side by side, let's visit two representative school districts—Boston and a "good suburban" school district in New York State.

In Massachusetts today, passing the new state test is now a requirement for earning a high school diploma—as it is, or soon will be, in most states. No longer can a district simply grant a student a diploma for showing up, going to class, and earning passing grades. In order to graduate, all students must pass the same standardized exam, which is given in 10th grade. Those who don't pass the first time will have several opportunities to take the test again.

But what is the students' reality? For the purposes of this article, I would like to leave aside serious questions about both the value and validity of the test itself and focus on the immediate consequences of this new policy. The Massachusetts Comprehensive Assessment System (MCAS) test has been severely criticized on a number of grounds by Anne Wheelock, Walter Haney, and other researchers. FairTest and the Massachusetts Coalition for Authentic Reform in Education have also put forward proposals for better assessment systems (see http://www.fairtest.org/).

Four years ago, about 4,900 ninth-graders began their high school careers in the Boston public schools. Today, as I write, there are approximately 3,400 12th-graders. Nearly one-third—1,500 students—have dropped out of the class in three years. Among those who remain, 1,648 students—almost half the group that hopes to graduate this spring—have not passed the MCAS test despite having taken it numerous times. Unless something changes suddenly, only about one-third of the students who started out together four years ago will cross the stage in their caps and gowns. The statistics are similar in most urban American school districts.

Isn't this just an urban problem? Not at all. Let me take you to a "good" suburban district in New York State, one that has long been considered a "lighthouse" district known for its innovative practices. When I recently began consulting in this district, I asked what the dropout rate was. No one knew for sure, but everyone thought it was very low. So we began to look at the data together.

We discovered that only eight out of 10 students who start out in ninth grade end up with a diploma four years later—even after accounting for transfers. But a problem looms that is more serious still. Right now in New York State, all districts are allowed to grant two different kinds of high school diplomas: a so-called local diploma and a Regents diploma, which requires that students pass state exams and take a much more academically rigorous course of study. Beginning with the class of 2005, all students will be required to pass Regents Examinations and meet more rigorous standards in order to receive a high school diploma. There will be no more local diplomas. In this "good" suburban district, of the students who graduated last year, only about 60% received a Regents diploma. The rest got a local diploma, which will not be an option under the new state requirements.

So the real scorecard for this district looks like this at the moment: of the 500 or so ninth-graders who started out together, 100 will have dropped out before graduation. Of the remaining 400, only 240 will receive a Regents diploma. In other words, more than half the students who start out in ninth grade do not meet the state standards for a high school diploma that are to become effective in just two years. To the great credit of the leadership in this district, as I write, this new challenge is being widely discussed among teachers, parents, and community members, and, with strong support from the local corporate community, solutions are being sought. No longer is the district resting on its reputation. There are stirrings of a deep urgency for change.

Let me give you one glimpse of another—and more frightening—juxtaposition of new and old reality. I was recently asked to lead a retreat for a large group of Midwestern suburban public school superintendents. During the meals and in between the sessions, there was much discussion of what one superintendent called the "Sovietization" of American public education. These superintendents, like virtually all others with whom I've spoken in the last year, were deeply concerned about the implications of NCLB, passed more than a year ago with strong bipartisan support. That law requires that all schools improve student achievement (as measured on annual standardized tests in grades 1 through 8) by at least 5% every year—or suffer serious penalties. Many superintendents are concerned that the law will encourage districts to set their initial "benchmarks" very low, so that they can easily show progress—a trick many factories and communes used in the Soviet Union in order to meet production quotas. Many also doubt that the law is enforceable or that it will result in improved student learning. Nevertheless, it's the new reality for these superintendents, and they know it.

Now let me describe what has not changed for them. I showed the group of superintendents an excerpt of a tape featuring an English teacher in a suburban district teaching a 10th-grade class. The teacher reviewed the moral "problem" faced by the protagonist in a short story that the students had read. He talked about an imaginary problem that a boy might face if he wanted to ask a girl out on a date but had no money—a topic that caused some amusement and much nervous laughter—and then he asked students to begin to write a story of their own with a central problem, compose just the first paragraph, and then pass it on to the next author, who would write another paragraph and pass it on, and so on until the story was completed. In other words, the students were to undertake a group writing project.

I asked the superintendents to discuss whether they thought this was effective teaching and what their criteria were for judging. The overwhelming majority said that it was effective because they observed that students were engaged. The students appeared to be paying attention, and there were no discipline problems.

True enough. But there wasn't much thinking going on, either. The students were asked factual-recall questions only and then given a writing assignment that was more suited to an elementary school class, in my opinion. They were not asked for their interpretations of the story. They were not asked to discuss a real moral dilemma in their lives and compare it with the one in the story. And they were not asked to write an essay in which they would have to analyze a theme or an idea and provide supporting evidence. In other words, there was no intellectual rigor to the engagement; students were not being asked to use their minds for anything more than factual recall. Nor did the superintendents comment on the often demeaning manner in which this teacher interacted with the women and minority students in the class.

In order to graduate from high school, these 10th-graders must now pass state tests. They should also have the skills required to succeed in college, to vote intelligently, to serve on juries, and to add value to the knowledge economy—all tasks that will require much more rigorous teaching if students are to be adequately prepared. Sadly, the overwhelming majority of superintendents did not see the gap between what these students were being taught and what they, as soon-to-be adults, must know and be able to do.

But their responses were hardly unique. My colleagues at the Harvard Graduate School of Education and I have shown this videotape to numerous audiences of education leaders in the last several years with the same result. In fact, when I've asked groups to grade the lesson, the average is a B+. But even more stunning is the range of grades that groups of educators in the same room—often from the same district—give the lesson: from an A to a D.

In summary, the new reality is that, in the last few years, with the increased emphasis on accountability and more and more high-stakes testing, the consequences of poor performance on standardized tests for students and for educators have grown steadily more serious. The policy theory—what some might call the theory of change—behind this new reality is that, if you raise the bar with tough new tests and raise the stakes for failure, performance will improve. But the theory is fatally flawed. It does not take into account the fundamental fact that, while we have a few examples of good individual schools, we do not know what a school system looks like in which all students master intellectual competencies at a high level. One simply doesn't exist anywhere in this country. Nor does the theory of change take into account the fact that we do not even have agreement on what good teaching looks like! Teaching is still considered an "art," performed in the privacy of one's classroom by people who prefer to think of themselves as self-employed. The number of school districts in this country that have effective teacher and principal supervision (not evaluation) programs in place can probably be counted on one hand.

Sadder still is the fact that the failure of this new accountability system is not likely to be blamed on the policy makers who passed the new laws. No, it is the victims—teachers, students, and their families—who will be held accountable. Ultimately, what is most likely to be "proved" a failure is the entire concept of public education. I do not believe that the intention of policy makers is to cripple or destroy public education. But I do think that most of the people—Democrats and Republicans alike—who pass these new laws know little or nothing about the daily reality of schools. I also believe that they do not have any idea how to create a very different kind of education and accountability system. It is this lack of informed, imaginative thinking and policy making that led me to write my most recent book, *Making the Grade: Reinventing America's Schools*, and to offer proposals for very different school, district, state, and national accountability systems.

Most of the people who pass the laws know little about the daily reality of schools.

But it took a trip to Denmark to confirm my hunches about what's possible and what works—and to give me a sense of hope for the future of public education. In the spring of 2001, I had the opportunity to accompany a small group of educators on a study tour of the Danish education system, sponsored by Marc Tucker and Judy Codding of the National Center on Education and the Economy. It is beyond the scope of this article to recount all that I learned on this trip, but let me describe a few highlights, from which we might learn. (Readers who want more in-depth information on the Danish education system should see the reports Marc Tucker and his colleagues have written at http://www.ncee.org/.)

Ten years ago, education reform in Denmark did not begin with new laws mandating more testing, as it did in the U.S. It began, instead, with a national conversation about values, about what it meant to be an educated citizen, as Denmark approached the 21st century. These discussions were promoted by the Danish Ministry of Education and took place throughout the country. The result is that today even elementary teachers know what skills students need to master for a knowledge economy and to be contributing citizens in a thriving democracy. The Danes decided that both education goals were of equal importance, as they began working to create much more rigorous education standards for all students.

Next, the ministry developed various incentives and policies that encouraged the creation of many different kinds of secondary schools and colleges, all of them rigorous, but which allowed students to develop mastery in different ways—some through conventional academic preparation, others in more of a technical or trade school environment. It is important to note, though, that these different kinds of schools were all considered "college prep," and a correspondingly diverse array of what we would call community colleges has been developed in parallel. The result: all Danish students graduate from high school "college ready," and almost all go on for some kind of post secondary education. In Denmark, there are many ways of becoming well educated, and there are carefully constructed safety nets for even the most educationally challenged and unmotivated students. There are almost no school dropouts in Denmark, despite the fact that the system is now educating an increasingly diverse population.

Meanwhile, the Danish tradition of small schools in which teachers spend as much as eight years with the same group of students continues to be the norm. Danes have long understood the importance of relationships in motivating students to want to achieve and of a more "personalized" approach to teaching and learning—ideas that I explore at length in *Making the Grade*.

The Danes have also long understood that computer-scored tests "dumb down" the curriculum because computers cannot assess the most important intellectual competencies, such as critical thinking and problem-solving ability. So the kinds of standardized tests that have become the daily reality in virtually all U.S. public schools do not exist in Denmark. Instead, the Danes have created a comprehensive national system of oral and written examinations at both the elementary and secondary levels. Even more significant, these exams are developed, administered, and scored by educators—usually from a neighboring school or district. The results are used to continuously improve the curriculum and to guide teachers' professional development.

In short, the Danish system works. Nearly all students are educated to high standards and motivated as learners. Educators are esteemed, and morale seems excellent. The Danes are justifiably proud of what they've accomplished. Can the system be imported "as is" into the U.S.? Of course not. But perhaps one of the most significant lessons I learned on my trip was the importance of having leaders and policy makers who truly understand—and are committed to—public education. I was told that nearly two-thirds of the Danish Parliament consists of individuals who are or have been educators. Perhaps this explains how and why the Danes have moved so far ahead internationally in creating an education system that meets the demands of the 21st century.

While it may be a well-intentioned attempt at ensuring greater accountability and educational equality, thus far the high-stakes testing approach to change appears to be increasing our rates of failure and dropping out. Thus it works to widen the gap between education's haves and have-nots. At a deeper level, this reform strategy leaves unanswered the fundamental question of what good lessons look like that teach all students to use their minds well as citizens, workers, and lifelong learners. Nor does it answer the questions of what school systems must do to ensure that all educators master the new skills needed to teach such lessons and to motivate students to *want* to learn. Rather than waste so much time arguing over the merits of more testing, policy makers, business and community leaders, and educators must learn to work together in new ways to "reinvent" the American education system so that all students can find both challenge and joy in learning. The Danes may have a few lessons to teach us.

TONY WAGNER is co-director of the Change Leadership Group at the Harvard Graduate School of Education, Cambridge, Mass. His most recent book, Making the Grade: Reinventing America's Schools, *has just been released in paperback by RoutledgeFalmer. This article was adapted from the introduction to the new edition. He can be reached through his website at http://www.newvillageschools.org/. ©2003, Tony Wagner.*

UNIT 3

Striving for Excellence: The Drive for Quality

Unit Selections

14. **A Balanced School Accountability Model: An Alternative to High-Stakes Testing**, Ken Jones
15. **Turning Accountability on Its Head: Supporting Inspired Teaching in Today's Classrooms**, Kristin L. Droege
16. **Accountability with a Kicker: Observations on the Florida A+ Accountability Plan**, Dan Goldhaber and Jane Hannaway
17. **No Flower Shall Wither; or, Horticulture in the Kingdom of the Frogs**, Gary K. Clabaugh
18. **The Power of Testing**, Matthew Gandal and Laura McGiffert
19. **Why Students Think They Understand—When They Don't**, Daniel T. Willingham
20. **The Homework Wars**, David Skinner
21. **Studying Education: Classroom Research and Cargo Cults**, E.D. Hirsch Jr.

Key Points to Consider

- Identify some of the different points of view on achieving excellence in education. What value conflicts can be defined?
- What are some assumptions about achieving excellence in student achievement that you would challenge? Why?
- What can educators do to improve the quality of student learning?
- Have there been flaws in American school reform efforts in the past 20 years? If so, what are they?
- Has the Internet affected the critical thinking skills of students? Defend your answer.

Links: www.dushkin.com/online/
These sites are annotated in the World Wide Web pages.

Awesome Library for Teachers
http://www.awesomelibrary.org

Education World
http://www.education-world.com

EdWeb/Andy Carvin
http://edwebproject.org

Kathy Schrock's Guide for Educators
http://www.discoveryschool.com/schrockguide/

Teacher's Guide to the U.S. Department of Education
http://www.ed.gov/pubs/TeachersGuide/

The debate continues over which academic standards are most appropriate for elementary and secondary school students. Discussion regarding the impact on students and teachers of state proficiency examinations goes on in those states or provinces where such examinations are mandated. We are still dealing with how best to assess student academic performance. Some very interesting proposals on how to do this have emerged.

There are several incisive analyses of why American educators' efforts to achieve excellence in schooling have frequently failed. Today, some interesting proposals are being offered as to how we might improve the academic achievement of students. The current debate regarding excellence in education clearly reflects parents' concerns for more choices in how they school their children.

Many authors of recent essays and reports believe that excellence can be achieved best by creating new models of schooling that give both parents and students more control over the types of school environments available to them. Many believe that more money is not a guarantor of quality in schooling. Imaginative academic programming and greater citizen choice can guarantee at least a greater variety of options open to parents who are concerned about their children's academic progress in school.

We each wish the best quality of life that we can attain, and we each desire the opportunity for an education that will optimize our chances to achieve our objectives. The rhetoric on excellence and quality in schooling has been heated, and numerous opposing concepts of how schools can reach these goals have been presented for public consideration in recent years. Some progress has been realized on the part of students as well as some major changes in how teacher education programs are structured.

In the decades of the 1980s and 1990s, those reforms were instituted to encourage qualitative growth in the conduct of schooling intended to be what education historian David Tyack once referred to as "structural" reforms. Structural reforms consist of demands for standardized testing of students and teaching, reorganization of teacher education programs, legalized actions to provide alternative routes into the teaching profession, efforts to recruit more people into teaching, and laws to enable greater parental choice as to where their children may attend school. These structural reforms cannot, however, in and of themselves produce higher levels of student achievement. We need to explore a broader range of the essential purposes of schooling, which will require our redefining what it means to be a literate person. We need also to reconsider what we mean by the "quality" of education and to reassess the essential purposes of schooling.

When we speak of quality and excellence as aims of education, we must remember that these terms encompass aesthetic and affective as well as cognitive processes. Young people cannot achieve the full range of intellectual capacity to solve problems on their own simply by being obedient and by memorizing data. How students encounter their teachers in classrooms and how teachers interact with their students are concerns that encompass both aesthetic and cognitive dimensions.

There is a real need to enforce intellectual standards and yet also to make schools more creative places in which to learn, places where students will yearn to explore, to imagine, and to hope.

Compared to those in the United States, students in European nations appear to score higher in assessments of skills in mathematics and the sciences, in written essay examinations in the humanities and social sciences, and in the routine oral examinations given by committees of teachers to students as they exit secondary schools.

What forms of teacher education and in-service re-education are needed? Who pays for these programmatic options? Where and how will funds be raised or redirected from other priorities to pay for this? Will the "streaming and tracking" model of secondary school student placement that exists in Europe be adopted? How can we best assess academic performance? Can we commit to a more heterogeneous grouping of students and to full inclusion of handicapped students in our schools? Many individual, private, and governmental reform efforts did not address these questions.

Other industrialized nations champion the need for alternative secondary schools to prepare their young people for varied life goals and civic work. The American dream of the common school translated into what has become the comprehensive high school of the twentieth century. But does it provide all the people with alternative diploma options? If not, what is the next step? What must be changed? For one, concepts related to our educational goals must be clarified and political motivation must be separated from the realities of student performance.

Policy development for schooling needs to be tempered by even more "bottom-up," grassroots efforts to improve the quality of schools that are now under way in many communities in North America. New and imaginative inquiry and assessment strategies need to be developed by teachers working in their classrooms, and they must nurture the support of professional colleagues and parents.

Excellence is the goal: the means to achieve it is what is in dispute. There is a new dimension to the debate over assessment of academic achievement of elementary and secondary school students. In addition, the struggle continues of conflicting academic (as well as political) interests in the quest to improve the quality of preparation of our future teachers, and we also need to sort these issues out.

No conscientious educator would oppose the idea of excellence in education. The problem in gaining consensus over how to attain it is that the assessment of excellence of both teacher and student performance is always based on some preset standards. Which standards of assessment should prevail?

A Balanced School Accountability Model:
An Alternative to High-Stakes Testing

The health of our public schools, Mr. Jones argues, depends on defining a new model of accountability—one that is balanced and comprehensive. And it needs to be one that involves much more than test scores.

By Ken Jones

FOR SOME time now, it has been apparent to many in the education community that state and federal policies intended to develop greater school accountability for the learning of all students have been terribly counterproductive. The use of high-stakes testing of students has been fraught with flawed assumptions, oversimplified understandings of school realities, undemocratic concentration of power, undermining of the teaching profession, and predictably disastrous consequences for our most vulnerable students. Far from the noble ideal of leaving no child behind, current policies, if continued, are bound to increase existing inequities, trivialize schooling, and mislead the public about the quality and promise of public education.

What is needed is a better means for evaluating schools, an alternative to the present system of using high-stakes testing for school accountability. A new model, based on a different set of assumptions and understandings about school realities and approaches to power, is required. It must be focused on the needs of learners and on the goals of having high expectations for all rather than on the prerequisites of a bureaucratic measurement system.

PREMISES

In the realm of student learning, the question of outcomes has often been considered primary: what do we want students to know and be able to do as a result of schooling? Once the desired outcomes have been specified, school reform efforts have proceeded to address the thorny questions of how to attain them. Starting from desired outcomes is an important shift in how to think about what does or does not make sense in classroom instruction.

In the realm of school accountability, however, little attention has been paid to corresponding outcome-related questions. It has simply been assumed that schools should be accountable for improved student learning, as measured by external test scores. It has been largely assumed by policy makers that external tests do, in fact, adequately measure student learning. These and other assumptions about school accountability must be questioned if we are to develop a more successful accountability model. It would be well to start from basic questions about the purposes and audiences of schools. For what, to whom, and by what means should schools be held accountable? The following answers to these questions provide a set of premises on which a new school accountability system can be based.

For what should schools be accountable? Schools should be held accountable for at least the following:

• *The physical and emotional well-being of students.* The caring aspect of school is essential to high-quality education. Parents expect that their children will be safe in schools and that adults in schools will tend to their affective as well as cognitive needs. In addition, we know that learning depends on a caring school climate that nurtures positive relationships.

• *Student learning.* Student learning is complex and multifaceted. It includes acquiring not only knowledge of disciplinary subject matter but also the thinking skills and dispositions needed in a modern democratic society.

• *Teacher learning.* Having a knowledgeable and skilled teacher is the most significant factor in student learning and should be fostered in multiple ways, compatible with the principles of adult learning. Schools must have sufficient time and funding to enable teachers to improve their own performance, according to professional teaching standards.

• *Equity and access.* Given the history of inequity with respect to minority and underserved student populations, schools must be accountable for placing a special emphasis on improving equity and access, providing fair opportunities for all to learn to high standards. Our press for excellence must include a press for fairness.

• *Improvement.* Schools should be expected to function as learning organizations, continuously engaged in self-assessment and adjustment in an effort to meet the needs of their students. The capacity to do so must be ensured and nurtured.

To whom should schools be accountable? Schools should be held accountable to their primary clients: students, parents, and the local community. Current accountability systems make the state and federal governments the locus of power and decision making. But the primary clients of schools should be empowered to make decisions about the ends of education, not just the means, provided there are checks to ensure equity and access and adherence to professional standards for teaching.

By what means should schools be held accountable? To determine how well schools are fulfilling their responsibilities, multiple measures should be used. Measures of school accountability should include both qualitative and quantitative approaches, taking into account local contexts, responsiveness to student and community needs, and professional practices and standards. Because schools are complex and unique institutions that address multiple societal needs, there should also be allowances for local measures, customized to meet local needs and concerns. A standardized approach toward school accountability cannot work in a nation as diverse as the U.S.

Given these premises, what are the proper roles of a government-developed and publicly funded school accountability system?

• It should serve to improve student learning and school practices and to ensure equity and access, not to reward or punish schools.

• It should provide guidance and information for local decision making, not classify schools as successes or failures.

• It should reflect a democratic approach, including a balance of responsibility and power among different levels of government.

A BALANCED MODEL

An accountability framework called the "balanced scorecard" is currently employed in the business world and provides a useful perspective for schools.[1] This framework consists of four areas that must be evaluated to give a comprehensive view of the health of an organization. The premise is that both outcomes and operations must be measured if the feedback system is to be used to improve the organization, not just monitor it. In the business context, the four components of the framework are: 1) financial, 2) internal business, 3) customer, and 4) innovation and learning.

Applying this four-part approach to education, we can use the following aspects of school performance as the components of a balanced school accountability model: 1) student learning; 2) opportunity to learn; 3) responsiveness to students, parents, and community; and 4) organizational capacity for improvement. Each of these aspects must be attended to and fostered by an evaluation system that has a sufficiently high resolution to take into account the full complexity and scope of modern-day schools.

1. Student learning. Principles of high-quality assessment have been well articulated by various organizations and should be followed.[2] What is needed is a system that

- is primarily intended to improve student learning; aligns with local curricula;
- emphasizes applied learning and thinking skills, not just declarative knowledge and basic skills;
- embodies the principle of multiple measures, including a variety of formats such as writing, open-response questions, and performance-based tasks; and
- is accessible to students with diverse learning styles, intelligence profiles, exceptionalities, and cultural backgrounds.

Currently, there is a mismatch between what cognitive science and brain research have shown about human learning and how schools and educational bureaucracies continue to measure learning.[3] We now know that human intellectual abilities are malleable and that people learn through a social and cultural process of constructing knowledge and understandings in given contexts. And yet we continue to conduct schooling and assessment guided by the outdated beliefs that intelligence is fixed, that knowledge exists apart from culture and context, and that learning is best induced through the behaviorist model of stimulus/response.

Scientific measurement cannot truly "objectify" learning and rate it hierarchically. Accurate decisions about the quality and depth of an individual's learning must be based on human judgment. While test scores and other assessment data are useful and necessary sources of information, a fair assessment of a person's learning can be made only by other people, preferably by those who know the person best in his or her own context. A reasonable process for determining the measure of student learning could involve local panels of teachers, parents, and community members, who review data about student performance and make decisions about promotion, placement, graduation, and so on.

What is missing in most current accountability systems is not just a human adjudication system, but also a local assessment component that addresses local curricula, contexts, and cultures. A large-scale external test is not sufficient to determine a student's achievement. District, sense of efficacy and professionalism and a heightened sense of job dissatisfaction and has become a factor in the attrition that is contributing to the growing teaching shortage.[17] Principals must share leadership with teachers and others as a means of sustaining capacity.

To be an effective collective enterprise, a school must develop an internal accountability system. That is, it must take responsibility for developing goals and priorities based on the ongoing collection and analysis of data, it must monitor its performance, and it must report its findings and actions to its public. Many schools have not moved past the stage of accepting individual teacher responsibility rather than collective responsibility as the norm.[18] States and districts must cooperate with schools to nurture and insist upon the development of such collective internal norms.

THE NEW ROLE OF THE STATE

For a balanced model of school accountability to succeed, there must be a system in which states and districts are jointly responsible with schools and communities for student learning. Reciprocal accountability is needed: one level of the system is responsible to the others, and all are responsible to the public.

The role of state and federal agencies with respect to school accountability is much in need of redefinition. Agencies at these levels should not serve primarily in an enforcement role. Rather, their roles should be to establish standards for local accountability systems, to provide resources and guidance, and to set in place processes for quality review of such systems. Certainly there should be no high-stakes testing from the state and federal levels, no mandatory curricula, and no manipulation through funding. Where there are clear cases of faulty local accountability systems—those lacking any of the four elements discussed above (appropriate assessment systems; adequate opportunities to learn; responsiveness to students, parents, and community; or organizational capacity)—supportive efforts from the state and federal levels should be undertaken.

Are there any circumstances in which a state should intervene forcibly in a school or district? If an accountability system is to work toward school improvement for all schools, does that system not need such "teeth"? This question must be addressed in a way that acknowledges the multi-level nature of this school accountability model. One might envision at least three cases in which the state would take on a more assertive role: 1) to investigate claims or appeals from students, parents, or the community that the local accountability system is not meeting the standards set for such systems; 2) to require local schools and districts to respond to findings in the data that show significant student learning deficiencies, inequity in the opportunities to learn for all students, or lack of responsiveness to students, parents, or communities; and 3) to provide additional resources and guidance to improve the organizational capacity of the local school or district.

Is it conceivable that a state might take over a local school or district in this model? Yes, but only after the most comprehensive evaluation of the local accountability system has shown that there is no alternative—and then only on a temporary basis.

It is of great importance to the health of our public schools that we begin as soon as possible to define a new model for school accountability, one that is balanced and comprehensive. Schools can and should be held accountable to their primary clients for much more than test scores, in a way that supports improvement rather than punishes deficiencies. The current model of using high-stakes testing is a recipe for public school failure, putting our democratic nation at risk.

REFERENCES

1. Robert S. Kaplan and David P. Norton, "The Balanced Scorecard—Measures That Drive Performance," *Harvard Business Review*, January/February 1992, pp. 71-79.
2. National Forum on Assessment, *Principles and Indicators for Student Assessment Systems* (Boston: FairTest, 1993), available at www.fairtest.org/k-12.htm.
3. Lorrie A. Shepard, "The Role of Assessment in a Learning Culture," *Educational Researcher*, October 2000, pp. 4-14.
4. Debra Smith and Lynne Miller, *Comprehensive Local Assessment Systems (CLASs) Primer: A Guide to Assessment System Design and Use* (Gorham: Southern Maine Partnership, University of Southern Maine, 2003), available at www.usm.maine.edu/smp/tools/primer.htm; and "Nebraska School-Based, Teacher-Led Assessment Reporting System (STARS)," www.nde.state.ne.us/stars/index.html.
5. Richard J. Stiggins, *Student-Centered Classroom Assessment* (Columbus, Ohio: Merrill, 1997).
6. Paul Black and Dylan Wiliam, "Inside the Black Box: Raising Standards Through Classroom Assessment," *Phi Delta Kappan*, October 1998, pp. 139-48; and Paul Black et al., *Working Inside the Black Box: Assessment for Learning in the Classroom* (London, U.K.: Department of Educational and Professional Studies, King's College, 2002).
7. Terry Crooks, "Design and Implementation of a National Assessment Programme: New Zealand's National Education Monitoring Project (NEMP)," paper presented at the annual meeting of the Canadian Society for the Study of Education, Toronto, May 2002.
8. Jeannie Oakes, "Education Inadequacy, Inequality, and Failed State Policy: A Synthesis of Expert Reports Prepared for *Williams v. State of California*," 2003, available at www.decentschools.org/experts.php.
9. Jeannie Oakes, "What Educational Indicators? The Case for Assessing the School Context," *Educational Evaluation and Policy Analysis*, Summer 1989, pp. 181-99.
10. Linda Darling-Hammond, *Standards of Practice for Learning Centered Schools* (New York: National Center for Restructuring Education, Schools, and Teaching, Teachers College, 1992).
11. Adam Urbanski, "Teacher Professionalism and Teacher Accountability: Toward a More Genuine Teaching Profession," unpublished manuscript, 1998.
12. Jacqueline Ancess, *Outside/Inside, Inside/Outside: Developing and Implementing the School Quality Review* (New York: National Center for Restructuring Education, Schools, and Teaching, Teachers College, 1996); New Zealand Education Review Office, *Frameworks for Reviews in Schools*, available at www.ero.govt.nz/EdRevInfo/Schedrevs/SchoolFramework.htm; Debra R. Smith and David J. Ruff, "Building a

Culture of Inquiry: The School Quality Review Initiative," in David Allen, ed., *Assessing Student Learning: From Grading to Understanding* (New York: Teachers College Press, 1998), pp. 164-82.

13. Kavitha Mediratte, Norm Fruchter, and Anne C. Lewis, *Organizing for School Reform: How Communities Are Finding Their Voice and Reclaiming Their Public Schools* (New York: Institute for Education and Social Policy, Steinhardt School of Education, New York University, October 2002).

14. Phillip Schlechty, *Systemic Change and the Revitalization of Public Education* (San Francisco: Jossey-Bass, forthcoming).

15. Fred M. Newmann, M. Bruce King, and Mark Rigdon, "Accountability and School Performance: Implications from Restructuring Schools," *Harvard Educational Review*, Spring 1997, p. 47.

16. Judith Warren Little, "Teachers' Professional Development in a Climate of Educational Reform," *Educational Evaluation and Policy Analysis*, vol. 15, 1993, pp. 129-51; and Milbrey W. McLaughlin and Joan Talbert, *Professional Communities and the Work of High School Teaching* (Chicago: University of Chicago Press, 2001).

17. Richard M. Ingersoll, *Who Controls Teachers' Work? Power and Accountability in America's Schools* (Cambridge, Mass.: Harvard University Press, 2003).

18. Charles Abelman et al., *When Accountability Knocks, Will Anyone Answer?* (Philadelphia: Consortium for Policy Research in Education, University of Pennsylvania, CPRE Research Report Series RR-42, 1999).

KEN JONES is the director of teacher education, University of Southern Maine, Gorham.

From *Phi Delta Kappan*, April 2004, pp. 584-590. Copyright © 2004 by Phi Delta Kappa International. Reprinted by permission of the publisher and author.

Article 15

Turning Accountability on Its Head:
Supporting Inspired Teaching In Today's Classrooms

By Kristin L. Droege

Using test scores as the sole indicator of students' and teachers' knowledge and skills is harming students and driving the best teachers from the profession, Ms. Droege fears.

WHEN YOU go for a walk with my sister, she has a way of making you interested in rocks. She points out things in the environment that you might otherwise walk right past without ever noticing. And she can explain to you how and why they got there and in what geological era they formed; you can understand her, and suddenly you want to know more. She is very smart. She has a bachelor's degree in geology from Duke University and a master's degree in environmental science from the University of Montana. She will complete a master's degree in education at Loyola College this year. My sister is well educated, and her enjoyment of learning is infectious. For the last three years, she has been a teacher in a California public elementary school. When she first started teaching elementary school, the parents of her students laughed because their children kept coming home with rocks in their lunch boxes. This spring my sister accepted a new teaching position in a private school in another state, where she will have the freedom and support to teach according to a curriculum and philosophy that inspire her.

Recently I read an article in *Education Week* by Patrick Bassett, the current president of the National Association of Independent Schools. In it, he referred to research by the Abell Foundation indicating that clear links could be found between teachers' verbal and cognitive abilities and the achievement of their students. Further, it indicated that verbal ability, the selectivity of the college attended, and the college achievement of the teacher were good predictors of teaching quality.

The research has been challenged, but isn't the conclusion sensible? Intelligent, articulate, well-educated individuals make better teachers. Who would have guessed? Over and over, in teacher recruitment statements, ad campaigns, and union materials, we hear that all it really takes is "heart." You must love children. You must be caring, compassionate, tolerant, and patient. But never "You must be smart. You must be well educated. You must be insightful and observant, with a breadth of knowledge."

Primarily, we don't make these statements because, on Monday morning when the school doors open, we have to fill the slots. Whether we like to think of it that way or not, our system demands that a certain number of teachers be present every school day, and if we set our criteria too high, the slots won't fill. Certainly, filling spaces became the priority in California in 1996 with the decision to implement class-size reduction. Almost overnight, schools and districts had to fill teaching positions from an already-depleted pool of applicants. With a college degree—in almost any major, from any accredited college, and with a mediocre grade-point average—most applicants could obtain an emergency credential and a job as a teacher.

The decision to implement class-size reduction was made for political reasons, not educational ones. Unfortunately, political reasoning guides most educational choices, and many of these decisions will continue to exacerbate the problem of recruiting and retaining high-quality teachers. Oddly enough, politicians are hanging these choices on the hook of "accountability." We will hold all teachers accountable for the success of their students, even though we have hired many teachers who were once mediocre students, who have never experienced very good teaching themselves, and who have little knowledge of how to teach. Accountability will take the form of test scores, even though we know that intelligence and learning are much broader and more complex concepts. There will be more federal money for school districts that implement curriculum packages that are proven—proven to raise test scores. And last summer, the *New York Times* reported that the National Blue Ribbon Award for Outstanding Schools will be awarded based exclusively on—you guessed it—test scores.

Curriculum developers know how to raise test scores. They create a process that is foolproof: any teacher can follow the directions and read the required passages, and average test scores will rise. Take Open Court as an example, the literacy curriculum adopted by the Los Angeles Unified School District (LAUSD). Many elementary teachers in LAUSD are required to devote three full hours per day to literacy instruction using the Open Court curriculum, frequently to the exclusion of any instruction at all in the areas of science or social studies. Several of my students have reported working in LAUSD schools that have monitors who walk the halls dropping into classrooms to ensure that the teacher is working on the required page of the Open Court curriculum manual for that day.

Test scores do not measure skills and strategies such as perseverance, cooperation, ingenuity, patience, creativity, originality, and flexibility of thinking.

The developers of Open Court have integrated a number of strategies and approaches into their curriculum. It appears to be a reasonably well formulated blend of traditional and progressive techniques for teaching reading, writing, and communication skills. It is, without doubt, very thorough. In fact, lessons even come with a script. The teacher can read or memorize the scripted passage that goes along with the day's lesson. For instance, after reading a story about a pet dog, the children are encouraged to take part in reflective thinking, a strategy linked to enhanced comprehension because it brings personal relevance to the story. The teacher, using Open Court, guides the student, not by reflecting on her own life experiences, but by reading her script: "I remember when I had a dog...." This, whether she had one or not. Does this sound like the career choice of an intelligent, articulate, well-educated professional?

Test scores are one component of education and one component of measuring success in our society. But they represent only a narrow view of the student being sent out into the world. Test scores do not measure skills and strategies such as perseverance, cooperation, ingenuity, patience, creativity, originality, and flexibility of thinking.

The ability to raise test scores is, similarly, one component of a teacher's quality. But, again, it is a narrow view of the teacher who is in charge of the educational success of a new classroom of students every year. Test scores do not reflect the teacher's skills or strategies for assessing students' diverse learning styles, adapting instruction to individual levels or needs within a classroom, observing students for signs of understanding or confusion, or infusing curriculum with personality, excitement, and imagination to make it inspiring.

The field of education must focus on creating a professional system that invites and attracts the best candidates into the field and then keeps them there by making sure they have outlets for intellectual challenge, professional growth, and creativity. This is truly an issue of educational leadership and vision on the part of school administrators and districts, who can choose to develop either a "foolproof" system or a system of and for professionals that will benefit all students in ways that motivate and inspire both adults and students.

KRISTIN L. DROEGE is an assistant professor in the Teaching/Curriculum Program in the Graduate Education Department, California State University, Dominguez Hills, Carson, Calif. She is founder of Mountain View Montessori Charter School in Victorville, Calif., and a former teacher at the elementary and undergraduate levels.

Accountability with a Kicker: Observations on the Florida A+ Accountability Plan

The A+ Accountability Plan in Florida predated NCLB but has similar provisions. Thus, the authors realized, a study of how the system has played out in Florida might allow us to see where NCLB is leading us.

BY DAN GOLDHABER AND JANE HANNAWAY

IN 1999, FLORIDA implemented a major reform of its accountability system, called the A+ Accountability Plan. A unique aspect of the A+ Plan is its explicit attempt to invoke market forces by allowing students in low-performing schools that meet specified criteria to receive vouchers that can be redeemed at an eligible public or private school. It is this "opportunity scholarship" (the portion of the A+ Plan that allows for vouchers) that set the accountability system in Florida apart from that of any other state at that time.

Since then, the Supreme Court's *Zelman* decision ruled that using vouchers for religious private schools is permissible.[1] In addition, the No Child Left Behind (NCLB) Act requires that all schools failing to achieve adequate yearly progress (AYP) implement a program similar to the opportunity scholarships in that it would allow students to choose alternative public schools. In many ways, the accountability program begun by Florida in 1999 was a precursor to the type of accountability systems that NCLB is now requiring states to implement. Thus studying Florida's school and district responses to the provisions of the A+ Plan may yield important insights into what we should expect to see elsewhere.

Much of the controversy and debate over the passage of NCLB focused on its accountability and voucher provisions. Many of those in favor of such reforms argued that public schooling was (and is) a closed system, unlikely to change in any fundamental way without the "kicker" increased competition would provide. The basic argument was that competition would provide schools with a clear incentive either to perform well or to risk losing students to higher-quality alternatives offered at the same price.[2] In short, the theory that competition can improve education presumes that inefficiencies resulting from the monopoly of the public school system are the cause of low performance in American education.[3] For a variety of reasons, however, it is not at all clear that schools will respond to increased market competition in the same way that the classic competitive model predicts for industry. Most important, they may have trouble discerning what changes would be beneficial to students or implementing effective reforms.

The research we report here is part of a larger effort focusing on how schools in Florida are responding to a new accountability system with many of the same provisions as NCLB. We will briefly describe publicly reported information on school performance in Florida since the inception of the A+ Plan, and then, using evidence gathered from our case studies, we will attempt to provide a more nuanced picture of the program's effect on schools—particularly the relationship between school accountability grades and the threat of vouchers.

THE A+ PLAN AND SCHOOL PERFORMANCE

At the time it was implemented, the Florida voucher program was unique in that it was established by law as an integral part of the state's education accountability system. With the A+ Plan, students in schools that receive a grade of F in two out of any four years and currently have an F grade are eligible to receive vouchers that can be used at another, nonfailing public school or at a private school, including a religious school. Schools' grades are based on their students' performance on the FCATs (Florida Comprehensive Achievement Tests)—the state tests in math, reading, and writing—and on dropout rates. The value of the vouchers awarded for students to attend private schools in 2002-03 ranged from $3,463 to $4,311 for basic K-12 education.[4] In short, the program is broad based, institutionalized, and reasonably well funded. (For further details on the Florida A+ Plan, see www.firn.edu/doe/index.html.)

In the first year of the A+ Plan, only two schools were identified as voucher-eligible. At that time, 119 students from these schools took advantage of the vouchers: 67 attended another Florida public school, and 52 attended a private Catholic school. No other schools met the criteria for voucher eligibility until 2002-03, when 10 additional schools were identified. From these newly voucher-eligible schools, more than 500 students chose to use opportunity scholarships to attend private schools, while over 870 students chose to attend another Florida public school in 2002-03.[5]

During this period many schools could have been considered "voucher-threatened" because they had already received one F, and an additional F grade would have placed them in the voucher-eligible category. Table 1 shows the distribution of schools by grade and by year.

Schools can move out of the voucher-threatened F category by increasing FCAT scores above certain thresholds.[6] This provision distinguishes the Florida program from two other publicly funded voucher programs in Milwaukee and Cleveland. In those cities, all students meeting certain income requirements are eligible to receive vouchers, regardless of the performance of their school. Because voucher eligibility in these cities is determined by individual student characteristics rather than school characteristics, voucher eligibility is beyond the control of the schools. Florida's system offers schools a clear option for avoiding voucher eligibility. This structural distinction is important because it provides immediate and direct incentives for schools to improve student performance.

By contrast, schools competing in an open market might compete for students in a variety of ways, such as establishing particular niches (for example, a music-oriented school) or offering various programs and services that parents may value (like sports teams) but that may have little to do with academic achievement. In Florida, the first line of defense for a low-performing school is clear and narrowly specified: improve student achievement. This situation is similar to the situation that underperforming schools now face with NCLB.

Changes in average test scores in Florida schools show that F, or voucher-threatened, schools do in fact gain more than higher-ranked schools. Some have attributed this gain, which is particularly pronounced on the writing portion of the test, to genuine school improvements.[7] However, it is unclear whether gains are attributable to the threat of vouchers or whether they represent statistical artifacts, such as regression to the mean.[8] Indeed, they could be the result of some other factors, such as the social stigma associated with the F grade or an increase in resources for F schools.

Table 1. Distribution of Schools by Grade and Year

School Grade	1998-99	1999-2000	2000-01	2001-02
A	203	579	591	894
B	314	266	413	553
C	1,236	1,165	1,120	725
D	613	397	307	185
F	78	4	0	64
Total	2,444	2,411	2,431	2,421

Some Glimpses into Behavioral Responses

In the course of our case studies, we visited five schools, interviewing the principals and conducting focus groups with teachers and parents to assess their views of the A+ Plan and their responses to the particular grades their schools had received. Because we were necessarily focusing on a small number of schools, we chose schools at the opposite extremes of the performance distribution in order to detect possibly distinct differences in response.

Our expectation was that high-performing schools would be operating securely beneath the radar screen of accountability policies and would be affected very little by them, if at all. In 1999, two of our case study schools received F grades, and three received A grades. In the subsequent two years, one F school received a grade of C, and one received a grade of D. The 1999 A schools had more variance, but two of them received a subsequent grade of A. Not surprisingly, the F schools had a much higher percentage of students eligible for free/reduced priced lunch than the A schools, and their average class size was smaller. All of the schools, except School 5, had a relatively large percentage of students with disabilities. School 5 housed both a multilingual magnet school that attracted students from across the district and a regular school program for students living in the school neighborhood and had an exceptionally high percentage of gifted students.[9]

Our case study visits to schools provided an opportunity to hear about the accountability system from school personnel most likely to be affected by it. We share their responses not to provide information from which to generalize, but rather to suggest questions and hypotheses for later investigation and systematic analysis.

Four general themes emerged. First, both A schools and F schools felt tremendous pressure as a consequence of the A+ Plan, which led them to narrow their instructional focus. This was counter to our expectations. Second, districts responded by providing significant amounts of additional resources to F schools. Third, the accountability results seemed to trigger new dynamics in the allocation of personnel. Fourth, the social stigma of an

F—not the threat of vouchers, per se—appeared to be the most important issue for those school people we interviewed. Essentially, our case study findings muddy the waters by suggesting alternative hypotheses for the improved performance of Florida schools, especially F schools. In addition, it seems that this grading system has significant behavioral consequences for schools at the top of the grading distribution, as well.

Instructional focus. The instructional focus in both A schools and F schools narrowed significantly, according to our subjects. This response from the A schools was somewhat surprising. The principals in A schools explained that parents paid attention to and cared about the grade, as did the teachers, which resulted in pressure to do whatever it might take to perform well on the test. One principal stated, "Even though they know better than to believe that any one test can show how good we are, they still want us to get an A."

At the same time, parents reported ambivalence about the time and attention given to test preparation. One A school put off all field trips and projects until after the FCATs in the spring. While parents lamented this and knew their own child's life chances would not be affected by his or her test results, they nonetheless claimed to be "type A personalities" who still "wanted to see their school with the highest grade." When one A school's grade dropped to C the next year, the principal reportedly had to expend considerable effort in explaining to parents what happened and reassuring them that the school was still a top school. The principal and teachers in one of the A schools also described the pressure they felt from other schools in the district to maintain their own school's A status. Evidently, other schools were envious of the school's A grade, had suggested it was not fully deserved, and wanted to see the school stumble. Florida's simple A-to-F grading scheme is easily understood and carries a certain amount of symbolic value (everyone knows what an A or an F means), a fact that is probably important in understanding the effects of the system.

Teachers and students feel the greatest tension. Teachers at one A school cried when describing the pressure they felt to maintain their school's grade. They also reported, as did parents, the tremendous pressure that students experience. One parent stated, "My daughter gets so nervous at testing time that she pulls her hair out." While most A school teachers believed that standards and some level of accountability were good for schools, they felt the system had "gone from one extreme to the other," at a high cost to education. One teacher explained that, "before [the accountability pressure], you could walk through the building and see fabulous things going on…. Now you walk into classrooms and see kids sitting at their desks, dead silent, doing workbooks, and that's truly a crime." Another teacher added more emphatically, "It is the most criminal form of child abuse that I have seen." Newspaper accounts paint a similar picture:

Across Florida, playgrounds are empty at recess. Cafeterias clear out early. After school, video arcades remain deserted. The children are in classrooms. Morning, noon, afternoon, and evenings, if parents cooperate, they are composing essays, cramming concepts, and endlessly drilling…. For more than six months, especially the last six weeks [before the FCAT], the Florida Comprehensive Assessment Tests have become both the omnipresent Holy Grail and bogeyman for students and teachers.[10]

"Ask children how many days there are until the FCAT, and they know," commented one teacher,[11] because many schools have daily countdowns to the FCAT. One elementary school even planned a lock-in the week before the test, as children studied through the night. The assistant principal explained that "it's sort of like cramming for exams."[12] Summarizing her school's views of its grade, one principal commented, "We are an A school, and we hate it."

In F schools, the views were somewhat different. Both principals and teachers saw greater merit in the accountability system and its contribution to the school's improved performance. One principal reported that "accountability overall is great…. All too often kids from certain backgrounds are expected to be low performing, nothing is expected of them." Accountability changed that. This principal also believed that the test results had real information value for teachers, who "didn't know that they weren't doing a good job." The principal felt that this shock helped open them to coaching and professional development.

Another principal reported that, when the school's F grade was first announced, "Teachers were in disbelief…. They began to search within themselves and think about what they were doing in the classroom." As a consequence, teachers thought their individual performance—and that of the school—was definitely better than it was five years earlier. The accountability program was a "rude awakening" for them, reported one teacher. "It made us feel we needed to do something, to make a change." Another teacher added, "It made us learn that we could pull inner resources that we didn't know we had…. People came together in a community to fight for improvement. We feel more motivated than ever now."

While the F grade appeared to motivate principals and teachers in new ways, it did not appear to have much of an effect on parents. One principal said, "If there was ever a legitimate reason to be upset, that was one of them," but the parent reaction was almost nonexistent. He added, "I don't know how tuned in they are." The other F school principal painted a similar picture, noting that, while a few families left the school, only "a small number of parents are truly aware." Some teachers were a bit resentful at the lack of parental input, stating, "The F was put right onto the teachers.... No responsibility was placed on parents, and I don't think that's right."

The fact that parents at F schools were not moved to action or even knowledgeable about the issue cuts to the core of the standard theory favoring vouchers, which sees informed clients or consumers as the primary regulators of system quality. It is certainly possible that, over time, parents in low-performing schools would become better informed, especially if vouchers became an actual option for them. What our findings do suggest is that the mechanisms triggered by the threat of vouchers may be very different from the mechanisms triggered by actual eligibility for vouchers. That is, information alone may be sufficient to trigger parental responses in schools where parents are "tuned in," but where parents are unlikely to be well informed, a school's grade is probably an insufficient stimulus for action.

Schools not only became more focused on test preparation in general but also concentrated intently on specific testing areas: F schools worked on writing in particular. Recall that a school must fail in all three subject areas—writing, reading, and math—to receive an F. One F school's improvement plan focused on a single subject per year to get the school in shape. Writing came first "because that is the easiest one to pass, then the next year reading, and the next year, we'll take math.... With writing there's a script; it's pretty much first we did this, then we did this, and finally we did that, and using that simple sequencing in your writing would get you a passing grade." In the first year of the accountability program, only 17% of the students in the school passed writing; the next year, 71% passed; and the year after that, 81% passed. The principal claimed they were the most improved school in the state. The school also improved in reading and math, but not enough to receive passing grades for those subjects.

The pattern of performance improvement of F schools across the state also indicates a strong focus on writing in these schools. Moreover, it appears that the movement to passing status for F schools was most heavily driven by improvement on the writing portion of the state assessment. In short, the concentration on writing appears to pay off and, indeed, may yield the highest benefit (in terms of achieving passing status) for a given level of effort. The 78 voucher-threatened schools in 1999 improved enough to avoid a second F grade in 2000. Of these, 57% improved in multiple areas of the test; however, all the schools that moved above the minimum threshold in only one area increased performance on the *writing* portion of the assessment. This improvement on the writing assessment guaranteed that 100% of the schools that received an F grade in 1999 would not become voucher-eligible. It is also the case for the four schools receiving an F grade in 2000, all of which improved enough to meet the minimum criteria for writing in 2001.

These findings raise questions inherent in any accountability system. Does the system lead to a narrowing of the curriculum or teaching to the test, and, if so, is that a good or bad outcome? The answer most likely depends on the characteristics of the schools and the characteristics of individual students. For example, statements by principals, teachers, and parents with whom we spoke indicate that the opportunity costs for narrowing the curriculum were greater for the A schools than for the F schools. At the same time, the principal and teachers in one A school reported putting greater effort into early identification of the lowest-performing students and giving them special attention because the accountability system specifically took account of the performance of these students. Therefore, while the average student in an A school may be worse off as a consequence of the accountability system, the very low-performing students in those top schools may be better off. In F schools, according to our discussions with school personnel, many of the students may be better off with the accountability system in place.

Additional resources. The F schools that we visited received significant amounts of new financial resources and technical assistance from their districts. One school reported receiving as much as $300,000 in additional funding, much of it for reducing class size. The principal of the other F school reported that nearly 25% of the activities in the school were a consequence of new funding. In addition to class-size reduction, new funding supported staff development, the purchase of books and technology, and an after-school tutoring program staffed by the school's teachers. Some of this funding was transferred directly to the school budget, and some of it remained in the district budget and was therefore difficult to sort out using administrative records. In addition to extra financial support, the district office provided instructional specialists who made regular visits to the school to coach teachers in tested subjects, particularly writing.[13] One teacher said he "would go to an F school any day since you could count on great resources and support," but he would be hesitant to move to a D or C school. This sentiment was also reflected in some newspaper accounts. For instance, one administrator reported being grateful for the increased scrutiny directed at his school, since it came with additional resources. "Failing meant that we finally got the resources we needed all along to help our kids improve," said the principal of an F school.[14]

The state accountability system may be triggering new practices in allocating district resources. For example, the F school that had improved its writing score so dramatically was anticipating losing its additional support for writing in the next year. It is critical to understand the nature of these ebbs and flows in order to determine the contributions that policies such as vouchers make to student performance. In other words, while the accountability system may be the stimulus for targeting resources in new ways, the new resources themselves, rather than the threat of vouchers, may be an important part of the explanation for improved student performance. Furthermore, a performance-based accountability system may also alter the structure of resource allocation—from a system based on some notion of equity to one based on adequacy.[15]

Personnel allocation shifts. Shifting personnel at both the school and district levels appears to be occurring as a result of the A+ Plan. Principals in the F schools, for example, were replaced. One principal also reported that he had the authority to restructure the entire staff in the school, although he did not act on it. There are also more subtle shifts occurring. Some of the schools we visited reported difficulty in recruiting teachers for fourth and fifth grades, where testing was heavy. In one school, a fourth-grade teacher with an allegedly sterling reputation refused to teach again in fourth grade because it required that instruction be tied closely to preparation for state testing. She moved to second grade, where state testing does not occur, because, as she explained, "There I can actually teach." In another school, which had dropped from an A to a C in 2000, teachers made use of their free periods to work with fourth- and fifth-graders identified as at risk in terms of test performance, in order to provide more intensive instruction and to prepare them for the test. Indeed, in this school, performance was raised to an A again in 2001.

We might expect that, as schools and districts acquire more experience and more information on the relative performance of different teachers, more marked and systematic shifts might occur in personnel allocation both within and across schools. These shifts might affect not only the assignment of teachers to particular schools, grades, and subjects, but also the way in which teachers allocate their time during the school day. As we saw above, some teachers were assisting the needy students of other teachers during their free periods in order to ensure a high grade for the school. To some extent, teacher preferences for teaching assignments also have to be taken into account. One might make the assumption that teachers would not want to teach in F schools, but, as we discovered, at least some teachers stated a preference for employment in F schools over higher-ranked schools in order to have access to additional resources.

The findings on the allocation of financial resources and personnel suggest several reasons why the A+ Plan may create ripple effects throughout districts that differ substantially, depending on the circumstances of the district as a whole. For example, the case studies indicate that voucher-threatened schools garner substantial additional resources, many of which are apt to appear in district budgets rather than in school budgets. Given resource limitations, however, we might not expect to see this kind of reallocation in districts with large numbers of voucher-threatened schools or districts that have chronically low-performing (C or D) schools but are not under the threat of vouchers. This reallocation did, in fact, elicit a negative reaction from one teacher in an A school, who stated, "Our district makes sure no school gets two F's. They go right in and lower class size to 10 or 12, and then we have to struggle to get a part-time art teacher." Another potential ripple effect may occur within the labor market, as teachers with records of high performance are called upon, perhaps through some incentive system, to work in the more troubled schools, while teachers with lower performance records find it difficult to get a school assignment.

Vouchers versus social stigma. Florida's F schools appear to be making disproportionately large improvements in student performance, and some analysts have attributed the improvement to the fact that these schools are voucher-threatened. When using simple aggregate statistics, it is exceedingly difficult to distinguish between the effect of a voucher threat associated with a grade of F and the effect of the social stigma associated with that grade. In both cases, we would expect similar school responses. Discussions with teachers, however, suggest that, for them at any rate, the stigma is far more important than the threat of vouchers. One teacher claimed, "I don't even think I thought about vouchers." Another said, "With that stigma [of an F], it was one of the hardest years I've ever taught. All your buddies are at other schools with C or D or A or B. No matter what they say, they look at you and their look asks, 'What do you do over there? Why is your school an F?'" The principal reported that teachers were "devastated" at the external perception of their school as a failing school. Principals, however, did feel tremendous pressure from the district when it appeared that vouchers might cause the district to lose students.

These observations suggest that the Florida accountability system, with it value-laden and symbolic labeling of performance (A through F), triggers more than one corrective force, depending on the level of the system one is observing. District officials worry about losing students and resources to vouchers; teachers worry about the stigma associated with a low grade; both district officials and teachers no doubt prefer to avoid these scenarios altogether if possible. Principals appear to be in the middle, for they are agents of the district in moving their schools to higher performance. As one would expect given this classic principal/agent situation, we uncovered some (though not many) explicit attempts by the district to direct the behavior of principals and their schools. The most obvious example was a district offering financial incentives for schools to adopt a whole-school reform model, which would specify a curriculum and include professional development. We may see more such attempts as time passes, perhaps built into principal and teacher contracts.

A CAT-AND-MOUSE GAME: STATE RESPONSE

Policy can sometimes evolve like a game of cat and mouse. While we have identified ways in which schools have responded to the Florida A+ accountability policies, leading some to conclude that the schools have beaten the system in certain ways, this is not the whole story. In December 2001, three years after the A+ Plan was put into place, the state announced sweeping changes in how schools would subsequently be graded. One major change was that grades would take into account student progress over the year, not just the overall level of performance. Therefore, simply achieving a passing grade would now be insufficient; the state had raised the bar, especially for the lowest-performing students in each grade.

A second major change was that less weight would be given to the writing portion of the state test and more to the reading portion. Writing would be only one of six performance elements taken into consideration, while reading would now be incorporated into three of these elements. We will have to wait and see what behavioral responses, if any, these new measures will evoke in schools.

CONCLUSION

What conclusions can be drawn from these school visits and firsthand accounts? First, the A+ Plan so far appears to have had a significant impact on the instructional focus of all schools—both high-performing and low-performing. More specifically, both the case studies and the actual FCAT results show that administrators and teachers are targeting instruction to improve FCAT scores, particularly on the writing portion of the exam. Allowing tests to influence instruction in this way may be good or bad, depending both on the quality of the FCAT and on one's personal opinion of the utility of standardized testing. Furthermore, as we have suggested, the costs and benefits are likely to vary by school characteristics and, perhaps, by individual student characteristics.

Second, it is clear at this point that distinguishing between "voucher effects" and other effects of the A+ Accountability Plan is rather difficult. The evidence of the reallocation of resources, for example, suggests that researchers must be very careful about jumping to any conclusions about "pure" voucher effects. Moreover, it is apparent that we will need to gather a great deal of information on the actual resources in the schools, above and beyond those that show up in school-based budgets, if we are to fully understand the impacts of the A+ Plan. Similarly, we need to understand and account for shifts in personnel assignments that may result from the accountability system.

Third, the case studies suggest that there is a very real and tangible social stigma attached to being judged a low-performing or failing school, at least for teachers. More surprising is the fact that A schools also feel considerable social pressure to maintain their standing. Indeed, social pressure and reputation far overshadowed any threat of vouchers, according to the principals, teachers, and parents whom we interviewed. One reason for the seeming lack of concern about vouchers at the school level is that relatively few vouchers have actually been issued in Florida. At the time of our school visits, only two schools (A. A. Dixon Elementary School, and Spencer Bibbs Elementary School) were voucher-eligible, and fewer than 100 students were actually using vouchers. Thus for most school officials, teachers, and parents, the possibility of vouchers affecting their school may have seemed remote. In addition, as we have suggested, the threat of vouchers may be more strongly felt at the district level, where financial responsibility for the schools rests. More time may be required for this concern to be conveyed to the schools in systematic ways.

Finally, our assessment of the implications of shifting resources and social stigma suggests that the consequences of having F or voucher-eligible schools in one district may be quite distinct from the effects in another, depending in part on the condition of other schools in each district, the resources available to the district, and any internal maneuvering that might result over time in inequitable resource allocation. The case studies demonstrate that the impacts of the A+ Plan are sometimes unanticipated, thereby increasing the challenge for any researchers who wish to fully understand the general equilibrium effects of a system that is still dynamic and evolving.

Policy is, of course, a moving target, and the real long-term impact of the many accountability systems—either individually or together—that are now working their way through the states will not be clear for some time.

REFERENCES

1. *Zelman v. Simmons-Harris* is the U.S. Supreme Court ruling handed down in June 2002, which upheld Cleveland's voucher program providing tuition assistance to students attending private religious schools.

2. See Milton Friedman, *Capitalism and Freedom* (Chicago: University of Chicago Press, 1962); and John E. Chubb and Terry M. Moe, *Politics, Markets, and America's Schools* (Washington, D.C.: Brookings Institution, 1990). Voucher advocates also often make equity arguments, claiming vouchers provide a cost-effective escape for students who are unfairly trapped in chronically low-performing public schools because their parents do not have the financial means to move to a better neighborhood or to pay tuition for a private school.

3. The validity of this assumption is not clear. Empirical studies comparing the effectiveness of public and private schools have yielded findings that are far from conclusive. See, for example, James S. Coleman, Thomas Hoffer, and Sally Kilgore, *Public and Private Schools* (Chicago: National Opinion Research Center, Report to the National Center for Education Statistics, 1981); Glen C. Cain and Arthur S. Goldberger, "Public and Private Schools Revisited," *Sociology of Education,* vol. 56, 1983, pp. 208-18; Karl L. Alexander and Aaron M. Pallas, "School Sector and Cognitive Performance: When Is a Little a Little?," *Sociology of Education,* vol. 56, 1985, pp. 115-28; Dan D. Goldhaber, "Public and Private High Schools: Is School Choice an Answer to the Productivity Problem?," *Economics of Education Review,* vol. 15, 1996, pp. 93-109; idem, "School Choice: An Examination of the Empirical Evidence on Achievement, Parental Decision Making, and Equity," *Educational Researcher,* December 1999, pp. 16-25; and Patrick J. McEwan, "The Potential Impact of Large-Scale Voucher Programs," *Review of Educational Research,* vol. 70, 2000, pp. 103-39.

4. This amount would have covered tuition costs in over 90% of the state's private schools, and receiving schools cannot charge

students more than the voucher value. In addition to adjustments for district costs, the value of the voucher also varies by grade level and program.

5. As of November 2002, opportunity scholarship payments were made to private schools for 522 students. A few students were still awaiting final eligibility decisions before payments were made.

6. Initially they could be reclassified if they increased performance on any single portion of the test—math, reading, or writing. This provision was changed for the school year 2001-02, and schools are now required to meet points criteria that take into account both performance and improvement in math, reading, and writing.

7. Jay P. Greene, "Vouchers in Charlotte," *Education Matters*, vol. 1, 2001, pp. 55-60.

8. Gregory Camilli and Katrina Bulkley, "Critique of 'An Evaluation of the Florida A-Plus Accountability and School Choice Program,'" *Educational Policy Analysis Archives*, vol. 9, 2001, available at http://epaa.asu.edu/epaa/v9n7/.

9. More detailed information on the case study schools is available from the authors upon request.

10. Bill Hirschman, Heidi Hall, and Kelly Patrick, "Pressure, Tension Fuel FCAT Drills," *Fort Lauderdale Sun-Sentinel*, 13 February 2000, p. A-1.

11. Ibid.

12. Andrew Dunn, "Schools Kick Off FCAT Preparation," *Tallahassee Democrat*, 23 January 2001.

13. Corroborating these reports, our survey results showed that teachers in F schools reported significantly more often than teachers in other schools that specialists or "master teachers" modeled lessons for them.

14. Holly Stepp and Luisa Yanez, "Bottom-Rung Schools Climb Up FCAT Ladder," *Miami Herald*, 10 April 2001, p. B-1.

15. William Clune, "The Shift from Equity to Adequacy in School Finance," *Educational Policy*, vol. 8, 1994, pp. 376-94; and Allan Odden and William Clune, "School Finance Systems: Aging Structures in Need of Renovation," *Educational Evaluation and Policy Analysis*, vol. 20, 1998, pp. 157-77.

DAN GOLDHABER is a research associate professor in the Daniel J. Evans School of Public Affairs, University of Washington, Seattle, and an affiliated scholar with the Urban Institute, Washington, D.C, where JANE HANNAWAY is the center director of the Education Policy Center. An earlier version of this article was presented at the annual meeting of the Association of Public Policy and Management, Washington, D.C., November 2001. The research reported here is part of a larger multi-year project evaluating the Florida A+ Accountability Plan being conducted by David Figlio, Dan Goldhaber, Jane Hannaway, and Cecilia Rouse. It is supported by the Annie E. Casey Foundation, Atlantic Philanthropic Services, the Smith Richardson Foundation, the Spencer Foundation, the National Institute of Child Health and Human Development, and the U.S. Department of Education, but the views presented are those of the authors.

From *Phi Delta Kappan,* April 2004, pp. 598-605. Copyright © 2004 by Phi Delta Kappa. Reprinted by permission from the publisher and author.

Article 17

No Flower Shall Wither;
or,
Horticulture in the Kingdom of the Frogs

by Gary K. Clabaugh

In olden times, when hope still mattered, a little boy named Horace was in love with flowers. When they bloomed, Horace was very, very happy; and when they withered, he was very, very sad.

Now Horace was a small frog, living in the Kingdom of the Frogs. In this realm, Bullfrogs reigned supreme because of their ability to croak very loudly and remain hidden for long periods in the muck at the bottom of ponds.

Happily for Horace, Bullfrogs professed a great love of flowers. In fact, the Kingdom's residents were compelled to pay tribute to support community greenhouses where small frogs sent their seedlings. Bullfrogs preferred private greenhouses for their own seedlings.

One fine day the Bullfrogs began harrumphing that the state-run greenhouses were in an awful mess. In *A Kingdom at Risk*, a blue-ribbon Bullfrog panel even proclaimed, "If an enemy dominion were in charge of our greenhouses, their condition would be a cause for war." Bullfrogs were fond of finding causes for wars.

Few stopped to consider that public greenhouses operated under Bullfrog rules and that Bullfrogs determined their resources. Fewer still seemed to notice that public greenhouse conditions mirrored public conditions in the Kingdom (bad neighborhoods, bad greenhouses; better neighborhoods, better greenhouses).

When Horace came of age and it was time to make his way in the world, he thought and thought about what to do. "I know!" exclaimed Horace with a smile, "I shall become a licensed horticulturalist"—certification being necessary for state greenhouse employment—"and bring flowers to bloom."

In the Kingdom of the Frogs, learning vital things—such as how to remove Bullfrog bunions or assist Bullfrog tax avoidance—required lengthy and focused schooling. Horticultural training was far easier. Colleges, largely controlled by Bullfrog trustees, saw horticultural programs as a source of ready revenue and little more. Bullfrogs even set up easier "alternative routes" to certification—"Grow for the Kingdom," for example—just in case traditional routes were too tough. "Such alternatives," Bullfrogs earnestly croaked, "open careers in horticulture to bright people who are enthusiastic about plant growth."

Horace wondered, "Why is it so easy to become a horticulturalist when other important things are hard?" Nonetheless, he took the standard training and learned as much as he could. Meanwhile, the Bullfrogs continued to stoke dissatisfaction regarding public greenhouses.

When Horace graduated he found a position in a public greenhouse in one of the poorer neighborhoods of the Kingdom. There were many such neighborhoods. Horace quickly discovered that he and his fellow horticulturalists had little say about how the communal greenhouse was run. Horace was not permitted to whitewash the greenhouse glass, so his sun-sensitive plants soon were scalded. He had no control over the greenhouse heat; so his cool-weather plants soon were cooked. Greenhouse managers even decided what type of fertilizer he should use.

If leggy seedlings needed pinching back, Horace wasn't permitted to do it. Seedling owners had to be consulted, and then greenhouse management made the final decision. Horace was not even permitted to apply insecticide or pull a weed. Only administrators, who in turn were controlled by a greenhouse board operating under strict Bullfrog rules, could make such decisions.

Horace would fill in the requisite pink slips requesting spraying or weeding, but nothing came of them. In consequence, Horace's plants soon were sucked dry by white flies, mealy bugs, and aphids, while weeds stole their nourishment.

It wasn't clear to Horace why the greenhouse was run that way. Some said Bullfrog mandates left the manager little choice. Others blamed it on the manager's desire to be a Bullfrog. Still others thought it was because greenhouse board members had no horticultural training and knew little about growing flowers.

In this Kingdom it was customary for agronomical ignoramuses to control horticultural affairs. Even the Bullfrog Secretary of Horticulture had no knowledge of plant husbandry—though he was well connected at the pond. In lieu of knowledge he substituted croaky solemnity. He regularly admonished greenhouse managers, for instance, to "demand higher expectations at all levels." In self-defense, greenhouse managers afterward declared that when plants didn't thrive, it was some horticulturalist's fault.

Article 17. No Flower Shall Wither; or, Horticulture in the Kingdom of the Frogs

Meanwhile Horace was realizing how important it was that he had no control over how plants were sprouted and first raised as seedlings. By the time plant owners brought them to the greenhouse, their all-important early growth period was over. Horace would get seedlings that were leggy from insufficient sun, stunted from inadequate fertilizer, or wilted from too little water, and often it was too late for him to undo the damage.

Old-timers told Horace that there was a time when struggling seedlings were put into a smaller greenhouse and given special care. But Bullfrogs declared that as many plants as possible should be put in the main greenhouse. Thus Horace received seedlings requiring more care than he could give.

Horace and his co-workers also controlled their seedlings only part of the day, five days a week, 180 days of the year. The rest of the time, and that was a great deal of time indeed, seedlings were "cared for" by their owners. That gave them ample opportunity to undo whatever Horace did.

It wasn't that the seedling owners were all indifferent. Many cared about their plants, but they were too besieged or uninformed to care properly. You see, small frogs were underpaid, often out of work, and sometimes homeless. Many were sick, and without health care. All that was because only Bullfrogs mattered in the Kingdom of the Frogs.

No matter what shape seedlings were in when he got them, Horace tried his best to make them thrive. In the end, though, the damaged condition of many new seedlings, inane greenhouse rules, incessant hectoring of Bullfrog officials, and seeing his work undone by plant owners combined to grind Horace down.

About this time the Frog King emerged from the muck on the bottom of his pond, swam to the surface, stuck his thick Bullfrog head out of the water, and croaked a royal decree. "Henceforth," he thrummed mightily," no flower shall wither!" And with that he dove back into the muck.

Little additional money followed for public greenhouses, but new mandates did. Bullfrog officials declared, for instance, that all public greenhouses must measure and report plant development. "Henceforth," the Bullfrogs croaked, "public greenhouse plant growth must be assessed, the results proclaimed, and horticulturalists held accountable." (There was no mention of measuring plant growth in the private greenhouses that served the Bullfrog's seedlings.)

Accountable Horace struggled mightily, but the neglected seedlings given him proved his undoing. He just couldn't get them all to measure up. Soon Horace was under the greenhouse manager's baleful stare. Sternly he said to Horace, "Too many of your plants are not meeting standards." Horace started to explain, "But there is so much I don't contro—" "Ah, ah, ah!" the manager interrupted. "I had hoped you wouldn't offer excuses! Truly professional growers just admit they must do a better job."

Horace wasn't the only horticulturalist whose damaged plants often failed to thrive. So many plants were stunted that the Bullfrogs threatened to label the greenhouse "dangerously substandard." "If that happens," the greenhouse administrator warned, "I'm not going down alone!" Then he began drawing up the Bullfrog-mandated Seedling Safety Plan.

Plant owners began thinking about transferring their seedlings to other greenhouses. Bullfrogs assured them it was every plant owner's right. Practically, though, their choices were limited to the same poor neighborhood. Oddly, the Bullfrogs knew that would happen, though they never said so.

Soon Bullfrog corporations began taking over communal greenhouses, operating them for profit. Just as many seedlings withered as before, but the Bullfrogs were much more contented.

The greenhouse season came to an end and there was sadness in Horace's eyes that had never been there before. He was unsure into what realm he was withdrawing. He also wondered what made him weary before his life had truly begun. Yes, Horace still loved flowers. Only now, when he saw a blossom, he found it difficult not to think of all the seedlings that had no real chance to bloom.

It was then that Horace's "miracle plant" came into flower. When Horace had received this seedling, it was in sad, sad shape. But it evidenced an uncanny resilience, responding eagerly to Horace's tender care. Yes, every time the plant went home, it came back worse for wear. But Horace would nurse it back to health, and the plant gained even more vigor.

When Horace's "miracle plant" finally came into bloom, it was a wonderful thing! Covered with fleshy pink blossoms that had blood-red interiors, it revealed a beauty that took Horace's breath away. "I've never seen anything so magnificent!" Horace said, as his weariness fled and the sadness left his eyes.

Horace spent the vacation recovering and considering his future. Eventually, because of that one glorious plant, he decided to return to the greenhouse for a second year. When he did, Horace found that things were worse than ever. Thanks largely to Bullfrog mandates, love of flowers was either an afterthought, or not thought of at all. The focus was on growth charts and standards instead.

Horace still was determined to once again do his very best. "Few worthwhile things are easy," he thought. But beneath that surface hopefulness, his sadness and weariness already were reemerging.

THE END

Gary K. Clabaugh, Ed.D., is a professor in the Department of Education at La Salle University in Philadelphia.

From *Educational Horizons*, Winter 2004, pp. 99-102, by Gary K. Clabaugh. Copyright (c) 2004 by Gary K. Clabaugh. Reprinted by permission of the author.

The Power of Testing

Just as medical tests help diagnose and treat patients, rigorous and meaningful education assessments can help ensure the academic health of all students.

By Matthew Gandal and Laura McGiffert

Our society relies on testing. We expect tests to tell us whether our water is safe to drink, our cholesterol is too high, or the dishwasher we want to buy is the best value. These tests help us ensure our safety, take care of our health, and spend money wisely.

In medicine, no one seriously questions the connection between testing and appropriate medical treatment. A patient may present certain obvious symptoms, but before making a diagnosis, a doctor will routinely order a battery of tests to isolate the specific condition causing those symptoms. Once these tests have identified the problem, the doctor can offer a treatment plan.

We may complain about the quantity, cost, or inconvenience of these tests, but we do not question their basic value. We expect our doctors to stay up-to-date on the latest testing methods, and we demand that our health plans provide coverage for the tests that we need.

When it comes to education, testing holds the same power to bring about the result we all want—academically healthy students. Although some may raise legitimate concerns about the adequacy of some tests now in use, we should not discount the validity or utility of testing altogether.

Imagine that every child had an annual education checkup—a set of assessments created to measure agreed-on expectations. The results of this checkup would help teachers chart a course for individual student improvement. The federal No Child Left Behind Act offers exactly this sort of checkup to U.S. schools and teachers. By the 2005-2006 school year, schools in every state will assess students in reading and math annually in grades 3-8, and again before they graduate from high school. Science assessments in key grades will follow in 2007-2008.

No Child Left Behind puts tremendous pressure on states to create new assessments within a tight timeline. At least 36 states will have to develop more than 200 new tests within the next few years to comply with the federal law. If the end result is quantity without quality, little value will be added. If these assessments are of high quality, however, they have the potential to add significant value to school improvement efforts.

High Expectations for All

Doctors treat each patient differently on the basis of his or her individual needs, yet they base their judgments on conventions widely held across the profession. A thermometer is the same in Indianapolis or Miami, as are a blood pressure gauge and a scale. What do these measures have in common? Each reports results against a common standard. A fever is a fever, regardless of where you live.

Similarly, we should hold students to the same achievement standards regardless of their race, their socioeconomic status, or where they attend school. Unfortunately, this does not always happen. Teachers' expectations for their students differ; an A awarded in one school can mean something very different in another school. And students in disadvantaged communities are disproportionately held to lower standards.

Useful education assessments must make clear what they measure, and they must measure what we value most.

Challenging all students to meet common standards should be non-negotiable. These standards must be more than just minimum requirements; they must be anchored in the challenging content and skills that students need to succeed. The highest-performing school systems around the world use this formula of common standards and assessments. Students in these countries routinely outperform U.S. students on international assessments, not because they have more talent, but because their schools expect more from them (TIMSS International Study Center, n.d.).

If these international comparisons are not convincing enough, we can find plenty of other evidence of the need for common, high standards. Too many students graduate from high school unprepared for the challenges that lie ahead. Increasing numbers of students at four-year colleges need remedial education in reading, writing, or mathematics. Employers tell a similar story: 34 percent of job applicants tested by major U.S. firms in 2001 lacked sufficient reading and math skills to do the jobs that they sought (American Management Association, 2001).

It Matters What We Measure

Useful medical tests must provide relevant and reliable information. A doctor would not order an X-ray to determine treatment for a sore throat, or a throat culture to treat a broken ankle. Doctors need tests that reveal information about a patient's particular condition.

Similarly, useful education assessments must make clear what they measure, and they must measure what we value most. In other words, states must tightly align assessments and standards to provide valid and meaningful information to educators.

Many states have found it difficult to accomplish this goal. Such alignment requires states to rely less on off-the-shelf, norm-referenced tests. These tests are not well aligned with most states' standards, and they report results against a norm, or average, rather than show whether students have met standards.

But even states that have developed their own tests have had trouble measuring their standards well. Our analyses of more than a dozen state tests designed to support standards-based instruction found that many tests are unbalanced, over-sampling some standards and under-sampling others. The more advanced content and skills usually get short shrift. For example, Achieve's research has found that although most states' middle school math standards emphasize the foundations of algebra and geometry, more than 60 percent of the questions on their 8th grade tests dealt with computation, whole-number operations, and fractions.

In contrast, Massachusetts is an encouraging example of a state that has established a well-aligned system of standards and tests. The state's 10th grade exams in English and math are among the most robust assessments in the United States. They are based on clear and challenging standards, and they measure the depth and breadth of those standards well. Students must read and write thoughtfully to do well on the Massachusetts English language arts tests, and they must demonstrate their understanding of both basic and advanced mathematics to do well on the mathematics tests. These exams will count for graduation this year for the first time, and although this requirement has engendered some debate, most people in the state agree that the tests measure what matters most (Achieve, 2002a).

Using Data to Inform Practice

The patient's examination is over, the relevant tests have been completed, and the results have come back. Now, with all the information in hand, the doctor can offer a diagnosis and prescribe treatment. He or she may pronounce that the patient is in perfect health, or may recommend antibiotics, physical therapy, or even surgery. The important question is what happens after the results come back.

Just as in medicine, assessments in education are a means to an end. Assessments provide information on where students and schools need to improve, and they may provide incentives for students and schools to make the necessary improvements. But tests alone cannot create improvement. Educators, parents, and students must do the work of raising student achievement.

To make this possible, schools must get test results in a timely and useful manner. Waiting six months to see how students scored is of little value in helping those students improve. In addition, states must provide the test data in a form that educators can understand and use, with a freer degree of specificity than just a number on a scale. For example, a particular score in phonemic awareness conveys more to a teacher than an overall score in reading and certainly more than a score in English language arts. Specific results that identify students' particular strengths and weaknesses enable teachers to target instruction to meet the needs of each student.

New York City has dramatically altered how it reports results on state assessments in order to make them useful in classrooms. Partnering with the Grow Network, the city provides every parent, teacher, and principal with clear reports and instructional tools linking the data to state standards. Innovative technology can disaggregate the data to the individual level, allowing teachers to identify which students need help with which concepts, instead of requiring the entire class to review all topics. This approach has met with remarkable approval from educators and parents, who now find the data from the state tests much more useful (Grow Network, n.d.).

Meaningful data turn a diagnosis into action, thereby enabling educators to respond to individual student needs. They also make assessments a helpful tool for educators rather than simply an accountability hammer.

Beyond Large-Scale Tests

Doctors routinely pair their own clinical observations with an objective test—like a blood cell count—to identify an illness. This practice allows them to get the most coherent and complete information and make an accurate diagnosis.

Educators, too, get the best information about their students when they compile data from a number of sources, including classroom assignments, quizzes, diagnostic tests, and large-scale assessments. Together, these tools paint a fuller picture of student performance than a single assessment can.

Large-scale state tests play a crucial role in monitoring and encouraging school improvement, but they are not enough. To tap the power of testing, schools and teachers need access to diagnostic assessments that give them immediate feedback on student performance throughout the school year. As states add new large-scale tests to meet the requirements of No Child Left Behind, school districts have the chance to drop duplicative tests and invest instead in diagnostic tools. Spring Branch Independent School District in Texas has done this to great effect by developing lessons, quizzes, and tests directly aligned to the standards that teachers can use in their classrooms at any time (Achieve, 2002b).

The Real High Stakes

With the results of medical tests in hand, doctors have an ethical duty to give their patients the best possible care, regardless of the complexity of the disease. In fact, they can be held responsible if they do not provide appropriate treatment.

We, too, must provide the best education for all students—not just those who are easy to educate. Indeed, we are delinquent if we pass students through the grades and award them diplomas even if they are unprepared for the opportunities and challenges that await them. The real high stakes for these youngsters will come when they arrive at college or the workplace and lack the skills to succeed.

Like doctors who do not act responsibly, schools whose students consistently fail to meet expectations should face consequences. Rather than just a heavy stick, these consequences should include a combination of assistance and sanctions. In Kentucky and North Carolina, for example, the state assigns teams of distinguished educators to help low-performing schools develop and implement improvement plans that often focus on boosting the ability of teachers to teach to the state standards. Both states have seen a dramatic decline in the number of low-performing schools (Mandel, 2000). But ultimately, if assistance does not lead to improved performance, states must take stronger actions—including reconstitution or state takeover.

The Challenge Ahead

Standards, testing, and accountability have become the policy framework within which schools in every state must operate. For schools and students to reap the benefits of standards-based reform, we need clear and rigorous standards, assessments aligned to those standards, results reported in meaningful ways, and appropriate incentives and consequences. States and districts also must work in tandem to align curriculum, diagnostic assessments, and high-quality professional development for teachers.

A few critics will always condemn the use of testing in schools. However, with students' futures at stake, we must not abandon the very tools that have the power to transform teaching and learning. We must make our education assessments stronger and take advantage of the information they provide to ensure that all of our graduates are academically healthy.

References

Achieve, Inc. (2002a). *Three paths, one destination: Standards-based reform in Maryland, Massachusetts, and Texas*. Washington, DC: Author.

Achieve, Inc. (2002b). *Aiming higher: Meeting the challenges of education reform in Texas*. Washington, DC: Author.

American Management Association. (2001). *AMA survey on workplace testing: Basic skills, job skills, psychological measurement*. New York: Author.

Grow Network. (n.d.). *About the Grow Network* [Online]. Available: www.grownetwork.org

Mandel, D. R. (2000). *Transforming underperforming schools: A strategy for Tennessee 2000*. Berkeley, CA: MPR Associates.

TIMSS International Study Center. (n.d.). *Third international mathematics and science study—1995* [Online]. Available: http://timss.bc.edu/timss 1995.html

---

Matthew Gandal is Executive Vice President of Achieve, Inc., an organization created by governors and corporate leaders to help states improve their schools and raise academic standards; www.achieve.org.
Laura McGiffert is Director of Achieve's Mathematics Achievement Partnership.

From *Educational Leadership*, February 2003, pp. 39-42. Copyright © 2003 by Matthew Gahndal and Laura McGiffert. Reprinted by permission of the authors.

Article 19

Why Students Think They Understand— When They Don't

How does the mind work—and especially how does it learn? Teachers make assumptions all day long about how students best comprehend, remember, and create. These assumptions—and the teaching decisions that result—are based on a mix of theories learned in teacher education, trial and error, craft knowledge, and gut instinct. Such gut knowledge often serves us well, but is there anything sturdier to rely on?

Cognitive science is an interdisciplinary field of researchers from psychology, neuroscience, linguistics, philosophy, computer science, and anthropology who seek to understand the mind. In this regular American Educator column, we will consider findings from this field that are strong and clear enough to merit classroom application.

By Daniel T. Willingham

Question: Very often, students will think they understand a body of material. Believing that they know it, they stop trying to learn more. But, come test time, it turns out they really don't know the material. Can cognitive science tell us anything about why students are commonly mistaken about what they know and don't know? Are there any strategies teachers can use to help students better estimate what they know?

Answer: There are multiple cues by which each of us assess what we know and don't know. But these cues are fallible, which explains why students sometimes think that they know material better than their classroom performance indicates.

* * *

How do we know that we know something? If I said to you, "Could you name the first President of the United States?" you would say, "Yes, I could tell you that." On the other hand, if I said, "Could you tell me the names of the two series of novels written by Anthony Trollope?" you might say, "No." What processes go into your judgment of what you know? The answer may at first seem obvious: You look in your memory and see what's there. For the first question, you determine that your memory contains the fact that George Washington was the first U.S. President, so you answer "yes." For the second question, if you determine that your memory contains little information about Trollope (and doesn't include the novel series named *Barchester* and *Palliser*), you would answer "no."

But, if the mechanism were really so simple, we would seldom—if ever—make mistakes about what we know. In fact, we do make such mistakes. For example, we have all confidently thought that we knew how to get to a destination, but then when put to the test by actually having to drive there, we realize that we don't know. The route may seem familiar, but that's a far cry from recalling every turn and street name.

The feeling of knowing has an important role in school settings because it is a key determinant of student studying (e.g., Mazzoni & Cornoldi, 1993). Suppose a third-grader has been studying the Vikings with the goal of understanding where they were from and what they did. At what point does the third-grader say to him or herself: "I understand this. If the teacher asks me, 'Who were the Vikings?' I could give a good answer."

Every teacher has seen that students' assessments of their own knowledge are not always accurate. Indeed, this inaccuracy can be a source of significant frustration for students on examinations. The student is certain that he or she has mastered some material, yet performs poorly on a test, and may, therefore, conclude that the test was not fair. The student has assessed his or her knowledge and concluded that it is solid, yet the examination indicates that it is not. What happened? What cues do students use to decide that they *know* something?

Cognitive science research has shown that two cues are especially important in guiding our judgments of what we know: (1) our "familiarity" with a given body of information and (2) our "partial access" to that information. In this column, I'll discuss how these two cues can lead students to believe that they know material when they don't. And, in the box, I suggest ways that teachers can help students develop more realistic self-assessments of their knowledge.

"Familiarity" Fools Our Mind into Thinking We Know More than We Do

The idea of familiarity is, well, familiar to all of us. We have all had the experience of seeing someone and sensing that her face is familiar but being unable to remember who that person is or how we know her.

Psychologists distinguish between *familiarity* and *recollection*. Familiarity is the knowledge of having seen or otherwise experienced some stimulus before, but having little information associated with it in your memory. Recollection, on the other hand, is characterized by richer associations. For example, a young student might be familiar with George Washington (he knows he was a President and maybe that there's a holiday named after him), whereas an older student could probably recollect a substantial narrative about him. (See Yonelinas, 2002, for an extended review of the differences between recollection and familiarity.)

Although familiarity and recollection are different, an insidious effect of familiarity is that it can give you the feeling that you know something when you really don't. For example, it has been shown that if some key words of a question are familiar, you are more likely to think that you know the answer to the question. In one experiment demonstrating this effect (Reder, 1987), subjects were exposed to a variety of word pairs (e.g., "golf" and "par") and then asked to complete a short task that required them to think at least for a moment about the words. Next, subjects saw a set of trivia questions, some of which used words that the subjects had just been exposed to in the previous task. Subjects were asked to make a rapid judgment as to whether or not they knew the answer to the question—and then they were to provide the answer.

If the trivia question contained key words from the previous task (e.g., "What term in golf refers to a score of one under par on a particular hole?"), those words should have seemed familiar, and may have led to a feeling of knowing. Indeed, Reder found that subjects were likely to say that they knew the answer to a question containing familiar words, irrespective of whether they could actually answer the question. For questions in which words had not been rendered familiar, subjects were fairly accurate in rapidly assessing their knowledge.

A similar effect was observed in an experiment using arithmetic problems (Reder & Ritter, 1992). On each trial of this experiment, subjects saw an addition or multiplication problem (e.g., 81 + 35) and they had to rapidly decide whether they would calculate the answer or answer from memory. If they chose to calculate, they had 20 seconds to do so; if they chose to answer from memory, they had just 1.4 seconds. Sometimes problems repeated, so subjects might have had the answer to a complex problem in memory. Subjects were paid depending on their speed and accuracy, so the decision about whether or not to calculate was important. As in the trivia question experiment, subjects were accurate in knowing when they could retrieve an answer from memory and when they needed to calculate it—except in one situation, when the experimenters repeated a two-digit problem but changed the operation (e.g., addition to multiplication). In that case, subjects were just as likely to try to retrieve an answer from memory for a problem they had actually just seen (e.g., 81 + 35) as they were for a problem they had *not* just seen but which used familiar operands (e.g., 81–35). The experimenters argued that subjects made their judgment about whether to calculate based on the familiarity of the problem components, not on the whether the answer was in memory.

"Partial Access": Our Mind Is Fooled When We Know Part of the Material or Related Material

A second basis for the feeling of knowing is "partial access," which refers to the knowledge that an individual has of either a component of the target material or information closely related to the target material. Suppose I ask you a question and the answer doesn't immediately come to mind, but some related information does. For example, when I ask for the names of the two series of Trollope novels, you readily recall *Barchester* and you know I mentioned the other series earlier; you even remember that it started with the letter P, and you believe it had two or three syllables. Your quick retrieval of this partial information will lead to a feeling of knowing the relevant information—even if *Palliser* is not actually in your memory.

The effect of partial access was demonstrated in an experiment (Koriat & Levy-Sadot, 2001) in which subjects were asked difficult trivia questions. If subjects couldn't answer a particular question, they were asked to judge whether they would recognize the answer if they saw it (i.e., to make a feeling-of-knowing judgment). The interesting twist: Some of the questions used categories for which lots of examples came to mind for their subjects (e.g., composers) and matching questions used categories for which few examples came to mind (e.g., choreographers)—that is, these subjects could easily think of at least a few famous composers, but couldn't think of more than one or two choreographers, if any.

The results showed that whether or not they could actually recognize the right answer, people gave higher feeling-of-knowing judgments to questions using many-example categories (e.g., "Who composed the music for the ballet *Swan Lake*?") than to questions using few-example categories (e.g., "Who choreographed the ballet *Swan Lake*?"). The experimenters argued that when people see the composer question, the answer doesn't come to mind, but the names of several composers do. This related information leads to a feeling of knowing. Informally, we could say that subjects conclude (consciously or unconsciously), "I can't retrieve the *Swan Lake* composer right now, but I certainly seem to know a lot about composers. With a little more time, the answer to the question could probably be found." On the other hand, the choreographer question brings little information to mind and, therefore, no feeling of knowing.*

These studies, and dozens of others like them, confirm two general principles of how people gauge their memories. First, people do not assess their knowledge directly by inspecting the contents of memory. Rather, they use cues such as familiarity and partial access. Second, most of the time these cues provide a reasonable assessment of knowledge, but they are fallible.

If a student believes that he knows material, he will likely divert attention elsewhere; he will stop listening, reading, working, or participating.

How Students End Up with "Familiarity" and "Partial Access" to Material

If a student believes that he knows material, he will likely divert attention elsewhere; he will stop listening, reading, working, or participating. Mentally "checking out" is never a good choice for students, but all the more so when they disengage because they *think* they know material that, in fact, they do not know. The feeling of knowing becomes a problem if you have the feeling without the knowing. There are some very obvious ways in which students can reach this unfortunate situation in a school setting. Here are several common ones:

1. Rereading. To prepare for an examination, a student rereads her classnotes and textbook. Along the way, she encounters familiar terms ("familiar" as in she knows she's heard these terms before), and indeed they become even more familiar to her as she rereads. She thinks, "Yes, I've seen this, I know this, I understand this." But feeling that you understand material as it is presented to you is not the same as being able to recount it yourself.

---

* Another important aspect of this phenomenon is that the accuracy of partially retrieved information is irrelevant to the feeling of knowing. In an experiment illustrating this phenomenon, Asher Koriat (1993) asked subjects to learn strings of letters. Later, subjects were asked to recall as many letters as possible and then judge whether they would sucessfully recognize the entire letter string from among several choices. Subjects' confidence that they would recognize the letter string increased with the number of letters that they had recalled, regardless of whether or not those letters were correct. The more they thought they were pulling out of memory, the more confident they were that they really knew the whole string and would recognize it when they saw it.

As teachers know, this gap between feeling that you know and genuine recollection can cause great frustration. I have frequently had exchanges in which one of my students protests that despite a low test grade, he or she really knew the material. When I ask a general question or two, the student struggles to answer and ends up sputtering, "I can't exactly explain it, but I know it!" Invariably, a student with this problem has spent a great deal of time reading over the course material, yielding a lot of familiarity, but not the necessary and richer recollective knowledge.

2. Shallow Processing. A teacher may prepare an excellent lesson containing a good deal of deep meaning. But this deep meaning will only reside in a student's memory if the student has actively thought about that deep meaning (see "Students Remember...What They Think About," *American Educator*, Summer 2003, www.aft.org/american_educator/summer2003/cogsci.html). Let's say, for example, that a teacher has prepared a lesson on the European settlement of Australia and on the meaningful issue of whether that settlement should be viewed as a colonization or invasion. But, let's say that a given student did not process and retain the deep meaning intended by the lesson. He did absorb key terms like "Captain Cook" and "Aborigines." His familiarity with these key terms could mislead him into believing he was ready for a test on the subject.

3. Recollecting Related Information. Sometimes students know a lot of information *related* to the target topic, and that makes them feel as though they know the target information. (This is analogous to the subjects in the experiment who knew the names of many composers and so felt that they knew who composed *Swan Lake*.) Suppose that a fifth-grade class spent three weeks studying weather systems, including studying weather maps, collecting local data, keeping a weather journal, learning about catastrophic weather events like hurricanes, and so on. In preparation for a test, the teacher says that there will be a question on how meteorologists use weather maps to predict hurricanes. When the student hears "weather map," she might recall such superficial information as that they are color coded, that they include temperature information, and so on; she feels she knows about weather maps and doesn't study further. In fact, she hasn't yet come to understand the core issue—how weather maps are used to predict weather. But her general familiarity with the maps has tricked her into believing she had the necessary knowledge when she didn't. (Ironically, the problem of recollecting related information is most likely to occur when a student has mastered a good deal of material on the general topic; that is, he's mastered related material, but not the target material. It's the knowledge of the related material that creates the feeling of knowing.)

Cognitive science research confirms teachers' impressions that students do not always know what they think they know. It also shows where this false sense of knowledge comes from and helps us imagine the kinds of teaching and learning activities that could minimize this problem. In particular, teachers can help students test their own knowledge in ways that provide

How To Help Students See When Their Knowledge is Superficial or Incomplete

What can be done to combat spurious feelings of knowing in students? Remedies center on jostling students away from a reliance on familiarity and partial access as indices of their knowledge, and encouraging (or requiring) them to test just how much knowledge they recall and understand.

- *Make it clear to students that the standard of "knowing" is the "ability to explain to others," not "understanding when explained by others."* I have found the following analogy helpful in explaining the difference in the two types of knowing: You and a friend are watching a movie that only you have seen before. As the plot unfolds, each event, even those meant to be surprising, seems predictable and familiar. Yet if your friend asks you, "How does it end?" you can't quite remember. To truly know about a movie (or a mathematical concept or historical event), you must be able to discuss it in your own words.

- *Require students to articulate what they know in writing or orally, thereby making what they know and don't know explicit, and therefore easier to evaluate, and easier to build on or revise.* Suppose that you've just gone over a rather tricky point in class. You want to be sure that they've understood the lesson. As we all know, asking "Does everyone understand the main point here?" yields only silence. Calling on one student makes it clear to that student whether or not he or she understands the main point, but brings little benefit to other students. An alternative is to have students pair off and then take turns explaining the main idea to each other. (This will work best if the teacher provides clear criteria by which students can judge each other's answers; otherwise it can be a case of the blind leading the blind.) The process of having to explain aloud to someone else makes it clear to students whether or not they understand what they are meant to understand. The process breaks the ice of silence, and if the teacher afterwards asks if there are questions, students are usually more willing to ask for help. Indeed, observing the pairs will usually make the extent of students' understanding clear to the teacher.

- *Begin each day (or selected days) with a written self test.* The teacher may pose a few questions reviewing the material from the previous lesson. The success of this strategy depends on students writing their answers rather than having the class shout out answers or calling on students who raise their hands. Again, the question you pose will likely lead to a feeling of knowing in most students because it is material they were recently taught. If, moments after hearing the question, they hear the answer provided by another student, they will likely think, "Sure, right, I knew that" because of this feeling of knowing. To get an accurate assessment of memory, each student must see whether he or she can recollect it.

- *Ask students to do self tests at home or in preparing for examinations.* For students who are a bit older, teachers can facilitate this process by organizing "study buddies" who agree to meet at least once before an examination, or at regular intervals, to test one another. Study buddies ask one another questions to ensure that they understand the material, and then go over whatever they don't understand. This procedure brings several benefits. It's another way to force students to actually recall information, rather than to simply recognize what is in the book. The process of generating questions for a partner is also an excellent way to encourage students to think deeply about the material; it is tantamount to asking oneself, "What is really important here? What must I know about this material?" That students pose questions for each other means that students will share their perspectives on the material—a point that one student missed or understood dimly will be supported by the other student's knowledge.

- *Help students prepare for examinations with study guides.* All students, but especially younger students, need help identifying the core information to be tested. Teacher-developed study guides are an excellent way to be sure that students are aware of the critical questions and key elements of the answers. Whether they study alone or with a buddy, the guide assures that all students will tackle the most difficult concepts or materials being tested.

—*DW*

more accurate assessments of what they really know—which enables students to better judge when they have mastered material and when (and where) more work is required.

References

Koriat, A. (1993). How do we know that we know? *Psychological Review, 100,* 600-639.

Koriat, A. & Levy-Sadot, R. (2001). The combined contribution of the cue-familiarity and accessibility heuristics to feelings of knowing. *Journal of Experimental Psychology: Learning, Memory, and Cognition, 27,* 34-53.

Mazzoni, G. & Cornoldi, C. (1993). Strategies in study time allocation: Why is study time sometimes not effective? *Journal of Experimental Psychology: General, 122,* 47-60.

Reder, L. M. (1987). Strategy selection in question answering. *Cognitive Psychology, 19,* 90-138.

Reder, L. M. & Ritter, F. (1992). What determines initial feeling of knowing? Familiarity with question terms, not with the answer. *Journal of Experimental Psychology: Learning, Memory, and Cognition, 18,* 435-451.

Yonelinas, A. P. (2002). The nature of recollection and familiarity: A review 30 years of research. *Journal of Memory and Language, 46,* 441-517.

Daniel T. Willingham is associate professor of cognitive psychology and neuroscience at the University of Virginia and author of Cognition: The Thinking Animal. *His research focuses on the role of consciousness in learning.*

From *American Educator,* Winter 2003/2004, pp. 38-41, 48. Copyright © 2003 by American Educator, the quarterly journal of the American Federation of Teachers, AFL-CIO. Reprinted by permission of the AFT and the author.

The Homework Wars

By David Skinner

The American child, a gloomy chorus of newspapers, magazines and books tells us, is overworked. All spontaneity is being squeezed out of him by the vice-like pressures of homework, extracurricular activities, and family. "Jumping from Spanish to karate, tap dancing to tennis—with hours of homework waiting at home—the overscheduled child is as busy as a new law firm associate," reports the *New York Times*. The article goes on to describe a small counter-trend in which some parents are putting a stop to the frenzy and letting their children, for once in their little harried lives, simply hang out or, as one of the insurgent parents explains, enjoy an informal game of pickup.

What's this? A game of catch is news? And this is said to be sociologically significant? Something must be amiss in the state of childhood today. The common diagnosis is that too much work, too much ambition, and an absence of self-directedness are harming American children. In an influential 2001 article in the *Atlantic Monthly*, David Brooks, author of *Bobos in Paradise*, christened the overachieving American child the "Organization Kid." Reporting on the character of the generation born in the early 1980s, in which he focused on those attending some of America's most prestigious colleges, Brooks found a youth demographic of career-oriented yes-men, with nary a rebel in the bunch. Called team players and rule-followers, they are best captured by a 1997 Gallup survey Brooks cites in which 96 percent of teenagers said they got along with their parents.

In this hyper-productive, overachieving setting, a curious educational debate has broken out. The parents of the younger K-12 worker-bees are revolting against the reportedly increasing amounts of homework assigned their children. A major lightning rod for this debate has been *The End of Homework*, a book by Etta Kralovec and John Buell, whose argument found an appreciative audience in *Time, Newsweek*, the *New York Times, People* magazine, and elsewhere. For a novel polemic against a long-established educational practice, such a widespread hearing suggests that the issue has struck a chord with many American families. Understanding the book's argument—its strengths and weaknesses—is not necessary to understanding the debate over homework, but it is helpful to understanding the overall tenor of this controversy.

THE END OF HOMEWORK

What makes *The End of Homework* stand out is that it was written by academics. Etta Kralovec holds a doctorate in education from the Teachers College at Columbia University and, for over 12 years, she directed teacher education at the College of the Atlantic. John Buell, too, has spent time on the faculty at the College of the Atlantic. Now a newspaper columnist, the onetime associate editor of *The Progressive* has authored two books on political economy. In an afterword, the authors say *The End of Homework* grew out of a series of interviews with high school dropouts, many of whom cited homework as a reason they discontinued their education. This snapshot of homework's dire effect, unfortunately, requires much qualification.

Kralovec and Buell show little restraint when describing the problems brought on by the reported increase in home-work. Attacking the proposition that homework inculcates good adult habits, the authors cite the historical trend in psychology away from viewing children as miniature adults, but then quickly lose perspective. "In suggesting that children need to learn to deal with adult levels of pressure, we risk doing them untold damage. By this logic, the schoolyard shootings of recent years may be likened to 'disgruntled employee' rampages." Nor do Kralovec and Buell inspire confidence by quoting a report attributing a spate of suicides in Hong Kong to "distress over homework." The report they cite is from the *Harare Herald* in Zimbabwe, not exactly a widely recognized authority on life in Hong Kong.

ON THE BACKS OF CHILDREN

The End of Homework's alarmist tone is best captured, however, in its uncritical acceptance of a 1999 report from the American Association of Orthopedic Surgeons (AAOS) "that thousands of kids have back, neck, and shoulder pain caused by their heavy backpacks." The book's cover photo even shows two little kids straining like packmules under the weight of their bookbags. It so happens that orthopedic professionals themselves, at the AAOS no less, dispute the report. To pick a recent example, a study presented at the 2003 meeting of the AAOS, based on interviews with 346 school-age orthopedic patients, found only one patient who attributed his back pain to carrying a bookbag.

Kralovec and Buell's case against homework is further diminished by the book's clear political agenda. Indeed, the telltale signs of an overriding left-wing social critique are sadly abundant. Twice inside of 100 pages, the same unilluminating quotation is trotted out from "the great radical sociologist C. Wright Mills," whose influence on this book, however, pales next to that of Harvard economist Juliet B. Schor. Schor is most famous for her controversial 1992 bestseller *The Overworked American: The Unexpected Decline of Leisure*, which argued that American adults were losing their disposable time to the steady encroachments of longer work schedules. But the book's primary findings were contradicted by existing research and just about every mainstream expert asked to offer an opinion on the subject.

Nevertheless, Schor's laborite call for a new consensus on the proper number of hours and days that should be devoted to employment (approximately half of current levels) finds an echo in *The End of Homework*'s call to American families to throw off their homework shackles and reclaim the evenings for family time. Indeed, one notices in this book more than a little overwrought socialist rhetoric. For example, after bemoaning the failure of standards-based reforms to improve achievement scores, the authors comment that the continued emphasis on homework "fits the ideological requirement of those who maintain the status quo in our economy and politics" and that homework "serves the needs of powerful groups within our society."

The book's other patron saint is Jonathan Kozol, the influential left-wing author of *Savage Inequalities* who has done more than anyone to swamp mainstream education debate with radical social criticism. In the style of Kozol, whom they cite a dozen or so times, Kralovec and Buell binge on the theme of equality when they should be carefully picking over social science data, insisting that homework "pits students who can against students who can't." And when they're not raising the specter of class warfare, Kralovec and Buell are lecturing readers on their unwillingness to recognize its insidious influence: "We suspect that many Americans may be unwilling to acknowledge the existence of an entrenched class system in the United States that serves to constrain or enhance our children's life chances." Economic inequalities, the authors inveigh, fly in the face of "our most cherished values, such as democracy and freedom." Typical of their tempestuous approach to this discrete pedagogical question, Kralovec and Buell devote their final chapter to "Homework in the Global Economy."

Hidden amid the authors' polemic, however, is a persuasive and warranted case against an educational practice of limited value. Homework, in some cases, deserves to be attacked, which makes it all the more a pity that Kralovec and Buell couldn't confine themselves to their primary subject. Their opinion that "homework is almost always counterproductive for elementary schoolchildren" is not the product of some left-wing fever swamp and deserves further consideration.

HOW MUCH?

Kralovec and Buell's more serious case against homework begins with a standard social-science discussion of the difference between coorelation and causality. But as often happens in critical examinations, the fact that there obvious limits to human understanding is used to argue for a radical skepticism when it comes to the methods and aims of research. One author's qualifiers and caveats become, in the hands of his opponents, arguments for the proposition that it is impossible to know anything about what condition brought about which effect. So what if students who did a lot of homework performed well on achievement exams? Maybe it was the case that they did a lot of homework because they were high-achieving students?

Down that road, many a worthy illusion comes undone, but few useable lessons can be drawn. Down the opposite road, however fraught it may be with epistemological limitations, we can nevertheless develop a vague picture of solid educational practice.

University of Missouri professor of psychological sciences Harris Cooper, whose research on homework is widely cited by critics on both sides of the debate, including Kralovec and Buell, offers conditional support for the practice. "Is homework better than no homework at all?" he asks in a 1980s literature review. On the basis of 17 research reports examining over 3,300 students, Cooper found that 70 percent of comparisons yielded a positive answer. In terms of class grades and standardized test scores, he found that "the average student doing homework in these studies had a higher achievement score than 55 percent of students not doing homework." Break down such average findings, however, and this modest advantage gained through homework is lost through other variables.

Perhaps the most commanding factor in deciding the homework question is age or grade level. "Older students benefited the most from doing homework," writes Cooper. "The average effect of homework was twice as large for high school as for junior high school students and twice as large again for junior high school students as for elementary school students." This raises interesting questions about homework's distribution among age groups.

Much of the homework controversy is fueled by stories of very young children burdened with lengthy assignments and complicated projects that require extensive parental involvement. Searching for evidence that such work is important to their child's education and development, the parent of a fifth grader will find only cold comfort in the research examined by Cooper. "Teachers of Grades 4, 5, and 6 might expect the average student doing homework to outscore about 52 percent of equivalent no-homework students." A 2 percentile-point advantage gained by a practice that could be interrupting dinner, stealing family time, and pitting child against parent hardly seems enough to justify the intrusion.

For high school students, however, homework can do a lot of good. "If grade level is taken into account," Cooper finds, "homework's effect on the achievement of elementary school students could be described as 'very small,' but on high school students its effect would be 'large.'" If the average fourth- through sixth-grade student who does homework can expect only a 2 percentile-point advantage over one who does none, junior high school students doing homework can expect a 10 percentile-point advantage and high school students a 19 percentile-point advantage. What's more, this effect translates into high achievement not only in class grades—which more readily reflect a positive homework effect—but also on standardized tests, which are quite significant to a student's educational future.

WHAT KIND

There are other wrinkles worth attending to. For one, Cooper himself still favors homework, but possibly not the kind that is causing the most heartache and the most headaches. "Not surprisingly, homework produced larger effects if students did more assignments per week. Surprisingly, the effect of homework was negatively related to the duration of the homework treatment—treatments spanning longer periods produced less of a homework effect." Which is to say, homework comprised of short regular assignments is probably the most effective.

One underlying lesson here should cause many enemies of homework to groan. Kralovec and Buell, for example, marshal the classic complaint, usually made by children, that homework is boring, repetitive, and basically has nothing to do with the developing child's true self. Interesting homework—the fun stuff that allows a child to express himself, that supposedly promotes "creativity" and "critical thinking" and "planning skills"—does not come off well in Cooper's study. Examining broad national and statewide studies of the relationship between time spent on homework and its effects, Cooper found that the correlations between time spent and positive effects increased "for subjects for which homework assignments are more likely to involve rote learning, practice, or rehearsal. Alternately, subjects such as science and social studies, which often involve longer-term projects, integration of multiple skills, and creative use of non-school resources show the smallest average correlations." Note the collision of opposing pedagogical trends: improving standards by increasing homework and the movement away from rote learning. Indeed, there may be nothing more unhelpful to a student than a teacher of high standards who doesn't want to bore his students.

JUST DON'T DO IT

Interestingly, no one involved in the fight over homework has argued that parents might consider encouraging their children to put in less effort on homework that is overly time-consuming and pedagogically unproductive. Which seems a pity. Why shouldn't a parent tell his overworked fifth-grader to spend less time on that big assignment on American subcultural narratives? Or occasionally have him not do his homework at all? A little civil disobedience might be a useful way of sending a message to a teacher whose assignments are overly ambitious. And if the child gets a lower grade as a result, then it's a small price to pay. It's not as if his entire educational future is on the line.

The homework critics never suggest such a course of action, needless to say, but not because it might undermine teachers' authority, a result they otherwise happily pursue. Odd as it sounds, the fight against homework is largely about achievement, specifically about setting the price of officially recognized excellence at an acceptable rate. Reading Kralovec and Buell and the many newspaper and magazine articles depicting the rebellion against homework, one comes away with an impression in keeping with David Brooks's "Organization Kid," but with an egalitarian twist. The whole movement reflects an organization culture that wants high grades to be possible for all kids, regardless of their varying levels of ability or willingness to work, regardless of what other commitments these children have made, regardless of the importance of family.

TIME AND HOMEWORK

A significant underlying question remains to be addressed. The evidence that there is a widespread homework problem—that too many students are carrying too heavy a homework load—is largely anecdotal. There are some empirical indications of a modest increase in homework over the last 20 years or so, but other indications suggest the problem is being overstated. While some parents and families may have rather serious homework problems, these would generally appear to be private problems, hardly in need of national or even local solutions.

At least there is a consensus on standard reference points. One constant in this debate are the data gathered from the University of Michigan's 1997 Child Development supplement to the Panel Study of Income Dynamics and 1981 Study of Time Use in Social and Economic Accounts, a collection of time-use studies of children. Often appearing in the press cheek-by-jowl with quotes from overstretched parents, most reporting on the study suggests its findings support the conclusion that American children lack for leisure time amid demands imposed on them by parents and school. But the study's authors, who arguably know more than anyone about how American children are actually spending their time day-in and day-out, do not see the story this way. In fact, in a *New York Times* article, the study's primary researcher, Sandra L. Hofferth, dismissed the whole notion that the American child is over-worked and overoccupied. "I don't believe in the 'hurried child' for a minute.... There is a lot of time that can be used for other things."

On the question of homework, Hofferth and co-author John F. Sandberg reject the claim that homework has seen a significant general increase. The average amount of time spent studying for 3- to 12-year-olds has increased from 1981 to 1997, but the vast majority of those increases (studying and reading are measured separately) are concentrated among 3- to 5-year-olds (reading) and 6- to 8-year-olds (studying). "The main reason for the increase in studying among 6- to 8-year-olds was an increase in the proportion who did some studying at all, from one-third to more than one-half. The fact that significant increases in reading occurred among 3- to 5-year-olds probably reflects parents' increasing concern with preparing children for school."

Which is to say, homework appears to be increasing most where there was no homework before, and among age groups for whom it will do the least good. Far from a situation of the straw breaking the camel's back, we see many unburdened camels taking on their first tiny handfuls of straw, and a number of others carrying little if any more than they did in the past. This is where the story of the debate over homework takes a major turn. While arguably some American children have been turned into walking delivery systems for wicked educators bent on upsetting the home life of innocent American families, this is clearly not true across the board. In fact, one might say that a good number of American children and teenagers are already deciding how much time they want to spend on homework, and the amount of work they've opted for is not exactly back-breaking.

The Brookings Institution recently weighed in on the homework debate on this very point, arguing that "almost everything in this story [of overworked students] is wrong." Like Hofferth and Sandburg, Tom Loveless, the Brookings author, points out that most of the increase noted in the University of Michigan study is concentrated among the youngest subjects who are reading earlier and being introduced to homework at a younger age. The most telling finding in the Brookings report, however, is that "the typical student, even in high school, does not spend more than an hour per day on homework." Needless to say, this picture is quite different from the homework situation described by Kralovec and Buell, to say nothing of the dire drama described over and over in newspaper and magazine stories.

THE NUMBERS

The 1997 University of Michigan time-use studies do report average increases for time spent on homework against a 1981 benchmark, but analysis by the Brookings Institution shows these increases are nearly negligible. The amount of time 3- to 5-year-olds spent studying increased from 25 minutes per week in 1981 to 36 minutes per week in 1997. This translates to an increase of two minutes a night if studying takes place five nights a week. The next group, 6- to 8-year-olds, as mentioned, saw the biggest increase, from 52 minutes a week to 2 hours and 8 minutes a week, which translates to an average increase of 15 minutes a night, bringing average homework time to a grand total of 25 minutes or so a night. The oldest group, 9- to 12-year-olds, saw only an increase of 19 minutes on average per week, an increase of less than four minutes a night. Other data culled by Brookings from the University of Michigan study show that over one-third of 9- to 12-year-olds reported doing no homework. Indeed, half of all 3- to 12-year-olds said that they were doing no homework whatsoever, despite data showing a small average increase in homework for this group.

Other research supports these findings. The National Assessment of Education Progress (NAEP) reports that a significant number of 9- and 13-year-olds are assigned no homework at all. Between 1984 and 1999, at least 26 percent and as much as 36 percent of 9-year-olds reported receiving no homework assignments the day before filling out the questionnaire. Among 13-year-olds, the numbers show a relatively large and increasing number of students assigned no homework: 17 percent in 1988, increasing to 24 percent in 1999. As for older students, the 1999 National Center for Education Statistics (NCES) reports that 12 percent of high school seniors said they were doing no homework during a typical week. Of the remaining 88 percent, most said they spent less than 5 hours a week doing homework. This, remember, is in high school, where teachers assign more work, students are expected to do more work, and homework is agreed to have the most benefits. And yet, the above NCES number tells us that most high school students who do homework spend less than an hour a day, five days a week, doing it. According to the NAEP, only about a third of 17-year-olds have more than one hour of homework a night.

What about examining the homework habits of students who go on to college, thus controlling for the downward pull of low performers in high school? In the national survey of college freshmen performed by the University of California at Los Angeles, a surprising number report having worked no more than one hour a night as high school seniors. In 1987, only 47 percent of college freshmen surveyed said they had done more than five hours of homework a week. By 2002, that number had fallen to 34 percent—meaning only about one-third of American college freshman said they'd spent more than one hour a night on homework as high school seniors. As the Brookings report comments, such a homework load makes American high schoolers look underworked compared with their peers in other developed nations.

PLEASED WITH OURSELVES

The evidence suggests that while a significant portion of students are not carrying an insupportable burden of homework, a small percentage of students work long hours indeed—and some of them not for any good reason. We are giving the wrong kind of homework and in increasing quantities to the wrong age groups. As the Brookings report notes, 5 percent of fourth graders have more than 2 hours of homework nightly. Whether such a figure is surprising or not may merely be a question of expectations, but it hardly seems reasonable to expect 9-year-olds to be capable of finishing such quantities of after-school work. Still, that a small percentage of students are unnecessarily overworked does not justify the national press coverage and research interest this story has generated.

Why the homework controversy has received the attention it has may result from our national preference for stories that make our children seem one and all to be high achievers. Also, it's no secret that many professional and upper-class parents will undertake extraordinary measures to help their children get ahead in school in order to get ahead in the real world: These children are sent to elite schools that liberally assign homework, even as they are signed up for any number of organized activities in the name of self-improvement. And, of course, this segment of the population does more than its share to direct and set the tone for press coverage of news issues of interest to families. That surely helps explain spectacular headlines like "The Homework Ate My Family" (*Time*), "Homework Doesn't Help" (*Newsweek*), and "Overbooked: Four Hours of Homework for a Third Grader" (*People*).

So, while the overworked American child exits, he is not typical. Strangely enough, he seems to be more of an American ideal—drawn from our Lake Woebegone tendency of imagining that we're so good and hard-working, we might be too good and too hard-working. Thus do we ask ourselves why Johnny is doing so much homework, when in fact he is not.

Mr. Skinner is assistant managing editor of the Weekly Standard. *From "The Homework Wars" by David Skinner,* The Public Interest, *Winter 2004, pages 49-60.*

From *The Public Interest,* No. 154 Winter 2004, pages 49-60. Copyright © 2004 by National Affairs, Inc. Reprinted with permission of the author and Public Interest.

Article 21

Studying Education

CLASSROOM RESEARCH AND CARGO CULTS

E. D. HIRSCH JR.

We really ought to look into theories that don't work, and science that isn't science. I think the educational... studies I mentioned are examples of what I would like to call cargo cult science. In the South Seas there is a cargo cult of people. During the war they saw airplanes with lots of good materials, and they want the same thing to happen now. So they've arranged to make things like runways, to put fires along the sides of the runways, to make a wooden hut for a man to sit in, with two wooden pieces on his head for headphones and bars of bamboo sticking out like antennas—he's the controller—and they wait for the airplanes to land. They're doing everything right. The form is perfect. It looks exactly the way it looked before. But it doesn't work. No airplanes land. So I call these things cargo cult science, because they follow all the apparent precepts and forms of scientific investigation, but they're missing something essential, because the planes don't land.

—Richard P. Feynman, "Cargo Cult Science,"
Surely You're Joking, Mr Feynman!: Adventures of a Curious Character (Norton, 1985).

After many years of educational research, it is disconcerting—and also deeply significant—that we have little dependable research guidance for school policy. We have useful statistics in the form of test scores that indicate the achievement level of children, schools, and districts. But we do not have causal analyses of these data that could reliably lead to significant improvement. Richard Feynman, in his comment on "cargo cult science," identifies part of the reason for this shortcoming—that while educational research sometimes adopts the outward form of science, it does not burrow to its essence. For Feynman, the essence of good science is doing whatever is necessary to get to reliable and usable knowledge—a goal not necessarily achieved by merely following the external forms of a "method."

The statistical methods of educational research have become highly sophisticated. But the quality of the statistical analysis is much higher than its practical utility. Despite the high claims being made for statistical techniques like regression analysis, or experimental techniques like random assignment of students into experimental and control groups, classroom-based research (as contrasted with laboratory research) has not been able to rid itself of uncontrolled influences called "noise" that have made it impossible to tease out the relative contributions of the various factors that have led to "statistically significant" results. This is a chief reason for the unreliability and fruitlessness of current classroom research. An uncertainty principle subsists at its heart. As a consequence, every partisan in the education wars is able to utter the words "research has shown" in support of almost any position. Thus "research" is invoked as a rhetorical weapon—its main current use.

In this essay I shall outline some fundamental reasons why educational research has not provided dependable guidance for policy, and suggest how to repair what it lacks. On a positive note, there already exists some reliable research on which educational policy could and should be based, found mainly (though not exclusively) in cognitive psychology. In the end, both naturalistic research and laboratory research in education have a duty to accompany their findings with plausible accounts of their actual implications for policy—as regards both the relative cost of the policy in money and time and the relative gain that may be expected from it in comparison with rival policies. Including this neglected dimension might wonderfully concentrate the research mind, and lead to better science in the high sense defined by Feynman.

A TALE OF TWO STUDIES

The November 2001 issue of *Scientific American* includes an article called "Does Class Size Matter?" about the policy consequences of research into the beneficial effects of smaller class size. The centerpiece of the article is the famous multimillion dollar star (Student/Teacher Achievement Ratio) study—considered to be a methodological model for educational research—which showed with exemplary technique that reducing class size will enhance equity and achievement in early grades.

But when California legislators dutifully spent $5 billion to reduce class size in early grades, the predicted significant effect did not result. Educational researchers, including the authors of the *Scientific American* article itself, complained that the California policy was implemented with "too little forethought and insight." Presumably this complaint implies that there are many factors that affect educational outcomes, and that we should not rely on a single one like class size. This after-the-fact criticism is valid. But if the California legislators had searched for useful "insight" in the star research they would have been disappointed. "Forethought and insight" cannot compensate for the deeper problem that *the process of, generalizing directly from classroom research is inherently unreliable.*

"WHOLE SCHOOL" PROGRAMS

Also in November 2001, there appeared an article in *Education Week* that summarized research into the multimillion dollar "whole-school reform" effort ("Whole School Projects Show Mixed Results"), According to the article, the researchers could not reliably discriminate between those programs that worked well and those that did not. The evaluators blamed the inconclusiveness of the results on uneven implementation of the various programs by the schools—an unhelpful observation. As a consequence, neither the expensive "whole-school" programs nor the expensive research into their effectiveness can usefully guide policy across the nation—which was a chief aim of the enterprise.

These are but two recent examples of the general inconclusiveness of educational research. The historical record—like these two particular studies—supports Feynman's contention that even when educational research follows the external forms of science, it misses the essence. It dutifully gathers complex data, and uses control groups and experimental groups, and it applies sophisticated statistical techniques. In rare cases, as in the star study, it follows the still more rigorous practice of purely random assignment of students to the experimental and control groups. But even after researchers have dutifully followed "all the apparent precepts and forms of scientific investigation," the planes don't land. The test score gaps between social classes do not narrow.

What is missing from this research? How, for example, might the star study have been made scientifically more solid, and ultimately more useful for the policymakers of California? These improvements would not have been achieved by using the now widely advocated technique of random assignment, since random assignment was in fact used. In fact, it was not the experimental structure of star but its intellectual structure that was deficient. This multimillion dollar study does not hazard a clear and detailed theoretical interpretation of its own findings. It does not, for example, answer such nitty-gritty questions as: What are the various causal factors that make smaller class size more effective for earlier grades than for later ones? Could there be alternative and even more reliable ways of achieving similar or higher student gains? Much of the literature I have read in connection with star quietly assumes that smaller class size is itself the causal agent. But even the more sophisticated interpretations of star which posit deeper causal factors do not systematically explore the following critical issue: Given the probable causes of student gain, are there even more effective and less costly ways of applying those causes and achieving the same or greater gains? If, for example, an important causal advantage of smaller class size is more interaction time between student and teacher, are there alternative, less expensive policies for achieving more interaction time and even greater student gains? These are the questions that a policymaker needs to have answered, and it is the duty of the informed researcher on the ground—not the beset legislator—to ponder and answer those questions.

Traditionally, scientific work is considered "good" if its results foster deeper theoretical understanding. One of the most disdainful remarks in the sciences is that a piece of work is "a-theoretical." It's true that in common parlance the word "theory" has an overtone of impracticality. Scientists, however, regard the formulation of theories about deep causal factors to be the motive force of scientific progress—a view that has rightly replaced an earlier just-the-facts conception of scientific advance. The star study is a first-rate illustration of the way in which the a theoretical tradition in education research hinders its utility. Wolfgang Pauli once remarked about a scientific paper: "It is not even wrong." That is exactly what can be said about the star study, and by extension many other classroom studies. Most of them are profoundly a-theoretical. They neither enable good policy inferences nor advance the research agenda. And they have other problems as well.

DIFFICULT AND UNDEPENDABLE RESEARCH

An apologetic argument heard in education schools is that educational research can never be as clean and decisive as controlled laboratory experiments because, on ethical grounds, one cannot treat children like rats in a maze. Admittedly, there is truth in this defense. Even the most carefully conducted school research must operate in circumstances that preclude certainty. Unfortunately, however, the limitations of classroom research eliminate not only certainty, but also the very possibility of scientific consensus—a very serious problem indeed.

If we take an example of the best educational research—say the Tennessee class-size experiment—and ponder why it fails to serve policymakers well, some very basic reasons present themselves. The star researchers were at pains not to interfere with anything in the school setting except class size. Had they manipulated other factors, they would have introduced unmanageable uncertainties into the analysis. They wanted to disclose what might be expected if the only policy change was the reduction of average class size from 24 to 15. Given such careful control and analysis, why was class-size reduction so much less effective in California than it seemed to be in Tennessee?

There's one immediate and self-evident answer: In some settings, class-size reduction helps an average .2 of a standard deviation; in other settings it helps only .075 of a standard deviation (neither effect being much to write home about).

CLASS SIZE

This simple restating of the results, while almost too obvious to mention, goes straight to the heart of one educational research problem: the fact that results cannot be generalized. Such research carries with it an implicit claim to reproducibility in other settings. Otherwise, why undertake it? But its multiplex character almost guarantees non-reproducibility. If just one factor such as class size is being analyzed, then its relative contribution to student outcomes (which might be co-dependent on many other real-world factors) may not be revealed by even the most careful analysis. On the other hand, if other classroom factors had been experimentally controlled at the same time, then it would be extremely hard if not impossible to determine—even by the most sophisticated means—just which of the experimental interventions caused or failed to cause which improvements. And if a whole host of factors are simultaneously evaluated as in "whole-school reform," it is not just difficult but, despite the claims made for regression analysis, impossible to determine relative causality with confidence.

In his essay on cargo cult science, Feynman described how one researcher managed with great persistence finally to obtain a reliable result in studying rats in a maze. Here is his description:

> There have been many experiments running rats through all kinds of mazes, and so, on—with little clear result. But in 1937 a man named Young did a very interesting one. He had a long corridor with doors all along one side where the rats came in, and doors along the other side where the food was. He wanted to see if he could train the rats to go in at the third door down from wherever he started them off. No. The rats went immediately to the door where the food had been the time before.
>
> The question was, how did the rats know, because the corridor was so beautifully built and so uniform, that this was the same door as before? Obviously there was something about the door that was different from the other doors. So he painted the doors very carefully, arranging the textures on the faces of the doors exactly the same. Still the rats could tell. Then he thought maybe the rats were smelling the food, so he used chemicals to change the smell after each run. Still the rats could tell. Then he realized the rats might be able to tell by seeing the lights and the arrangement in the laboratory like any commonsense person. So he covered the corridor, and still the rats could tell. He finally found that they could tell by the way the floor sounded when they ran over it. And he could only fix that by putting his corridor in sand. So he covered one after another of all possible clues and finally was able to fool the rats so that they had to learn to go in the third door. If he relaxed any of his conditions, the rats could tell.

As mentioned, given ethical constraints, the likelihood of conducting such a scientifically rigorous experiment on American schoolchildren would appear to be rather low.

CONTEXTUAL VARIABLES

There are other fundamental difficulties standing in the way of generalization from classroom research. Young children learn slowly. The cumulative effects of interventions are gradual, extending over years. Yet most educational research is conducted over spans measured in months rather than years, ensuring that effect sizes will tend to be small. These effects may be rendered almost invisible by another difficulty—the fact that the process of schooling is exceedingly context-dependent. Children's learning is deeply social, lending each classroom context a different dynamic. Moreover, learning is critically dependent on students' relevant prior knowledge. Neither of these contextual variables, the social and the cognitive, can be experimentally controlled in real-world classroom settings. The social context of schooling depends on unpredictable interactions between teachers and students, and among students themselves. And what students bring to a classroom depends not only on what they previously learned in school, but also—as is well established—on unpredictable knowledge they gained outside of school.

Detailed analyses of the contextual factors that influence learning are greatly to be desired, of course, but progress in understanding those contextual factors is unlikely to result from coarsegrained classroom studies. Progress is more likely to result from highly controlled "artificial" experiments that reveal the fine-grained underlying causes. It used to be thought that damp, low-lying air causes "swamp fever." (The other term for swamp fever, "malaria," means "bad air.") That theory of the cause of the disease was accepted by medical science as long as researchers stuck to coarse-grained observations which indicated that if you live in a swamp you are likely to get swamp fever from the bad air. It was not until the disease was put under the microscope that progress began to be made in determining the true causes and vectors of malaria. Medical science continues to advance as it becomes allied with ever more refined laboratory understandings. Its most striking and reliable advances have occurred since medicine became closely tied to biochemistry at a still more fine-grained level—the molecular. By analogy, it is plausible to think that progress in educational research, if it occurs at all, will follow this sort of pattern.

TEACHER QUALITY

Another hard-to-control contextual variable is, of course, teacher quality. One argument of this essay is that deep-lying principles of learning are more reliable than specific teaching methods, because a decision about which teaching methods will be most effective will depend on unpredictable contextual variables, with the result that the same underlying principle may require very different methods in different contexts. This means that the teacher's role as the on-the-spot translator of principles into methods is critical. But teacher training, though crucial, is not my subject here. Leaving aside the vexed and critical question of "teacher quality," the two other uncontrolled-for context variables that I mentioned—the social and the cognitive—are so important that their influences alone tend to drown out most experimental interventions. That will be true even when (as in star) the number of students being sampled is large enough to allow the hopeful assumption that the variables will cancel out. In those cases, the influence of contextual variables has been so great that the effect-sizes of most experimental interventions have been small.

The smallness of effect sizes has prompted disinterested scholars like H.J. Walberg, Barak Rosenshine, and Jeanne Chall to analyze whole masses of relevant studies on given educational topics to see if a reliable pattern emerges. These meta-studies are the most dependable sources of the meager insights that educational research has uncovered. But the end result of these painstaking analyses is that most conclusions still remain insecure, and still reflect the uncertainty and ambiguity of the underlying studies.

To summarize so far: Educational data are difficult to apply in a dependable way because of contextual variables that change from classroom to classroom and: from year to year, and that drown out the effects of single or multiple interventions. Clearly, therefore, one major assumption of educational research needs to be examined and modified—i.e., the assumption that data about what works in schools could be gathered from schools and then applied directly to improve schools.

CHANGING THE THOUGHT MODEL

Is there a way in which this inherent uncertainty principle in educational data can be diminished? Yes, by placing less reliance on traditional educational research that makes inferences from school data and applies those inferences directly back to schools.

Here is an example of traditional educational research in action from the government's educational database called eric:

ERIC NO: ED394125 TITLE: Vocabulary Teaching Strategies: Effects on Vocabulary Recognition and Comprehension at the First Grade Level. author: Peitz, Patricia; Vena, Patricia publication date: 1996

ABSTRACT: A study examined teaching methods for vocabulary at the first grade level. The study compared teaching vocabulary in context and teaching vocabulary in isolation. Subjects were 32 culturally diverse first-grade students from varying socio-economic backgrounds. The sample consisted of 14 boys and 18 girls, heterogeneously grouped. Two teacher-made tests were used, each consisting of 30 multiple choice items: Test a, to test vocabulary in isolation; and Test b, to test vocabulary in context. Target words for the tests were taken from the Dolch list, the Harris-Jacob list, and the reading material used in the classroom on a regular basis. Both tests were administered as pretests prior to instruction. After a 3-month period of instruction, Tests a and b were readministered as posttests to determine students' vocabulary growth. Results indicated that there was no significant difference in vocabulary acquisition by the sample. Results also indicated that, although there was vocabulary growth with both methods, the sample group's growth in vocabulary taught in isolation was greater than that of the vocabulary taught in context. Findings suggest that both methods of learning vocabulary will enable children to increase their vocabulary base and should be used. (Four tables of data are included; contains 37 references, 4 appendixes containing lists of vocabulary in context and in isolation, and related literature on vocabulary building.)

To paraphrase, there seems to be a slight benefit to teaching high-frequency vocabulary words in isolation rather than in context, but no significant difference in vocabulary growth as between the two methods. If the experiment had been made on a grander scale with thousands of students, random assignments, and a duration longer than three months, the data might have shifted in favor of teaching words in context. To repeat, however, it is unlikely that the results of a more massive experiment would supply dependable guidance. Again, we simply do not know enough about the uncontrolled factors at play in either sort of result to move confidently from research to policy.

But suppose a policymaker had to form a decision on how teachers should best achieve first-grade vocabulary enhancement (an extremely important issue). What decision should be made? Someone who read the work of cognitive scientists (rather than classroom reports) would find well-tested advice on how to teach vocabulary. They would find a consensus that, depending on the prior knowledge of students, both isolated and contextual methods need to be used—isolated instruction for certain high-frequency words students may not know or may not recognize by sight, like the prepositions "about," "under," "before," "behind," but carefully guided contextual instruction for other words. Teachers and administrators would learn that word meanings are acquired gradually over time through multiple exposures to whole systems of related words, and that the most effective type of contextual word study is an extended exposure to coherent subject matters.

WORD STUDY

This scientific consensus arose not just from classroom educational research but principally from laboratory studies and theoretical considerations unconnected to the classroom. One theoretical consideration, for instance, is that a top-of-the-class 17-year-old high-school graduate knows around 60,000 different words. That averages out to a learning rate of 11 new words a day from age two. Although this estimate varies in the literature from 8 to 18, its range implies by any reckoning a word-acquisition rate that cannot be achieved by studying words in isolation. There is notable cognitive research on the subject of vocabulary acquisition. Synthesis of this research is a more dependable guide to education policy than the data derived from classrooms.

If we follow this line of thought where it leads, we come to the conclusion that the most reliable guidance to what works in school is not to be found by looking at data from schools but rather by looking at inferences from the laboratory. ("By indirections find directions out.") Of course, these scientific inferences must prove themselves in the schools; they can't be permitted to produce worse educational outcomes than we had before. But because of the variability of the local contexts from which the school data is taken, the probability that an inference from school data is wrong is much greater than the probability that a scientific consensus is wrong.

Education-school proponents of "qualitative" research criticize quantitative research by taking note of the variability of classroom contexts, and claiming that all education, like all politics, is local. (They use the term "situated learning.") They pride themselves on following "ethnographic" methods, and taking into account the uniqueness of the classroom context. They rightly object that quantitative research tries to apply oranges to apples. But if their descriptions do not disclose something general that I could confidently apply to my own classroom, their studies are not very useful. And if their inferences did have general application, then the value of an "ethnographic" rather than a straightforward general description would lie in the literary vividness of a concrete example. But literary value is rarely claimed or observed in these productions.

Descriptive educational research suffers a fundamental shortcoming. To describe is to select what is important to describe out of an uncountable multitude of classroom happenings. How do I know that the chosen events are the ones that have made a difference? Overt behaviors like calling on shy students or building medieval castles out of milk cartons may or may not be the behaviors that have mainly caused one classroom to learn more about medieval castles than another. To be useful, even in the abstract, the descriptions would have to be selected on the basis of a prior theory about what is important to be described. This begs the research question. What is important to be described is what careful research should be trying to find out, not what it should be taking for granted. Although advocates of qualitative research are right to point out the unreliability of quantitative analyses like the star study, they need to apply a similar skepticism to their own efforts.

SCIENTIFIC THEORY

The reliability picture changes dramatically when we apply consensus science to education. Cognitive scientists have reached agreement, for example, about the chief ways in which vocabulary is acquired. This theory gained consensus because it explains data from many kinds of studies and a diversity of sources. While incomplete in causal detail, it explains more of what we know about vocabulary acquisition than does any other theory. When we apply it, we are no longer applying oranges to apples, but well-validated general principles to particular instances, in confidence that the principles will work when accommodated to the classroom or other context.

One might object that teachers should not have to think back to first principles every time they make lesson plans. Highly probable maxims that work most of the time (Francis Bacon called them "middle axioms") get us through the day. True enough, but for reasons I have already advanced, classroom research has been undependable in offering middle-level generalizations. Its maxims tend to be overgeneralized beyond their highly uncertain sphere of validity, so they are often inapplicable to particular circumstances. Teachers who were to read a different research report such as ERIC ED246392 or ED392012 would conclude they should favor the words-in-context approach.

Yet neither conclusion would be warranted. According to more general principles gleaned from cognitive science, it would be premature for teachers to follow either approach without further consideration. If students in a particular class already know and recognize by sight critical foundational words like "under," "over," "about," "beside," beneath," it wastes class time chiefly to use a words-in-isolation approach. This more general maxim is grounded not just in classroom research but in an interpretation of data from a diversity of domains.

Middle axioms are inherently probabilistic, and, in education, the probabilities change greatly in different circumstances. A teacher needs not just practical maxims but also underlying general principles that can guide their intelligent application. The wider public shows an understanding of this truth in the adage "teaching is an art, not a science." This is another way of saying that the variabilities of classrooms demand a flexible application of deep general principles, not a mechanical application of methods and maxims.

WHAT ARE "RELIABLE GENERAL PRINCIPLES"?

Fifty years ago, psychology was dominated by the guru principle. One declared an allegiance to B.F. Skinner and behaviorism, or to Piaget and stage theory, or to Vygotsky and social theory. Today, by contrast, a new generation of "cognitive scientists," while duly respectful of these important figures, have leavened their insights with further evidence (not least, thanks to new technology), and have been able to take a less speculative and guru-dominated approach. This is not to suggest that psychology has now reached the maturity and consensus level of solid-state physics. But it is now more reliable than it was, say, in the Thorndike era with its endless debates over "transfer of training."

To lend some credence to the proposition that general cognitive principles tend to be more dependable than maxims from direct classroom research, I shall now outline some issues in cognitive science about which a degree of consensus has been reached. Shrewd applications of these consensus principles would almost certainly enhance classroom learning, and ought also to encourage a shift in the way policymakers use educational data and research.

Prior knowledge as a prerequisite to effective learning. I have put this principle first, because so many other principles and policy implications flow from it. If "fortune favors the prepared mind," so does learning. One of the themes currently dominant in our education schools is that learning should be based on the mastery of formal habits of thinking rather than on "mere facts," that learning how to think is more important than mere accumulation of "factoids." The modicum of truth in this widely-held notion would appear to go something like this: After a student has reached a certain threshold of enabling knowledge, then acquiring a habit of critical thinking may be more valuable than acquiring a few more facts.

But it would be a profound mistake, uncountenanced by cognitive science, to suppose that skillful thinking can be mastered independently of broad subject-matter knowledge. The fallacy of derogating content is obvious in mathematics, where everyone concedes that skill and understanding in multiplication depend on a preparatory knowledge of addition. And the principle of preparatory knowledge applies not just to math, but to most other intellectual domains.

The research that offers the most dramatic evidence that relevant prior knowledge is critical to thinking skill is the area of expert-novice studies. The expert learns more from a given experience than a novice does, even though the novice has much more still to learn, That's because being presented with too many not-yet-interpreted items overloads and confuses the mind, whereas prior knowledge makes experience salient and meaningful (see "meaningfulness" below), and the expert need interpret less novelty than the non-expert.

Meaningfulness. A lot of learning is, of necessity, pretty meaningless. The connection between the sound and the sense of many words is entirely arbitrary. That the words "brother" or "sister" sound like they do is, for a child, just a brute fact that has to be learned. But, once the arbitrary sound-sense connection is learned, the meaningfulness of those words ensures that they will be remembered. Meaningfulness implies connectedness by experiential association (episodic memory), by schematic structure (semantic memory), or by emotional associations. In the expert-novice experiments, it is thought that prior knowledge enables the expert not only to connect the elements of an experience, but also to pick out what is meaningful and salient in it. Moreover, prior knowledge enables the expert to deduce more from the experience than the novice can. A novice looking at the outside of an Italian villa wouldn't understand that it has an unseen central courtyard; the expert, equipped with prior knowledge, would comprehend the unseen interior courtyard as well as the exterior walls.

The familiar distinction between "rote learning" and "meaningful learning" is thus well grounded—if understood liberally. But, since not all learning is inherently meaningful to a child (e.g. "sis-tuh," "bruh-thuh") one of the tasks of teaching is to make it so. A brilliant kindergarten teacher once described to me some tricks she used to teach children the names of the numbers. One trick was to bring in a pretzel, "Look, this is the shape of the number 8." She plopped it into her mouth. "Look, I ate it! I 8 it." It's hard to believe that this method of making "rote learning" meaningful, which incidentally invoked the children's prior knowledge of the verb "to eat," could have been easily forgotten by the children.

The right mix of generalization and example. Learning in school requires generalization. Nothing could be more abstract and general than arithmetic. But to acquire the concepts of addition, subtraction, multiplication, and division (or as Lewis Carroll would have it: "Ambition, Distraction, Uglification, and Derision"), you have to learn more than the abstract conceptions. You have to work with a lot of examples. No one advocates saying to first graders "ok, kids, this is the commutative law of addition. You memorize that—and never mind fiddling around with all those beans." The beans or their equivalent are absolutely essential.

CONTEXT AND EXAMPLE

The optimal mode for learning most subjects is through a carefully devised combination of the general concept and well-selected examples. This idea of teaching by both precept and example is so old—going back to the earliest literature in many cultures—that its confirmation in experiment is no surprise. Examples serve a number of functions that can't be retailed here. Researchers say that it's important to get the right mix and number of examples. If arithmetic exercises are too numerous and similar, time will be wasted. It is important to vary the angle of attack in examples, to illustrate different key aspects of the underlying concepts, and not to forget that explicit restatements of the general concept are equally important. The way we store these concepts is typically enmeshed with models or examples. One famous experiment showed that the concept "bird" is stored (by North Americans) as something about the size of a robin, not the size of a hummingbird or ostrich. Concept and example are deeply connected with one another in how we think and remember as well as how we learn.

Attention determines learning. Although "motivation" and "interest" are perennial themes of education, and important to any practicing teacher, it is sobering to discover from cognitive science that motivation is only an indirect and dispensable aid to learning. Intention to learn, whether internally imposed by intrinsic interest and ambition, or imposed from outside through rewards and punishments, may be sometimes a condition for learning, but it is not a necessary or sufficient condition. Some things that we involuntarily pay attention to are learned and remembered better than things we are trying to learn and remember. What is learned is that which is paid attention to, and, typically, what is paid attention to is what is learned.

Attention is an aspect of our "working memory," a function that lasts just a few seconds. Out of the whirr of perceptual features that impinge on working memory every instant, we attend only to a salient few. That few is very, very limited in number, even for the most brilliant minds. A famous article about the limited number of things we can attend to at one time was called 'The Magical Number Seven, Plus or Minus Two" (by G.A. Miller, first published in 1956). In some cases the limiting number is nearer to four. An expert with prior knowledge will be able to attend to many more things than a novice, not because of greater mental capacity, but because of "chunking." For an expert, noticing one thing is automatically to notice a myriad of things implied by it and known to be chunked with it, whereas the novice has to get through dozens of connections, which, because of the limitations of working memory, is impossible.

One chief aim of education is to enable the mind to transcend the narrow constraints of working memory by concentrating an immense wealth of individual elements into a single symbol or name that can be attended to all at once. This concentration effect is one of the marvels of language, and it illustrates the immense importance of imparting a sufficient vocabulary. As individuals and societies learn more, they form and learn new names for these large complexes of concepts and perceptions. By means of effective names and symbols, the vastness of what an ordinary school child can retain, use, and pay attention to in, say, mathematics, exceeds the capacity of the most learned doctors of fourteenth-century Oxford.

MEMORY

If the attended-to things are given meaning by A being connected with what we already know, we will learn (remember) them. If we do not attend to them and do not accommodate them to some known structure, we will usually not learn them. Although this finding is not surprising to common sense, it is a sobering reminder that we should not be overly distracted by the vast and unreliable literature on what will or will not properly motivate students—a debate that seems baffling to many teachers, since what motivates some students does not motivate others. A teacher's job is to ensure meaningful attention by as many students as possible towards that which is to be learned—using whatever methods may come to hand, including, above all, giving students the preparatory knowledge that will make attention meaningful.

Rehearsal (repetition) is usually necessary for retention. How long something will be remembered is typically determined by how often it has been attended to. Rehearsal has the double purpose of retention and making meaningful connections between experiences. There is evidence that the need for rehearsal has a physical basis in the neuron structure of the brain. The need for repetition to maintain what is learned has been well understood in every culture. We teach children little poems or songs so they can retain the letters of the alphabet or the days of the months. All this the world knows well, however contemporary slogans may disparage it.

The disagreeable need for rehearsal is called in the educational parlance "drill and kill." Good teachers try to find ways of making rehearsal less obviously painful, when that is possible. But effective learning depends on rehearsal by one means or by another. In the old argument between "natural development" and "practice makes perfect," it is the latter that has the support of cognitive science.

Some useful findings can make practice effective. It has long been known that massed practice is less effective than distributed practice. Cramming for an exam is less effective for long-term retention than keeping up with assignments as you go along. Frequent classroom testing of students (another disparaged method) is a very effective distributed-practice technique. To test students shortly after they learn something rehearses that knowledge. Moreover, students' awareness that a test is coming focuses their attention during original learning—giving classroom tests a double whammy for learning. A maximally effective mode of practice is to rehearse something just shortly before getting rusty, thus gradually extending the time span between rehearsals. So superior is distributed practice to massed practice that the cognitive scientist Ulrich Neisser was moved to poetry:

> You can get a good deal from rehearsal
> If it just has the proper dispersal.
> You would just be an ass
> To do it en masse:
> Your remembering would turn out much worsal.

Automaticity (through rehearsal) is essential to higher skills. Rehearsal serves other purposes beyond long-term retention and the constructing of meaningful connections. It also serves to make certain operations non-conscious and automatic. An obvious example is reading. The beginning reader must consciously correlate sound and symbol, and consciously move the eye from left to right, and consciously form the symbols into words. The beginning student does not have much "channel capacity" left for paying attention to what the words are saying. Since working memory can attend to just a few things at a time, the meaning of the sentence and even its component sounds are likely to spill into oblivion. As these underlying processes become more and more unconscious and automatic, the possibility grows for meaningful reading, and finally for thinking about the meaning. The processes do not become automatic just because children grow older, as the term "development" is often used to imply. Skills become automatic by being practiced.

What is true for reading is also true for other activities. Obvious examples come from sports; the more one has to think about all the motions required for hitting a tennis ball well, the less one is likely to do so. In sports no one doubts the need to gain automaticity. And it is no less true of other skills including academic ones. Automaticity frees up the working memory and allows it to concentrate on higher-order thinking.

Implicit instruction of beginners is usually less effective. A theme in the literature of American education research is that natural, real-world simulations (hands-on projects), in which the student gains knowledge implicitly, are superior to the artificial, step-by-step methods of traditional schooling. It is initially plausible that exposure to the complex realities of reading—the "whole language" method—would lead to more sophisticated reading skill than stumbling along step by step with the bricks and mortar of the alphabetic code. The more general question is this, however: Should students be immersed right away in complex situations that simulate real life—the method of implicit learning—or should they first be provided with explicit modes of instruction that are focused on small chunks deliberately isolated from the complexities of actual situations?

COGNITIVISTS

The answer one gets from cognitivists is complex. A teacher needs to engage in both implicit and explicit teaching. Because of the limitations of working memory, a step-by-step, explicit approach is good for beginners. A new tennis player has to be able to hold the racket and hit the ball over the net, and usually needs instruction in those sub-skills before going on to play a game. On the other hand, it's hard to see how one could gain knowledge of the ways subskills work together except in an actual game. Successful coaches provide guided practice in isolated subskills, and also in how to put them together in real-world simulations.

Since the resolution of the implicit-explicit debate is that teachers should use both, the main point of considering the issue here is that explicit learning has been subjected to widespread "research-based" condemnation in education schools. Hence the subject forms a good illustration of the contrast between educational research and cognitive research.

There's a dramatic experiment in the literature. At issue was the problem of how "to teach people to discern the sex of day-old chicks. The proto-sexual characteristics are extremely subtle and variable, and even after weeks of guidance from a mentor, trainees rarely attain a correctness rate of more than 80 per cent. Learning this skill has important financial implications for egg-producing farmers, and chick-sexing schools have been set up in Canada and California. The school training, which involves implicit learning from real-world live chicks, lasts from six to 12 weeks.

It occurred to two cognitive scientists familiar with the literature on implicit vs. explicit learning that these chick-sexing schools might present an experimental opportunity. They wondered if they could construct a more efficient learning program based on their knowledge of the literature. They decided to capitalize on the experience of a Mr. Carlson, who had spent 50 years sexing over 55 million chicks. From a set of 18 chick photographs representing the different types, Mr. Carlson was able to identify the range of critical features distinctive to each sex, and on the basis of his trait-analysis, a single-page instruction leaflet was created. Training was to consist in looking at this analytical leaflet for one minute.

To conduct the experiment, people without any chick-sexing experience were randomly divided into two groups, one of which looked at the leaflet. Thereafter, both groups were tested. Those who did not study the leaflet scored about 50 percent, that is, at the level of pure chance. Those who looked at the leaflet scored 84 percent, which was even better than the scores achieved by professional chick-sexers. Alan Baddeley, the distinguished psychologist from whose book this example was taken, interprets the experiment as "an extremely effective demonstration that . . . one minute of explicit learning can be more effective than a month of implicit learning."

CHICK-SEXING

Reading and other academic skills are, at least in some respects, analogous to chick-sexing. Mr. Carlson's 50 years of experience enabled him to isolate the proto-sexual traits of chicks into an analytical chart that could be learned in 60 seconds. This feat is analogous in its form to the achievement of ancient scholars in isolating the phonemic structure of speech into an alphabet of 26 letters. Their work, one of the great intellectual feats of human history, can now be recited or sung by a non-precocious preschooler by the age of four. Teachers and students can then be trained in the approximately 43 phonemes of English and their various correlations with the 26 alphabetic letters by using focused, analytical techniques. There is now ample evidence that carefully planned explicit instruction in phoneme-letter correlations is the fastest and surest way of empowering all beginners to decode alphabetic writing. In instances like these, explicit instruction with clearly defined goals is superior to implicit instruction and constitutes the most effective use of that precious commodity, school time.

Implicit rather than explicit learning is, as we have seen, the superior method for vocabulary growth, since word acquisition occurs over a very long period, and advances very, very gradually along a broad front. On the other hand, explicitly learning a few foundational words is much faster than implicitly learning them. It may be that explicit learning is best for a limited number of foundational elements, while implicit learning is best for advancing slowly on a broad front. It is not yet clear whether this division of labor between explicit and implicit learning applies to domains other than vocabulary growth, but even after that issue is sorted out, common sense will remain a valuable classroom commodity.

OF CONVERGENCE AND CONSENSUS

In recommending skepticism towards the findings of classroom research, I have at the same time counseled confidence in the findings of cognitive science as the more reliable guide to educational practice. Cognitive science, in contrast to school-based research, gathers data from many sources and explains why they converge on a consensus interpretation. I do not mean that cognitive research is always good or that educational research is always bad. The difference in the two fields is that, whereas classroom research, in the nature of the case, rarely converges on a consensus view, cognitive science has recently begun to do so.

The principle of independent convergence has always been the hallmark of dependable science. In the nineteenth century, for example, evidence from many directions converged on the germ theory of disease. Once policymakers accepted that consensus, hospital operating rooms, under penalty of being shut down, had to meet high standards of cleanliness. The case has been very different with schools. Educational policymakers, in the grip of their own strong sentiments of in thrall to the latest bulletins from the education research front, have authorized experimentation upon children on a vast scale, often under assumptions that conflict with the relevant scientific consensus.

What policymakers should demand from the research community is consensus. This has been achieved in some cases. Under the aegis of the National Institutes of Health, a high degree of consensus has been reached among both mainline psychologists and school-based researchers regarding effective modes of teaching early reading. This work is notable for having integrated both laboratory and classroom research and for having supplied theoretical accounts of the underlying causal processes at a detailed level.

Policymakers can further demand that laboratory researchers take the plunge that they have not yet taken and offer us theoretical extrapolations to classrooms. On the other side, policymakers can demand that classroom researchers take the extra effort and study needed to offer theoretical descriptions (de-

Morality has always been a concern of educators. There has possibly not been a more appropriate time to focus attention on ethics and on standards of principled conduct in our schools. The many changes in American family structures in past years make this an important public concern, especially in the United States. We are told that all nations share concern for their cherished values. In addition to discerning how best to deal with moral and ethical educational issues, there are also substantive value controversies regarding curriculum content, such as the dialogue over how to infuse multicultural values into school curricula. On the one hand, educators need to help students learn how to reason and how to determine what principles should guide them in making decisions in situations where their own well-being and/or the well-being of another is at stake. On the other hand, educators need to develop reasoned and fair standards for resolving the substantive value issues to be faced in dealing with questions about what should or should not be taught.

There is frustration and anger among some American youth, and we must address how educators can teach moral standards and ethical decision-making skills. This is no longer simply something desirable that we might do; it has become something that we *must* do. How it is to be done is the subject of a national dialogue that is now occurring.

Students need to develop a sense of genuine caring both for themselves and others. They need to learn alternatives to violence and human exploitation. Teachers need to be examples of responsible and caring persons who use reason and compassion in solving problems in school.

Some teachers voice their concerns that students need to develop a stronger sense of character that is rooted in a more defensible system of values. Other teachers express concerns that they cannot do everything and are hesitant to instruct on morality and values. Most believe that they must do something to help students become reasoning and ethical decision makers.

What teachers perceive to be worthwhile and defensible behavior informs our reflections on what we as educators should teach. We are conscious immediately of some of the values that affect our behavior, but we may not be as aware of what informs our preferences. Values that we hold without being conscious of them are referred to as tacit values—values derived indirectly after reasoned reflection on our thoughts about teaching and learning. Much of our knowledge about teaching is tacit knowledge, which we need to bring into conscious cognition by analyzing the concepts that drive our practice. We need to acknowledge how all our values inform and influence our thoughts about teaching.

Teachers need to help students develop within themselves a sense of critical social consciousness and a genuine concern for social justice. Insight into the nature of moral decision making should be taught in the context of real current and past social problems and should lead students to develop their own skills in social analysis relating to the ethical dilemmas of human beings.

There is a need for teachers to develop principles of professional practice that will enable them to respond reasonably to the many ethical dilemmas that they now face. Knowledge of how teachers derive their sense of professional ethics is developing; further study of how teachers' values shape their professional practice is very important. Schooling should not only transmit national and cultural heritages, including our intellectual heritage; it should also be a fundamentally moral enterprise in which students learn how to develop tenable moral standards in the contexts of their own world visions.

The controversy over teaching morality deals with more than the tensions between secular and religious interests in society. We argue that the construction of educational processes and the decisions about the substantive content of school curricula involve moral issues as well.

One of the most compelling responsibilities of schools is that of preparing young people for their moral duties as free citizens of free nations. Governments have always wanted schools to teach the principles of civic morality based on their respective constitutional traditions. Indeed when the public school movement began in the 1830s and 1840s, the concept of universal public schooling as a mechanism for instilling a sense of national identity and civic morality was supported. In every nation, school curricula have certain value preferences embedded in them.

For whom do the schools exist? Is a teacher's primary responsibility to his or her client, the student, or to the student's parents? Do secondary school students have the right to study and to inquire into subjects not in officially sanctioned curricula? What are the moral issues surrounding censorship of student reading material? What ethical questions are raised by arbitrarily withholding information regarding alternative viewpoints on controversial topics?

Teachers cannot hide all of their moral preferences. They can, however, learn to conduct just and open discussions of moral topics without succumbing to the temptation to indoctrinate students with their own views.

Teaching students to respect all people, to revere the sanctity of life, to uphold the right of every citizen to dissent, to believe in the equality of all people before the law, to cherish freedom to learn, and to respect the right of all people to their own convictions—these are principles of democracy and ideals worthy of being cherished. An understanding of the processes of ethical decision making is needed by the citizens of any free nation; thus, this process should be taught in a free nation's schools.

What part ought the schooling experience to play in the formation of such things as character, informed compassion, conscience, honor, and respect for self and others? The issue of public morality and the question of how best to educate to achieve responsible social behavior, individually and collectively, are matters of great significance today.

Article 22

Practicing Democracy in High School

In Massachusetts, Hudson High School has implemented reforms that build participatory democracy.

By Sheldon H. Berman

How can we engage students in meaningful learning and help them become effective citizens? Developing a strong academic program is crucial, but educators also need to create a school culture that welcomes all students, helps them learn to work together, and convinces them of their ability and responsibility to make the world a better place.

For the past 10 years, the Hudson Public School District has been working on two goals: bringing consistency, student-centered instruction, and high standards to our academic curriculum; and creating a school environment that nurtures students' social, emotional, ethical, and civic development.

To foster social-emotional learning and civic engagement, our K-12 social development program teaches social skills, creates a sense of community in the classroom, and gives students opportunities to use their knowledge to effect changes in their school and community.

For the elementary level, we use a social skills development curriculum called Second Step, which is produced by the Committee for Children. Our elementary and middle school teachers nurture positive classroom relationships through Responsive Classroom, a program developed by the Northeast Foundation for Children. For elementary and middle school classrooms, we have implemented conflict resolution and peer mediation programs developed by Educators for Social Responsibility. Service learning has become a natural extension of K-12 academic learning and serves as a solid base for building a sense of community.

These layered programs combine citizenship instruction in the academic curriculum with practicing citizenship in the classroom and school culture. Most of these programs, however, focus on the elementary and middle school level. We wanted to develop programs for the high school that would appropriately address adolescent development.

Fostering Responsibility

We began by creating a yearlong core course for the 9th grade that focuses on ethics and civic engagement. English and social studies teachers collaborate on examining an essential question: What is an individual's responsibility for creating a just society? Using the Facing History and Ourselves curriculum, students study the roots of the Holocaust and the Armenian Genocide. Our teachers have added a study of the genocide in Rwanda and U.S. treatment of Native Americans.

By asking how genocide can become state policy, the curriculum confronts students with the human potential for passivity, complicity, and destructiveness. It raises significant ethical questions and sensitizes students to injustice, inhumanity, suffering, and the abuse of power. This academically challenging curriculum helps students realize that complex problems do not have simple answers. Students confront their own potential for passivity and complicity, their prejudices and intolerance, and their moral commitments.

To expand students' sense of social responsibility, the course requires students to develop a service-learning project that helps foster a more just society. As a result, students begin to see that they are either part of the solution or part of the problem. There are no bystanders in one's moral life.

> Clustering enables students to enjoy the advantages of a small school and the curricular and extracurricular benefits of a larger school.

Building Community

Studies of social development show that creating a sense of community in classrooms and schools has a powerful impact on adolescents' social development. Resnick's study (1997) of factors that prevent at-risk behavior highlighted the importance of adolescents feeling connected to individuals at school and to the school as a whole. In a multiyear, social development program study, Schaps, Battistich, & Solomon (in press) found that the sense of community among students had a favorable impact on their conflict resolution skills, reading comprehension skills, reasoning about social

ANNUAL EDITIONS

Resource Organizations

- Character Education Partnership, 809 Franklin St., Alexandria, VA 22314; (800) 988-8081; www.character.org.
- Collaborative for the Advancement of Social and Emotional Learning, Dept. of Psychology (M/C 285), The University of Illinois at Chicago, 1007 W. Harrison St., Chicago, IL 60607-7137; (312) 413-1008; www.casel.org.
- Second Step, Committee for Children, 2203 Airport Way S., Ste. 5000, Seattle, WA 98134; (800) 634-4449; www.cfchildren.org/program_fss.shtml.
- National Center for Learning and Citizenship, Education Commission of the States, 707 17th St., Ste. 2700, Denver, CO 80202-3427; (303) 299-3629; www.ecs.org/html/ProjectsPartners/clc/clc_fmain.htm.
- Developmental Studies Center, 2000 Embarcadero, Ste. 305, Oakland, CA 94606; (800) 666-7270; www.devstu.org.
- Educators for Social Responsibility, 23 Garden St., Cambridge, MA 02138; (800) 370-2515; www.esrnational.org.
- Facing History and Ourselves Foundation, 16 Hurd Rd., Brookline, MA 02146; (617) 232-6919; www.facinghistory.org.
- Responsive Classroom, Northeast Foundation for Children, 71 Montague City Rd., Greenfield, MA 01301; (800) 360-6332; www.responsiveclassroom.org.
- Open Circle Social Competency Program, Stone Center, Wellesley College, 106 Central St., Wellesley, MA 02181-8268; (781) 283-2847; www.wellesley.edu/opencircle.

and moral issues, and interest in helping others. To enhance this connection to a community, we have moved to a semester-based block schedule, which gives students greater opportunity to work in depth and to build stronger relationships with their teachers.

We have also divided our 1,000-student high school into eight smaller communities. Data on effective high schools (Wasley, 2002) indicate that small schools outperform larger schools academically; experience fewer incidents of violent and disruptive behavior; and help students feel less anonymous and more willing to participate actively in school activities.

We started by creating an 8th and 9th grade middle school within the high school, with two teams for each grade. Each team includes approximately 110 students who take all of their core courses from cohesive, interdisciplinary teaching teams. The team identity brings a greater sense of community to these transition years.

In grades 10-12, in spring 2003, we created four groups, which we call *interest-based clusters*. To create a common bond among students in each cluster, we organized the clusters thematically around four broad areas of student interest: communications, media, and the arts; science, health, and the environment; technology, engineering, and business; and public policy, education, and social service. Using data from career-interest surveys, we organized the clusters into relatively equal and compatible groups.

To build a sense of community, we have scheduled an hour each week for cluster meetings in which students and faculty gather together to discuss school governance issues, plan cluster-based service projects, or hear school-to-career speakers. Each cluster includes approximately 130 students from all three upper grade levels. In contrast to the teams in the 8th and 9th grades, these students may take courses from any teacher in the school; however, because both students and teachers select their clusters on the basis of interest in a theme, most students will take a significant number of their classes from their cluster's teachers. This cluster model allows closer contact between teachers and students and fosters a more close-knit community. Clustering enables students to enjoy the advantages of a small school and the curricular and extracurricular benefits of a larger school.

The thematic organization does not restrict students' exploration of other careers or academic areas but instead offers students ways to delve more deeply into subjects with other similarly interested students. It also gives them service-learning and school-to-career experiences that support decision making about their future direction. Because students will remain in a cluster for three years, work on projects and issues together, and address differences of opinion through discussion, they will come to know a group of teachers and students well.

In the past, our service-learning program for the upper grades was centered in classrooms. Now, each cluster's students and teachers will be working together on more extensive and varied service-learning projects that relate to the cluster's theme. For example, the science, health, and environment cluster may develop a variety of short-term or multiyear environmental service projects, such as expanding the school's current conservation work on the nearby Assabet River or the schoolwide recycling program. The public policy, education, and social service cluster may work on issues of confronting prejudice and appreciating diversity, such as planning for and implementing a diversity awareness week for the entire school. By formulating these projects themselves and often continuing them for several years, students will experience greater depth and commitment in their service.

Building on our current school-to-work program, which includes extensive internships, job-shadowing opportunities, and workshops offered by local business partners, the clusters will further help students see relationships between coursework and the world outside school and offer school-to-career experiences to help them consider their future goals. Speakers and presentations, for example, will provide ideas about career opportunities or discussions of current social issues relevant to the cluster's theme.

Clusters will also allow the flexible formation of smaller groups and advisories to discuss such topics as college and career planning, conflict resolution skills, or world events that are of concern to students.

Democratic Governance

High school students' involvement in decision making is effective in fostering moral growth. *Just communities*—an approach to student self-governance proposed and developed by Kohlberg—offers students hands-on practice in democratic governance. In a study of just communities (Power, Higgins, & Kohlberg, 1989), small groups of approximately 100 students practiced democracy during weekly town meetings in which each person, including each adult, had one vote. In these meetings, students made decisions about the management, care, and direction of the school. Because the issues were meaningful to students and their decisions had direct consequences for the group, each student developed a personal sense of responsibility to the community and learned to argue issues with an increasingly sophisticated level of moral reasoning.

The typical high school curriculum and schedule, however, usually allow little time for student self-governance. Typical representative democracy in a high school—usually a student council—involves very few students. Those who serve are often the most active and popular—those who may be least in need of the experience of democratic engagement.

Knowing that active participation in a democratic community is the best way to foster tolerance, respectful dialogue, civic engagement, and moral responsibility among adolescents, we decided to build a participatory governance structure. We have designed our new high school, which opens in September 2003, with group spaces large enough for entire clusters to meet for discussions. The hour that our weekly schedule allocates will provide time for effective and participatory deliberation of issues.

Clusters will be the principal governance units in the school, providing opportunities for participatory, student-led, democratic governance. The governance meetings will replicate Kohlberg's concept of just communities. Students will select, discuss, and take action on topics of concern to them. Each cluster will meet as a whole group and in smaller groups to discuss school and cluster issues. They will make decisions about cluster activities and make proposals and policy recommendations for consideration by the entire school. Within each cluster and its smaller groups, student agenda committees with rotating memberships will decide on the cluster's program of activities. This regular participation in decision making will build commitment to the school and cluster. Sometimes the topics for discussion in clusters will be of particular interest to that cluster, but sometimes they will be topics of interest to all students in the school.

> To provide common bonds among students in each cluster, we organized the cluster thematically around four broad areas of student interest.

A typical four-week schedule for cluster meetings might include one week for flexible small-group governance meetings to discuss an issue; a second week for a whole-cluster governance meeting discussing the same issue; a third week for small-group work on service projects in classrooms; and a fourth week for a large-group meeting to hear a speaker.

Whole-School Discussions

For the past two years and prior to establishing the clusters this past spring, we piloted this governance concept, engaging the entire student body in small-group, student-led discussions of issues selected by students. The first whole-school dialogue focused on the question, "What can we do to improve the school?" An all-voluntary group of approximately 110 students facilitated the small-group dialogues and then compiled the list of issues of greatest concern to students. To prepare for facilitating these discussions, many of the student volunteers had undergone one-day training programs. So far, the school has participated in about a dozen whole-school discussions on a variety of topics.

The first issue raised by students was the quality and selection of food offered by our food service program. All students met in small groups to discuss areas of dissatisfaction and recommendations for improvement. After the discussions, students volunteered to work with our food service director to research available options and implement some of the students' ideas. The result has been a wider selection of sandwiches, soups, yogurts, and a salad bar. Students and faculty are continuing their research by visiting other schools' food service programs to make further recommendations for improving the organization of the food service.

Another topic selected by students was the lack of integration of students from other countries into the school culture. Approximately 15 percent of Hudson's high school students come from other countries, such as Brazil, Portugal, Mexico, and Guatemala. Student volunteers interested in the issue produced a video based on interviews about students' feelings of isolation within the school. Again in small groups, student facilitators showed the tape and led discussions on how to create a more inclusive school community. One of the results of this discussion was a program called *Friends*, in which students volunteer to buddy with students from other countries. The group of approximately 100 members has held a number of events—including a special luncheon at a local Brazilian restaurant—and has set up peer mentoring and regular group meetings.

As the school moved to a clustering governance structure, students were eager to discuss how the democratic clustering model would work. Some students were enthusiastic; others were wary. These whole-school conversations have been powerful vehicles for engaging students in practicing democracy and in formulating our governance policies. To lend authority to these discussions, the students and faculty have approved a constitution that includes a community council composed of teacher and student representatives from each cluster. This council replaces our traditional student council and votes on decisions that affect the entire school.

Our Future Citizens

Although we are still in the early stages of implementation, students and faculty are committed to this model for improving school culture, student motivation, teacher instruction, and civic engagement. Implementing democratic governance and small democratic groups in a large public school is not only doable; it brings public schools closer to their historic mission. These democratic clusters build rich relationships between faculty and students, a meaningful instructional program, a stimulating professional culture for staff, and a respectful and responsible student body. But most important, participating in a democratic community enables young people to enter the adult world with the skills, values, and commitment to actively participate in our civic community.

References

Power, C., Higgins, A., & Kohlberg, L. (1989). *Lawrence Kohlberg's approach to moral education.* New York: Columbia University Press.

Resnick, M., et al. (1997). Protecting adolescents from harm: Findings from the national longitudinal study on adolescents' health. *Journal of the American Medical Association, 278,* 823–832.

Schaps, E., Battistich, V., & Solomon, D. (in press). Community in school as key to student growth: Findings from the Child Development Project. In R. Weissberg, J. Zins, & H. Walberg (Eds.), *Building school success on social and emotional learning.* New York: Teachers College Press.

Wasley, P. (2002). Small classes, small schools: The time is now. *Educational Leadership, 59* (5), 6-10.

Sheldon H. Berman is Superintendent of the Hudson Public Schools, 155 Apsley St., Hudson, MA 01749; shelley@concord.org. Hudson High School is a First Amendment School in a project sponsored by ASCD and the First Amendment Center of the Freedom Forum.

From *Educational Leadership,* September 2003 pp. 35-38. Reprinted by permission of the Association for Supervision and Curriculum Development. Copyright © 2003 by ASCD. All rights reserved. The Association for Supervision and Curriculum Development is a worldwide community of educators advocating sound policies and sharing best practices to achieve the success of each learner. To learn more, visit ASCD at www.ascd.org

Article 23

Values: The Implicit Curriculum

A school's culture can help foster students' sense of personal and social responsibility.

Linda Inlay

Whether teachers intend to or not, they teach values. Teachers' behaviors are, in fact, moral practices that are deeply embedded in the day-to-day functioning of the classroom (Jackson, Boostrom, & Hansen, 1993). Likewise, a school's culture communicates values through the ways in which faculty, parents, and students treat one another and through school policies on such issues as discipline and decision making.

In his eight-year study of more than 1,000 classrooms, Goodlad found a "great hypocrisy" (1984, p. 241) in the differences between what schools espouse as values and what students experience. This disparity produces cynical students who don't take seriously what schools say about character (Postman & Weingartner, 1969).

A ropes course can teach students mutual trust and foster group cohesion.

At River School, a charter middle school of approximately 160 students, we work hard to develop an entire school culture that teaches character through the explicit curriculum of reading, writing, and arithmetic and through an implicit curriculum of values—what Adlerian psychologist Raymond Corsini called the implicit four *R*s: responsibility, respect, resourcefulness, and responsiveness (Adler, 1927/1992; Ignas & Corsini, 1979). My introduction to this school-wide approach to character education began 30 years ago when school director and Catholic nun Sr. Joan Madden, who was collaborating with Corsini in implementing what they called Individual Education, hired me as a teacher. She told me, "You are not teaching subjects. You are teaching who you are."

At River School, we rarely talk about character—nor do we have posters or pencils that trumpet values—because we know that the most effective character education is to model the values that we want to see in our students. We attempt to align every part of our school—from assessment to awards, from decision making to discipline—to encourage and foster students' character development. Our mission is to help students cultivate a strong sense of self through demonstrations of personal and social responsibility.

Fostering Personal Responsibility

We have barely spent a month in our school's new location when the fire alarm goes off. We have not yet established our safety protocols, and two of our students have pulled the fire alarm while horsing around, a typical middle school antic. Before I even get back to my office, the two students who pulled the alarm have voluntarily acknowledged the mistake that they made. They decide to "clean up their mistake" by apologizing to the affected people on campus, from the caretakers in the toddler program to the senior citizens in the Alzheimer's Center. One student voluntarily talks with the fire chief about her error. The mistake becomes an important lesson, as all mistakes should be.

These students are willing to be accountable for their actions. We view negative behavior as a sign of neediness, and we respond with positive contact, not just discipline of the behavior. Humans resist the diminution of spirit that comes with typical messages implying that they are "bad" or "wrong." These students have instead heard a call to responsibility:

> You made a mistake. To be human means making mistakes and learning from them.
>
> What do you think you should do to clean up this mistake?

Teachers focus on creating an atmosphere in which it is emotionally safe to make mistakes. We acknowledge when we have made a mistake and work hard not to get angry at students' mistakes. Within this emotionally safe terrain, we hold students accountable for their actions, allowing them to experience appropriate and natural consequences. Parents know, for example, that they are not responsible for bringing their children's forgotten homework to school.

The view of responsibility is the essential notion of our systems approach to character and relates to our underlying assumption about human beings. Humans are self-determining creatures; we have free will to make choices. Because of our ability to think, discern, and reflect, we want to make our own choices.

If humans have free will and the capacity to choose, then experiencing the consequences of "good" or "poor" choices is how humans learn to make choices. At the River School, we organize our school's curriculum and culture to provide many age-appropriate choices so that students learn, through trial and error, what works and what doesn't work for growing as independent learners and human beings.

The middle school years are about testing limits and shedding the old skin of the elementary school years, and we expect our students to cross boundaries as a way to learn about choice, consequences, freedom, and responsibility. Students say that they notice that our discipline system is different because we treat them like adults, even when they don't act like adults. We trust in our students' innate ability to make good decisions for themselves—with practice over time.

We define responsibility as an attitude that reflects a willingness to see oneself as cause, instead of victim. Students who see themselves as active rather than passive don't blame others. They see the mistake or the situation as the result of the choices that they have made. If the situation is out of their control, they see their responses to the situation as their own choice to be positive or to be negative.

This approach lessens extrinsic control, nurtures our students' intrinsic motivation to learn, and increases their self-confidence to meet and overcome challenges.

Fostering Social Responsibility

Self-determination is one side of human need; a sense of community and belonging is the other. Our vision of students developing fully as individuals cannot occur without the community being a safe place that accepts the different qualities of each individual. Particularly in middle school, we see students struggling to meet these two needs. They desperately want to belong, so they assume the external trappings and mannerisms of their peer group. At the same time, they try to break away from traditions and develop their individual identities.

To grow as individuals, students must believe that the school community accepts individual differences. One test of a school's effectiveness in teaching social responsibility is how well students treat those who are socially inept on the playground. Most of the time, our students respect one another. When they do not, the school community has opportunities to learn about making our school safe for everyone.

In preparation for the annual Thanksgiving feast, a student writes notes of appreciation on the placemats of each of her classmates.

Last year, for example, students were picking on a classmate who we suspected had a mild form of autism. With the student's consent, we devoted several team meetings to helping the school community understand why he sometimes stared at others or made odd noises. As a result of these conversations, students began to include him at lunch tables, lessened the teasing considerably, and defended him when teasing occasionally occurred. Such open conversations help each student become aware of how he or she makes a difference to every other student in school.

How do we teach *responsiveness,* this value of being responsible for one another? We begin with the recognition that we need to fulfill our students' needs for significance ("I matter") and for belonging (being part of a community) by structuring the school's culture so that we listen to students, take their concerns seriously, and depend on them.

We organize students into homeroom advisories in which the homeroom teacher is their advocate. The homeroom groups further divide into smaller "listening groups" that meet every other week with their teachers to share concerns and acknowledge successes. These meetings provide one of the ways in which we allow students to participate in solving problems in the school.

In one case, for example, someone was trashing the boys' bathroom. Student advisories discussed the problem, and one homeroom class volunteered to monitor the bathrooms throughout the day. Instead of the unspoken code of silence often practiced by middle schoolers, students reported the boy involved because they trusted that he would be treated with respect in the discipline process. In another case, students disliked some features of the dress code that had been developed by the student council and teachers. Students presented a proposal for changes at a staff meeting and did such an outstanding job of responding to the purposes of the dress code that the changes were approved.

We also take time to listen to students' ideas and questions as we develop the school's curriculum, modeling responsiveness by taking their concerns seriously. We follow the approach of the National Middle School Association (2002) to curriculum integration by asking students to develop their own questions for dealing with particular standards. The student question "What do you wish you could say but don't have the courage to say?" was the impetus for a unit last year that studied the First Amendment; various positions on evolution; and Galileo, Gandhi, Susan B. Anthony, and other figures who dared to take an unpopular stand.

> **Students who see themselves as active rather than passive don't blame others. They see the mistake or the situation as the result of the choices that they have made.**

If a student has problems with a teacher, he or she can call on a facilitator to mediate a conference. The purpose of a facilitating conference with a teacher is not to question his or her authority or to find out who is wrong and who is right. The goal of the conference is common understanding; the teacher works to understand the student's point of view and the student works to understand the teacher's point of view. Earlier this year, for example, a student felt picked on by his teacher and asked for a conference. Following the protocol of the facilitating conference, the teacher began with an "invitation" and asked, "What do you want to say to me?" After the student spoke, the teacher rephrased what the student said, and after the teacher spoke, the student rephrased what the teacher said. Through this active listening format, each came to a better understanding of the reasons for the other's behavior, and their relationship and classroom interactions improved.

We use this same conference format with students, faculty, and parents. Facilitators for conflicts are usually the advisors or the principal, with new teachers learning these communication skills primarily through observation and special training during faculty meetings. In some situations, students facilitate their own conflicts in listening groups, or they ask teachers to allow them time to do so. Last year, for example, two students began harassing each other on Halloween, when one laughed at the other's costume. When their conflict came to a head four months later, a facilitating conference helped them come to a resolution. They apologized to each other without being asked to and were friendly for the rest of the year.

Once understanding occurs, both sides can reach a solution together. Conflicts in the community become opportunities to learn how to deal with differences, to learn how to listen and solve problems. In this way, we empower our students to voice their beliefs and opinions more effectively. Whether expressing their beliefs and opinions about personal relationships, the dress code, or the First Amendment, students have to think through the logic and rationale of their position. This active engagement results in improved critical thinking skills, and the students develop a sense of responsibility for their community and their learning.

Students also learn that the community depends on them as they perform community chores, offer community service, and plan school meetings and events. When the school's environment meets students' needs for significance and belonging, students are more likely to cooperate with others and look toward the common good.

Throughout our school, the implicit message is clear: We deeply respect our students, not just because they are our students, but because all human beings have the right to be respected in these ways. The seminal ideas of our program are not new. We have simply translated them into practical, day-to-day applications embedded in the school setting so that the entire school's culture becomes our implicit curriculum. Everything that we do and say teaches character.

References

Adler, A. (1927/1992). (Trans. C. Brett.) *Understanding human nature.* Oxford, UK: One World Publications.

Goodlad, J. (1984). *A place called school.* New York: McGraw-Hill.

Ignas, E., & Corsini, R. J. (1979). *Alternative educational systems.* Itasca, IL: F. E. Peacock Publisher.

Jackson, P., Boostrom, R., & Hansen, D. (1993). *The moral life of schools.* San Francisco: Jossey-Bass.

National Middle School Association. (2002). NMSA position statement on curriculum integration [Online]. Available: www.nmsa.org/cnews/positionpapers/integrativecurriculum.htm

Postman, N., & Weingartner, C. (1969). *Teaching as a subversive activity.* New York: Delacourt Press.

Linda Inlay is Director of the River School, 2447 Old Sonoma Rd., Napa, CA 94558; linlay@nvusd.k12.ca.us.

//
THE MISSING VIRTUE

Lessons from dodge ball & Aristotle

Gordon Marino

Americans are inclined to ring the moral alarm and then hit the snooze button. After the latest moral crisis on Wall Street (I won't go into the sexual-abuse crisis), there were loud cries for more ethics classes. Not a bad idea, but if you are going to talk with students about ethics, which is something I do for a living, it helps to know where they are calling from. In the mid-sixties, Philip Rieff (*The Triumph of the Therapeutic*) apprized us of the fact that therapy had become the organizing motif in much of Western culture and, as a result, our understanding of moral character was shifting. Rieff was right. In the early eighties, the moral philosopher Alastair Macintyre (*After Virtue*) observed that for postmodern men and women, candor, rather than moral accountability, had become a cardinal virtue. Over the years, I have taken some soundings in my ethics classes and have been surprised to find that a cardinal virtue that everyone used to salute now evokes a shrug.

In *Nichomachean Ethics,* Aristotle invites us to think about the connection between moral character and happiness. He asks, Can you be happy and a cad? Definitely not. If that is the case, which moral virtues are essential to happiness? Before unveiling Aristotle's recipe, I press my students, "Which moral virtues do you believe are indispensable to the good life?" A hand shoots up; respect gets the first vote, then compassion, and this year, a sense of humor comes in the third. After a while, some of the more traditional virtues such as wisdom and justice are invited in. Honesty eventually makes it onto the blackboard without my prompts. Raising my voice and making a vee with my eyebrows, I nudge them, "Is there something missing?" Students look around puzzled, as if to say, OK, what's the trick?

"What about courage?" "Oh yeah, I guess so," is invariably the grudging response. Save for the two years that I taught at the Virginia Military Institute, I have never seen courage hit the top of the list. I hector my captive audience, "How can you be honest without courage? Truth telling, for example, only becomes difficult when there are unpleasant consequences for being honest." The sermonette continues, "And if you can't bear the consequences, you will be unwilling to tell the truth."

I close with an object lesson. Suppose it is the end of the spring semester and you did not hand your paper in for your ethics class. The professor believes that, in the interest of fairness, all students ought to have the same amount of time to work on their term papers and so has promised to dish out an F to anyone who does not hand the essay in on time. The deadline is fast approaching. You planned to write your term paper when you were on break in Cancún, but you never got around to it. You are a junior, planning to apply to medical school in the fall. No paper, and you are sure to get a D in the course and torpedo your chances for admission. Still, there is hope. While the professor may be a martinet, he is also a trusting soul. You could easily get a few extra days if you told him you were suffering from mononucleosis or that your grandmother died. What will it be? Truth and consequences or a white, maybe gray, lie?

My students at Saint Olaf College are as morally earnest as any I have ever taught, but there can be no denying that the death rates of grandparents rise here at semester's end as much as they do at other campuses. Unless he is even more afraid of getting caught in a lie, the student who cannot control his fears will start working up a short story on deadline day. Again, trying to give a boost to the ancient virtue, I pace dramatically and repeat, "You can't be an honest coward." Usually delivered in midsemester, this is one of my better half-time speeches. Students seem to walk out of class thinking (if only for a few hours) that courage is essential to the life they aspire to, and I shuffle out speculating on how courage could ever have become an afterthought.

Courage was touted as a keystone virtue in the post–World War II era in which I grew up. It was then common to hear stories about boys who would not be allowed back into their homes until they faced down some bully. Television, movies, and popular literature emphasized the signal importance of grace under pressure. The president was famous for having penned a Pulitzer Prize–winner called *Profiles in Courage*. A quick study of the "self help" literature of the nineteenth century also hints that our ancestors thought of courage as the bedrock of moral character. Again, what prompted the demotion of courage?

Prior to the war in Vietnam, the values of the military were widely respected and well represented in the larger culture. The qualities that were imagined necessary for good soldiering were incorporated into our notions of an ideal moral life. But as many Americans came to see the military as misguided and worse, a pall was cast over traditionally martial virtues, such as honor and courage. At best, the teaching elite now thinks of the military as a necessary evil and the virtues associated with the guardian class have become déclassé. (It will be interesting see how the military's reputation fares after the second Gulf War.) As the subconscious reasoning goes, courage is good for people intent upon combat but useless for less primitive, more pacific people.

Aristotle, however, taught that we acquire virtuous dispositions by practicing the actions that we want to be disposed toward. In accord with Aristotle, our moralists today rightly recommend diversity workshops as a means to develop a tolerant disposition. Yet in most of our lives there is very little opportunity for getting practice in coping with physical fear. Indeed, last year after much dispute, dodge ball was bounced out of many public schools. Those who defended the game argued that it helped develop mettle. Those who argued against it noted that some students found big red balls being hurled at their skulls traumatic. Guess who won the debate? And yet, the ramifications of regarding courage as a moral elective are potentially catastrophic, not only for our ability to tell the truth, but for our foreign policy as well. A nation of people who cannot tolerate feeling afraid might be unduly inclined to send their subcontracted military into actions that will quiet the sources of their fears. Courage by proxy is no courage at all.

Gordon Marino *is a philosophy professor and the director of the Hong Kierkegaard Library at Saint Olaf College in Northfield, Minnesota.*

From *Commonweal*, April 25, 2003, pp. 12-13. © 2003 by Commonweal Foundation. Reprinted by permission.

UNIT 5
Managing Life in Classrooms

Unit Selections

25. **Heading Off Disruptive Behavior**, Hill M. Walker, Elizabeth Ramsey, and Frank M. Gresham
26. **How Disruptive Students Escalate Hostility and Disorder—and How Teachers Can Avoid It**, Hill M. Walker, Elizabeth Ramsey, and Frank M. Gresham
27. **Good Behavior Needs to Be Taught: How a Social Skills Curriculum Works**, Hill M. Walker, Elizabeth Ramsey, and Frank M. Gresham
28. **True Blue**, M. Christine Mattise
29. **A Profile of Bullying**, Dan Olweus

Key Points to Consider

- Describe some of the myths associated with bullying behavior. How do you see the reality of bullying? What do you think school policy and teachers in particular can do to control bullying?

- Prepare your own roadmap of how you would create positive and productive approaches to the classroom instruction of middle-school-age children. Summarize your ideas about what features would lead to effective classroom management in a given school system.

Links: www.dushkin.com/online/
These sites are annotated in the World Wide Web pages.

Classroom Connect
http://www.classroom.com

Global SchoolNet Foundation
http://www.gsn.org

Teacher Talk Forum
http://education.indiana.edu/cas/tt/tthmpg.html

All teachers have concerns regarding the "quality of life" in classroom settings. All teachers and students want to feel safe and accepted when they are in school. There exists today a reliable, effective knowledge base on classroom management and the prevention of disorder in schools. This knowledge base has been developed from hundreds of studies of teacher/student interaction and student/student interaction that have been conducted in schools in North America and Europe. We speak of managing life in classrooms because we now know that there are many factors that go into building effective teacher/student and student/student relationships. The traditional term *discipline* is too narrow and refers primarily to teachers' reactions to undesired student behavior. We can better understand methods of managing student behavior when we look at the totality of what goes on in classrooms, with teachers' responses to student behavior as a part of that totality. Teachers have tremendous responsibility for the emotional climate that is set in a classroom. Whether students feel secure and safe and whether they want to learn depends on the psychological frame of mind of the teacher. Teachers must be able to manage their own selves first in order to effectively manage the development of a humane and caring classroom environment.

Teachers bare moral and ethical responsibilities for being witnesses to and examples of responsible social behavior in the classroom. There are many models of observing life in classrooms. Arranging the total physical environment of the room is a very important part of the teacher's planning for learning activities. Teachers need to expect from students the best work and behavior that they are capable of achieving. Respect and caring are attitudes that a teacher must communicate to receive them in return. Open lines of communication between teachers and students enhance the possibility for congenial, fair dialogical resolution of problems as they occur.

Developing a high level of task orientation among students and encouraging cooperative learning and shared task achievement will foster camaraderie and self-confidence among students. Shared decision making will build an *esprit de corps*, a sense of pride and confidence, which will feed on itself and blossom into high-quality performance. Good class morale, well managed, never hurts academic achievement. The importance of emphasizing quality, helping students to achieve levels of performance that they can feel proud of having attained, and encouraging positive dialogue among them leads them to take ownership in their individual educative efforts. When that happens, they literally empower themselves to do their best.

When teachers (and prospective teachers) discuss what concerns them about their roles (and prospective roles) in the classroom, the issue of discipline—how to manage student behavior—will usually rank near or at the top of their lists. A teacher needs a clear understanding of what kinds of learning environments are most appropriate for the subject matter and ages of the students. Any person who wants to teach must also want his or her students to learn, to acquire basic values of respect for others, and to become more effective citizens.

There is considerable debate among educators regarding certain approaches used in schools to achieve a form of order in classrooms that also develops respect for self and others. The dialogue about this point is spirited and informative. The bottom line for any effective and humane approach to discipline in the classroom, the necessary starting point, is the teacher's emotional balance and capacity for self-control. This precondition creates a further one—that the teacher wants to be in the classroom with his or her students in the first place. Unmotivated teachers cannot motivate students.

Helping young people learn the skills of self-control and motivation to become productive, contributing, and knowledgeable adult participants in society is one of the most important tasks that good teachers undertake. These are teachable and learnable skills; they do not relate to heredity or social conditions. They can be learned by any human being who wants to learn them and who is cognitively able to learn them. There is a large knowledge base on how teachers can help students learn self-control. All that is required is the willingness of teachers to learn these skills themselves and to teach them to their students. There are many sound techniques that new teachers can use to achieve success in managing students' classroom behavior, and they should not be afraid to ask colleagues questions and to develop peer support groups with whom they can work with confidence and trust.

Teachers' core ethical principles come into play when deciding what constitutes defensible and desirable standards of student conduct. Teachers need to realize that before they can control behavior, they must identify what student behaviors are desired in their classrooms. They need to reflect, as well, on the emotional tone and ethical principles implied by their own behaviors. To optimize their chances of achieving the classroom atmosphere that they wish, teachers must strive for emotional balance within themselves; they must learn to be accurate observers; and they must develop just, fair strategies of intervention to aid students in learning self-control and good behavior. A teacher should be a good model of courtesy, respect, tact, and discretion. Children learn by observing how other persons behave and not just by being told how they are to behave. There is no substitute for positive, assertive teacher interaction with students in class.

This unit addresses many of the topics covered in basic foundations courses. The selections shed light on classroom management issues, teacher leadership skills, and the rights and responsibilities of teachers and students. In addition, the articles can be discussed in foundations courses involving curricula and instruction. This unit falls between the units on moral education and equal opportunity because it can be directly related to either or both of them.

The differences between baseline and intervention groups were highly significant. The research concluded that the registered changes in bully/victim problems and related behavior patterns were likely to be a consequence of the intervention program and not of some other factor. Partial replications of the program in the United States, the United Kingdom, and Germany have resulted in similar, although somewhat weaker, results (Olweus & Limber, 1999; Smith & Sharp, 1994).

In 1997–1998, our study of 3,200 students from 30 Norwegian schools again registered clear improvements with regard to bully/victim problems in the schools with intervention programs. The effects were weaker than in the first project, with averages varying between 21 and 38 percent. Unlike the first study, however, the intervention program had been in place for only six months when we made the second measurement. In addition, we conducted the study during a particularly turbulent year in which Norway introduced a new national curriculum that made heavy demands of educators' time and resources.

Nonetheless, the intervention schools fared considerably better than the comparison schools. Surveys of the comparison schools, which had set up anti-bullying efforts according to their own plans, showed very small or no changes with regard to "being bullied" and a 35 percent increase for "bullying other students" (Olweus, in press). Because we have not yet analyzed the questionnaire information, we cannot fully explain this result, but it is consistent with findings from a number of studies showing that inexpert interventions intended to counteract delinquent and antisocial behavior often have unexpectedly negative effects (Dishion, McCord, & Poulin, 1999; Gottfredson, 1987; Lipsey, 1992).

> Most students in a classroom with bully/victim problems are involved in or affected by the problems.

In the most recent (1999–2000) evaluation of the Olweus Bullying Prevention Program among approximately 2,300 students from 10 schools—some of which had large percentages of students with immigrant backgrounds—we found an average reduction by around 40 percent with regard to "being bullied" and by about 50 percent for "bullying other students" (Olweus, in press).

The Need for Evidence-Based Intervention Programs

Coping with bully/victim problems has become an official school priority in many countries, and many have suggested ways to handle and prevent such problems. But because most proposals have either failed to document positive results or have never been subjected to systematic research evaluation, it is difficult to know which programs or measures actually work and which do not. What counts is how well the program works for students, not how much the adults using the program like it.

Recently, when a U.S. committee of experts used three essential criteria (Elliott, 1999) to systematically evaluate more than 500 programs ostensibly designed to prevent violence or other problem behaviors, only 11 of the programs (four of which are school-based) satisfied the specified criteria.[2] The U.S. Department of Justice's Office of Juvenile Justice and Delinquency Prevention and other sources are now providing financial support for the implementation of these evidence-based "Blueprint" programs in a number of sites.

In Norway, an officially appointed committee recently conducted a similar evaluation of 56 programs being used in Norway's schools to counteract and prevent problem behavior (Norwegian Ministry of Education, Research, and Church Affairs, 2000) and recommended without reservation only one program for further use. The Olweus Bullying Prevention Program is one of the 11 Blueprint programs and the program selected by the Norwegian committee.

Norway's New National Initiative Against Bullying

In late 2000, Norway's Department of Education and Research and Department of Children and Family Affairs decided to offer the Olweus Bullying Prevention Program on a large scale to Norwegian elementary and junior high schools over a period of several years. In building the organization for this national initiative, we have used a four-level train-the-trainer strategy of dissemination. At Norway's University of Bergen, the Olweus Group Against Bullying at the Research Center for Health Promotion trains and supervises specially selected *instructor candidates*, each of whom trains and supervises key persons from a number of schools. The key persons are then responsible for leading staff discussion groups at each participating school. These meetings typically focus on key components and themes of the program (Olweus, 1993, 2001b).

The training of the instructor candidates consists of 10–11 whole-day assemblies over 16 months. In between the whole-day meetings, the instructor candidates receive ongoing consultation from the Olweus Group by telephone or through e-mail.

In implementing this train-the-trainer model in the United States with financial support from the U.S. Department of Justice and the U.S. Department of Health and Human Services, we have made some modifications to accommodate cultural differences and practical constraints. In particular, we have reduced the number of

Figure 2
The Olweus Bullying Prevention Program

General Prerequisite

- Awareness and involvement of adults

Measures at the School Level

- Administration of the Olweus Bully/Victim Questionnaire (filled out anonymously by students)
- Formation of a Bullying Prevention Coordinating Committee
- Training of staff and time for discussion groups
- Effective supervision during recess and lunch periods

Measures at the Classroom Level

- Classroom and school rules about bullying
- Regular classroom meetings
- Meetings with students' parents

Measures at the Individual Level

- Individual meetings with students who bully
- Individual meetings with victims of bullying
- Meetings with parents of students involved
- Development of individual intervention plans

---

whole-day assemblies to four or five and have granted greater autonomy to individual schools' Bullying Prevention Coordinating Committees than is typical in Norway.

So far, 75 instructor candidates have participated in training, and more than 225 schools participate in the program. Recently, Norway's government substantially increased our funding to enable us to offer the program to more schools starting in 2003.

We see Norway's national initiative as a breakthrough for the systematic, long-term, and research-based work against bully/victim problems in schools. We hope to see similar developments in other countries.

Notes

1. More information about the Olweus Bullying Prevention Program is available at www.colorado.edu/cspv/blueprints/model/BPPmaterials.html or by contacting nobully@clemson.edu or olweus@psych.uib.no.
2. The four school-based programs are Life Skills Training, Promoting Alternative Thinking Strategies (PATHS), the Incredible Years, and the Olweus Bullying Prevention Program. For more information about the Blueprints for Violence Prevention's model programs, visit www.colorado.edu/cspv/blueprints/model/overview.html.

References

Dishion, T. J., McCord, J., & Poulin, F. (1999). When interventions harm: Peer groups and problem behavior. *American Psychologist, 54,* 755–764.

Elliott, D. S. (1999). Editor's introduction. In D. Olweus & S. Limber, *Blueprints for violence prevention: Bullying Prevention Program.* Boulder, CO: Institute of Behavioral Science.

Gottfredson, G. D. (1987). Peer group interventions to reduce the risk of delinquent behavior: A selective review and a new evaluation. *Criminology, 25,* 671–714.

Lipsey, M. W. (1992). Juvenile delinquency treatment: A meta-analytic inquiry into the variability of effects. In T. D. Cook, H. Cooper, D. S. Corday, H. Hartman, L. V. Hedges, R. J. Light, T. A. Louis, & F. Mosteller (Eds.), *Meta-analysis for explanation: A casebook* (pp. 83–125). New York: Russell Sage.

Nansel, T. R., Overpeck, M., Pilla, R. S., Ruan, W. J., Simons-Morton, B., & Scheidt, P. (2001). Bullying behaviors among U.S. youth: Prevalence and association with psychosocial adjustment. *Journal of the American Medical Association, 285,* 2094–2100.

Norwegian Ministry of Education, Research, and Church Affairs. (2000). *Rapport 2000: Vurdering av program og tiltak for å redusere problematferd og utvikle sosial kompetanse.* (Report 2000: Evaluation of programs and measures to reduce problem behavior and develop social competence.) Oslo, Norway: Author.

Olweus, D. (1973). *Hackkycklingar och översittare. Forskning om skolmobbing.* (Victims and bullies: Research on school bullying.) Stockholm: Almqvist & Wicksell.

Olweus, D. (1978). *Aggression in the schools: Bullies and whipping boys.* Washington, DC: Hemisphere Press (Wiley).

Olweus, D. (1983). *The Olweus Bully/Victim Questionnaire.* Mimeo. Bergen, Norway: Research Center for Health Promotion, University of Bergen.

Olweus, D. (1991). Bully/victim problems among schoolchildren: Basic facts and effects of a school-based intervention program. In D. Pepler & K. Rubin (Eds.), *The development and treatment of childhood aggression* (pp. 411–448). Hillsdale, NJ: Erlbaum.

Olweus, D. (1992). Bullying among schoolchildren: Intervention and prevention. In R. D. Peters, R. J. McMahon, & V. L. Quincy (Eds.), *Aggression and violence throughout the life span.* Newbury Park, CA: Sage.

Olweus, D. (1993). *Bullying at school: What we know and what we can do.* Cambridge, MA: Blackwell. (Available from AIDC, P.O. Box 20, Williston, VT 05495; (800) 216-2522)

Olweus, D. (1996). *The Revised Olweus Bully/Victim Questionnaire.* Mimeo. Bergen, Norway: Research Center for Health Promotion, University of Bergen.

Olweus, D. (1999). Norway. In P. K. Smith, Y. Morita, J. Junger-Tas, D. Olweus, R. Catalano, & P. Slee (Eds.), *The nature of school bullying: A cross-national perspective* (pp. 28–48). London: Routledge.

Olweus, D. (2001a). Peer harassment: A critical analysis and some important issues. In J. Juvonen & S. Graham (Eds.), *Peer harassment in school* (pp. 3–20). New York: Guilford Publications.

Olweus, D. (2001b). *Olweus' core program against bullying and anti-social behavior: A teacher handbook.* Bergen, Norway: Research Center for Health Promotion, University of Bergen.

Olweus, D. (2002). *Mobbing i skolen: Nye data om omfang og forandring over tid.* (Bullying at school: New data on prevalence and change over time.) Manuscript. Research Center for Health Promotion, University of Bergen, Bergen, Norway.

Olweus, D. (in press). Bullying at school: Prevalence estimation, a useful evaluation design, and a new national initiative in Norway. *Association for Child Psychology and Psychiatry Occasional Papers.*

Olweus, D., & Alsaker, F. D. (1991). Assessing change in a cohort longitudinal study with hierarchical data. In D. Magnusson, L. R. Berg-

IV. Effective Programs for Preventing Antisocial Behavior

In spite of huge advances in our knowledge of how to prevent and treat antisocial behavior in the past decade, the Surgeon General's Report on Youth Violence indicates that less than 10 percent of services delivered in schools and communities targeting antisocial behavior patterns are evidence-based (see Satcher, 2001). As these children move through schools without effective intervention services and supports, their problems are likely to become more intractable and ever more resistant to change. This is simply not necessary. Effective, manageable programs exist.

Effective programs require an upfront investment of time and energy, but they more than "pay for themselves" in terms of teaching time won back.

We highlight three promising interventions—Second Step, First Step to Success, and Multisystemic Therapy—as examples of, respectively, universal, selected, and indicated interventions. The coordinated implementation of these or similar programs can make a remarkable difference in the orderliness of schools and classrooms and in the lives of antisocial youth (not to mention the victims of their aggression).

Second Step, a social skills training program for K-9 students, is described in detail. It was recently rated as the number one program for ensuring school safety by a blue ribbon panel of the U.S. Department of Education. Evaluations of Second Step have found results ranging from decreases in aggression and disruption among 109 preschool and kindergarten children from low-income, urban homes (McMahon, 2000) to less hostility and need for adult supervision among over 1,000 second- to fifth-grade students (Frey, Nolen, Van Schoiack-Edstrom, and Hirschstein, 2001).

First Step, is an intensive intervention for highly aggressive K-3 students. Experimental studies with kindergartners have found great improvments in their overall classroom behavior and academic engagement, and substantial reductions in their aggression during implementation and over many years following the end of intervention (see Walker, Kavanagh, Stiller, Golly, Severson, and Feil, 1998; Epstein and Walker, 2002). Similarly, studies involving two sets of identical twins enrolled in regular kindergarten programs found that exposure to the program produced powerful behavior changes upon introduction of the intervention that were maintained throughout the program's implementation (Golly, Sprague, Walker, Beard, and Gorham, 2000). These types of positive effects have also been replicated by other investigators. The First Step program has been included in six national reviews of effective early interventions for addressing oppositional and/or aggressive behavior in school.

Multisystemic Therapy (MST) is a family-focused intervention conducted by a trained therapist. It is aimed at the most severely at-risk youth, those who have been or are about to be incarcerated, often for violent offenses. Very often, the student has already been assigned to an alternative education setting. The therapist teaches parents the skills they need to assist their antisocial child to function more effectively across a range of social contexts. Daily contact between the student and therapist is common in the early stages of MST and reduces to several times per week as the intervention progresses. Therapists periodically talk to teachers to find out about the children's behavior, attendance, and work habits. Most importantly, teachers need to let therapists know when they perceive incremental improvements in the children's behavior—the therapists use this information to guide their work with the families. According to the Blueprints for Violence Prevention Project, MST has been found to reduce long-term rates of being re-arrested by 25 to 70 percent, to greatly improve family functioning, and to lessen mental health problems (Blueprints, 2003). (To find out if MST is available in your area, visit) **www.mstservices.com**

As the research clearly shows, these three programs have the potential to prevent countless acts of aggression and positively influence both school and family functioning.

Disruptive student behavior will decrease and teaching time will increase, allowing all children to learn more. Office discipline referrals will decrease, freeing up school staff to address other school needs like supporting instruction. Effective programs do require an upfront investment of time and energy, but over the school year, and certainly over the school career, they more than "pay for themselves" in terms of teaching time won back.

An obvious subtext in the article has been that elementary schools—and especially K-3 teachers—must bear the burden of preventing antisocial behavior. This may come as a surprise since behavior problems seem so much more severe as children age. But if there's one uncontestable finding from the past 40 years of research on antisocial children, it's this: The longer students are allowed to be aggressive, defiant, and destructive, the more difficult it is to turn them around. While high schools can, and should, do what they can to help antisocial students control themselves, elementary schools can, and should, actually help antisocial children to become socially competent.

Hill M. Walker is founder and co-director of the Institute on Violence and Destructive Behavior at the University of Oregon, where he has been a professor since 1967. Walker has published hundreds of articles; in 1993 he received the Outstanding Research Award from the Council for Exceptional Children and in 2000 he became the only faculty member to receive the University of Oregon's Presidential Medal. Elizabeth Ramsey is a school counselor at Kopachuck Middle School in Gig Harbor, Wash., and a co-author of the Second Step program. Frank M. Gresham is distinguished professor and director of the School Psychology Program at the University of California-Riverside. He is co-author of the Social Skills Rating System and co-principal investigator for Project REACH. The Division of School Psychology in the American Psychological Association selected him for the Senior Scientist Award. Together, Walker, Ramsey, and Gresham wrote Antisocial Behavior in School: Evidence-Based Practices, on which this article is based.

References

Blueprints for Violence Prevention (2003). Multisystemic Therapy online at **www.colorado.edu/cspv/blueprints/model/programs/MST.html**

Burns, B. (2002). Reasons for hope for children and families: A perspective and overview. In B. Murns & K.K. Hoagwood (Eds.), *Community treatment for youth: Evidence-based interventions for severe emotional and behavioral disorders* (pp. 1–15). New York: Oxford University Press.

Caprara, G., Barbaranelli, C., Pastorelli, C., Brandura, A., & Zimbardo, P. (2000). Prosocial foundations of children's academic achievement. *Psychological Science, 11*(4), 302–306.

Catalano, R., Loeber, R., & McKinney, K. (1999). School and community interventions to prevent serious and violent offending. *Juvenile Justice Bulletin*. U.S. Department of Justice, Office of Juvenile Justice and Delinquency Prevention, Washington, D.C.

Eddy, J.M., Reid, J.B., & Curry, V. (2002). The etiology of youth antisocial behavior, delinquency and violence and a public health approach to prevention. In M.R. Shinn, H.M. Walker, & G. Stoner (Eds.), *Interventions for academic and behavior problems II: Preventive and remedial approaches*, (pp. 27–51). Bethesda, Md.: National Association for School Psychologists.

Epstein, M. & Walker, H. (2002). Special education: Best practices and First Step to Success. In B. Burns & K. Hoagwood (Eds.), *Community treatment for youth: Evidence-based intervention for severe emotional and behavioral disorders* (pp. 177–197). New York: Oxford University Press.

Frey, K.S., Nolan, S.B., Van Schoiack-Edstrom, L., and Hirschstein, M. (2001, June). "Second Step: Effects on Social Goals and Behavior." Paper presented at the annual meeting of the Society for Prevention Research, Washington, D.C.

Golly, A., Sprague, J., Walker, H.M., Beard, K., & Gorham, G. (2000). The First Step to Success program: An analysis of outcomes with identical twins across multiple baselines. *Behavioral Disorders, 25*(3), 170–182.

Gresham, F.M. (1991). Conceptualizing behavior disorders in terms of resistance to intervention. *School Psychology Review, 20*, 23–36.

Gresham, F.M., Lane, K., & Lambros, K. (2002). Children with conduct and hyperactivity attention problems: Identification, assessment and intervention. In K. Lane, F.M. Gresham, & T. O'Shaughnessy (Eds.), *Children with or at risk for emotional and behavioral disorders* (pp. 210–222). Boston: Allyn & Bacon.

Grossman, D., Neckerman, M., Koepsell, T., Ping-Yu Liu, Asher, K., Beland, K., Frey, K., & Rivara, F. (1997). Effectiveness of a violence prevention curriculum among children in elementary school: A randomized, control trial. *Journal of the American Medical Association, 277*(20), pp. 1605–1611.

Herrnstein, R. (1961). Relative and absolute strength of response as a function of frequency of reinforcement. *Journal of the Experimental Analysis of Behavior, 4*, 267–272.

Herrnstein, R. (1974). Formal properties of the matching law. *Journal of the Experimental Analysis of Behavior, 21*, 486–495.

Kauffman, J. (1999). How we prevent emotional and behavioral disorders. *Exceptional Children, 65*, 448–468.

Kazdin, A. (1993). Adolescent mental health: Prevention and treatment programs. *American Psychologist, 48*, 127–141.

Kellam, S., Rebok, G., Ialongo, N., & Mayer, L. (1994). The course and malleability of aggressive behavior from early first grade into middle school: Results of a developmental epidemiologically-based prevention trial. *Journal of Child Psychology and Psychiatry, 35*(2), 259–281.

Loeber, D. & Farrington, D. (2001). *Child delinquents: Development, intervention and service needs*. Thousand Oaks, Calif.: Sage.

Loeber, R., Dishion, T., & Patterson, G. (1984). Multiple-gating: A multistage assessment procedure for identifying youths at risk for delinquency. *Journal of Research in Crime and Delinquency, 21*, 7–32.

Loeber, R. & Farrington, D. (Eds.). (1998). *Serious and violent juvenile offenders: Risk factors and successful interventions*. Thousand Oaks, Calif.: Sage.

Loeber, R. & Farrington, D.P. (2001) *Serious and violent juvenile offenders: Risk factors and successful interventions*. Thousand Oaks, Calif.: Sage.

Mayer, G.R. & Sulzer-Azanoff, B. (2002). Interventions for vandalism and aggression. In M. Shinn, H. Walker, & G. Stoner (Eds.), *Interventions for academic and behavior problems II: Preventive and remedial approaches* (pp. 853–884). Bethesda, Md.: National Association of School Psychologists.

McMahon, S.D., et al. (2000). "Violence Prevention: Program Effects on Urban Preschool and Kindergarten Children." *Applied and Preventive Psychology, 9*, 271–281.

Patterson, G. (1982). *A social learning approach, Volume 3: Coercive family process*. Eugene, Ore.: Castalia.

Patterson, G.R., Reid, J.B., & Dishion, T.J. (1992). *Antisocial boys*. Eugene, Ore.: Castalia.

Reavis, H.K., Taylor, M., Jenson, W., Morgan, D., Andrews, D., & Fisher, S. (1996). *Best practices: Behavioral and educational strategies for teachers*. Longmont, Colo.: Sopris West.

Reid, J.B., Patterson, G.R., & Snyder, J.J. (Eds.). (2002). *Antisocial behavior in children and adolescents: A developmental analysis and the Oregon Model for Intervention*. Washington, D.C.: American Psychological Association.

Satcher, D. (2001). *Youth violence: A report of the Surgeon General*. Washington, D.C.: U.S. Public Health Service, U.S. Department of Health and Human Services.

Severson, H. & Walker, H. (2002). Proactive approaches for identifying children at risk for sociobehavioral problems. In K. Lane, F.M. Gresham, & T. O'Shaughnessy (Eds.), *Interventions for children with or at-risk for emotional and behavioral disorders*, pp. 33–53. Boston: Allyn & Bacon.

Snyder, J. (2002). Reinforcement and coercion mechanisms in the development of antisocial behavior: Peer relationships. In J. Reid, G. Patterson, & L. Snyder (Eds.), *Antisocial behavior in children and adolescents: A developmental analysis and model for intervention*, pp. 101–122. Washington, D.C.: American Psychological Association.

Snyder, J. & Stoolmiller, M. (2002). Reinforcement and coercive mechanisms in the development of antisocial behavior. The family. In J. Reid, G. Patterson, & J. Snyder (Eds.), *Antisocial behavior in children and adolescents: A developmental analysis and model for intervention* (pp. 65–100). Washington, D.C.: American Psychological Association.

Sugai, G. & Horner, R., & Gresham, F. (2002) Behaviorally effective school environments. In M. Shinn, H. Walker, & G. Stoner (Eds.). *Interventions for academic and behavior problems II: Preventive and remedial approaches* (pp. 315–350). Bethesda, Md.: National Association of School Psychologists.

Walker, H.M. (1995). *The acting-out child: Coping with classroom disruption*. Langmont, Colo.: Sopris West.

Walker, H.M., Horner, R.H., Sugai, G., Bullis M., Spraque, J.R., Bricker, D. & Kaufman, M.J. (1996). Integrated approaches to preventing antisocial behavior patterns among school-age children and youth. *Journal of Emotional and Behavioral Disorders, 4,* 193–256.

Walker, H., Kavanagh, K., Stiller, B., Golly, A., Severson, H., & Feil, E. (1997). *First Step to Success: An early intervention program for antisocial kindergartners,* Longmont, Colo.: Sopris West.

Walker, H., Kavanagh, K., Stiller, B., Golly, A., Severson, H., & Feil, E. (1998). First Step: An early intervention approach for preventing school antisocial behavior. *Journal of Emotional and Behavioral Disorders, 6*(2), 66–80.

Walker, H. & Severson, H. (1990). *Systematic screening for behavioral disorders.* Longmont, Colo.: Sopris West.

Walker, H.M., Nishioka, V., Zeller, R., Severson, H., & Feil, E. (2000). Causal factors and potential solutions for the persistent under-identification of students having emotional or behavioral disorders in the context of schooling. *Assessment for Effective Intervention, 26*(1) 29–40.

Wolf, M.M. (1978). Social validity: The case for subjective measurement, or how applied behavior analysis is finding its heart. *Journal of Applied Behavior Analysis, 11,* 203–214.

From *American Educator,* Winter 2003-2004, pp. 6, 8-21, 46. Copyright © 2003 by American Educator, the quarterly journal of the American Federation of Teachers, AFL-CIO. Reprinted by permission of the AFT and the author.

Article 26

How Disruptive Students Escalate Hostility and Disorder— and How Teachers Can Avoid It

Managing unruly behavior is one of the most difficult, frustrating, and even frightening parts of being a teacher. Intervening when children are young with evidence-based programs is the "Gold Standard" for preventing, or at least greatly reducing, disruptive behavior. Ideally, chronically disruptive students should be placed in high-quality alternative education settings where they can receive long-term, intensive interventions. Meanwhile, the reality is that teachers face such behavior regularly, especially from older students, and they need strategies they can start using today. In this article, our authors look closely at the moments before a volatile student becomes totally unmanageable and suggest how to defuse the situation.

With these high-need students, no behavior management strategy is going to work all of the time—but some are more effective than others. None of these strategies will turn an antisocial student into an angel, but they will give you a much better chance of completing your day's lessons.

—EDITORS

By Hill M. Walker, Elizabeth Ramsey, and Frank M. Gresham

A teacher, Ms. Smith, instructs her class to take out their reading books and begin writing definitions of key words for the story on pages 25-33. The class begins organizing for the assignment—except Mike, who sits sulking at his desk. Ms. Smith approaches Mike and the following exchange occurs:

Ms. Smith: "Mike, I told the class to get ready for the assignment, but you aren't. Is there something the matter?" (Mike ignores Ms. Smith's question and avoids eye contact with her.)

Ms. Smith: "Mike, I asked you a question, Now what's the problem here?"

Mike: "There ain't no problem here, except you! I don't want to do this dumb work. Leave me alone."

Ms. Smith (now angry): "If you're going to be in my class, you will have to do your work like everyone else. Also, when I speak to you, I expect an answer. I don't like your attitude and I will not tolerate it in my classroom. You better watch yourself or you'll be in the office." (This is not the first exchange of this type between Mike and Ms. Smith. Both carry residual anger from these prior episodes.)

Mike (laughs sarcastically): "Get off my case! I don't give a damn about you or this stupid class. Go ahead and write me up!"

Ms. Smith tells Mike to leave the room and report to the vice principal. Mike goes ballistic, calls the teacher an obscene name, and pounds the wall as he strides out of the room. He continues to curse loudly as he leaves the classroom. Ms. Smith writes up the incident as insubordination and submits her report to the principal's office.

* * *

Teachers, as well as parents and peers, are often inadvertently trapped in escalating, negative social interactions like the one above. These interactions are extremely disruptive to the learning environment and damaging to interpersonal relationships. Such behavior, if not brought under control, can also trigger a broader group of students to behave in disruptive ways.

Defiant, aggressive students like Mike (who are generally referred to with the clinical term "antisocial") are often highly agitated and bring to school a history of noncompliance with parents' instructions and commands (Walker, Colvin, and Ramsey, 1995). Their pattern of oppositional behavior can be triggered by seemingly innocuous requests and instructions given by teachers throughout the school day (Colvin and Sugai, 1989). At school, these students are perceived as touchy; often they "train" the social environment to handle them with kid gloves. This posturing behavior pattern allows them to escape or avoid many reasonable requests made by teachers, peers, and parents.

Inevitably, even the kid gloves fail to keep antisocial students calm and engaged in their schoolwork. What to do? In this article we review some of what are known to be the most—and least—effective teacher responses to these students' provocative behavior.

I. Ineffective Reactions to Bad Behavior

Having rarely been taught the best strategies for dealing with antisocial students, teachers typically try a number of techniques in a desperate attempt to control the students' behavior. Most of these techniques, unfortunately, are of limited effectiveness—some may even fuel the bad behaviors of concern. Examples of teacher strategies that can fuel and strengthen problem behaviors are reprimanding, arguing, escalating hostile interactions, and attempting to force compliance. These approaches are fruitless in dealing with antisocial students because they come to school well versed in the "science" of coercion, having had extensive practice at home. When teachers issue an instruction with which these students do not want to comply, they escalate their noncompliance to higher and higher intensity levels until the instruction is withdrawn. This is called the behavior escalation game and it is a game teachers cannot win and should not play (Walker, 1995).

Ironically, the teacher's direct effort to stop the student from engaging in acting-out behavior is the very thing that strengthens and maintains it.

Take a second look at the interaction between Ms. Smith and Mike, as it characterizes the behavior escalation game. This aversive process between the teacher and student occurs in thousands of classrooms daily, disrupting the classroom ecology and damaging teacher-student relationships. Teachers who respond "normally" to such situations (i.e., by engaging in the escalation), usually end up on the losing side of the confrontation. Walker (1995) has noted that this sort of escalating interaction progresses as follows:

1. The student is sitting in class in a highly agitated state, which may or may not be noticeable.
2. The teacher assigns a task or gives a direction to the student, either individually or to a group of which the student is a member.
3. The student refuses to engage in the requested task.
4. The teacher confronts the student about his or her refusal.
5. The student questions, argues with, and/or defies the teacher.
6. The teacher reprimands the student and demands compliance.
7. The student explodes and confronts the teacher, and the situation escalates out of control.

This scenario is played out in front of roughly 30 or more very interested observers (i.e., classmates). If the student "wins" the escalation game and forces the teacher to concede, then the teacher's ability to manage the classroom may be severely damaged. Other students may lose respect for the teacher and may resent the fact that a single student, rather than the teacher, can essentially control the classroom. In contrast, if the teacher "wins" and is successful in establishing his or her authority over the student, this victory is likely to be short-lived and prove to be very costly in the long run. The student may feel humiliated in front of his or her peers and will likely harbor feelings of long-term resentment toward the teacher. Typically, these students find ways to "get even" with the teacher. Thus, the teacher may "win the battle," but end up "losing the war."

To better understand why teachers' normal reactions to aggressive and defiant behavior are not highly effective, we'll begin by looking at three of the most common reactions: giving attention to the misbehavior, ignoring it, and escalating commands to the offender. Next, we'll offer strategies that teachers can use to avoid and escape hostile interactions with students. And lastly, we'll discuss the best way to deliver directions to antisocial students.

Giving Attention

Generally, teachers are very alike in their approaches to managing antisocial behavior. Most often, they respond in ways designed to persuade or encourage the acting-out child to stop disrupting the class and to behave more appropriately. But in fact, both the positive social attention from peers (e.g., laughing at the jokes that interrupt a lesson) and the negative social attention from teachers (e.g., telling the student to be quiet) function to fuel the inappropriate behavior—making it much more likely in the future. Ironically, the teacher's direct effort to stop the student from engaging in acting-out behavior is the very thing that strengthens and maintains it.

Teachers typically respond rapidly to an antisocial student's inappropriate behavior because it disrupts the classroom ecology and is highly aversive. Teachers' efforts to manage problem behaviors are almost always directed toward making the student stop the inappropriate behavior as soon as possible. But their success in accomplishing this goal varies considerably (see Walker, 1995).

The antisocial student learns that it is much easier and more efficient to obtain peer and teacher attention by engaging in disruptive, noncompliant behavior than by completing work, following classroom rules, and/or developing friendships with peers. The antisocial student acquires a repertoire of disruptive behaviors and adopts tactics that force teachers and peers to respond to these highly aversive behaviors, often in a negative way. Even though the teacher's social attention is often negative, critical, and disapproving, it still functions to maintain the problem behavior. Many acting-out students appear to thrive on the hostile confrontations they have with teachers; their ability to confront, irritate, and otherwise make life miserable for their teachers is rewarding.

Ignoring

Sometimes, teachers attempt to control the acting-out, disruptive behaviors of students by simply ignoring them. This strategy is based on the mistaken notion that the inappropriate behavior is maintained *exclusively* by teacher attention. This response is typically ineffective for at least three reasons. First, the attention students receive from peers (positive or negative) provides a huge amount of reinforcement for the student's bad behavior. So teachers who ignore behavior that is maintained primarily by peer social attention will have no impact.

Second, teachers understandably find it almost impossible to ignore seriously disruptive behavior for any length of time because antisocial students escalate their demands for attention. Theoretically, if all reinforcement (by teachers and peers) is continually withheld, then the behavior will eventually stop, but total extinction can take a very long time. In reality, teachers will eventually have to respond to highly escalating behaviors, which then reinforces and strengthens the escalation.

Third, in some cases the student does not use his behavior to gain attention, but to avoid academic tasks in the classroom. If the student's escalation is serving this function, then simply ignoring the problem behavior will not be an effective response.

Escalating Commands

One of the most common mistakes that teachers make in trying to control the inappropriate behavior of antisocial children is the use of escalating commands or reprimands. Examples include statements such as: "You will do what I say," "You won't talk to me that way," or "I told you to begin work now!" Sometimes, these techniques will result in a temporary reduction in inappropriate behavior; other times, they will produce no noticeable effect on behavior.

General Rules for Avoiding Escalation

Walker and Walker (1991) provided three general rules that will help teachers avoid becoming engaged in hostile interactions with students:

- *Do not initiate contact with a student when he or she appears to be agitated.* The teacher should wait until the student's agitated mood passes before initiating an interaction that involves an instruction. When a student is agitated, a teacher's directive is likely to be perceived as an aversive, provocative event, especially when it is delivered in the presence of other students. In certain situations, the teacher can inquire about the student's problem, but she should not pair the inquiry with a command at that time if at all possible.

- *Do not allow yourself to become "engaged" through a series of questions and answers initiated by an agitated student.* Once the teacher realizes that the student is asking questions just to be provocative or to delay working, the teacher should not respond to the student's questions or comments about the situation and, especially, should not argue with the student. If the student asks a question, the teacher should ignore it or simply restate what the student needs to do. The teacher should indicate that the question will be answered after the student does as instructed. If the student refuses, the teacher should leave him or her alone until the agitated state passes.

- *Do not attempt to force the student's hand.* If the student chooses not to comply, the teacher should not try to coerce him or her through such tactics as hovering and waiting, using social punishment (e.g., glaring, verbal reprimands, or social intimidation), or threatening future sanctions. The teacher should never touch, grab, or shake a student in any way—in this or other situations. If the situation calls for a consequence such as losing recess or taking a trip to the principal's office, the consequence should be applied promptly and with a minimum of verbalization. If the situation does not call for such action, the teacher should leave the student's presence and terminate the interaction.

Studies of classroom interactions have shown that teachers tend to fall into a pattern of paying extra attention to chronically disruptive children's bad behavior and very little attention to their good behavior (even though teachers do pay attention to the good behavior of nondisruptive children). Specifically, researchers have found that (1) interactions with generally disruptive students are more likely to be negative than positive; (2) the teacher is much more likely to reprimand the disruptive children's inappropriate behavior than to praise their appropriate behavior; and (3) disruptive children tend to monopolize the teacher's time (Mayer & Sulzer-Azaroff, 2002). Falling into a negative pattern of interacting is understandable given the children's aversive behavior. But it means that many opportunities to reinforce good behavior are lost. And, over time, disruptive children perceive that they are treated in a more critical way than others.

Clearly, hostile teacher-student interactions are frustrating for teachers who have to deal with antisocial students. Frequently, the harder the teacher tries to control the student's behavior, the less effective these efforts are. This process can be physically and emotionally draining. In the next section, we illustrate principles and procedures for managing student agitation. This information provides extremely valuable ammunition to teachers in avoiding, escaping from, and terminating angry interactions that often damage teacher-student relationships, waste teaching time, and threaten the teacher's ability to control the classroom.

II. Managing Hostile Interactions

What should teachers do to keep agitated students from erupting? The key strategy is for teachers to get out of these escalating interactions as quickly as possible. Of course, it is not always clear when students are in the agitated state that is a precursor to behavior escalation—teachers can get drawn into the early stages of behavioral escalation before they realize what is happening. But as soon as they realize that the student is agitated, teachers can use the following *avoidance* and *escape* strategies.

Avoidance

An important concept in dealing with escalating behavior cycles is to "pick your battles" and to know when to leave students alone. If an antisocial student does not immediately engage in an assignment, it is often best to wait and give him or her leeway (i.e., the benefit of the doubt). These students quite often engage in delaying tactics as a way of (1) provoking teachers (and parents), (2) engaging them in negative interactions, and (3) asserting their control and independence in certain situations.

The teacher who forces compliance with a direction in a rigid, prescribed timeframe will find that this strategy seldom produces a good result with antisocial students. Waiting for a reasonable period of time (and ignoring the student's passive noncompliance) is often a reasonable alternative to direct confrontation. Many times, the students will engage in the assigned task if left alone and given sufficient time. It is vital, however, that the teacher not reinforce students' delaying tactics by either reprimanding them or showing signs of irritation and disapproval. Such teacher behavior will fuel rather than deflate the students' bad behaviors; students often are reinforced by "getting a rise" out of the teacher.

If it is obvious that a student is not going to engage in the assigned task and seeks to wait the teacher out, the teacher will have to address the situation. In so doing, the teacher obviously does not want to communicate that the antisocial student does not have to play by the same rules as the rest of the class. In these cases, the teacher should approach the student quietly and inquire as to why he or she is not engaging in the assigned task. The teacher should speak in a low voice, remain calm, and try to keep the situation as private as possible. If the student begins to escalate by arguing or questioning, the teacher should *immediately* disengage and state something like the following: "If you need some time to yourself, go ahead and take it. You can sit quietly as long as you do not bother other students. Let me know if you need some help with the assignment or have questions."

The teacher should leave the student alone and allow him or her to deal with the situation without further assistance. In this way, it becomes the student's responsibility to cope with the situation. But the teacher should also make it abundantly clear that the student must complete the assigned task (either now or later) and that lost time will have to be made up. Neither the student nor his or her classmates should be left with the impression that delaying tactics will result in a reduction of assigned work. Walker (1995) suggests that teachers using this strategy ought to communicate the following to the student:

- The student can't take control of the situation by arguing with the teacher or asking provocative questions. As long as the teacher is willing to answer such questions or argue, the student, not the teacher, is in control of the situation. This is a trap that must be avoided *at all costs*. In most cases, it leads to a worsening situation.
- When the student is ready to work, the teacher will be there to provide any assistance and support required.
- The student will not be able to reduce the assigned work by showing signs of agitation, sulking, or using delaying tactics.
- The student will not be able to provoke or anger the teacher through verbal or physical means (e.g., being unresponsive, sulking, or arguing).

> By calibrating the nature and timing of directions, teachers can reduce the chances that the directions will be seen as provocative.

Escape

Inadvertently, teachers often find themselves in an escalating situation by simply answering questions, providing assistance, or clarifying instructions. As soon as a teacher realizes what the student is doing, she should escape the interaction and disengage with the student. A typical example of escaping is as follows:

Ms. Smith: "Mike, you had a question about the assignment?"

Mike: "I don't have a clue what you want me to do." (Ms. Smith repeats the directions given to the class for the assignment.)

Ms. Smith: "Does that help? Do you understand what I want you to do now?"

Mike: "I guess, but I'm not going to do it because it's too hard for me. You know I hate math!"

Ms. Smith (realizing she's about to get trapped): "Mike, I have explained the assignment to you. You know what you have to do and your job is to do it. If you want help, I'll give it to you. You have 15 minutes left to complete the assignment." (Ms. Smith disengages and walks away from Mike's desk. Mike sulks for a while and gradually becomes more and more agitated. He raises his hand and Ms. Smith approaches the desk.)

Ms. Smith: "Yes, Mike?"

Mike begins to hassle Ms. Smith about the assignment and how his parents think it is unreasonable. Ms. Smith says nothing to Mike in response and simply walks away. Mike goes ballistic, throws his math book across the room, and curses. Ms. Smith sends Mike to the principal's office on a discipline referral.

An interaction that ends with sending a student to the front office may not seem like a success. But escaping, no matter how the student reacts, is always a better bet than arguing with or reprimanding the student in an attempt to force compliance. Arguing or reasoning with Mike in his current emotional state would have gained nothing. In fact, it would have made the situation much worse. It is likely that Mike would have become extremely aggressive with the teacher had she issued escalating prompts and attempted to force Mike to comply. Escaping terminates the hostile interaction as quickly as possible, thereby doing minimal damage to the relationship between the teacher and the student and preserving teaching time.

Escaping is also a safe strategy. It is never a good idea to allow teacher-student interactions to escalate out of control, particularly when students are older, more mature, and physically stronger than many teachers. Juvenile courts frequently place adjudicated youth in schools without informing teachers and administrators of their backgrounds. These students often have histories of assault and have committed other serious crimes. As such, escalating social interactions with these students often carry considerable risks to teachers and peers.

Angry, escalating episodes that teachers must avoid or escape are almost always precipitated by teachers delivering directions. Antisocial children tend to perceive adult directives as provocations rather than reasonable requests and are masterful at resisting them. Note, however, that by calibrating the nature and timing of directions, teachers can reduce the chances that the directions will be seen as provocative. The following section reviews some critical issues related to teacher directives and provides guidelines for the delivery and use of this important technique for teaching and managing groups of students in the classroom and other settings.

III. Delivering Directions

Researchers have classified two major types of directions that adults give to children: alpha commands and beta commands (Williams and Forehand, 1984). Alpha commands involve clear, direct, and specific instructions to students without additional verbalizations, and they allow a reasonable period of time for a response. In contrast, beta commands are vague and/or contain multiple directives; either way, they do not provide a clear criterion for compliance or sufficient opportunity to comply. Beta commands also include excess verbalizations from the person issuing the command. As a result, the student receiving the beta command has no opportunity to comply and is often confused. From preschool through grade 12, alpha commands are associated with higher levels of compliance than beta commands. Beta commands should be avoided whenever possible.

The use of alpha commands has a long history in the military. Training in military leadership strongly emphasizes the use of clear, specific, and forceful commands to prevent misunderstanding and to increase compliance. The following are some examples of alpha commands:

> "Matt, I want you to pick up your room as soon as you finish dinner."

> "Luke, tell me what time you have to be at baseball practice today."

> "Merilee, go see the vice principal right now about yesterday's absence."

The following are some examples of beta commands:

> "Matt, your room is always such a mess! Why don't you clean it up instead of waiting for me to do it for you? I get so tired of always picking up after you!"

> "Lisa, stop talking to Laura unless you are discussing today's assignment. Besides, you are only supposed to be talking if you've finished all your work!"

> "Mike, it's time for you to get to work. So get to it and don't let me catch you loafing again or you'll have to stay in for recess!"

When students do not comply with commands (alpha or beta), it's natural for teachers to then make demands in an attempt to force compliance. But with antisocial students, demands have a good chance of resulting in defiance. Defiance can be explosive, sometimes violent, and, as has been noted, often highly damaging to the teacher-student relationship. Instead of giving in to the temptation to make demands, teachers should consider the following guidelines in giving commands to maximize their effectiveness and to manage the classroom more efficiently (Walker, 1995). The teacher should:

- Use only as many commands as needed in order to teach and manage the classroom effectively. Research has shown that rates of noncompliance increase as the number of commands increases (Walker, 1995).
- Try to limit the number of *terminating* commands given in favor of *initiating* commands. Terminating commands direct the student to stop doing something inappropriate (e.g., "Don, stop talking to Frank right now!"). Initiating commands direct the student to start doing something positive or productive (e.g., "Mike, read this passage out of your book aloud to the class").
- Give only one command at a time. If a series of separate tasks is involved, give distinct commands for each task.
- Be specific and direct. Get the student's attention, establish eye contact, and describe what is wanted in a firm voice using alpha command language that is easily understood.
- Allow a reasonable time (at least 10 seconds) for the student to respond.
- Do not repeat the command more than once if the student does not comply. Instead, use some other consequence or action (like in-class time-out for younger students or being sent to the principal's office for older students) to deal with the noncompliance in this situation.
- Give commands while standing next to the student instead of from a distance. This is particularly important with antisocial students.

Compliance with teacher instructions is typically a major problem with antisocial students and, on occasion, a problem with many students. It is a key source of conflict between teachers and students. The skilled use of avoidance, escape, and alpha commands will prevent many conflicts in the classroom, foster better relationships with antisocial students, and save a great deal of teaching time.

References

Colvin, G. & Sugai, G. (1989). *Managing escalating behavior.* Available from Behavior Associates, P.O. Box 5317, Eugene, OR 97405.

Mayer, G.R., & Sulzer-Azaroff, B. (2002). Interventions for vandalism and aggression. In M. Shinn, H. Walker, & G. Stoner (Eds.), *Interventions for academic and behavior problems II: Preventive and remedial approaches* (pp. 853-884). Bethesda, Md. National Association of School Psychologists.

Walker, H. & Walker, J. (1991). *Coping with noncompliance in the classroom: A positive approach for teachers.* Austin, Tex: Pro-Ed.

Walker, H.M. (1995) *The acting-out child: Coping with classroom disruption.* Longmont, Colo.: Sopris West.

Walker, H.M., Colvin, G., & Ramsey, E. (1995) *Antisocial behavior in school: Strategies and best practices.* Pacific Grove, Calif.: Brooks/Cole, Inc.

Williams, C. & Forehand, R. (1984). An examination of predictor variables for child compliance and noncompliance. *Journal of Abnormal Child Psychology, 12,* 491-504.

Hill M. Walker is co-director of the Institute on Violence and Destructive Behavior at the University of Oregon, where he has been a professor since 1967. Elizabeth Ramsey is a school counselor at Kopachuck Middle School in Gig Harbor, Wash. Frank M. Gresham is distinguished professor and director of the School Psychology Program at the University of California-Riverside. Together, Walker, Ramsey, and Gresham wrote *Antisocial Behavior in School: Evidence Based Practices*, on which this article is based.

From *American Educator,* Winter 2003/2004, pp. 22, 24-27, 47. Copyright © 2003 by American Educator, the quarterly journal of the American Federation of Teachers, AFL-CIO. Reprinted by permission of the AFT and the author.

Article 27

Good Behavior Needs To Be Taught
How a Social Skills Curriculum Works

Social skills training may sound at first like just another requirement to be piled onto teachers and crammed into precious teaching time—just another thing that parents, not teachers, should be doing. But school requires a unique set of social skills like sitting quietly, sharing, and discussing problems. Learning them can be difficult even for well-behaved children; for children from chaotic homes, such skills may never be learned without direct instruction, modeling, and practice. So social skills training benefits a wide range of students and can be a worthwhile investment even for schools with moderate or mild levels of student misbehavior. In just 30 minutes once or twice a week, teachers or counselors can deliver the training and avoid countless acts of bad behavior. In the long run, teaching time will be won back, not lost.

Hill M. Walker, Elizabeth Ramsey, and Frank M. Gresham

Cliff Heights Elementary School was nearly overwhelmed with bad behavior. It is located in a working-class neighborhood in Chicago, and serves approximately 800 students from low- and middle-income families. Violent behavior, including random acts of assault and vandalism and occasional drive-by shootings, characterize the daily life of this neighborhood.

Before the implementation of Second Step, Cliff Heights teachers and staff were frustrated with the number of students in their classrooms who had low academic skills and poor school adjustment records. Teachers had to spend most of their time dealing with bad behavior; there were playground fights almost every day, despite the new requirement that two classroom teachers supervise recess, in addition to the three regular playground supervisors. At the same time, a small, vocal group of parents was asking Cliff Heights to do something about the situation. They were very concerned about drugs, gangs, and the disrespectful behavior toward adults and property they saw in the school.

Cliff Heights was lucky to have Ms. Gilfrey, a fulltime counselor, who ran anger-management, social skills, and self-esteem groups for selected students. They seemed to be effective and were popular with teachers, parents, and students; however, only a small number of students in the school were being reached by each group. Clearly, another strategy was needed if the problems at Cliff Heights were to be adequately addressed.

Ms. Gilfrey, together with the principal, decided to devote an entire staff meeting to a problem-solving session focused on what the school could do to decrease students' aggressive, disruptive, and sometimes dangerous behavior. Teachers were concerned about Ms. Gilfrey's groups since they were held during class time and pulled out the very students who most needed academic instruction and support.

As an alternative to the groups, Ms. Gilfrey described Second Step, a social and emotional skills training program that can be used classwide or schoolwide from preschool through grade nine. It is a "universal" intervention that supports good behavior in all children, but most especially in marginal children who are on the brink of becoming antisocial. Second Step teaches the same skills at each grade level—empathy, impulse control, social problem solving, and emotion management—to reduce impulsive and aggressive behavior and to increase social competence. Lesson content varies according to grade level, but all students have opportunities for modeling, practice, and reinforcement of skills.

In addition to its easy-to-use curriculum, the program offers training for educators, program evaluation materials, parent education videos, and teachers' and administrators' guides that explain the underpinnings of the program and support implementation. Because the curriculum relies on the instructional skills most teachers already have, the recommended training consists of a one-day session for teachers—though teachers also have the option of using training videos and a discussion guide. (Schools or districts can also designate a Second Step coordinator who would participate in a three-day training and then be able to train new teachers as needed.) At each grade level, multimedia kits contain everything teachers will need—from songs and puppets for preschoolers to videos and overhead transparencies for adolescents. In elementary grades, the primary lesson format is an 11" x 17" photo lesson card. The photo illustrates a story that stimulates discussion and initiates role-playing exercises.

The Cliff Heights teachers were interested in the program but were hesitant to take on anything more. They already felt extremely stressed by the demands and pressures of increasing class sizes, the complex needs of their students, reduced resources, and the diversity of students' backgrounds and behavioral characteristics.

Ms. Gilfrey was determined to make a violence prevention program work at Cliff Heights. Too often, she had helped at-risk students make positive behavioral changes, only to watch them confront negative reactions from peers. Another recurring problem had been that, even when students were able to improve socially, the improvement tended to be restricted largely to her office (i.e., the training setting) and was reflected only in students' talk, and not in actual behavior. Getting students to behave well throughout the school day tended to be difficult and ephemeral.

Following the staff meeting, however, Ms. Gilfrey decided that schoolwide implementation would have to be put on hold. She decided to approach only the third-grade teachers to conduct a trial test of the program.

Ms. Gilfrey struck a deal with the third-grade teachers: She agreed to take primary responsibility for preparing and teaching the lessons if the classroom teachers would make 30 minutes of classtime available twice a week for a two-month period. The teachers were also asked to participate in all role-play activities included in the lessons. After two lessons, one third-grade teacher, Mr. Michaelson, decided he would teach the curriculum himself. There were modifications he wanted to make, including teaching the lessons at different times during the day. Ms. Gilfrey agreed and made herself available for support and assistance.

After one month of leading students through the curriculum and demonstrating how to teach it, Ms. Gilfrey asked the other teachers to teach the lessons themselves. She offered to stay in the classroom and help when necessary as the teachers assumed the responsibility for Second Step. Apparently, the third-grade teachers had spoken with Mr. Michaelson, who was quite pleased with the program, and he had encouraged them to take charge of teaching it. It quickly became clear that Ms. Gilfrey's presence was not needed to teach and manage Second Step successfully. The teachers were able to integrate Second Step instruction into their ongoing teaching activities and were able to review, practice, and reinforce the skills taught as students displayed them throughout the school day.

During this time, Ms. Gilfrey also trained all playground supervisors as well as the school principal. Her goal was for everyone (herself included) to help the third-graders practice the key social skills they were learning—especially when conflict arose. This was a smart move on Ms. Gilfrey's part: It is extremely important that each student be recognized and praised by teachers, counselors, playground supervisors, the principal, and school support staff for displaying these skills in natural school settings.

Within two months of Second Step's implementation, the principal observed a substantial decline in office referrals and the number of playground incidents reported to the front office—and support increased among the faculty for schoolwide implementation over the next few years. These results are consistent with the findings from formal evaluations of Second Step. In one such evaluation, trained observers recorded students' behavior in intervention and nonintervention classrooms and found that in Second Step classrooms, aggression decreased 29 percent from fall to spring—but in nonintervention classrooms, aggression went up 41 percent. At the same time, while positive and neutral behavior increased by 10 percent in Second Step classrooms, it increased by just one percent in nonintervention classrooms. The following fall, six months after the end of the Second Step intervention, students who had been exposed to Second Step were still better behaved (see Grossman et al, 1997).

Second Step is available nationwide through the Committee for Children. To learn more about it, visit www.cfchildren.org/program_ss.shtml. To request a free preview of the curricula, call 800-634-4449, ext. 200 or use the Web site's online request form.

From *American Educator*, Winter 2003/2004, pp. 16-17. Copyright © 2003 by American Educator, the quarterly journal of the American Federation of Teachers, AFL-CIO. Reprinted by permission of the AFT and the author.

True Blue

An American educator brings her anti-bullying program to South African schools.

by M. Christine Mattise, M.Ed.

Where could she be?

"She was sad and ran away," the children reported, "and now we can't find her!"

I was aware of the recess bell ringing loudly, the crunching of many small feet on the snow. The sounds faded away slowly as I herded the classes inside, until there was only silence.

A flicker of red behind a tree caught my eye—her small rubber boot. I found her sitting there, hugging her knees and whimpering.

Her body was fine—she had been missing for less than 15 minutes—but her spirit was shattered. We talked quietly about what had happened and, in a few minutes, she uncurled and we walked inside.

As the guidance counselor at an elementary school in a small New Hampshire town, I thought I had been dealing effectively with this bullying situation, in which several children had set their sights on this one girl.

Traditional interventions (small group, individual counseling, classroom guidance, parent conferences) were obviously having little or no effect. The bullies had stuck with their project relentlessly, using snide looks, vicious whispering and a systematic plan to totally isolate one child on the playground.

The victim had suffered obediently in silence, believing what the bullies said about her—that she was unattractive, slow to learn, had a weird laugh and that no one wanted to play with her or be her friend. How did she come to accept the negative self-images? Why did she abandon her own right to be free from fear on the playground?

These children had no language or context to understand why their hurtful behaviors were so painful and damaging.

That became my goal: I would create this absent language for children in schools. I called it "Hurt-Free Schools."

Little did I realize that educators on a distant continent were involved in a similar, even more desperate, search for this new language. Far away in a land of both great beauty and great pain, other schools were struggling to stop the damages caused by bullies.

My pledge to create a language of empowerment for children led me to South Africa, a country struggling to recover from a giant among all-time bullies, apartheid. Interestingly, my journey to South Africa began in Glasgow, Scotland, at a university conference where I presented my anti-bullying program. There, I engaged in a lively discussion with a South African educator that ended with my half-humorous, utterly sincere offer to come to South Africa to teach the Hurt-Free model. I've spent the past three summers doing just that.

It didn't matter whether the school was located in Nashua or Kwa-Zulu Natal, we were both looking for the same thing: a way to teach and empower all children to claim their universal right to live in emotional, social and physical safety within a climate of peace and mutual respect.

As my work evolved, I developed the basic foundation for my vision: the positive presence of a school community that promises to work together to weave a web of emotional, social and physical safety around every child.

Of all the elements of a Hurt-Free School, I believe the most vital concept is that it is child-friendly.

I constantly remind myself of the child curled in the snow, now grown. What strategies could have made a difference for her in that bullying situation? What tools could she have used to understand her rights and to get the help she needed?

I believe that every intervention designed to build a climate of safety in school must be easily understood, developmentally appropriate and, most important, give children real tools they can use on the playground.

I chose the rainbow to embody my child-friendly vision. The "Rainbow of Safety," as I call it, meets all of my criteria: universal and protective, honoring individuality and celebrating diversity.

The words of children say it all:

It's a rainbow that goes over the whole school. Everyone is under it; no one is left out.

Even when there's a really scary storm with thunder and lightning, it makes you feel good to know that you might get to see a rainbow when the rain stops.

I don't have to be afraid to tell a bully to stop on my own because I know that other kids will come over to help me.

I know how and when to ask for help from an adult if I don't feel safe.

THE COLOR OF SAFETY

The Rainbow of Safety uses four colors to help children process decisions about their behaviors in school.

It is important to set firm guidelines regarding the use of these colors.

Children need to be reminded that the colors stand for the decisions they make about what they say or do. Young children should be reassured that choices can be changed, turning mistakes and missed opportunities into better decisions in the future.

True Blue is the first color of our rainbow. This universal color of the sky represents the best of humankind: equity, respect, acceptance, kindness, responsibility and tolerance. True Blue is what we reach for under the Rainbow of Safety.

Again, my trip to South Africa reminded me of the universal message behind True Blue. Just as *life, liberty and the pursuit of happiness* have meaning to Americans, the word *ubuntu* has meaning to South Africans.

The Zulu word *ubuntu* describes our relationships to one another. Though difficult to define, *ubuntu* is, to me, the connection to one another that makes us uniquely human. To experience our humanity most fully, we must honor these bonds to one another, intertwining our journeys through life with mutual concern and respect.

The first time I used *ubuntu* to describe True Blue was in front of about 100 girls sitting cross-legged on the floor. The girls looked at each other, eye to eye, recognizing their mother tongue. It passed between them like a shock of electricity, leaving proud smiles and straightened shoulders.

I have adapted this word as one of the elements of the Rainbow of Safety in South Africa. *Ubuntu* in school means that we must work together if we want a safe school. If even one child is afraid to be hurt on the playground, our school is not a safe place.

When we are all watching for one another's safety, we know that:

- If you are hurt on the playground, someone will come over to see if you are all right.
- If you are alone, you are welcome to join in a game.
- If you are being teased by a bully, other children will come and tell the bully to stop.
- If you need help, ask an adult.

In real life, we know, adults struggle to reach True Blue behavior. How then can a child be expected to meet such lofty ideals?

The Rainbow of Safety uses the image of the traffic light (or robot in South Africa) to help children strive to be as Blue as possible. By using a universal image, like a real traffic light with cars approaching an intersection, children may look to the Rainbow's traffic light to guide them safely through their behavior decisions in school.

Growing Green is a comfortable, friendly color for most American children. It encourages them to act upon their best intentions, yet supports them if they fall short of their goals. Children are works in progress who must be given encouragement and as many successful experiences as possible.

Caution Yellow teaches children that thoughtless choices can take away others' rights and have significant impact on a school's level of safety. Children are urged to stop, think and make choices that turn Yellow behavior back to Green with words like:

I'm sorry.
I should not have said that.
I didn't mean to hurt you.
I'll try harder to pay more attention to your rights/feelings next time.

Yellow provides a concrete tool to help even the very young child grasp the subtle concepts behind social climate theory.

The Rainbow of Safety addresses the "spectator syndrome," which bullying depends upon for its ongoing survival. Choosing to look away, doing nothing or not seeking adult help when needed are unacceptable options in a Hurt-Free School. Children are taught that such choices jeopardize the safety of all and can turn Caution Yellow into Danger Red if better choices aren't made.

Danger Red hurts! It is never acceptable under the Rainbow of Safety. It differs from Yellow in that it represents a deliberate choice to hurt another person. Red behavior becomes bullying when it is hurtful, deliberate, repeated and continues even after the bully has been told to stop.

Our school now overflows with Rainbow of Safety language. Traffic lights are found in hallways and classrooms. Mini-traffic lights are on every student's desk, used in some cases as part of individual behavior contracts with teachers. Students use giant rainbow sunglasses, visors and teddy bears to role-play real-life behavior challenges.

If students are not listening attentively, the teacher stops and says quietly, "I will wait until your listening turns back to Green."

The morning announcements talk about True Blue with a behavior challenge such as: "Telling the truth is not as hard as it may seem. If you start to say something Yellow, stop and change it to Green."

The Rainbow of Safety offers a plan—indeed, a set of tools—to give schools the strategies they need to make every school day count for every child.

Rather than accept the hopelessness that keeps bullying alive, the Rainbow of Safety offers a neutral language that teaches all children to claim their rights to safety while respecting those of others.

So not only can you find that little girl curled up in the snow, but you can offer her tools to rejoin life, with safety and comfort, on the playground and in the classroom.

M. Christine Mattise, an elementary school guidance counselor in New Hampshire, has lectured extensively about bullying and violence-prevention character education in the U.S. and abroad. The author of several books, she can be reached through her websites: www.hurt-free-character.com or www.bullying-in-school.com.

From *Teaching Tolerance*, Spring 2004, pp. 18-21. Copyright © 2004 by Southern Poverty Law Center. Reprinted by permission.

A Profile of Bullying at School

Bullying and victimization are on the increase, extensive research shows. The attitudes and routines of relevant adults can exacerbate or curb students' aggression toward classmates.

Dan Olweus

Bullying among schoolchildren is a very old and well-known phenomenon. Although many educators are acquainted with the problem, researchers only began to study bullying systematically in the 1970s (Olweus, 1973, 1978) and focused primarily on schools in Scandinavia. In the 1980s and early 1990s, however, studies of bullying among schoolchildren began to attract wider attention in a number of other countries, including the United States.

What Is Bullying?

Systematic research on bullying requires rigorous criteria for classifying students as bullies or as victims (Olweus, 1996; Solberg & Olweus, in press). How do we know when a student is being bullied? One definition is that

> a student is being bullied or victimized when he or she is exposed, repeatedly and over time, to negative actions on the part of one or more other students. (Olweus, 1993, p. 9)

The person who intentionally inflicts, or attempts to inflict, injury or discomfort on someone else is engaging in *negative actions*, a term similar to the definition of *aggressive behavior* in the social sciences. People carry out negative actions through physical contact, with words, or in more indirect ways, such as making mean faces or gestures, spreading rumors, or intentionally excluding someone from a group.

Bullying also entails an *imbalance in strength* (or an *asymmetrical power relationship*), meaning that students exposed to negative actions have difficulty defending themselves. Much bullying is *proactive aggression*, that is, aggressive behavior that usually occurs without apparent provocation or threat on the part of the victim.

Some Basic Facts

In the 1980s, questionnaire surveys of more than 150,000 Scandinavian students found that approximately 15 percent of students ages 8–16 were involved in bully/victim problems with some regularity—either as bullies, victims, or both bully and victim (bully-victims) (Olweus, 1993). Approximately 9 percent of all students were victims, and 6–7 percent bullied other students regularly. In contrast to what is commonly believed, only a small proportion of the victims also engaged in bullying other students (17 percent of the victims or 1.6 percent of the total number of students).

In 2001, when my colleagues and I conducted a new large-scale survey of approximately 11,000 students from 54 elementary and junior high schools using the same questions that we used in 1983 (Olweus, 2002), we noted two disturbing trends. The percentage of victimized students had increased by approximately 50 percent from

FIGURE 1
The Bullying Circle
Students' Modes of Reaction/Roles in an Acute Bullying Situation

A — The Bully/Bullies
Start the bullying and take an active part

B — Followers, Henchmen
Take an active part but do not start the bullying

C — Supporters, Passive Bully/Bullies
Support the bullying but do not take an active part

D — Passive Supporters, Possible Bully/Bullies
Like the bullying but do not display open support

E — Disengaged Onlookers
Watch what happens but do not take a stand

F — Possible Defenders
Dislike the bullying and think they ought to help (but do not)

G — Defenders of the Victim
Dislike the bullying and help or try to help the victim

Y — The Victim
The one who is exposed

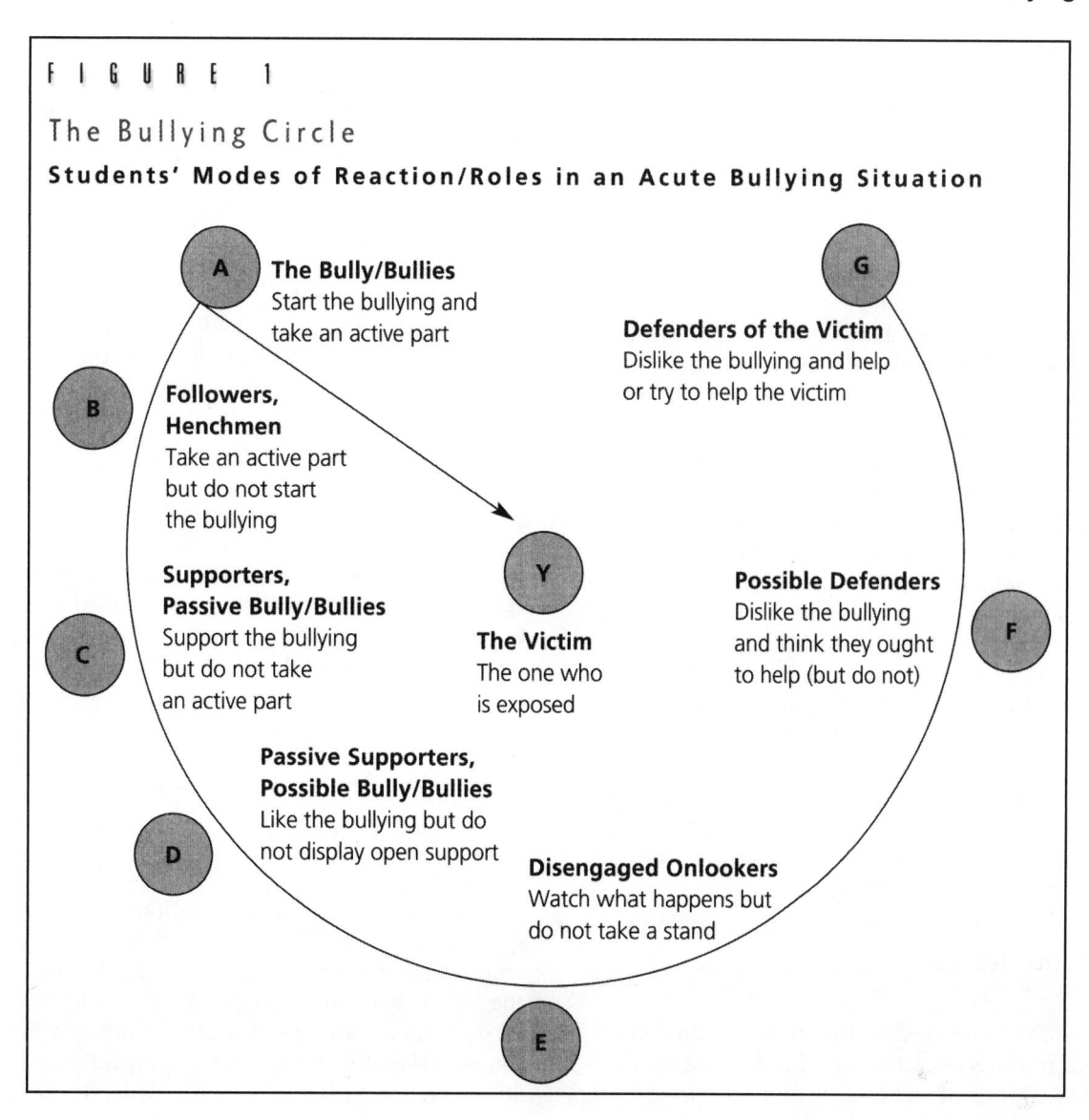

1983, and the percentage of students who were involved (as bullies, victims, or bully-victims) in frequent and serious bullying problems—occurring at least once a week—had increased by approximately 65 percent. We saw these increases as an indication of negative societal developments (Solberg & Olweus, in press).

The surveys showed that bullying is a serious problem affecting many students in Scandinavian schools. Data from other countries, including the United States (Nansel et al., 2001; Olweus & Limber, 1999; Perry, Kusel, & Perry, 1988)—and in large measure collected with my Bully/Victim Questionnaire (1983, 1996)—indicate that bullying problems exist outside Scandinavia with similar, or even higher, prevalence (Olweus & Limber, 1999; Smith et al., 1999). The prevalence figures from different countries or cultures, however, may not be directly comparable. Even though the questionnaire gives a detailed definition of bullying, the prevalence rates obtained may be affected by language differences, the students' familiarity with the concept of bullying, and the degree of public attention paid to the phenomenon.

Boys bully other students more often than girls do, and a relatively large percentage of girls—about 50 percent—report that they are bullied mainly by boys. A somewhat higher percentage of boys are victims of bullying, especially in the junior high school grades. But bullying certainly occurs among girls as well. Physical bullying is less common among girls, who typically use more subtle and indirect means of harassment, such as intentionally excluding someone from the group, spreading rumors, and manipulating friendship relations. Such forms of bullying can certainly be as harmful and distressing as more direct and open forms of harassment. Our research data (Olweus, 1993), however, clearly contradict the view that girls are the most frequent and worst bullies, a view suggested by such recent books as *Queen Bees and Wannabes* (Wiseman, 2002) and *Odd Girl Out* (Simmons, 2002).

Common Myths About Bullying

Several common assumptions about the causes of bullying receive little or no support when confronted with empirical data. These misconceptions include the hypotheses that bullying is a consequence of large class or school size, competition for grades and failure in school, or poor self-esteem and insecurity. Many also believe erroneously that students who are overweight, wear glasses, have a different ethnic origin, or speak with an unusual dialect are particularly likely to become victims of bullying.

All of these hypotheses have thus far failed to receive clear support from empirical data. Accordingly, we must look for other factors to find the key origins of bullying problems. The accumulated research evidence indicates that personality characteristics or typical reaction patterns, in combination with physical strength or weakness in the case of boys, are important in the development of bullying problems in individual students. At the same time, environmental factors, such as the attitudes, behavior, and routines of relevant adults—in particular, teachers and principals—play a crucial role in determining the extent to which bullying problems will manifest themselves in a larger unit, such as a classroom or school. Thus, we must pursue analyses of the main causes of bully/victim problems on at least two different levels: individual and environmental.

Victims and the Bullying Circle

Much research has focused on the characteristics and family backgrounds of victims and bullies. We have identified two kinds of victims, the more common being the *passive* or *submissive victim*, who represents some 80–85 percent of all victims. Less research information is available about *provocative victims*, also called *bully-victims* or *aggressive victims*, whose behavior may elicit negative reactions from a large part of the class. The dynamics of a classroom with a provocative victim are different from those of a classroom with a submissive victim (Olweus, 1978, 1993).

Bullies and victims naturally occupy key positions in the configuration of bully/victim problems in a classroom, but other students also play important roles and display different attitudes and reactions toward an acute bullying situation. Figure 1 outlines the "Bullying Circle" and represents the various ways in which most students in a classroom with bully/victim problems are involved in or affected by them (Olweus, 2001a, 2001b).

The Olweus Bullying Prevention Program

The Olweus Bullying Prevention Program,[1] developed and evaluated over a period of almost 20 years (Olweus, 1993, 1999), builds on four key principles derived chiefly from research on the development and identification of problem behaviors, especially aggressive behavior. These principles involve creating a school—and ideally, also a home—environment characterized by

- Warmth, positive interest, and involvement from adults;
- Firm limits on unacceptable behavior;
- Consistent application of nonpunitive, nonphysical sanctions for unacceptable behavior or violations of rules; and
- Adults who act as authorities and positive role models.

We have translated these principles into a number of specific measures to be used at the school, classroom, and individual levels (Olweus, 1993, 2001b). Figure 2 lists the set of core components that our statistical analyses and experience with the program have shown are particularly important in any implementation of the program.

> Our research data clearly contradict the view that girls are the most frequent and worst bullies.

The program's implementation relies mainly on the existing social environment. Teachers, administrators, students, and parents all play major roles in carrying out the program and in restructuring the social environment. One possible reason for this intervention program's effectiveness is that it changes the opportunity and reward structures for bullying behavior, which results in fewer opportunities and rewards for bullying (Olweus, 1992).

Research-Based Evaluations

The first evaluation of the effects of the Olweus Bullying Prevention Program involved data from approximately 2,500 students in 42 elementary and junior high schools in Bergen, Norway, and followed students for two and one-half years, from 1983 to 1985 (Olweus, 1991, in press; Olweus & Alsaker, 1991). The findings were significant:

- Marked reductions—by 50 percent or more—in bully/victim problems for the period studied, measuring after 8 and 20 months of intervention.
- Clear reductions in general anti-social behavior, such as vandalism, fighting, pilfering, drunkenness, and truancy.
- Marked improvement in the social climate of the classes and an increase in student satisfaction with school life.

quired in order to successfully bring about behavior change: (1) a consistently enforced schoolwide behavior code, (2) social-skills training, (3) appropriately-delivered adult praise for positive behavior, (4) reinforcement contingencies and response costs, and (5) time-out (see Wolf, 1978). Each of these techniques is briefly explained below.

Over the past three decades, an extensive body of research has developed on the effectiveness of these techniques for preventing and remediating problem behavior within the context of schools. Studies of the use of these techniques show that positive strategies (appropriate praise, social-skills training, providing free-time privileges or activities) are generally sufficient for developing and maintaining the appropriate behavior of most students. However, students with challenging behavior often also require sanctions of some type (e.g. time-out or loss of privileges) in order to successfully address their problems. Extensive research clearly shows that, to be most effective, intervention programs or regimens incorporating these techniques should be applied across multiple settings (classrooms, hallways, playgrounds, etc.), operate for a sufficient time period for them to work, and should involve teachers and parents in school-home partnerships whenever possible.

No single technique applied in isolation will have an enduring impact. Used together, however, they are effective—especially for antisocial students age 8 or younger. Assembling these techniques into feasible and effective daily routines can be done by individual teachers in well-run schools. But it is difficult, time-consuming, and fraught with trial and error. Among the fruits of the past several decades of research on this topic is a group of carefully developed and tested programs that integrate these techniques into entirely doable programs that don't overly distract teachers from their main job: teaching. Several are briefly described in this and the following section.

1. A Well-Enforced Schoolwide Behavior Code

A schoolwide behavior code creates a positive school climate by clearly communicating and enforcing a set of behavioral standards. The code should consist of 5 to 7 rules—and it's essential to carefully define and provide examples of each rule. Ideally, school administrators, teachers, related services staff, students, and parents should all be involved in the development of the code. But writing the code is just the first step. Too often, teachers and others complain, a behavior code is established—and left to wither. To be effective, students must be instructed in what it means, have opportunities to practice following the rules, have incentives for adhering to it (as described in the third and fourth techniques below), and know that violating it brings consequences.

One excellent, inexpensive program for teaching the schoolwide behavior expectations reflected in a code is called Effective Behavior Support (EBS). The principal features of EBS are that all staff (administrative, classroom, lunchroom, playground, school bus, custodial, etc.) recognize and abide by the same set of behavioral expectations for all students. The behavior expectations are explicitly taught to students and they are taught in each relevant venue. In groups of 30 to 45, students are taken to various parts of the school (e.g., the bus loading zone, cafeteria, main hallway, gym, and classrooms) to discuss specific examples of behaviors that would, and would not, meet the behavior expectations. Once they have learned the expectations, they are motivated to meet them by earning rewards and praise for their good behavior.

2. Social Skills Training

As discussed earlier, many antisocial students enter school without adequate knowledge of—or experience with—appropriate social skills. These skills must be taught, practiced, and reinforced. This is the purpose of social skills training. Skills taught include empathy, anger management, and problem solving. They are taught using standard instructional techniques and practiced so that students not only learn new skills, but also begin using them throughout the school day and at home. While the training is vital for antisocial students, all students benefit from improving their social skills—especially students "on the margin" of antisocial behavior. Social skills curricula are typically taught in one or two periods a week over the course of several months and in multiple grades.

3. Adult Praise

Adult praise (from teachers, parents, or others) is a form of focused attention that communicates approval and positive regard. It is an abundantly available, natural resource that is greatly underutilized. Researchers have found that teachers do tend to praise their regular students for good behavior, but they tend not to seize opportunities to praise antisocial students when they are behaving well (Mayer & Sulzer-Azaroff, 2002). This is indeed unfortunate because praise that is behavior specific and delivered in a positive and genuine fashion is one of our most effective tools for motivating all students and teaching them important skills. Reavis et al. (1996) note that praise should be immediate, frequent, enthusiastic, descriptive, varied, and involve eye contact. We would also suggest that the ratio of praise to criticism and reprimands be at least 4:1—and higher if possible. Although antisocial students may not immediately respond to praise because of their long history of negative interactions with the adults in their lives, when paired with other incentives (such as the type of reward system described below), the positive impact of praise will eventually increase.

Funding Early Interventions

With the research reviewed here, building support for the idea of early interventions should not be difficult—but finding funds could be if you don't know where to look. One source is Title I. Schools in which at least 40 percent of the students are poor should look into using the schoolwide provision of Title I to fund universal interventions. Under Title I schoolwide, you can combine several federal, state, and local funding streams to support school improvement programs. Insofar as students are identified as emotionally disturbed, their interventions can be funded by IDEA. The federal government also provides funding to reduce behavior problems through the Safe and Drug Free Schools and Communities Act. In this case, state education agencies receive funds to make grants to local education agencies and governors receive funds to make complementary grants to community-based organizations. Schools can also partner with mental health agencies, enabling services to be covered by insurance such as Medicaid and the State Children's Health Insurance Program. Plus, most states have funding streams that could support the programs described in this article. (For more information on funding, see chapter two of *Safe, Supportive, and Successful Schools: Step by Step*, available from Sopris West for $49; order online at

www.sopriswest.com/swstore/product.asp?sku=872)

4. Reinforcement Contingencies and Response Costs

Rewards and penalties of different sorts are a common feature of many classroom management strategies. Research shows that there are specific "best" ways to arrange these reinforcements to effectively motivate students to behave appropriately. These strategies are called individual reinforcement contingencies, group reinforcement contingencies, and response costs. Individual contingencies are private, one-to-one arrangements between a teacher or parent and a student in which specified, positive consequences are made available dependent ("contingent") upon the student's performance. Earning a minute of free time for every 10 or 15 math problems correctly solved, or attempted, is an example of an individual contingency.

Group contingencies are arrangements in which an entire group of individuals (e.g., a class) is treated as a single unit and the group's performance, as a whole, is evaluated to determine whether a reward is earned, such as an extra five minutes of recess. (Note: A group can fail to earn a reward, such as an extra five minutes of recess, but should not be penalized, such as by losing five minutes of the normal recess.) This strategy gets peers involved in encouraging the antisocial student to behave better. For example, if the antisocial student disrupts the class, instead of laughing at his antics, other students will encourage him to quiet down so that they can all earn the reward. To make it easier to keep track of students' behavior, reinforcement contingencies are often set up as point systems in which students must earn a certain number of points within a certain time period in order to earn a reward.

"Response costs" are a form of penalty that is added to the package of contingencies when working toward a reward is not quite enough to change students' behavior. Teachers can increase the effectiveness of contingencies by adding a response cost so that good behavior earns points and bad behavior subtracts points—making it much harder to earn a reward. (Response costs are the basis for late fees, traffic tickets, penalties in football, foul shots in basketball, and other sanctions in public life.)

5. Time-Out

Time-out is a technique of last resort in which students are removed for just five to 15 minutes from situations in which they have trouble controlling their behavior and/or their peers' attention is drawn to their inappropriate behavior. We recommend both in-classroom time-out for minor infractions and out-of-classroom time-out (the principal's office or a desginated time-out room) for more serious infractions. Students should be given the option of volunteering for brief periods of time-out when they temporarily cannot control their own behavior, but teachers should *never* physically try to force students into time-out. Finally, *in-class* time-out should be used sparingly and should *not* be used with older students. Older students who need to be removed from a situation can be sent to the principal's office or another "cool-down" room instead of having an in-class time-out.

The research foundation for these techniques is quite strong and the empirical evidence of their effectiveness is both persuasive and growing. For the past 40 years, researchers in applied behavior analysis have worked closely with school staff and others in testing and demonstrating the effectiveness of these techniques within real world settings like classrooms and playgrounds. Literally hundreds of credible studies have documented the effectiveness of each of these techniques—as well as combinations of them—in remediating the problems that antisocial children and youth bring to schooling. The research has also surfaced guidelines for the effective application of the techniques in school contexts (Walker, 1995).

Second, schools can, to a large and surprising extent, affect the level of aggression in young boys just by the orderliness of their classrooms. An intriguing longitudinal study dramatically illustrates the role of this variable in the development or prevention of aggressive behavior from first grade to middle school (Kellam, Rebok, Ialongo, and Mayer, 1994). After randomly assigning students to first-grade classrooms, researchers found that nearly half of the classrooms were chaotic and the remainder were reasonably well-managed. Of the boys in the study who began schooling in the top quartile of aggressive behavior (as rated by their teachers), those assigned to orderly classrooms had odds of 3:1 in favor of being highly aggressive in middle school. However, those boys assigned to chaotic classrooms had odds of 59:1 for being highly aggressive in middle school. This seminal finding suggests that poor classroom management by teachers in grade one is a huge, but preventable, factor in the development of antisocial behavior—and, conversely, that effective classroom management can have an enormous long-term positive effect on behavior. Thus, working closely with first-grade teachers (and, presumably, other early-grade teachers) on their behavior management can yield substantial future benefits for students and their schools by offsetting destructive outcomes.

Aggressive first-grade boys assigned to orderly classrooms had odds of 3:1 in favor of being highly aggressive in middle school. Those assigned to chaotic classrooms had odds of 59:1 for being highly aggressive in middle school.

But to some extent, this just begs the larger question: How can schools and their teachers create and sustain orderly classrooms? We summarize here the key findings and conclusions from 40 years of research. First, we present a three-tiered intervention model that matches the extent of children's behavioral problems to the power (and, therefore, cost) of the programs implemented. Second, we offer tools that can accurately and effectively identify students as young as kindergarten (and, in daycare or preschool settings, even at-risk three-year-olds can be identified) who are likely to become school behavior problems (and, later in life, delinquents and even adult criminals). Third, we review five techniques that, in combination, are at the heart of preventing antisocial behavior. Fourth, we describe specific programs with substantial and growing records of effectiveness that successfully incorporate all of the above into entirely doable, economical, and feasible school interventions. These programs can be purchased by schools from a variety of for-profit publishers and non-profit child and family services organizations. Some are inexpensive; the more expensive interventions tend to be individualized to meet the needs of highly aggressive children. All of the programs described in this article can be funded with either IDEA resources or school improvement funds. Programs for antisocial children, such as those described here, can also be funded in partnership with mental health agencies and/or through grants available through the Safe and Drug Free Schools division of the U.S. Department of Education. (See box, Funding Early Interventions.)

A. Three Levels of Intervention

Research has shown that the best way to prevent antisocial behavior is actually to start with an inexpensive school-wide intervention and then add on more intensive interventions for the most troubled kids. Building on work done by the U.S. Public Health Service, Hill Walker and his colleagues developed a model with three progressively more intensive levels of intervention to address challenging behavior within schools (Walker, Horner, Sugai, Bullis, Sprague, Bricker, and Kaufman, 1996). This model has proved to be very popular among educational researchers and has been broadly adopted by practitioners as a way to select and coordinate interventions. It is sometimes referred to in educational forums as "the Oregon Model." However, this approach is clearly a matter of public domain and is not owned by anyone. The three levels of intervention are known as "universal," "selected," and "indicated." Each is briefly described below.

"Universal" interventions are school or classroom practices that affect all students. Examples of universal interventions relevant to behavior are classwide social skills training and well-enforced school discipline codes. (Outside of education, the polio vaccination is an example of a "universal intervention.") It may seem odd to implement a program for all students when most teachers can easily identify children who have, or are developing, antisocial behavior. But schoolwide programs accomplish three things. First, they improve almost all students' behavior—and most students, even if they don't qualify as troublemakers, still need some practice being well-behaved. Second, universal interventions have their greatest impact among students who "are on the margins"—those students who are just beginning to be aggressive or defiant. Sometimes, systematic exposure to a universal intervention will be sufficient to tip them in the right direction. Third, the universal intervention offers a foundation that supports the antisocial students throughout the day by reinforcing what they are learning in their more intensive selected and indicated interventions; these latter interventions are more efficient and have a greater impact when they are applied in the context of a prior, well-implemented, universal intervention.

Approximately 80 to 90 percent of all students will respond successfully to a well-implemented universal intervention (Sugai et al., 2002). Once the school environment is orderly, the antisocial students pop up like corks in water. These students have "selected" themselves out as needing more powerful "selected" interventions that employ much more expensive and labor-intensive techniques. The goal with these students is to decrease the frequency of their problem behaviors, instill appropriate behaviors, and make the children more responsive to universal interventions (Sugai et al., 2002). While selected interventions typically are based in the school, to be their most effective they often require parental involvement. Nevertheless, even when parents refuse to participate, selected interventions still have positive effects and are well worth the effort.

The vast majority of antisocial students will start behaving better after being involved in universal and selected interventions, but schools can expect that a very small percentage of antisocial students (about one to five percent of the total youth population) will not. These are the most severe cases—the most troubled children from the most chaotic homes—and they require extremely intensive, individualized, and expensive interventions. These interventions, called "indicated," are typically family focused, with participation and support from mental health, juvenile justice, and social service agencies, as well as schools. Most non-specialized schools will find that running such an intervention is beyond their capacity. It's for such students that alternative education settings are necessary.

This three-tiered intervention model offers a structure that educators can use when they are reviewing and trying to coordinate programs. It ensures that all students' needs will be met efficiently—each child is exposed to the level of intervention that his behavior shows he needs. This is a very cost-effective model for schools because interventions become much more expensive as they become more specialized.

But it all begins with effective early screening.

B. Early Screening and Identification of Potentially Antisocial Students

Many fields have well-established practices to identify problems early and allow for more effective treatments. For instance, in medicine, routine screening procedures such as prostate-specific antigen (PSA) tests to detect prostate cancer, mammograms to detect breast cancer, and Papanicolaou (Pap) tests to detect the early states of cervical cancer have been routine for years. Unfortunately, similar proactive, early identification approaches are not commonly used to identify children with, or at risk of developing, antisocial behavior.

But research shows that early identification is absolutely critical: Children who have not learned appropriate, non-coercive ways to interact socially by around 8 years of age (the end of third grade) will likely continue displaying some degree of antisocial behavior throughout their lives (Loeber and Farrington, 1998). We also know that the longer such children go without access to effective and early intervention services (particularly after the age of 8), the more resistant to change their behavior problems will be (Gresham, 1991) and the more expensive it will be to induce the change.

Yet, as discussed previously, schools offer special education services to just one percent of students, though two to 16 percent manifest some form of antisocial behavior—and virtually no special education services are provided before students become adolescents. The technology (usually simple normed checklists and observation instruments, as described below) for identifying such children is gradually becoming more accurate for children at younger and younger ages (Severson and Walker, 2002).

A particularly valuable approach to screening is known as "multiple gating" (Loeber, Dishion, and Patterson, 1984). Multiple gating is a process in which a series of progressively more precise (and expensive) assessments or "gates" are used to identify children who need help with their behavior. One such screening procedure is the Systematic Screening for Behavior Disorders (SSBD) (Walker and Severson, 1990).

This screening procedure offers a cost-effective, mass screening of all students in grades one to six in regular education classrooms. The SSBD is made up of a combination of teacher nominations (Gate 1), teacher rating scales (Gate 2), and observations of classroom and playground problem behavior (Gate 3). It was nationally standardized on 4,500 students for the Gate 2 measures and approximately 1,300 students for the Gate 3 measures. It represents a significant advance in enabling the systematic and comprehensive screening of behavioral problems among general education students (Gresham, Lane, and Lambros, 2002). The major advantage of the SSBD is first, its ease of use, and second, its common set of standards for teachers to use in evaluating students' behavior; these standards remove most of the subjectivity that is endemic to the referral process commonly used in schools (Severson and Walker, 2002). If all schools employed universal screening (and backed it up with effective early interventions), an enormous amount of defiant and destructive behavior could be prevented—and innumerable teaching hours could be preserved.

Researchers have found that teachers do tend to praise their regular students for good behavior, but they tend not to seize opportunities to praise antisocial students when they are behaving well.

C. Key Features of Effective Interventions

When dealing with well-established antisocial behavior, a combination of the following techniques is usually retile ground in which antisocial behavior is bred. The negative effects tend to flow across generations much like inherited traits.*

By the time they are old enough for school, children who have developed an antisocial profile (due to either constitutional or environmental factors) have a limited repertoire of cooperative behavior skills, a predilection to use coercive tactics to control and manipulate others, and a well-developed capacity for emotional outbursts and confrontation.

...Then Comes School

For many young children, making the transition from home to school is fraught with difficulty. Upon school entry, children must learn to share, negotiate disagreements, deal with conflicts, and participate in competitive activities. And, they must do so in a manner that builds friendships with some peers and, at a minimum, social acceptance from others (Snyder, 2002). Children with antisocial behavior patterns have enormous difficulty accomplishing these social tasks. In fact, antisocial children are more than twice as likely as regular children to initiate unprovoked verbal or physical aggression toward peers, to reciprocate peer aggression toward them, and to continue aggressive behavior once it has been initiated (Snyder, 2002).**

From preschool to mid-elementary school, antisocial students' behavior changes in form and increases in intensity. During the preschool years, these children often display aversive behaviors such as frequent whining and noncompliance. Later, during the elementary school years, these behaviors take the form of less frequent but higher intensity acts such as hitting, fighting, bullying, and stealing. And during adolescence, bullying and hitting may escalate into robbery, assault, lying, stealing, fraud, and burglary (Snyder and Stoolmiller, 2002).

Although the specific form of the behavior changes (e.g., from noncompliance to bullying to assault), its function remains the same: Coercion remains at the heart of the antisocial behavior. As children grow older, they learn that the more noxious and painful they can make their behavior to others, the more likely they are to accomplish their goals—whether that goal is to avoid taking out the trash or escape a set of difficult mathematics problems. An important key to preventing this escalation (and therefore avoiding years of difficult behavior) is for adults to limit the use of coercive tactics with children—and for these adults to avoid surrendering in the face of coercive tactics used by the child. This has clear implications for school and teacher practices (and, of course, for parent training, which is not the subject of this article).

Frequent and excessive noncompliance in school (or home) is an important first indicator of future antisocial behavior. A young child's noncompliance is often a "gate key" behavior that triggers a vicious cycle involving parents, peers, and teachers. Further, it serves as a port of entry into much more serious forms of antisocial behavior. By treating noncompliance effectively at the early elementary age (or preferably even earlier), it is possible to prevent the development of more destructive behavior.

II. Early Intervention Is Rare

How many children are antisocial? How many are getting help early? To study the national incidence of antisocial behavior among children, researchers focus on two psychiatric diagnoses: oppositional defiant disorder and conduct disorder. Oppositional defiant disorder, the less serious of the two, consists of an ongoing pattern of uncooperative, angry behavior including things like deliberately trying to bother others and refusing to accept responsibility for mistakes. Conduct disorder is characterized by severe verbal and physical aggression, property destruction, and deceitful behavior that persist over time (usually one or more years). Formal surveys have generally indicated that between two and six percent of the general population of U.S. children and youth has some form of conduct disorder (Kazdin, 1993). Without someone intervening early to teach these children how to behave better, half of them will maintain the disorder into adulthood and the other half will suffer significant adjustment problems (e.g., disproportionate levels of marital discord and difficulty keeping a job) during their adult lives (Kazdin, 1993). (It is worth noting that on the way to these unpleasant outcomes, most will disrupt many classrooms and overwhelm many teachers.) When we add in oppositional defiant disorder (which often precedes and co-occurs with conduct disorder), estimates have been as

---

*It is important to note that the kind of coercive interaction described is very different from parents' need to establish authority in order to appropriately discipline their children. This is accomplished through the clear communication of behavioral expectations, setting limits, monitoring and supervising children's behavior carefully, and providing positive attention and rewards or privileges for conforming to those expectations. It also means using such strategies as ignoring, mildly reprimanding, redirecting, and/or removing privileges when they do not. These strategies allow parents to maintain authority without relying on the coercion described above and without becoming extremely hostile or giving in to children's attempts to use coercion.

**This unfortunate behavior pattern soon leads to peer rejection (Reid, Patterson and Snyder, 2002). When behaviorally at-risk youth are rejected and forsaken by normal, well-behaved peers, they often begin to form friendships amongst themselves. If, over several years (and particularly in adolescence), these friendships solidify in such a way that these youth identify with and feel like members of a deviant peer group, they have a 70 percent chance of a felony arrest within two years (Patterson et al., 1992).

Students with Emotional Disturbance Served by Age, Selected School Years

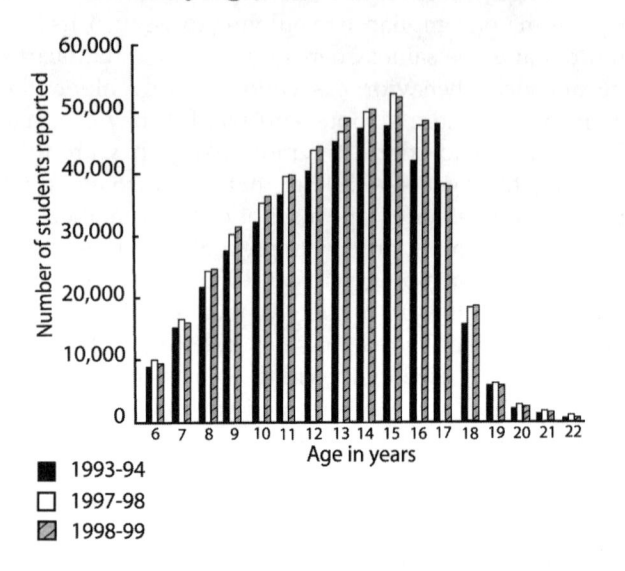

[Bar chart showing number of students reported by age in years (6-22) for school years 1993-94, 1997-98, and 1998-99. Numbers peak around age 15 at approximately 50,000 students.]

■ 1993-94
□ 1997-98
▨ 1998-99

high as 16 percent of the U.S. youth population (Eddy, Reid, and Curry, 2002).

In contrast, school systems typically identify (through the Individuals with Disabilities Education Act [IDEA]) slightly less than one percent of the public school population as having emotional and behavioral problems. Further, the great tendency of schools is to identify these behavioral problems quite late in a child's school career.

The figure above provides a stark example of this practice, which is more typical than not in today's public school systems. Walker, Nikiosha, Zeller, Severson, and Feil (2000) examined the number of K-12 students in the 1993-94, 1997-98, and 1998-99 school years who were certified as emotionally disturbed (the IDEA category that captures antisocial students). As the figure shows, the number of students certified as emotionally disturbed peaks around age 15 (approximately 50,000 cases) during the 1997-98 and 1998-99 school years. Similarly, the older data, from the 1993-94 school year, show the peak in referrals spread over the ages 14, 15, and 17. These results suggest that a large number of students, who were no doubt in need of supports and services for emotional disturbance in their elementary and middle school years, were not referred, evaluated, or served under special education.* Only in adolescence, when their behavior problems had become so intractable and difficult to accommodate, were many of these students finally identified and served. This practice of delayed referral is the polar opposite of what research clearly shows is necessary.

Our society's social, cultural, and economic problems are spilling over into our schools. They are greatly complicating schools' central task of educating students safely and effectively. But the research is clear and growing: Even though many children and youth come from and return to chaotic, coercive home environments on a daily basis, they can still acquire sufficient behavioral control to succeed in school—and to allow classmates to learn in an orderly environment.

We have substantial knowledge about how to divert at-risk children, youth, and families from destructive outcomes.** We believe the problem is not one of knowing what to do, but of convincing schools to effectively use research-based intervention programs over the long term.

The remainder of this article is devoted to providing educators with guidelines and programs for early intervention that greatly reduce antisocial behavior. There are no magic bullets in the material presented herein. Dealing with the antisocial student population is difficult, frustrating, and, because schools tend to intervene too late, often without identifiable rewards. However, of all those who suffer from conditions and disorders that impair school performance, these students are among those with the greatest capacity for change—particularly when they first start school.

III. What Can Schools Do?

Schools are not the source of children's antisocial behavior, and they cannot completely eliminate it. But schools do have substantial power to prevent it in some children and greatly reduce it in others.

First, and in some ways most importantly, schools can help by being academically effective. The fact is, academic achievement and good behavior reinforce each other: Experiencing some success academically is related to decreases in acting out; conversely, learning positive behaviors is related to doing better academically. Kellam and his colleagues (1994), for example, showed experimentally that gains in first-grade academic achievement, as measured by standardized achievement tests, resulted in substantially reduced levels of aggression, according to behavior ratings by their teachers. And, confirming what common sense tells us, Caprara, Barbaranelli, Pastorelli, Bandura, and Zimbardo (2000) found that positive behaviors (like cooperating, sharing, and consoling) among very young children contributed to their later academic achievement.

---

*Kauffman (1999) suggests that the field of education actually "prevents prevention" of behavioral disorders through well-meaning efforts to "protect" difficult children from being labeled and stigmatized by the screening and identification process.

**Successful model programs have been reviewed and described extensively by Catalano, Loeber, and McKinney (1999), by Loeber and Farrington (2001), and by Reid and his colleagues (2002).

UNIT 6
Cultural Diversity and Schooling

Unit Selections

30. **An Unfinished Journey: The Legacy of *Brown* and the Narrowing Of the Achievement Gap**, Ronald F. Ferguson and Jal Mehta
31. **Against the Tide: Desegregated High Schools and Their 1980 Graduates**, Amy Stuart Wells, Jennifer Jellison Holme, Anita Tijerina Revilla, and Awo Korantemaa Atanda
32. **Minding the Gap**, Jennifer L. Hochschild
33. **Civic Education in Schools: The Right Time is Now**, Joyce Baldwin

Key Points to Consider

- What is multicultural education? To what does the national debate over multiculturalism in the schools relate? What are the issues regarding it?

- How would you define the equity issues in the field of education? How would you rank order them?

- What are the ways that a teacher can employ to help students understand the concept of culture?

- Critique the slogan, "Every child can learn." Do you find it true or false? Explain.

DUSHKIN ONLINE Links: www.dushkin.com/online/
These sites are annotated in the World Wide Web pages.

American Scientist
http://www.amsci.org/amsci/amsci.html

American Studies Web
http://www.georgetown.edu/crossroads/asw/

Multicultural Publishing and Education Council
http://www.mpec.org

National Institute on the Education of At-Risk Students
http://www.ed.gov/offices/OERI/At-Risk/

Prospects: The Congressionally Mandated Study of Educational Growth and Opportunity
http://www.ed.gov/pubs/Prospects/index.html

man, G. Rudinger, & B. Törestad (Eds.), *Problems and methods in longitudinal research* (pp. 107–132). New York: Cambridge University Press.

Olweus, D., & Limber, S. (1999). *Blueprints for violence prevention: Bullying Prevention Program*. Boulder, CO: Institute of Behavioral Science.

Perry, D. G., Kusel, S. J., & Perry, L. C. (1988). Victims of peer aggression. *Developmental Psychology, 24*, 807–814.

Simmons, R. (2002). *Odd girl out*. New York: Harcourt.

Smith, P. K., Morita, Y., Junger-Tas, J., Olweus, D., Catalano, R., & Slee, P. (Eds.). (1999). *The nature of school bullying: A cross-national perspective*. London: Routledge.

Smith, P. K., & Sharp, S. (Eds.). (1994). *School bullying: Insights and perspectives*. London: Routledge.

Solberg, M., & Olweus, D. (in press). Prevalence estimation of school bullying with the Olweus Bully/Victim Questionnaire. *Aggressive Behavior*.

Wiseman, R. (2002). *Queen bees and wannabes*. New York: Crown.

Dan Olweus is Research Professor of Psychology and Director of the Olweus Group Against Bullying at the Research Center for Health Promotion at the University of Bergen, Christies Gate 13, N-5015 Bergen, Norway; olweus@psych.uib.no.

From *Educational Leadership*, March 2003, pp. 12-17. Copyright © 2003 by Dan Olweus. Reprinted with permission of the author.

UNIT 4
Morality and Values in Education

Unit Selections

22. **Practicing Democracy in High School**, Sheldon H. Berman
23. **Values: The Implicit Curriculum**, Linda Inlay
24. **The Missing Virtue: Lessons From Dodge Ball & Aristotle**, Gordon Marino

Key Points to Consider

- What is character education? Why do so many people wish to see a form of character education in schools?
- Are there certain values about which most of us can agree? Should they be taught in schools? Why, or why not?
- What can teachers do to help students become caring, morally responsible persons?
- Do you agree with Aristotle that virtue can and should be taught in shools? Explain.

Links: www.dushkin.com/online/
These sites are annotated in the World Wide Web pages.

Association for Moral Education
http://www.amenetwork.org/

Child Welfare League of America
http://www.cwla.org

Ethics Updates/Lawrence Hinman
http://ethics.acusd.edu

The National Academy for Child Development
http://www.nacd.org

duced from laboratory research) of the causal factors that have produced the classroom results they report. This was the theoretical element so glaringly absent in the star study. The nation needs both groups—basic researchers and school-level researchers, acting in concert to begin a tradition of hard theoretical effort at the most profound and intricate level. Without greater theoretical sophistication we are unlikely to achieve greater practical results. With it, educational research could begin to earn the high gratitude and prestige that it currently lacks but which, given its potential importance, it could someday justify.

Recently, an impressive book on educational research has appeared called *Evidence Matters* (Brookings Institution, 2002). It contains a fine essay by Thomas D. Cook and Monique R. Payne advocating the method followed in the star study—random assignment of students into experimental and control groups. The Cook and Payne essay argues that randomization is the most convincing way to determine whether the outcomes of educational interventions have statistical significance. Currently, the method of random assignment is advocated as the herald of a new research era.

One may concede to Cook and Payne and others that the practice of random assignment may yield more convincing evidence of statistical significance than other methods of data gathering, but that is not to concede that statistical significance is itself a reliable guide to educational policy. When an intervention yields effects that have statistical significance, we can infer only that the effects are not accidental in the given circumstances. As was evident in the star study, we cannot necessarily be confident that the observed effect size will be repeated in new circumstances.

Brute empirical data does not speak its own meaning. The main policy use of educational research is to enable us to make good predictions about which interventions will yield significant effects in new situations—by understanding of the root causes of the observed effects. In a domain as causally complex as mass education, "statistical significance" no matter how rigorously derived must be interpreted with a wary eye.

For instance, it is dangerous to predict long-term benefits from short-term results. Random assignment research has shown short-term gains from teaching "metacognitive" reading strategies (such as looking for the main idea). At the same time, cognitive theory predicts that the rate of student improvement with such interventions will not only reach a ceiling but will ultimately slow down a student's progress in reading—an important illustration that theory (based on extensive data) is more important and useful than ad hoc data.

In short while the new stress on random assignment is welcome, it doesn't affect the validity of Feynman's strictures about the limitations of method in educational research. A companion volume to *Evidence Matters* needs to be issued entitled *Theory Matters.* By all means let us use random assignments where plausible in educational data gathering. But then let us interpret the results warily in light of the deepest and most detailed theoretical insights into root causes that science has currently achieved.

In commenting on a draft of this essay, a federal administrator of research who has pursued both classroom and laboratory research observes that, ideally, the relationship between classroom research and cognitive science ought to parallel the collegial and fruitful relationship between medical research and biochemistry. This hopeful analogy, he concedes, could not be validly drawn in describing the educational research of the past, but he is determined to make the analogy more applicable in the future. Godspeed!

Mr. Hirsch is professor emeritus of education and humanities at the University of Virginia and a visiting scholar at the Hoover Institution.

From *Policy Review,* October/November 2002, pp. 51-69. Copyright © 2002 by Hoover Institution/Stanford University. Reprinted by permission of Policy Review.

Morality has always been a concern of educators. There has possibly not been a more appropriate time to focus attention on ethics and on standards of principled conduct in our schools. The many changes in American family structures in past years make this an important public concern, especially in the United States. We are told that all nations share concern for their cherished values. In addition to discerning how best to deal with moral and ethical educational issues, there are also substantive value controversies regarding curriculum content, such as the dialogue over how to infuse multicultural values into school curricula. On the one hand, educators need to help students learn how to reason and how to determine what principles should guide them in making decisions in situations where their own well-being and/or the well-being of another is at stake. On the other hand, educators need to develop reasoned and fair standards for resolving the substantive value issues to be faced in dealing with questions about what should or should not be taught.

There is frustration and anger among some American youth, and we must address how educators can teach moral standards and ethical decision-making skills. This is no longer simply something desirable that we might do; it has become something that we *must* do. How it is to be done is the subject of a national dialogue that is now occurring.

Students need to develop a sense of genuine caring both for themselves and others. They need to learn alternatives to violence and human exploitation. Teachers need to be examples of responsible and caring persons who use reason and compassion in solving problems in school.

Some teachers voice their concerns that students need to develop a stronger sense of character that is rooted in a more defensible system of values. Other teachers express concerns that they cannot do everything and are hesitant to instruct on morality and values. Most believe that they must do something to help students become reasoning and ethical decision makers.

What teachers perceive to be worthwhile and defensible behavior informs our reflections on what we as educators should teach. We are conscious immediately of some of the values that affect our behavior, but we may not be as aware of what informs our preferences. Values that we hold without being conscious of them are referred to as tacit values—values derived indirectly after reasoned reflection on our thoughts about teaching and learning. Much of our knowledge about teaching is tacit knowledge, which we need to bring into conscious cognition by analyzing the concepts that drive our practice. We need to acknowledge how all our values inform and influence our thoughts about teaching.

Teachers need to help students develop within themselves a sense of critical social consciousness and a genuine concern for social justice. Insight into the nature of moral decision making should be taught in the context of real current and past social problems and should lead students to develop their own skills in social analysis relating to the ethical dilemmas of human beings.

There is a need for teachers to develop principles of professional practice that will enable them to respond reasonably to the many ethical dilemmas that they now face. Knowledge of how teachers derive their sense of professional ethics is developing; further study of how teachers' values shape their professional practice is very important. Schooling should not only transmit national and cultural heritages, including our intellectual heritage; it should also be a fundamentally moral enterprise in which students learn how to develop tenable moral standards in the contexts of their own world visions.

The controversy over teaching morality deals with more than the tensions between secular and religious interests in society. We argue that the construction of educational processes and the decisions about the substantive content of school curricula involve moral issues as well.

One of the most compelling responsibilities of schools is that of preparing young people for their moral duties as free citizens of free nations. Governments have always wanted schools to teach the principles of civic morality based on their respective constitutional traditions. Indeed when the public school movement began in the 1830s and 1840s, the concept of universal public schooling as a mechanism for instilling a sense of national identity and civic morality was supported. In every nation, school curricula have certain value preferences embedded in them.

For whom do the schools exist? Is a teacher's primary responsibility to his or her client, the student, or to the student's parents? Do secondary school students have the right to study and to inquire into subjects not in officially sanctioned curricula? What are the moral issues surrounding censorship of student reading material? What ethical questions are raised by arbitrarily withholding information regarding alternative viewpoints on controversial topics?

Teachers cannot hide all of their moral preferences. They can, however, learn to conduct just and open discussions of moral topics without succumbing to the temptation to indoctrinate students with their own views.

Teaching students to respect all people, to revere the sanctity of life, to uphold the right of every citizen to dissent, to believe in the equality of all people before the law, to cherish freedom to learn, and to respect the right of all people to their own convictions—these are principles of democracy and ideals worthy of being cherished. An understanding of the processes of ethical decision making is needed by the citizens of any free nation; thus, this process should be taught in a free nation's schools.

What part ought the schooling experience to play in the formation of such things as character, informed compassion, conscience, honor, and respect for self and others? The issue of public morality and the question of how best to educate to achieve responsible social behavior, individually and collectively, are matters of great significance today.

Article 25

Heading Off Disruptive Behavior

*How Early Intervention Can Reduce Defiant Behavior—
and Win Back Teaching Time*

By Hill M. Walker, Elizabeth Ramsey, and Frank M. Gresham

More and more children from troubled, chaotic homes are bringing well-developed patterns of antisocial behavior to school. Especially as these students get older, they wreak havoc on schools. Their aggressive, disruptive, and defiant behavior wastes teaching time, disrupts the learning of all students, threatens safety, overwhelms teachers—and ruins their own chances for successful schooling and a successful life.

In a poll of AFT teachers, 17 percent said they lost four or more hours of teaching time per week thanks to disruptive student behavior; another 19 percent said they lost two or three hours. In urban areas, fully 21 percent said they lost four or more hours per week. And in urban secondary schools, the percentage is 24. It's hard to see how academic achievement can rise significantly in the face of so much lost teaching time, not to mention the anxiety that is produced by the constant disruption (and by the implied safety threat), which must also take a toll on learning.

But it need not be this way in the future. Most of the disruption is caused by no more than a few students per class*—students who are, clinically speaking, "antisocial." Provided intervention begins when these children are young, preferably before they reach age 8, the knowledge, tools, and programs exist that would enable schools to head off most of this bad behavior—or at least greatly reduce its frequency. Schools are not the source of children's behavior problems, and they can't completely solve them on their own. But the research is becoming clear: Schools can do a lot to minimize bad behavior—and in so doing, they help not only the antisocial children, they greatly advance their central goal of educating children.

In recent decades, antisocial behavior has been the subject of intense study by researchers in various disciplines including biology, sociology, social work, psychiatry, corrections, education, and psychology. Great progress has been made in understanding and developing solutions for defiant, disruptive, and aggressive behavior (see Burns, 2002). The field of psychology, in particular, with its increasingly robust theories of "social learning" and "cognition," has developed a powerful empirical literature that can assist school personnel in coping with, and ultimately preventing, a good deal of problematic behavior. Longitudinal and retrospective studies conducted in the United States, Australia, New Zealand, Canada, and various western European countries have yielded knowledge on the long-term outcomes of children who adopt antisocial behavior, especially those who arrive at school with it well developed (see Reid et al., 2002). Most importantly, a strong knowledge base has been assembled on interventions that can head off this behavior or prevent it from hardening (Loeber and Farrington, 2001).

To date, however, this invaluable knowledge base has been infused into educational practice in an extremely limited fashion. A major goal of this article (and of our much larger book) is to communicate and adapt this knowledge base for effective use by educators in coping with the rising tide of antisocial students populating today's schools. In our book, you'll find fuller explanations

---

*In the AFT's poll, of the 43 percent of teachers who said they had students in their classes with discipline problems, more than half said the problems were caused by one to three students. Poll conducted by Peter D. Hart Research Associates, October 1995.

of the causes of antisocial behavior, of particular forms of antisocial behavior like bullying, and of effective—and ineffective—interventions for schools. And all of this draws on a combination of the latest research and the classic research studies that have stood the test of time.

In this article, we look first at the source of antisocial behavior itself and ask: Why is it so toxic when it arrives in school? Second, we look at the evidence suggesting that early intervention is rare in schools. Third, we look at a range of practices that research indicates should be incorporated into school and classroom practice. Fourth, in the accompanying sidebars we give examples of how these practices have been combined in different ways to create effective programs.

I. Where Does Antisocial Behavior Come from and What Does That Mean for Schools?

Much to the dismay of many classroom teachers who deal with antisocial students, behavior-management practices that work so well with typical students do not work in managing antisocial behavior. In fact, teachers find that their tried and true behavior-management practices often make the behavior of antisocial students much worse. As a general rule, educators do not have a thorough understanding of the origins and developmental course of such behavior and are not well trained to deal with moderate to severe levels of antisocial behavior. The older these students become and the further along the educational track they progress, the more serious their problems become and the more difficult they are to manage.

How can it be that behavior-management practices somehow work differently for students with antisocial behavior patterns? Why do they react differently? Do they learn differently? Do they require interventions based on a completely different set of learning principles? As we shall see, the principles by which they acquire and exercise their behavioral pattern are quite typical and predictable.

Frequent and excessive noncompliance in school (or home) is an important first indicator of future antisocial behavior.

One of the most powerful principles used to explain how behavior is learned is known as the Matching Law (Herrnstein, 1974). In his original formulation, Herrnstein (1961) stated that the rate of any given behavior matches the rate of reinforcement for that behavior. For example, if aggressive behavior is reinforced once every three times it occurs (e.g., by a parent giving in to a temper tantrum) and prosocial behavior is reinforced once every 15 times it occurs (e.g., by a parent praising a polite request), then the Matching Law would predict that, on average, aggressive behavior will be chosen five times more frequently than prosocial behavior. Research has consistently shown that behavior does, in fact, closely follow the Matching Law (Snyder, 2002). Therefore, how parents (and later, teachers) react to aggressive, defiant, and other bad behavior is extremely important. The Matching Law applies to all children; it indicates that antisocial behavior is learned—and, at least at a young enough age, can be unlearned. (As we will see in the section that reviews effective intervention techniques, many interventions—like maintaining at least a 4 to 1 ratio of praising versus reprimanding—have grown out of the Matching Law.)

First Comes the Family...

Antisocial behavior is widely believed to result from a mix of constitutional (i.e., genetic and neurobiological) and environmental (i.e., family and community) factors (Reid et al., 2002). In the vast majority of cases, the environmental factors are the primary causes—but in a small percentage of cases, there is an underlying, primarily constitutional, cause (for example, autism, a difficult temperament, attention deficit/hyperactivity disorder [ADHD], or a learning disorder). Not surprisingly, constitutional and environmental causes often overlap and even exacerbate each other, such as when parents are pushed to their limits by a child with a difficult temperament or when a child with ADHD lives in a chaotic environment.

Patterson and his colleagues (Patterson et al., 1992) have described in detail the main environmental causes of antisocial behavior. Their model starts by noting the social and personal factors that put great stress on family life (e.g., poverty, divorce, drug and alcohol problems, and physical abuse). These stressors disrupt normal parenting practices, making family life chaotic, unpredictable, and hostile. These disrupted parenting practices, in turn, lead family members to interact with each other in negative, aggressive ways and to attempt to control each others' behavior through coercive means such as excessive yelling, threats, intimidation, and physical force. In this environment, children learn that the way to get what they want is through what psychologists term "coercive" behavior: For parents, coercion means threatening, yelling, intimidating, and even hitting to force children to behave. (Patterson [1982] conducted a sequential analysis showing that parental use of such coercive strategies to suppress hostile and aggressive behavior actually increased the likelihood of such behavior in the future by 50 percent.)

For children, coercive tactics include disobeying, whining, yelling, throwing tantrums, threatening parents, and even hitting—all in order to avoid doing what the parents want. In homes where such coercive behavior is common, children become well-acquainted with how hostile behavior escalates—and with which of their behaviors ultimately secure adult surrender. This is the fer-

The concept of "culture" encompasses all of the life ways, customs, traditions, and institutions that a people develop as they create and experience their history and identity as a people. In the United States of America, many very different cultures coexist within the civic framework of a shared constitutional tradition that guarantees equality before the law for all. So, as we all have been taught, out of many peoples we are also one nation united by our constitutional heritage.

The civil rights movement in America in the 1950s and 1960s was about the struggle of cultural minorities to achieve equity: social justice before the law under our federal Constitution. The articles in this unit attempt to address some of these equity issues.

There is an immense amount of unfinished business before us in the area of intercultural relations in the schools and in educating all Americans regarding how multicultural our national population demographics really are. We are becoming more and more multicultural with every passing decade. This further requires us to take steps to ensure that all of our educational opportunity structures remain open to all persons regardless of their cultural backgrounds or gender. There is much unfinished business as well with regard to improving educational opportunities for girls and young women; the remaining gender issues in American education are very real and directly related to the issue of equality of educational opportunity.

Issues of racial prejudice and bigotry still plague us in American education, despite massive efforts in many school systems to improve racial and intercultural relations in the schools. Many American adolescents are in crisis as their basic health and social needs are not adequately met and their educational development is affected by crises in their personal lives. The articles in this unit reflect all of the above concerns plus others related to efforts to provide equality of educational opportunity to all American youth and attempts to clarify what multicultural education is and what it is not.

The "equity agenda," or social justice agenda, in the field of education is a complex matrix of gender- and culture-related issues aggravated by incredibly wide gaps in the social and economic opportunity structures available to citizens. We are each situated by cultural, gender-based, and socioeconomic factors in society; this is true of all persons everywhere. We have witnessed a great and glorious struggle for human rights in our time and in our nation. The struggle continues to deal more effectively with educational opportunity issues related to cultural diversity and gender.

The "Western canon" is being challenged by advocate's multicultural perspectives in school curriculum development. Multicultural educational programming, which will reflect the rapidly changing cultural demographics of North American schooling, is being advocated by some and strongly opposed by others. This controversy centers around several different issues regarding what it means to provide equality of opportunities for culturally diverse students. The traditional Western cultural content of general, social studies, and language arts curricula is being challenged as Eurocentric.

Helping teachers to broaden their cultural perspectives and to take a more global view of curriculum content is something that the advocates of culturally pluralistic approaches to curriculum development would like to see integrated into the entire elementary and secondary school curriculum structure. North America is as multicultural a region of the world as exists anywhere. Our enormous cultural diversity encompasses populations from many indigenous "First Americans" as well as peoples from every European culture, plus many peoples of Asian, African, and Latin American nations and the Central and South Pacific Island groups. There is spirited controversy over how to help all Americans to better understand our collective multicultural heritage. There are spirited defenders and opponents of the traditional Eurocentric curriculum.

The problem of inequality of educational opportunity is of great concern to American educators. One in four American children does not have all of the basic needs met and lives under poverty conditions. Almost one in three lives in a single-parent home, which in itself is no disadvantage, but under conditions of poverty, it often is. More and more concern is expressed over how to help children of poverty. The equity agenda of our time has to do with many issues related to gender, race, and ethnicity. All forms of social deprivation and discrimination are aggravated by great disparities in income and accumulated wealth. How can students be helped to have an equal opportunity to succeed in school?

Some of us are still proud to say that we are a nation of immigrants. In addition to the traditional minority/majority group relationships that evolved in the United States, new waves of immigrants today are again enhancing the importance of concerns for achieving equality of opportunity in education. In light of these vast sociological and demographic changes, we must ensure that we will remain a multicultural democracy.

The social psychology of prejudice is something that psychiatrists, social psychologists, anthropologists, and sociologists have studied in great depth since the 1930s. Tolerance, acceptance, and a valuing of the unique worth of every person are teachable and learnable attitudes. A just society must be constantly challenged to find meaningful ways to raise human aspirations, to heal human hurt, and to help in the task of optimizing every citizen's potential. Education is a vital component to that end. Teachers can incorporate into their lessons an emphasis on acceptance of difference, toleration of and respect for the beliefs of others, and the skills of reasoned debate and dialogue.

The struggle for optimal representation of minority perspectives in the schools will be a matter of serious concern to educators for the foreseeable future. From the many court decisions upholding the rights of women and cultural minorities in the schools over the past years has emerged a national consensus that we must strive for the greatest degree of equality in education as may be possible. The triumph of constitutional law over prejudice and bigotry must continue.

Article 30

The 50th Anniversary

An Unfinished Journey:
The Legacy of *Brown* and the Narrowing of the Achievement Gap

Why, Mr. Ferguson and Mr. Mehta wonder, does the achievement gap persist 50 years after *Brown* declared that black children must receive a truly equal education?

BY RONALD F. FERGUSON WITH JAL MEHTA

THE GOOD NEWS is that the achievement gaps between racial and ethnic groups in the U.S. are smaller than they were several decades ago. The bad news is that progress stopped around 1990.[1] The National Assessment of Educational Progress (NAEP) continues to show large differences between the average scores of blacks and Hispanics on the one hand and those of whites and Asians on the other.[2] Now, half a century after *Brown v. Board of Education*, while progress is evident and many milestones have been achieved—especially in the area of civil rights—policy measures focused on rights, resources, and required testing for students have not achieved their full promise for raising achievement and narrowing gaps between groups of students. And it is the failure to go behind the classroom door and foster high-quality instructional practices for all students, in all classrooms, in all schools that is strongly implicated in these disappointing results.

What we need today is a more determined, high-quality, research-based emphasis on improving what happens in classrooms. But before we look at just what sorts of practices we need to adopt, some historical background is in order.

HISTORICAL OVERVIEW

One hundred and seven years ago, the U.S. Supreme Court upheld the doctrine of "separate but equal" in *Plessy v. Ferguson*. The conflict was over passenger accommodations on the East Louisiana Railroad. Nonetheless, the doctrine of "separate but equal" was codified in state laws governing schools and virtually all other types of public accommodations in the South, where the majority of African Americans lived. Representing an eight-person majority, Justice Henry Brown wrote the following: "The object of the [14th] Amendment was undoubtedly to enforce the absolute equality of the two races before the law, but in the nature of things it could not have been intended to abolish distinctions based upon color, or to enforce social, as distinguished from political equality, or a commingling of the two races upon terms unsatisfactory to either."

Half a century later, the doctrine of separate but equal still dominated the South, but the question being litigated was whether enforced segregation in public schools deprived black children of equal protection under the U.S. Constitution. On 17 May 1954, Chief Justice Earl Warren issued the Court's decision in the cases subsumed into *Brown*. The Court's opinion granted that it might be possible with segregation to achieve equality of "tangible factors"—things that money can buy—but the Court rejected the idea that separate could be equal or that laws maintaining segregation could provide equal protection under the Constitution. Informed by the work of social scientists, including the black psychologist Kenneth Clark, the justices wrote the following about the harm that segregation was doing to black children: "To separate them from others of similar age and qualifications solely because of their race generates a feeling of inferiority as to their status in the community that may affect their hearts and minds in a way unlikely ever to be undone." Thus *Brown* was not merely about equality of resources; it was also about children's "hearts and minds" and "status in the community." The decision struck down the doctrine of separate but equal. It was a landmark event.[3]

In challenging the separate-but-equal doctrine of the Jim Crow South, the plaintiffs in Brown aimed to challenge white supremacist ideology and the moral injustice of forced segregation. In addition, they hoped that giving black children access to the schools and classrooms where white children studied would help to equalize educational resources and academic outcomes. Unfortunately, implementation of the court order was exceedingly slow and limited. Most of the school integration that actually happened in the South took place after the Civil Rights Act of 1964 and after other court orders took effect in the late 1960s and early 1970s. As discussed below, evidence regarding the impact of desegregation—when it finally happened—on achievement and other outcomes is mixed.

After the mid-1970s, forced integration was no longer the standard judicial remedy for segregation, and the desegregation cases, especially in the North, came to resemble the cases dealing with equity in school finance. They focused increasingly on state aid and compensatory education. James Ryan writes:

> In sum, school desegregation and school finance litigation have converged around money. That poor and minority schools will remain separate from white and wealthier schools [because they are in different political jurisdictions] appears to be taken as a given, and, if anything, is reinforced by the fact that advocates are fighting not over integration but resources.[4]

In the 1990s, courts began releasing districts from desegregation orders issued in the 1970s. The likely result is that court-ordered desegregation will soon be only a memory.

Around the same time that the Civil Rights Act of 1964 set the wheels in motion to enforce desegregation orders, the War on Poverty introduced the federal Head Start program in order to give children from disadvantaged homes a "head start" on school success. In addition, Title I of the Elementary and Secondary Education Act (ESEA) of 1965 was intended to supplement academic resources for low-income children who needed extra support in the early grades. Head Start and Title I were not explicitly race targeted, but a major motivation among their supporters was to reduce racial inequities. Over the years, recipients of services have included large numbers of poor minority children.

Title I is a funding stream that supplements school-level resources and is not a highly prescriptive intervention. Schools have great discretion in how the funds are used. Before the reforms of 1994, federal legislation targeted Title I funds to the early elementary grades, with the intention that funds should assist only those students in those grades who were most in need of supplemental support. However, reforms passed in 1994 encouraged support for students across all grade levels, not just the early elementary years. They also encouraged whole-school reforms in high-poverty schools and an increased emphasis on accountability.

Neither of the two large-scale evaluations of Title I has reached the conclusion that it substantially narrows achievement gaps between disadvantaged and middle-class students, as policy makers intended.[5] Reanalyses of the data and a quantitative synthesis of state-level studies have produced somewhat more optimistic conclusions, but none of the studies find effects that are impressively large.[6]

Increasing the long-term sustainability of the gains children make in Head Start almost certainly depends on improving the primary and secondary schools that Head Start graduates attend, including those assisted by Title I.

To put these findings in proper perspective, we should note that all the estimates depend on contestable decisions about how to determine what would have happened to Title I student achievement in the absence of Title I support. Even if Title I has failed to narrow the achievement gap between disadvantaged and middle-class students, it might nonetheless have helped to keep the gap from widening—and to a degree that existing studies have no way to reliably estimate. The most definitive and defensible methodology for this purpose would be to randomly assign some schools to a treatment group that receives Title I support and others to a control group that does not. The impact of Title I would be measured as the difference in achievement gains between treatment and control schools. There have been no such studies of Title I, probably because it would seem unfair to the control group.

Findings on the effectiveness of Head Start are somewhat more positive than those for Title I. Specifically, most studies find that Head Start improves school readiness, as measured by achievement test scores.[7] However, most also find that the initial advantage fades over the elementary years, so that achievement scores of Head Start graduates eventually resemble those of nonparticipants from similar backgrounds. The most likely reason for the fade-out is that Head Start graduates attend inferior schools that fail to motivate them sufficiently and don't build optimally on the skills they bring.[8] There is evidence (though not much) that with favorable conditions, fade-out is not inevitable. For example, preschool programs, including Head Start, have sometimes shown sustained benefits (including but not limited to test scores) all the way into adulthood.[9] Increasing the long-term sustainability of the gains children make in Head Start almost certainly depends on improving the primary and secondary schools that Head Start graduates attend, including those assisted by Title I.

While the federal government was introducing Head Start and Title I in the mid-1960s, local districts were continuing a century-old trend toward reducing class sizes for children from all backgrounds. Historically, classes have been larger in schools that blacks have attended.[10] However, class-size reductions have been larger for blacks than for whites. By 1990, the national pupil/

teacher ratio for all races and ethnicities in elementary school classrooms was only 70% of what it was in 1965 (18.9 pupils per teacher in 1990 versus 27.6 in 1965), and there was no clear remaining difference among racial groups.[11] Most of the reduction that took place after 1965 was complete by 1980.[12]

The period from the mid-1960s to the early 1980s was also a time when schools went "back to basics." The back-to-basics movement spread rapidly during the 1970s in response to media attention to such things as falling SAT scores. It was driven to a substantial degree by parents' concern that their children were not acquiring basic skills, and it produced systemic and results-based accountability reforms that were the precursors of those we have today, raising many of the same issues as today about "teaching to the test" and diluting curricula.

By 1985, 35 states were mandating statewide minimum competency testing (MCT), and 11 required students to pass such tests in order to graduate. Some also used the scores to determine eligibility for remedial programs and promotions.

Jennifer O'Day and Marshall Smith believe that the move to instruction focused heavily on basic skills in preparation for minimum competency tests was an important reason that black students' NAEP scores rose during the 1970s (for 9-year-olds) and during the 1980s (for 17-year-olds). Analysts who have looked closely at the timing of the gains are skeptical, for the following reasons. First, scores rose on tests even in states without MCT. Second, scores began to rise before MCT could have had much of an impact. Third, all states were reporting performance of their students on nationally normed achievement tests above the national average, which is a statistical impossibility. Fourth, the degree to which NAEP and SAT scores rose varied from place to place in ways that seem inconsistent with MCT as the explanation. It seems most likely that MCT and rising scores were both products of the movement to strengthen basic skills, but that MCT was not a key causal factor in the rise in NAEP scores.[13]

The critique that ultimately weakened the basic skills movement was that it did not focus enough on higher-order thinking. Students, it was argued, needed much more than basic skills. This meant they needed teachers who had more than basic skills themselves. Attention during the 1980s shifted to improving the quality of new teachers. Only three states required initial certification testing of new teachers in 1980, but by 1990, 42 states did so. States also adopted measures to encourage students, including minorities, to take more academically advanced courses.[14]

From the late 1980s to the present, the nation has searched actively at both the state and federal levels for ways to improve whole schools and whole school systems. Ideas about "systemic reform" and "standards-based accountability" have been influential at every level of policy making. The latter is most evident in the No Child Left Behind (NCLB) Act.

Compared to 1954, much has changed, and much has not. On the one hand, segregation is still widespread, and Gary Orfield reminds us that improving schools for the most disadvantaged children, given present levels of segregation and isolation, is a gargantuan task.[15] On the other hand, political leaders at all levels of the society are claiming public education as their number-one concern, and they are talking publicly and optimistically about prospects for improving outcomes for even the most disadvantaged children. That's certainly progress since 1954, but there remains a long way to go.

DESEGREGATION

In 1955, the Supreme Court issued the implementation order for *Brown* v. *Board of Education*, known as *Brown II*. In it, the Court ordered southern states to desegregate their schools with "all deliberate speed." However, it defined neither "desegregation" nor "all deliberate speed." Instead, the ruling left the interpretation and enforcement of *Brown II* to federal district courts in the South.[16] Under heavy pressure from local politicians, schools in the South remained heavily segregated, with just one out of 50 southern black children attending integrated schools in 1964.[17] For roughly a decade, the decision in *Brown* did little to raise achievement among southern black children, because it did little to affect the conditions of their schooling.

Southern patterns of segregation in public schools persisted until the Civil Rights Act of 1964 prohibited discrimination in all schools receiving federal dollars. Four years later, in another landmark decision, *Green* v. *County School Board*, the U.S. Supreme Court declared that segregated or dual systems of public education had to be dismantled "root and branch." The mandated desegregation applied to facilities, staff and faculty, extracurricular activities, and transportation. By 1970, southern schools were less segregated than schools in any other region of the country.

Desegregation in the North and West faced a different set of challenges, because large-scale white suburbanization after World War II had left too few whites in cities to achieve meaningful integration without crossing city/suburb lines. Interdistrict desegregation plans sprang up in the wake of the civil rights legislation, and segregation decreased in the North. But there was a limit to how far the movement would go. In 1974, in *Milliken* v. *Bradley*, the Supreme Court overruled a metropolitan-wide desegregation plan under which children from Detroit would have integrated with children from the mostly white suburbs. Absent a court finding that suburban districts had conspired to maintain segregation in Detroit schools, the Court ruled that there was no legal reason that the suburbs of Detroit should be part of the remedy.[18] This made it effectively impossible for Detroit to achieve extensive integration, since there were too few whites left in the city.

Instead, in a companion case, *Milliken* v. *Bradley II*, the remedy approved by the Court required the state of Michigan to help fund remedial and compensatory education programs. Court rulings in the *Milliken* cases, combined with continuing outmigration from cities to suburbs by the largely white middle class, effectively foreclosed the possibility of meaningful desegregation in the North and West. In recent years, segregation has begun to increase because of continuing suburbanization of whites and because courts are no longer writing and enforcing desegregation orders.

Achievement impacts of the desegregation orders. A number of studies in the 1960s and 1970s evaluated the effects of the desegregation orders on achievement. Reviews of this literature have pooled estimates from multiple studies to reach summary conclusions. They suggest the following: 1) white achievement is unaffected by desegregation; 2) desegregation does not lead to an increase in black mathematics achievement; 3) desegregation does tend to raise black reading scores, but by relatively small amounts (between .06 and .26 standard deviations); and 4) gains are likely to be greatest among the youngest children.[19]

These studies have been subject to a number of methodological criticisms, the most important of which is that the time frame for the majority of the studies is far too short.[20] Many of the studies estimate effects on achievement after only one year, and none estimate the effect of desegregation on the cumulative achievement of black students over a number of years.[21] Another problem is that the studies rarely attend to the details of implementation. Finally, it is unclear whether the effects of court-ordered plans from nearly three decades ago can fairly be generalized to today.

Other studies of the effects of integration. Beyond studies of court-ordered desegregation, a parallel literature seeks to understand whether natural variation in the level of school integration can explain differences in student achievement, controlling for family background. These studies use nationally representative data for schools that are not operating under desegregation orders, and so they cannot overcome the possibility that selection bias has affected their findings. That is, black families who send their children to integrated schools may differ in unmeasured ways from black families who do not. Therefore, some of the estimated effects that the studies attribute to integration might be the result of these unmeasured differences. For example, we know that in nationally representative data, more advantaged blacks are the ones more likely to attend integrated schools. Some characteristics, such as parental ambition, are not accounted for in the research. Thus the positive effect of integration is likely to be overestimated if more ambitious black parents are the ones more likely to integrate.

> Schools in high-poverty areas are less likely to offer college-preparatory classes, and they have much higher rates of teachers' teaching out of subject areas, greater teacher turnover, and lower test scores.

The best evidence may come from the *Equality of Educational Opportunity* study by James Coleman and his colleagues and from the National Education Longitudinal Survey (NELS) of 1972. By one measure, these studies show that blacks who attended predominantly white northern schools during the late 1960s and early 1970s scored 0.30 standard deviations higher than blacks who attended all-black northern schools. Meredith Phillips analyzed the same issue using the Prospects data—a nationally representative sample collected in the early 1990s to study the effects of Title I. Phillips finds effects of integrated schools on black reading achievement of about 13% of the black/white reading gap, but she finds no effect on math achievement. She speculates that the repeated findings in the literature that reading achievement is affected by integration but math achievement is not suggest that black students in integrated schools benefit not so much from better instruction or from more advanced curricula as from interaction with teachers and peers who speak the mainstream dialect.[22]

There has been some research on ways that integration affects other important outcomes besides test scores. The latter include higher rates of high school completion, college attendance, and college completion and lower rates of delinquency and teen childbearing.[23] Authors who emphasize this longer list of impacts are careful to point out that the advantages of integration probably come less from racial mixing than from middle-class educational environments:

> Unfortunately, the framing of the issue in racial terms often leads both Blacks and whites to conclude that desegregation plans assume that Black institutions are inferior and that Black gains are supposed to come from sitting next to whites in school. But the actual benefits come primarily from access to the resources and connections of institutions that have always received preferential treatment, and from the expectations, competition and values of successful middle-class educational institutions that routinely prepare students for college.[24]

Consistent with this view, there is a considerable body of literature that documents the reduced opportunities available in schools that have extremely high concentrations of poverty. Schools in high-poverty areas are less likely to offer college-preparatory classes, and they have much higher rates of teachers' teaching out of subject areas, greater teacher turnover, and lower test scores. Parents are less likely to be involved in school affairs, less able to ensure high standards, and less likely to pressure administrators to fire or transfer bad teachers.[25] While there has been considerable debate in the academic literature about how much these school-level factors affect achievement independent of student background, it is undeniable that the interaction of poverty, segregation, and inadequate school resources heavily disadvantages the poor and minority students who attend high-poverty schools.

Accordingly, the most striking effects of integration have been measured in case studies of interdistrict programs in which a limited number of city children are bused to suburban schools. For example, Amy Stuart

Wells and Robert Crain found that, of the city students they studied who remained in the suburban schools in the St. Louis metropolitan area, approximately 50% graduated from high school in 1994, compared to 24% of all students in central-city public schools.[26] Of the suburban stayers, 68% of those who graduated from high school went on to college; about two-thirds entered four-year colleges; the rest entered two-year colleges. Of the much smaller proportion who graduated from city schools, about 50% went to college, with one-third of those attending four-year institutions. James Rosenbaum's study of the Gautreaux Program concerned a semi-randomized program comparing families who moved to the Chicago suburbs with those who moved to other urban locations. Rosenbaum found greatly increased educational outcomes among suburban movers. Specifically, suburban students (who experienced both residential and school integration) were four times less likely to drop out of school, more than twice as likely to attend college, and almost seven times more likely to attend four-year colleges than their city counterparts.[27] Unfortunately, there are methodological problems with both the St. Louis and the Chicago studies, so their findings are far from definitive.

With a more robust study design, the federally sponsored residential mobility program, Moving to Opportunity (MTO), began operating in 1994 in Baltimore, Boston, Chicago, Los Angeles, and New York. Qualified households were low-income families with children living in public housing or Section 8 project-based housing in selected high-poverty census tracts. Families who volunteered for MTO were assigned randomly to one of three groups. The experimental group was offered rent subsidies that could be used only for private-market housing in census tracts with 1990 poverty rates under 10%. A "Section 8-only" comparison group received rental subsidies, but with no requirement to live in a low-poverty census tract. Members of the control group received no subsidy at all. Because of the random assignment design and careful implementation, this project is not subject to the concerns about selection bias that plague other studies.

The Baltimore study of MTO has reported education findings. Jens Ludwig, Helen Ladd, and Greg Duncan report that elementary school children in the experimental group score higher than those in the control group by about a quarter of a standard deviation in both reading and math. Elementary school children in the Section-8 only group score higher than the controls in reading but not math. Achievement data for adolescents are too limited to draw conclusions about effects on test scores. There are, however, some other conclusions:

> The teens in the experimental and Section 8-only groups experience a higher incidence of grade retentions than controls, and may experience more disciplinary actions and school dropout as well. These findings are generally robust to problems of missing data and to decisions about the specific estimation approach that is used.[28]

There is no way to know at this time what the long-term effects will be.

All in all, evidence on the impacts of racial and income mixing varies from study to study. A tentative conclusion is that a combination of racial and socioeconomic mixing often improves outcomes—particularly those other than test scores—for nonwhite students who might otherwise attend low-income segregated schools. However, the research generally suffers from methodological problems that limit our ability to draw firm, confident conclusions.

As the long struggle to achieve integration continues, supports and incentives for schools to maximize achievement outcomes for minority children after integration occurs need to be strengthened so that all children will be well served. The work that *Brown* and other desegregation cases began remains undone as long as segregation remains as extensive as it is and as long as children's "hearts and minds" are not nurtured in ways that propel them toward their potential in whatever schools they attend. To maximize the value of mixing, co-location of students under the same school-building roof must be only the first step in a more elaborate process of social and academic adjustment.

INSTRUCTIONAL QUALITY, TRACKING, AND ABILITY GROUPING

Why are the effects of integration so small? If integrated schools (especially middle-class ones) tend to be superior to segregated schools in their capacity to produce positive student outcomes, *and* if those capacities are applied effectively to benefit all students who attend them, then we should expect to find more positive gains from integration than most studies show. Surely, there is more potential for a poor child to thrive in a school that is mixed by race, ethnicity, and socioeconomic status than in one where teachers and administrators are overwhelmed by a high concentration of children who are poor and socially isolated from the mainstream society. Yet the research tells mixed stories about the degrees to which such potential has been harvested over the past several decades. One possibility is that, when poor and minority children entering a school are systematically different in preparation and identity from the children whom the school is accustomed to serving, integration without accommodation may yield far less than the full potential of the opportunity. In the following passage, Gloria Ladson-Billings provides an example of integration gone awry.

> Because of a clerical error I ended up in a "basic" English class during the first grading period of my sophomore year. ... I was excited about the opportunity to be in a class where African American students were the majority. In my previous English classes, the emphasis was on literature and composition. We read Dickens, Hardy, and Shakespeare. But in this class we were drilled in grammar and spelling. Each time we took a spelling test. Each week I got 100. In fact, I got an A on every assignment given. Nevertheless, on the first report card my grade was a C. When I questioned the teacher about it, she smiled and said, "Why Gloria,

a C is the highest possible grade in this class!" After a quick trip to my guidance counselor, ... I was returned to my rightful place in the college preparatory English class. The basic English teacher told me she was sorry to see me go and wished me well. I left that class confused and hurt. Why hadn't the teacher recognized that I had the ability to move out of it? And more importantly why didn't my classmates know that no matter how hard they worked, their efforts would only be rewarded with mediocre grades?[29]

The quotation reports an experience from the early 1960s. Even today, however, it remains true in racially integrated schools that black students are overrepresented in lower-level classes. It also seems to be common (or at least it remains a common perception) that lower-level classes are less well taught than those at higher levels.

Consequently, tracking and ability grouping are leading "suspects" for why integration has not produced greater benefits for minority children. These practices provide means by which students attending the same schools may nevertheless have different instructional experiences. Because of differences in their family backgrounds and academic preparation[30] and perhaps also because of bias, children are frequently grouped for instruction in combinations that are more homogeneous by race and socioeconomic background than the school is as a whole. However, grouping and tracking are not *necessary* in order for some children to be served less effectively than others, especially if schools do not accommodate well to the instructional needs of particular students.

Ability grouping in elementary school refers to practices that separate children for instruction either within or between classrooms, based on teachers' judgments. Ability grouping after elementary school often occurs in the context of what historically has been called tracking and has more recently been called "leveling" because "tracking" has acquired a pejorative connotation. Courses at higher levels cover more advanced material and may require more work. Currently, the standard arrangement is that no student is officially forbidden from entering a course at any level. Nonetheless, race, gender, and socioeconomic imbalances frequently develop. Explanations include differences in proficiency; in the advice received from parents, counselors, and teachers; and students' own preferences to be with their friends.[31]

For at least the past century, there have been recurrent debates among educators about whether ability grouping and tracking are helpful or harmful, especially for low achievers and minority students.[32] In its standard form, the debate confuses at least three questions.

The first question concerns whether groups at all levels receive the same quality of instruction and, if not, what the implications are for whether the grouping should continue. To the extent that research addresses this question, the most common conclusion is that children in lower-ability groups (and tracks) receive a lower quality of instruction than those in higher-ability groups (and tracks); therefore, grouping and tracking hurt students at the lower levels.[33]

Those who conclude that ability grouping hurts students in lower-level groups or tracks assume that the same students would receive superior instruction in more heterogeneous groups or classrooms. However, ample evidence indicates that, even in heterogeneous, mixed-ability classrooms, low-achieving students often receive inferior treatment.

Thomas Good cites multiple studies[34] to support including each of the following items on the list of ways that teachers treat "highs" and "lows" differently in the same classroom: waiting less time for low achievers to answer; giving low achievers answers or calling on someone else rather than offering clues or repeating or rephrasing questions; rewarding inappropriate behavior or incorrect answers by low achievers; criticizing low achievers more often for failure; praising low achievers less often for success; failing to give feedback to the public responses of low achievers; paying less attention to low achievers or interacting with them less frequently; calling on low achievers less frequently; seating low achievers farther away from the teacher; demanding less from low achievers; interacting with low achievers more privately than publicly and monitoring and structuring their activities more closely; grading tests or assignments in a different manner, in which the high achievers but not the low achievers are given the benefit of the doubt in borderline cases; having less friendly interaction with low achievers, including less smiling; providing briefer and less informative feedback to the questions of low achievers; providing less eye contact and other nonverbal communication of attention to low achievers; using fewer effective but time-consuming instructional methods with low achievers; and showing less acceptance and use of low achievers' ideas.

We think researchers are correct when they conclude that instruction for lower-level tracks is routinely inferior to what higher-level tracks receive in secondary schools. An analogous statement may apply to ability grouping in elementary schools. However, it does not follow directly that moving students into heterogeneously grouped arrangements will improve learning outcomes. As Good's list reminds us, even in heterogeneously grouped schools and classrooms, minority students in integrated schools may receive inferior instruction if they are overrepresented among low achievers or among students from whom not much is expected.[35]

It is important to note here that students in lower-level groups and classrooms may not even be exposed to important concepts that they need to know in order to preserve future learning options. Sometimes this drawback is offered as a reason to abolish ability grouping and tracking. Although circumstances surely exist in which the only way to give students what they need academically is to move them to heterogeneously grouped classrooms, there are also surely situations in which enriching the curriculum and quality of instruction while maintaining the ability-grouped regime is the most academically responsible option.

The second question to consider is whether ability grouping matters if the curriculum and the quality of instruction are similar across different grouping arrangements. The best studies to address this question are experimental and quasi-experimental studies in which students are randomly assigned or carefully matched to be grouped by ability, or not. In a meta-analysis of many such studies, James Kulik finds that the overwhelming conclusion is that ability grouping makes no difference to learning if there is no tailoring of curriculum or instruction to fit the proficiency of the group.[36] In other words, if what is taught is the same, classmates' proficiencies seem not to matter.

Kulik's analysis also indicates that, when students are placed in ways that match their proficiencies and when instruction and curriculum are tailored to their needs, students *at all levels* can benefit at least modestly from ability-grouped instruction. Less time is wasted on material that is too elementary or too advanced, and instruction that serves one student well is more likely to serve others well, too. Furthermore, contrary to the belief that ability grouping harms the self-esteem of low achievers, Kulik's review finds that ability grouping tends to lower self-esteem slightly among the high-achieving group and raise it slightly among the low-achieving group.

The third question concerns whether students are placed in ways that match their proficiencies and potentials. Even if instruction is of high quality and tailored, some students may be misplaced. If teachers or guidance counselors use race, gender, or socioeconomic status as an indicator of current or potential proficiency, there may be race, gender, or socioeconomic bias in the placements. However, most placements are predicted by measures of past performance (and sometimes parental education), leaving little independent explanatory power for race.

Ultimately, our conclusion is that how children are grouped for instruction seems less important than how well they are taught. For example, in the classroom that Gloria Ladson-Billings described above, it is not at all clear that merging the entire "basic" class with students from the higher-level section would have been the best option for Gloria's classmates. It is extremely clear, however, that the "basic" class was being poorly taught. Any simple, unidimensional, yes/no perspective with regard to ability grouping and tracking might be correct at some times and in some places, but it is surely wrong as a generalization.

And it is impossible to make a reliable generalization based on the existing literature about whether disproportionate placements in lower-level ability groups and curriculum tracks are an important part of the answer to the question of why integration produces such meager gains. Racial biases in placement may be common, but the few studies that seek to measure this bias, controlling for scores and past performance, tend not to find it.

CLASS SIZE

One of the most highly touted education policies of the Clinton years was a major class-size reduction initiative that distributed $1.3 billion to help school districts recruit, hire, and train new teachers for the 2000-01 school year. In December 2000, Congress appropriated an additional $1.6 billion to cover the class-size initiative during the 2001-02 school year. However, President Bush was not persuaded that class-size reductions should be a priority.

The Bush Administration's deemphasis on class size was surely informed by the work of economist Eric Hanushek, whose literature reviews over a period of two decades have been widely cited.[37] Hanushek tabulates the findings from what economists call education production function studies, which use data on child, family, classroom, school, and community characteristics as predictors of academic outcomes such as test scores and graduation rates. In most such studies, the data have been generated for purposes unrelated to the study and seldom include all of the variables that the researcher's theory suggests should be included. Indeed, a host of problems with both data and methodology make many of the studies heavily flawed.

Nonetheless, Hanushek's literature reviews tabulate estimates of the degree to which the "inputs" of class size, expenditures, teacher experience, and teacher education affect academic outcomes. Hanushek's well-known and widely quoted conclusion is that there is no consistent relationship between these school resources and school achievement. Instead, based on other work by himself and others,[38] he emphasizes that far and away the most important schooling input is teacher quality, but that teacher quality is difficult to measure with the types of data available for education production function analysis.

The first major challenge to Hanushek's summary of the literature came from statistician Larry Hedges and his colleagues. They argued that Hanushek's technique for summarizing the literature was likely to produce misleading results because it could easily fail to detect real effects. Analyzing most of the same studies as Hanushek, they found that several kinds of resources, including class size, have beneficial effects on student outcomes.[39]

In the debate that has ensued, each side has applied assumptions that, if correct, favor its own position. These assumptions are not testable, so there is an intellectual standoff. Our view is that the literature on education production functions is sufficiently flawed, especially in the way that it treats class size, that neither method is very reliable.

The latest and most effective challenge comes from economist Alan Krueger, who questions the way that Hanushek selected estimates from the education production function literature to include in his summaries. For example, Hanushek's 1997 review included 277 estimates of class-size effects from 59 different studies. Different numbers of estimates were taken from different studies. Two studies contributed 24 estimates each. Seventeen studies contributed only one each.

Since each estimate counted equally in the analysis, some studies counted much more than others. According to Krueger and Diane Whitmore, "The number of estimates Hanushek extracted from a study is systematically related to the study's findings, with fewer estimates taken from studies that tend to find positive effects of smaller classes or greater expenditures per student."[40] Krueger and Whitmore do not question Hanushek's motives, but they do question his judgment.

Consensus is growing among researchers, including all those cited above, that the only way to reliably estimate the effect of class size is by conducting experimental studies that randomly assign otherwise similar students (and teachers) to classes of different sizes. Experimental studies avoid most of the methodological pitfalls of education production function studies and are less controversial to interpret. In a perfectly executed class-size experiment, class-size differences would be the only systematic source of differential achievement among students who get assigned to different class sizes.

Tennessee's Project STAR, funded by the Tennessee state legislature in 1985, is the largest experimental study of class size ever conducted.[41] It randomly assigned 11,600 students and teachers to small classes (13 to 17 students) or large classes (22 to 25 students). Students began with their assigned class sizes in kindergarten and continued through third grade. A number of researchers have examined the Project STAR data, and all find, on average, that students in smaller classes outperformed those in the larger classes. Moreover, the effects were roughly twice as large for blacks as for whites. In addition, students from small classes kept their advantage in achievement all the way through high school (though in standardized units it diminished), and they were also more likely to take college admissions exams.[42] For each outcome variable, the advantage of small classes was greater for blacks than for whites.

There have been questions raised about whether imperfections in the way the experiment was executed might have biased the results. However, analyses that test the sensitivity of the results to such factors have found no evidence that imperfections in implementation distorted the findings.[43]

Alan Krueger and Diane Whitmore use the elementary school pupil/teacher ratio to predict the black/white test score gap for fourth-graders for the 1970s through the 1990s. They find that the relationship between falling class sizes and the narrowing of the gap is very close to what one would have predicted based on class-size effects estimated in Project STAR.[44] They are appropriately cautious, however, in acknowledging that there were many other forces aside from class size that could also have contributed to changes in the test score gap.

Recently, California and Wisconsin have joined Tennessee as sites for research on the importance of class size. The California class-size initiative, adopted in 1996, allocates additional funds per student to classes of 20 or fewer students. Evaluators have reported "a small positive gain in achievement" that is associated with smaller classes, but they acknowledge that it is difficult to know for sure that these gains are caused by the changes in class size, as opposed to other reforms in the same classrooms.[45] They also report that California schools serving low-income, minority, and English-language-learning students have had difficulty competing for additional teachers and have suffered a greater decline in the qualifications of teachers than other schools. Hence, these schools have been slower to implement the initiative and have received disproportionately less class-size reduction revenue (which accrues after class sizes are reduced). It is possible that disadvantaged students fortunate enough to be placed in smaller classes have benefited from this initiative, while those whose schools have been unable to implement it have suffered.

To the degree that research shows low-income and minority students benefit most from reduced class sizes, the California initiative seems poorly targeted. As other states design their own initiatives, they should pay close attention to the California experience, in order to avoid disadvantaging the students who most need the benefits of smaller class sizes.

In Wisconsin, the Student Achievement Guarantee in Education (SAGE) Program is a five-year effort initiated by the state department for the benefit of schools serving low-income students.[46] It is being implemented in 80 schools across the state. Researchers at the University of Wisconsin, Madison, are conducting an evaluation of the initiative involving 31 schools in 21 districts. The study design is quasi-experimental, not random assignment. Specifically, the evaluators are comparing academic progress in schools where class sizes are being reduced to 15 students per teacher in the early grades to that in similar schools that have regular class sizes. The black/white gap in baseline composite scores (for language arts, reading, and math) was roughly 0.75 standard deviations in both the SAGE and the comparison schools. (Other racial and ethnic groups represent such small percentages of the students that their scores are not reported separately.) Average scores for blacks in the SAGE schools were roughly equal to those for blacks in the comparison schools at the time that the study began, and the same was true for whites.

The evidence from the SAGE project shows that most of the advantage of small classes was concentrated among black first-graders.[47] From our examination of the published data, we conclude that the main story in SAGE appears to be that black first-graders in regular classes learn less than black or white children in small classes or white children in regular classes. This first-grade experience is the main source of differences by the end of third grade. During the second and third grades, all groups learn similar amounts, but black children who were in regular classes in first grade do not make up the deficit from having learned less in that first year. This is very similar to what occurred with Tennessee's Project STAR: most of the differential gain between small and larger classes was concentrated in the first year that a student spent in small classes and was roughly twice as large for blacks as for whites.

A MATTER OF BALANCE

Should policy makers focus more on instructional quality and less on reducing class size? In our view, until more extensive and definitive class-size research is conducted, class sizes larger than the low twenties are probably ill-advised, especially in elementary schools. Because we lack definitive evidence from other sources, our judgment is based primarily on what teachers themselves report. In surveys over the years by the Educational Research Service, there has been a consistent shift in teachers' responses from characterizing class size as a minor problem to characterizing it as a major problem at class sizes of 23 to 24 students.[48] (Note that classrooms of 22 to 25 were the *large* ones in the Tennessee experiment.) Based on both the Tennessee and Wisconsin findings, class sizes in the neighborhood of 15 seem warranted for black kindergartners and first-graders in low-income schools.

At the same time that class size should not be neglected, it would be wrongheaded not to make instructional quality the top priority. Researchers in Project SAGE are studying the skills and practices that make some teachers more effective in small classrooms than others. There needs to be more research of this type to inform teacher training and professional development. There also needs to be greater effort to attract skilled people to the profession. *Teacher quality matters.* In most research that tries to study it, variation in teacher quality accounts for more of the variation in student achievement than any other schooling input and even rivals parental background in importance.

The evidence is clear. Studies that track the differential progress of students who have different teachers find very large teacher-to-teacher differences in effectiveness. Teachers who score higher on standardized tests tend to produce students who score higher on achievement tests, but schools that blacks and Latinos attend often attract teachers with lower scores.[49] Concerns about teacher quality that began growing in the 1980s are thus entirely appropriate—indeed necessary—if the society is serious about raising levels of achievement among all groups of students. There are active debates under way about how to improve classroom instruction. Some favor an emphasis on attracting more talent to the teaching profession, while others work to refine teacher training and professional development. We believe that both emphases are important to pursue and potentially quite consequential.

CONCLUSION

It seems clear that the nation's future depends fundamentally on the degree to which schools and communities can raise skill levels among children of all racial, ethnic, and socioeconomic backgrounds. Achievement disparities among today's students foreshadow socioeconomic disparities among tomorrow's families. Large socioeconomic disparities among families are morally objectionable and politically dangerous for the future of a society.

As we stated at the outset, the U.S. has achieved substantial progress in narrowing gaps between racial groups since *Brown* v. *Board of Education* in 1954. At the same time, there have been missed opportunities, and the remaining gaps are large. Integration came too slowly and produced fewer benefits than it might have. Head Start failed to produce as many lasting benefits as it would have if the schools to which graduates matriculated had been strong enough to sustain the gains. Title I has been a disappointment, but it still has a great deal of potential. Class-size effects are only now beginning to be understood, though they might have been many years ago if there had been more support for experimental research in education. In addition, we need much more information about which types of teacher training and professional development produce the best outcomes for the children that trainees end up teaching. The fact that such information has not been developed using high-quality research standards and then widely shared represents an extremely important set of missed opportunities.

Yet the nation's habit of missing opportunities to improve the outcomes of education need not continue to such a degree. Recent assertions by political leaders regarding the need for more research-based practices and policy decisions are encouraging—especially if the focus is on improving classroom practices, complemented by results-based accountability. If practitioners, political leaders, and researchers can make real the promise of today's public discourse about the need to provide a high-quality education to all children, then the next 50 years might bring us closer to the end of the long journey toward equality that began with *Brown*. We are guardedly optimistic and ready to work with others to get there. There is reason to be hopeful.

3. Some possible reasons are explored in Ronald F. Ferguson, "Test-Score Trends Along Racial Lines 1971 to 1996: Popular Culture and Community Academic Standards," in Neil Smelser, William Julius Wilson, and Faith Mitchell, eds., *America Becoming: Racial Trends and Their Consequences* (Washington, D.C.: National Academy Press, 2001), pp. 348-90.

4. Of course, there are also large disparities within groups. Thus many whites and Asians do poorly, and many blacks and Latinos do quite well.

5. Southern whites were not ready to share their schools. Immediately following the decision, the Court provided for a "cooling off" period. As reported in the *Atlanta Constitution Daily Newspaper* on 18 May 1954, "Not until next autumn will [the Court] even begin to hear arguments from the attorneys general of the 17 states involved on how to implement the ruling. ... It is no time to indulge the demagogues on either side nor to listen to those who always are ready to incite violence and hate." An article in the *Jackson Mississippi Daily News* was less open-minded. Titled "Bloodstains on White Marble Steps," it proclaimed, "Human blood may stain Southern soil in many places because of this decision, but the dark red stains of that blood will be in the marble steps of the United States Supreme Court building. White and Negro children in the same schools will lead to miscegenation. Miscegenation leads to mixed marriages, and mixed marriages lead to mongrelization of the human race."

6. James E. Ryan, "Schools, Race, and Money," *Yale Law School Journal*, vol. 109, 1999, p. 272.
7. See Michael J. Puma et al., *Prospects: Final Report on Student Outcomes* (Washington, D.C.: Planning and Evaluation Service, U.S. Department of Education, April 1997); and L. F. Carter, *A Study of Compensatory and Elementary Education: The Sustaining Effects Study* (Washington, D.C.: Office of Program Evaluation, U.S. Department of Education, 1983).
8. Geoffrey D. Borman et al., "Coordinating Categorical and Regular Programs: Effects on Title I Students' Educational Opportunities and Outcomes," in Geoffrey D. Borman, Samuel C. Stringfield, and Robert E. Slavin, eds., *Title I: Compensatory Education at the Crossroads* (Mahwah, N.J.: Erlbaum, 2001), pp. 79-116; and Geoffrey D. Borman and Jerome V. D'Agostino, "Title I and Student Achievement: A Quantitative Synthesis," in Borman, Stringfield, and Slavin, pp. 25-58.
9. See the discussion of this point in Sheri Oden, Lawrence J. Schweinhart, and David P. Weikart, *Into Adulthood: A Study of the Effects of Head Start* (Ypsilanti, Mich.: High/Scope Press, 2000).
10. D. T. Campbell and P. W. Frey, "The Implications of Learning Theory for the Fade-Out of Gains from Compensatory Education," in Jerome Hellmuth, ed., *Compensatory Education: A National Debate*, vol. 3 (New York: Brunner/Mazel, 1970), pp. 185-223; Valerie E. Lee and Susan Loeb, "Where Do Head Start Attendees End Up? One Reason Why Head Start Effects Fade Out," *Educational Evaluation and Policy Analysis*, vol. 17, 1995, pp. 62-82; and Janet Currie and Duncan Thomas, "Does Subsequent School Quality Affect the Long-Term Gains from Head Start?" unpublished manuscript, University of California, Los Angeles, 1995.
11. Oden, Schweinhart, and Weikart, op. cit.; and W. Steven Barnett, "Benefits of Compensatory Preschool Education," *Journal of Human Resources*, vol. 27, 1992, pp. 279-312.
12. James Coleman et al., *Equality of Educational Opportunity* (Washington, D.C.: Government Printing Office, 1966); and Michael A. Boozer, Alan Krueger, and Shari Wolkon, "Race and School Quality Since *Brown v. Board of Education*," in *Brookings Papers on Economic Activity, Microeconomics* (Washington, D.C.: Brookings Institution Press, 1992), pp. 269-338.
13. Michael Boozer and Cecilia Rouse, "Intraschool Variation in Class Size: Patterns and Implications," Working Paper No. 5144, National Bureau of Economic Research, Cambridge, Mass., 1995. Boozer and Rouse suggest that the data may be hiding remaining differences, if black and white students are in different types of classes. They point out that, for each type of class, blacks may still, on average, be in larger classes.
14. *Digest of Education Statistics* (Washington, D.C.: National Center for Education Statistics, 2000), Table 65.
15. See Jennifer O'Day and Marshall S. Smith, "Systemic Reform and Educational Opportunity," in Susan Fuhrman, ed., *Designing Coherent Education Policy: Improving the System* (San Francisco: Jossey-Bass, 1993), pp. 250-312; and Office of Technology Assessment, *Testing in American Schools* (Washington, D.C.: Congress of the United States, 1992), chap. 1.
16. See the discussion and statistics in Ferguson, op. cit.
17. See, for example, Gary Orfield and John T. Yun, "Resegregation in American Schools," Civil Rights Project, Harvard University, June 1999.
18. In its "Ruling on Relief," issued on 31 May 1955, the district courts were advised to consider a number of factors in determining the meaning of "all deliberate speed." These included "problems related to administration, arising from the physical condition of the school plant, the school transportation system, personnel, revision of school districts and attendance areas into compact units to achieve a system of determining admission to the public schools on a nonracial basis, and revision of local laws and regulations which may be necessary in solving the foregoing problems."
19. Gary Orfield and Susan E. Eaton, *Dismantling Desegregation: The Quiet Reversal of* Brown v. Board of Education (New York: New Press, 1996), p. 7.
20. However, Orfield and Yun, op. cit., point out that there were "findings of intentional discrimination by both state and local officials, which intensified segregation in the metropolitan area."
21. Thomas Cook, *School Desegregation and Black Achievement* (Washington, D.C.: U.S. Department of Education, 1984); and Janet W. Schofield, "Review of Research on School Desegregation's Impact on Elementary and Secondary School Students," in James A. Banks and Cherry A. McGee Banks, eds., *Handbook of Research on Multicultural Education* (New York: Macmillan, 1995), pp. 597-617.
22. Robert L. Crain and Rita E. Mahard, "The Effect of Research Methodology on Desegregation-Achievement Studies: A Meta-Analysis," *American Journal of Sociology*, vol. 88, 1983, pp. 839-54.
23. Christopher Jencks and Susan E. Mayer, "The Social Consequences of Growing Up in a Poor Neighborhood," in Laurence E. Lynn, Jr., and Michael G. H. McGreary, eds., *Inner-City Poverty in the United States* (Washington D.C.: National Academy Press, 1990), pp. 111-86.
24. Meredith Phillips, "Do African-American and Latino Children Learn More in Predominantly White Schools?," unpublished paper, School of Public Policy and Social Research, UCLA, 2001. Cited with permission.
25. Susan E. Mayer, "How Much Does a High School's Racial and Socioeconomic Mix Affect Graduation and Teenage Fertility Rates?," in Christopher Jencks and Paul E. Peterson, eds, *The Urban Underclass* (Washington, D.C.: Brookings Institution Press, 1991), pp. 187-222.
26. Orfield and Eaton, p. 57.
27. Richard D. Kahlenberg, *All Together Now: Creating Middle-Class Schools Through Public School Choice* (Washington, D.C.: Brookings Institution Press, 2001).
28. Amy Stuart Wells and Robert L. Crain, *Stepping Over the Color Line: African American Students in White Suburban Schools* (New Haven: Yale University Press, 1997).
29. James E. Rosenbaum et al., "Can the Kerner Commission's Housing Strategy Improve Employment, Education, and Social Integration for Low-Income Blacks?," *North Carolina Law Revie*, vol. 71, 1993, pp. 1519-56; and James E. Rosenbaum, "Changing the Geography of Opportunity by Expanding Residential Choice: Lessons from the Gautreaux Program," *Housing Policy Debate*, vol. 6, 1995, pp. 231-69.
30. Jens Ludwig, Helen F. Ladd, and Greg J. Duncan, "Urban Poverty and Educational Outcomes," in William G. Gale and Janet R. Pack, eds., *Brookings-Wharton Papers on Urban Affairs 2001* (Washington, D.C.: Brookings Institution Press, 2001), p. 4.
31. Gloria Ladson-Billings, *The Dreamkeepers: Successful Teachers of African American Children* (San Francisco: Jossey-Bass, 1994), pp. 60-61.
32. Meredith Phillips et al., "Family Background, Parenting Practices, and the Black-White Test Score Gap," in Christopher Jencks and Meredith Phillips, eds., *The Black-White Test Score Gap* (Washington, D.C.: Brookings Institution Press, 1998), pp. 103-45.
33. See Signithia Fordham, *Blacked Out: Dilemmas of Race, Success, and Identity at Capital High* (Chicago: University of Chicago Press, 1996); and Ronald F. Ferguson, "A Diagnostic Analysis of Black-White GPA Disparities in Shaker Heights, Ohio," in Diane Ravitch, ed., *Brookings Papers on Education Policy, 2001* (Washington, D.C.: Brookings Institution Press, 2001), pp. 347-411.

34. James A. Kulik, *An Analysis of the Research on Ability Grouping: Historical and Contemporary Perspectives* (Storrs: National Center on the Gifted and Talented, University of Connecticut, 1992).

35. See Jeannie Oakes, *Keeping Track: How Schools Structure Inequality* (New Haven, Conn.: Yale University Press, 1985); Marilee K. Finley, "Teachers and Tracking in a Comprehensive High School," *Sociology of Education*, vol. 57, 1984, pp. 233-43; Frances Schwartz, "Supporting or Subverting Learning: Peer Group Patterns in Four Tracked Schools," *Anthropology and Education Quarterly*, vol. 12, 1981, pp. 99-121; Mary H. Metz, *Classrooms and Corridors: The Crisis of Authority in Desegregated Secondary Schools* (Berkeley: University of California Press, 1978); and Adam Gamoran and Mark Berends, "The Effects of Stratification in Secondary Schools: Synthesis of Survey and Ethnographic Research," *Review of Educational Research*, Winter 1987, pp. 415-35.

36. Thomas L. Good, "Two Decades of Research on Teacher Expectations: Findings and Future Directions," *Journal of Teacher Education*, July-August 1987, pp. 32-47.

37. Ronald F. Ferguson, "Teachers' Perceptions and Expectations and the Black-White Test Score Gap," in Jencks and Phillips, pp. 273-317; and idem, "Can Schools Narrow the Black-White Test Score Gap?," in Jencks and Phillips, pp. 318-74. These two reviews show that teachers have similar expectations for black students and white students with similar past patterns of performance. But that says nothing about the treatment of students with latent or unexpressed potential.

38. Kulik, op. cit.

39. Eric A. Hanushek, "The Economics of Schooling: Production Efficiency in Public Schools," *Journal of Economic Literature*, September 1986, pp. 1141-77; and idem, "Assessing the Effects of School Resources on Student Performance: An Update," *Educational Evaluation and Policy Analysis*, vol. 19, 1997, pp. 141-64.

40. Steven G. Rivkin, Eric A. Hanushek, and John F. Kain, "Teachers, Schools, and Academic Achievement," Working Paper No. 6691, National Bureau of Economic Research, Cambridge, Mass., 2000; and William L. Sanders and Sandra P. Horn, "The Tennessee Value-Added Assessment System (TVAA): Mixed Model Methodology in Educational Assessment," in Anthony J. Shinkfield and Daniel L. Stufflebeam, eds., *Teacher Evaluation: Guide to Effective Practice* (Boston: Kluwer Academic Publishers, 1995), pp. 337-50.

41. See Larry V. Hedges, Richard D. Laine, and Rob Greenwald, "Does Money Matter? A Meta-Analysis of Studies of the Effects of Differential Inputs on Student Outcomes," *Educational Researcher*, April 1994, pp. 5-14; Larry V. Hedges, Richard D. Laine, and Rob Greenwald, "Money Does Matter Somewhere: A Reply to Hanushek," *Educational Researcher*, May 1994, pp. 9-10; Rob Greenwald, Larry V. Hedges, and Richard D. Laine, "The Effect of School Resources on Student Achievement," *Review of Educational Research*, vol. 66, 1996, pp. 361-96; and Larry V. Hedges and Rob Greenwald, "Have Times Changed? The Relation Between School Resources and Student Performance," in Gary Burtless, ed., *Does Money Matter? The Effect of School Resources on Student Achievement and Adult Success* (Washington, D.C.: Brookings Institution Press, 1996), pp. 74-92.

42. Alan B. Krueger and Diane Whitmore, "Would Smaller Classes Help Close the Black-White Achievement Gap?," paper presented at Closing the Gap: Promising Approaches to Reducing the Achievement Gap, a Brookings Institution conference, January 2001, p. 5.

43. See Elizabeth Word et al., *Student/Teacher Achievement Ratio (STAR): Tennessee's K-3 Class Size Study, Final Summary Report, 1985-1990* (Knoxville: Tennessee State Department of Education, 1990); Barbara A. Nye et al., "The Lasting Benefits Study Seventh Grade: Executive Summary," Center of Excellence for Research and Policy on Basic Skills, Tennessee State University, Nashville, June 1994; Barbara A. Nye et al., "Tennessee's Bold Experiment: Using Research to Inform Policy and Practice," *Tennessee Education*, Winter 1993, pp. 10-17; Barbara Nye and Larry V. Hedges, "The Effects of Small Classes on Academic Achievement: The Results of the Tennessee Class Size Experiment," *American Educational Research Journal*, Spring 2000, pp. 123-51; and Frederick Mosteller, "The Tennessee Study of Class Size in the Early School Grades," *The Future of Children*, Summer/Fall 1995, pp. 113-27.

44. Krueger and Whitmore, op. cit.

45. Nye and Hedges, op. cit.; and Alan B. Krueger, "Understanding the Magnitude and Effect of Class Size on Student Achievement," Working Paper No. 121, Economic Policy Institute, Washington, D.C., October 2000.

46. Krueger and Whitmore, op. cit. See also David Grissmer, Ann Flanagan, and Stephanie Williamson, "Why Did the Black-White Score Gap Narrow in the 1970s and 1980s?," in Jencks and Phillips, pp. 182-226; and Grissmer et al., *Improving Student Achievement: What State NAEP Test Scores Tell Us* (Santa Monica, Calif.: RAND Corporation, 2000).

47. George Bohrnstedt, "Class Size Reduction in California: Early Findings Signal Promise and Concerns," 2001. Available at www.air.org/projects/csr.htm.

48. John A. Zahorik, "Reducing Class Size Leads to Individualized Instruction," *Educational Leadership*, September 1999, pp. 50-53.

49. Alex Molnar, Phillip Smith, and John Zahorik, "1999-2000 Evaluation Results of the Student Achievement Guarantee in Education (SAGE) Program," December 2000. Available at www.uwm.edu/Dept/CERAI/sage.html.

50. Glen E. Robinson and James H. Wittebods, "Class Size Research: A Related Cluster Analysis for Decision Making," Research Brief, Educational Research Service, Arlington, Va., 1986.

51. Ronald F. Ferguson, "Certification Test Scores, Teacher Quality, and Student Achievement," in David W. Grissmer and J. Michael Ross, eds., *Analytic Issues in the Assessment of Student Achievement* (Washington, D.C.: National Center for Education Statistics, 2000).

RONALD F. FERGUSON is a lecturer in public policy and a senior research associate at the Wiener Center for Social Policy Research and John F. Kennedy School of Government, Harvard University, Cambridge, Mass. JAL MEHTA is a graduate student in sociology and social policy at the Wiener Center for Social Policy Research and Department of Sociology, Harvard University. This article has been adapted from a chapter in *Achieving High Standards for All*, edited by Timothy Ready, Christopher Edley, and Catherine Snow (National Academy Press, 2002).

Article 31

The 50th Anniversary

Against the Tide:
Desegregated High Schools and Their 1980 Graduates

Adults who attended racially mixed high schools in the late 1970s, at the peak of school desegregation, are in a unique position to report on the experience and to reflect on how it affected students of different races. Having interviewed more than 500 people involved in six diverse high schools in the 1970s, including 242 graduates of the class of 1980, the authors find that school desegregation fundamentally changed the people who lived through it, yet had a more limited impact on the larger society.

BY AMY STUART WELLS, JENNIFER JELLISON HOLME, ANITA TIJERINA REVILLA, AND AWO KORANTEMAA ATANDA

IN THE LATE 1970s, a Jewish teenager named Bernard Rose[1] attended a racially diverse high school in New Jersey. He took the top-level classes, played two varsity sports, starred in the school play, and went on to a respected public university. In an interview shortly after his 40th birthday in 2002, Bernard looked back fondly on his high school experience, contrasting it to his years in an all-white grammar school where he was ostracized socially and "tormented" emotionally. In high school, he said, "I was popular with black people, I was popular with white people, I was popular." He added, "It was so much better than being a loser."

Bernard found solace in the fact that he was never singled out individually in his high school, which was 57% black, 36% white, and 7% Latino. He said the black students "didn't have anything against me personally. ... They were calling everybody that was white, 'white boy.'" And despite such racial taunts, the only time Bernard had a white/black altercation was when he accidentally hit a black student with a spit wad aimed at his white friend. "But even then, he didn't beat me up."

Certainly, Bernard said, there were problems, including prevalent resegregation across classrooms and cafeteria tables. He recalled traveling throughout the school day with the same 30 white students from one advanced class to the next, while the regular and remedial classes were filled mostly with black students. He does not remember learning much about the civil rights movement or African American history in school. In fact, he does not recall much discussion about race at all in his desegregated school.

At the same time, in Bernard's school and many others that were racially diverse at that time, students did get to know one another across racial lines, especially through such activities as athletics, drama, band, and student government. According to Bernard, by his senior year, students had transcended many racial barriers, and there was a "growing togetherness" evidenced by more racial mixing inside and outside of school. Parties in which black students and white students went to one another's homes, he said, were far more common by senior year. In fact, he commented that, if such social mixing could have continued, "you may have actually had, like, the creation of a truly integrated society."

But in June of 1980, in the midst of the Iranian hostage crisis and Ronald Reagan's presidential campaign, Bernard and his classmates graduated from high school and went on to higher education or full-time jobs. The integrated society Bernard talked about never came to be. In fact, he and other 1980 graduates of desegregated schools found that, after high school, their lives became more racially segregated. In college, Bernard recalled, even though the student body was racially diverse, the students on campus were divided physically and socially according to where they lived, which programs they were enrolled in, and the sororities and fraternities they joined.

Today, Bernard lives in an affluent suburb in New Jersey that is predominantly white. Though he lives not far geographically from his high school, which is now all black and Latino, he might as well live in another world. His young children are entering a predominantly white public school system that is highly ranked according to state test scores and is also highly competitive. Socially, he interacts mostly with Jewish friends and family. Most of his exposure to African Americans or Latinos comes through his work in the New York City-based welding company that he owns and operates. Either they are his employees, or they live in housing projects where his company installs metal bars on the windows.

A graduate of a racially mixed high school who drives his SUV from an affluent suburb to some of the poorest neighborhoods in New York City, Bernard has a special vantage point from which to assess racial inequality in the U.S. and to comment on the limited but valuable impact of school desegregation on our increasingly diverse society. When asked what school desegregation accomplished, he is quick to say that it did not fail, but it also did not do enough, because "the white people still went back to their white houses, and their white homes, and their white society."

Bernard's story epitomizes the experiences of many members of his generation who attended racially mixed schools. While the specifics vary across racial and ethnic groups, as well as school sites, much of what Bernard observed during and after high school speaks to larger social trends of the past 25 years: namely, that school desegregation policy was pushing against a powerful tide of racial segregation and inequality in our society and that it could not be expected to solve all the problems by itself. Furthermore, while graduates of desegregated schools say they are better prepared for a racially diverse society, many—especially the white graduates—find their adult lives and their children's lives more segregated than their schools were 20-plus years ago.

This spring, as we celebrate the 50th anniversary of *Brown v. Board of Education*, we need to listen to the voices of Bernard and others who lived through school desegregation and who can reflect on both its successes and limitations. These are the people we interviewed in our five-year study of six racially mixed high schools in different regions of the country.[2] Across these sites, we collected hundreds of historical documents and interviewed more than 500 people, including local leaders, district officials, and educators from these six high schools, as well as graduates of the class of 1980. We found that these former educators and students from racially mixed high schools have learned powerful lessons about race and education that Americans of all generations should heed before drawing conclusions about the value of school desegregation policy.

WHY THE CLASS OF 1980?

We chose to study the history of these six schools during the late 1970s because, despite the 1954 *Brown* ruling, most desegregation in this country did not occur until after 1968, when white resistance was finally overpowered by additional federal court orders and legislation. In fact, the late 1970s through the early 1980s were the peak years of school desegregation in the U.S. By 1988, ongoing efforts by the Reagan Administration and the first Bush Administration to dismantle these policies had begun to pay off, and school desegregation was in decline.[3]

The class of 1980, which entered kindergarten in 1967, moved through elementary school just as the old system of segregation was breaking down in the South and facing challenges in the North. National data show that members of this class were, on average, more likely to have classmates of other races than any class before them or the more recent classes of the last 15 years.[4]

Furthermore, our research suggests that the late 1970s was a particularly pivotal moment in the history of school desegregation policy across the country. By this time in many towns, the initial protests and racial conflict that occurred when students were first reassigned to desegregated schools in the early 1970s had subsided to some degree. According to many people we interviewed, this late-1970s era was a relatively more sedate time. Strong and vocal opposition to desegregation had died down, and the promise of a new, more racially integrated society was still alive, at least in those school districts that had not already lost most of their white students.[5] Yet, at the same time, this was a transition period, following Watergate and the Vietnam War, as the country sat on the verge of a conservative revolution that would quickly squelch any policies designed to further an agenda of racial equality.

In the middle of all this came the class of 1980—students born during the civil rights movement, at the very tail end of the Baby Boom, but who would come of age as adults during the Reagan years. And yet there was no research on what these students of 20-plus years ago experienced in their racially mixed high schools and how they believed that experience had influenced their lives as adults. Indeed, while there is a limited body of research on the long-term effects of school desegregation on African Americans, we found virtually no literature on white or Latino adults who had attended racially mixed schools.[6]

We believe that the stories told by the class of 1980 of cross-racial friendships, racial inequality, and missed opportunities within their racially mixed schools and the larger society are especially salient in light of the anniversary of *Brown* and the current move back to segregated schools. Below, we will briefly describe the circumstances that existed in each of the six high schools in the Seventies. Then we will present a summary of our major findings.

- Austin High School, Austin, Texas. Desegregated via majority-to-minority transfers from several different attendance areas; racial makeup during the 1970s: 15% African American, 19% Hispanic, and 66% white.

- Dwight Morrow High School, Englewood, New Jersey. Desegregated by receiving white students from Englewood Cliffs via a sending/receiving plan and by being the only public high school serving the racially diverse town of Englewood. Busing and reassignment occurred at the elementary level. Racial makeup during the 1970s: 57% African American, 7% Hispanic, and 36% white.
- John Muir High School, Pasadena, California. Desegregated originally by drawing from several diverse attendance areas and in the 1970s through mandatory busing. Racial makeup during the 1970s: 50% African American, 11% Hispanic, 35% white, 5% Asian/Pacific Islander.
- Shaker Heights High School, Shaker Heights, Ohio. Desegregated as the only high school in a district experiencing an influx of African American students from Cleveland. Efforts were made in Shaker Heights to integrate neighborhoods, and student reassignment occurred at the elementary level. Racial makeup during the 1970s: 39% "minority" (mostly African American) and 61% white.
- Topeka High School, Topeka, Kansas. Desegregated via assigned attendance areas; students were also reassigned at the junior high and elementary levels. Racial makeup during the 1970s: 20% African American, 8% Hispanic, 69% white.
- West Charlotte High School, Charlotte, North Carolina. Desegregated via court order to reassign students from white high schools to this historically black high school. Racial makeup during the 1970s: 50% African American and 50% white.

Overall, we interviewed a total of 242 graduates of these six high schools. They fell into the following categories: 79 African Americans, 136 whites, 21 Latinos, two Asians, and four people of mixed race. We interviewed six of these graduates a second time to elicit more in-depth portraits of the participants. Our central finding is that school desegregation fundamentally changed the people who lived through it, yet had a more limited impact on the larger society. Within this overarching finding are two overlapping and intertwined sets of findings that challenge any simple assumptions about the success or failure of school desegregation but also point to the limits of a policy that contradicts the racial status quo in American society.

SWIMMING AGAINST THE TIDE

Our first set of major findings reveals that public schools could achieve only so much integration and racial equality in the midst of a segregated and unequal society. Our data and analyses demonstrate that racially mixed public schools of the late 1970s were doing more than most other major institutions in our society—except perhaps the military—to bring people of different racial and ethnic backgrounds together and to foster equal opportunity. But they could not, on their own, come close to fulfilling the promise of *Brown* v. *Board of Education*.

Despite the very different social and political contexts and the divergent racial demographics of the six schools we studied, we found that their desegregation efforts bore several common characteristics.

Desegregation on white terms. In each of the six communities and schools in our study, policy makers and educators tried to make school desegregation as palatable as possible for middle-class white parents and students. On a political level, this made perfect sense. The idea was to stave off white and middle-class flight, which would leave the public schools politically and economically vulnerable. But in their attempts to meet the demands of these more powerful families, educators and officials too often ignored the needs of students of color and the poor.

Efforts to please white and more affluent parents manifested themselves in similar ways across the six communities. For instance, in these communities, as in most districts implementing school desegregation, African American and Latino students bore most of the burden of desegregation.[7] More often than not, it was the historically black or Latino public schools that were closed when districts were forced to desegregate their schools. As a result, black and brown students were more likely to be riding buses longer distances at younger ages than most white students in desegregating school districts. At least one historically black school was eventually closed in five of the six districts that we studied, and in all of these districts, black students, parents, and activists felt that their communities shouldered most of the burden to achieve racial balance in the schools.

What we learn from our data, however, is that this was not merely an issue of inconvenience—of getting up early and getting home late. Rather, this was an issue of pride and dignity, of white society saying there is nothing of value in the black or Latino community. As one white school district administrator in Austin, Texas, noted, "When you tell people that their schools are inferior, to some degree, you're telling them they're inferior."

Perhaps even more pervasive was the consistent resegregation of students across classrooms.

Same schools, different classes: uneven knowledge of and access to high-track classes. One of the most prevalent incentives that school officials used to keep white parents and students happy was the creation of high-track or gifted classes in each school. These tracks were ostensibly offered to challenge the most advanced students. But the racial overtones and implications cannot be ignored, as in school after school, these top-level classes were almost entirely white.[8]

We recognize that many factors affected the resegregation of students within desegregated schools—not the least of which was the unequal schooling that black and Latino students had received prior to desegregation, as well as the higher poverty rates of their families. But we also have a great deal of evidence in our data to suggest that white students were given more information about and easier access to honors, AP, or advanced classes. From practices that labeled students as "gifted" as early as kindergarten and then channeled them through the grade levels in the "appropriate" classes, to more subtle forms of sorting students that entailed teacher recommendations and support to get into the best classes, the schools and districts we studied managed to create incredible and consistent levels of within-school segregation.

At all six of the high schools we studied, white students such as Bernard said that they had many of the same students in all of their upper-level classes and that this group of students constituted a separate, predominantly white "school-within-a-school." For instance, a white 1980 graduate of Shaker Heights High School who was in all high-level classes noted: "You know, I mean this AP thing … was actually also like a school-within-a-school. And so in a way I was really insulated from a lot of … stuff." This graduate also noted that, while it was not always the same 20 students in every class, "it would be very unusual to see somebody, like a new face in one class, that you didn't see in any other class."

Over the long run, in five out of the six schools that we studied, even these practices, which often offended African American and Latino parents and students, were not enough to retain large numbers of white, middle-class families. But the effort to please white families and keep them from fleeing to whiter school districts just down the road illustrates how difficult it was for schools to live up to the goals of school desegregation given the larger societal forces working against them—including housing segregation, economic inequality, and racial politics.

"Colorblindness" as a goal. Against the backdrop of racial inequality described above, the educators, administrators, and graduates of the six schools we studied said that they rarely talked about issues of race in the late 1970s and that, overall, the goal of the era was to be totally "colorblind."[9] This goal was especially important in the eyes of the educators. In fact, it was a very rare exception to find an educator who had taught in one of these schools in the late 1970s who did not espouse this colorblind ideology.

Educators offered two central explanations for *why* colorblindness was so important. The first had to do with their prior experiences, particularly in the early 1970s, when in several of the districts and schools we studied there had been a great deal of racial tension and even "rioting." By the late 1970s, things had calmed down in these settings, and so colorblindness was seen as the best way to "keep the peace" and to "keep a lid on things." The educators argued that, by not talking about race and striving to be colorblind, they could prevent such incidents from happening again.

A second major rationale for the colorblind perspective adopted by educators was the simple and well-meaning argument that "people are people," no matter what color they are. From this, they concluded that teachers and students in these schools needed to treat people as individuals and not as members of a particular racial or ethnic group. This view was then seen as the most helpful way to get people to look beyond race and to emphasize personal connections across racial and ethnic groups, even as these high schools were, in many ways, organized around racial inequality.

Understanding this finding explains not only what colorblindness looked like in the six racially mixed schools, but also how it shaped and was shaped by the experiences of the educators and students. The colorblind ideology contributed largely to the uncertainty and contradictions about race that many of these graduates, especially the white graduates, express today. According to one white graduate of West Charlotte High School:

> [We] knew our mission was to make us all colorblind. That was the objective…. In the late 1970s, early 1980s, [for] everyone [to] be the same. That has since changed to embracing the differences through diversity…. It was [a] very different time and different objective.

Yet this graduate, like so many of those we interviewed, felt unprepared for this changed perspective because the colorblind view had served so many of them—especially the white graduates—so well, for so long.

Moving closer, staying apart. In spite of the resegregation of students across classes and the taboo against talking about race in their schools, the majority of the class of 1980 graduates we interviewed recalled becoming friends or at least acquaintances with people of another racial group while in high school. These interactions and cross-race friendships were most likely formed through extracurricular activities. Athletics, in particular, tended to facilitate cross-racial friendships, especially among boys, who often bonded with teammates of all colors as they played competitive sports. But other activities, including student government, drama, band, and chorus, also brought students together across racial lines. Furthermore, we found that, in a few of these schools, as the class of 1980 neared graduation, the racial barriers seemed to diminish, and social cliques—once extremely segregated by race—became slightly less so.

Still, throughout their high school years, the graduates we interviewed remembered that, while they learned a great deal from their interactions with students of other racial and ethnic groups, their closest friends tended to be of the same race, and the social cliques remained racially identifiable even as more students crossed their boundaries. It was in the two high schools in which white students were in the minority—Dwight Morrow and John Muir—that the social integration by senior year was most pronounced and that many white students, such as Bernard, found a reprieve from the more cliquish and socially exclusive predominantly white schools they had attended.

Of course, the ongoing segregation across racial and ethnic lines was partly the result of logistical and historical facts—e.g., who grew up with whom, who had attended elementary school and junior high with whom, and who lived near whom. For instance, we found that "close" friendships tended to involve the same race, even in the schools in which "everyone got along" fairly well. But there is no denying that divisions along racial lines were also the result of a powerful social hierarchy dividing students not only by race but also by social class and other factors, including physical attractiveness, skin color, and athletic ability. For instance, it was mostly the athletes or cheerleaders from minority racial backgrounds in any given school—usually African American or Latino students but sometimes white students—who were more likely to be accepted into the "popular crowd," often making these popular cliques the most integrated.

As an African American graduate of West Charlotte noted, "The black students who were in the clubs, student council, cheerleaders' squad, and things like that, they did congregate and go out with the white students after school. Maybe they did things after practice ... and you would see them talking more, or walking to class more together."

Still, even these popular "minority" students did not always feel fully accepted within these groups. Instead, they often found that these friendships went only "so far," meaning that in many instances students did not feel welcome or comfortable in the homes of students of different racial or ethnic backgrounds.

In addition, to the extent that there was any interracial dating in these schools, it tended to be the athletically gifted African American and Latino males who dated white females. It was very rare to find instances in which white boys had dated African American or Latino girls.

All of these findings suggest the many ways in which broader societal inequalities demarcated by race, class, and gender were reproduced in these schools. Such social hierarchies were entrenched in the local communities and thus easily permeated the school walls. Nonetheless, students reported that they had important cross-racial interactions that they could not have had in a one-race school. As we see below, these interactions changed them in some fundamental and long-lasting ways.

THAT WAS THEN, THIS IS NOW

Our second set of major findings examines the lives of the adult graduates and asks how they make sense of their desegregated school experiences more than 20 years later. We found that, overwhelmingly, graduates of all racial and ethnic backgrounds were glad they had attended a racially diverse high school but that their lives today and the experiences of their children—especially the children of the white graduates—are much more segregated than their experiences in high school.

Learning through experience. In spite of the findings noted above, all of the 242 graduates we interviewed expressed some gratitude for having attended desegregated high schools. Reflecting on those days, graduates from all racial backgrounds said that their high schools had provided them with one of their only opportunities to come together in a setting with people of other racial or ethnic backgrounds. Although this experience was not always easy and occasionally involved a great deal of pain and frustration, the graduates said that they obtained a valuable social education in these schools.

Ultimately, these graduates took away lessons that they said could not be learned any other way but through experience in a desegregated setting. As a mixed-race graduate from John Muir High School noted, her high school taught her invaluable "life lessons" that could not be learned through books. She contrasted her experience with that of people who went to more segregated schools, some of whom may "test really well, but you put them out in the real world, and ... they can't make it."

Thus graduates of all racial and ethnic backgrounds emphasized the importance of "living" through integration and stressed that the type of social education they received is not obtainable through books. They all pointed to the increased level of comfort they now have in racially diverse settings, especially settings in which they are in the minority.

Indeed, the lessons these graduates said they took with them from their high school experiences were all the more valuable because they now know just how unusual their diverse school experiences were. It was only when they had graduated from high school, these graduates now say, that they realized what they had gained in comparison with their peers who had not attended diverse schools and who now seem more close-minded, prejudiced, and fearful of other races. Still, there were important differences across racial and ethnic groups in terms of *what* the students learned about race and how it has helped them as adults.

For instance, the white graduates stressed that they gained a greater appreciation for other cultures in high school and that they were less likely to revert to stereotypes or make assumptions about others based on race. They also stressed their decreased fear of people of color and of predominately nonwhite environments. They frequently compared themselves to their white spouses and friends who did not attend diverse schools and who are often fearful in racially diverse or predominantly black or Latino settings.

Meanwhile, the graduates of color also stressed their greater sense of comfort in interracial settings. But these graduates emphasized that they were not simply prepared to get along with others, but that they had learned through experience how to cope better with the prejudice they were likely to encounter in predominantly white settings. In addition, many graduates of color said that high school left them better able to deal with life in a white-dominated society because they had learned that not all whites are racist. A number of graduates of color also observed that, through their daily interactions with whites in high school, they had learned that they could compete with whites academically, which gave them a confidence that they felt they would not have gained in a segregated high school.

Being prepared for "the real world." This finding highlights one of the central paradoxes of school desegregation policy: namely, it was designed to bring young people of different backgrounds together to help prepare them for adult lives in our racially and ethnically diverse society, and thus it should help the next generation overcome segregation in the United States. Clearly, what we learn from the stories of the graduates is that, while attending racially mixed schools did, for the most part, help them learn to "get along" with and feel more comfortable with people of different racial and ethnic backgrounds, such learning did not change the fact that the adult world is *highly segregated* in terms of housing, employment, social interaction, and settings for worship. Thus, even when the graduates of these high schools have actively sought more racially diverse environments—truer for graduates of color than for white graduates—there have not been a lot of options. In other words, the pattern of racial segregation that this generation was supposed to change after its experiences in desegregated schools proved to be much more powerful than the will of this single cohort of graduates.

Three-fourths of the whites we interviewed described their current neighborhoods as predominantly white. Meanwhile, 56% of African Americans and about two-thirds of Latinos reported living in diverse or predominantly white neighborhoods. Still, almost 20% of these African American graduates said that their white neighbors were moving out of their neighborhoods, making them more segregated. The fact that the graduates of color sought integrated neighborhoods at a higher rate than the white graduates says something about the economic benefits that some racial and ethnic groups derive from the current segregated system. In other words, the white graduates of desegregated schools have much stronger economic incentives not to change the status quo.

For the most part, after high school, these graduates entered a racially segregated housing market and, to a lesser extent, a segregated job market. In fact, we learned that these graduates were more likely to interact with members of other racial and ethnic groups at work than they were in most other realms of their lives. But even in these more diverse work settings, people of color are more likely to be in more subservient roles, and whites are more likely to be in leadership or management positions—a dynamic that mirrors the tracking in desegregated high schools and challenges meaningful cross-racial interactions on equal terms.

The increased segregation after high school appears to have begun immediately after graduation. For instance, the graduates who went on to college talked about the social milieu of their college campuses as being far more segregated than that of their high schools. They talked about students of different racial and ethnic groups occupying different areas of the campuses, with very few opportunities to mix and interact as they had in high school through extracurricular activities and common spaces.

And even for the minority of graduates—more graduates of color than white graduates—who sought and found housing in integrated neighborhoods, their social circles, including their churches, and most of their close friends tended to be of the same race. For instance, an African American graduate of Topeka High School, reflecting on whom he spent most of his free time with, noted that, even though he lived in a predominantly white neighborhood, he spent most of his free time with African Americans—his family and people from his church, where he ran a youth group. "I think that's just because I still spend a lot of social time there. The congregation ... is predominantly African American. The kids that I work with are predominantly African American. And so I think that has a lot to do with, you know, just who I spend most of the ... social time with." This finding forces us to face the mismatch between the policy of school desegregation and the racially divided society in which we now live.

A different time. Another extremely poignant finding from our study speaks directly to the contrast between the current social, political, and economic context and that of 25 years ago. The vast majority of 1980 graduates said that they see so many differences between when they went through high school and today, when they are making decisions regarding their own children's education. Gone are the days when political leaders focused on issues of equity and equal educational opportunities, as well as racial harmony. Today, the political climate lends itself to education policies that stress accountability and high-stakes testing. At the same time, the economy has created much more income inequality over the last two decades, leaving the haves—mostly upper-middle-class professionals—more focused than ever on maintaining their status by providing their children educational opportunities that other children do not have.

Thus the comparatively low-pressure era of the 1970s, when parents were not facing the prospect that their choice of a high school for their children could make or break their entire educational and possibly economic future, seems very distant now. The 1980 graduates recounted how much less pressure they and their parents felt about whether or not they attended the "best" high school—at least as defined by state tests and rankings. They contrasted that with their own anxiety about their children and whether or not they are in the "right" preschool program, one that will allow them to matriculate into the "right" elementary school and so on up through the education system.

In addition, graduates discussed the political and social differences between then and now. They noted that the focus today is much more on individual gains and less on changing society for the better. As one white graduate of West Charlotte High School commented in comparing her school days to those of her sons, who attend a predominantly white and affluent private school:

> Things seem a lot more materialistic to me now.... I mean, my kids and all those children are just in sixth grade this year. But already I'm seeing the clothes are important, you know, movies, the TV, all that and the computer, all that they have and that didn't seem as important to us. And you know, we had things ... it was important to be cool in certain respects, but it wasn't the material stuff. And you know, we were all coming off the Sixties still, and Seventies. I mean ... there was still a lot about women's rights, and it was a time people were still looking for equality and their place in the world, and that seemed to be more what was important. Not that that's not going on now, but it just seems to me *stuff* is important.

This pressure to make sure they get ahead and stay ahead was expressed by the white, upper-middle-class graduates in particular and translated into their seeking out schools with the best academic reputations and highest test scores, regardless of the racial makeup of the student body. And these graduates were often the ones with the resources to buy the homes or pay the tuition that would allow their children to attend such schools, which were often predominantly white or Asian and very affluent. In fact, of the white graduates we interviewed, 60% of those with school-age or nearly school-age children already enrolled them or planned to enroll them in public or private schools that fit this description. And this was true even as they lamented that their own children would not benefit from the racial diversity they had in their own school days.

Meanwhile, the graduates of color were more likely to seek out predominantly white schools or very racially diverse schools for their children. Indeed, about three-fourths of those with children in school or close to school age already had their children in or said they would enroll them in predominantly white or racially diverse schools. And despite these graduates' stronger commitment to racially diverse schools, their choices, too, were framed in terms of school quality more than integration. In other words, these African American and Latino graduates had a savvy understanding of how "green follows white"—meaning they knew that many middle- and upper-middle-class white parents are politically and economically able to demand high-quality programs in their children's schools.

This last finding speaks to the power of social trends, and the fear they foster, to override the life experiences of parents and supplant their desire for their own children to have cross-racial relationships similar to their own. While this shift in values is truer for the white and affluent graduates than for the graduates of color, its prevalence among both groups speaks to the difficulty in our racially unequal society of creating diverse schools that are good enough for those who have other choices—especially today, when the public policy tools needed to create such schools are being dissolved.

CONCLUSION

Reflecting on the late 1970s and the role of his generation of desegregated students in making any lasting change in society, Bernard Rose, a 1980 graduate of Dwight Morrow High School, noted that everybody is a product of his or her time. He said that in the late 1970s, in the post-Watergate and post-Vietnam era of high inflation, a poor economy, and lines at gas stations, there was a lot of political apathy, which was a stark contrast to the prior era of the civil rights movement.

By the time Bernard and his classmates got to high school, much of the hard work to get black, white, and Latino students together under one roof had been done by other people. It was clear that the struggle for more racial equality needed to go to the next level, which would involve more than just desegregating the public schools. It would have meant pursuing integrated housing and seeking greater economic equality. But, as we know now, this next level was never achieved, and the schools were left holding the bag as the society clearly abandoned any notions of broader social change. In Bernard's words describing that time:

> The desegregation had taken place, people died for the cause, you know, the tumult was over with. [We were on to] smoothing out the rough edges and really, you know, trying to take it to the next level. Well, that would have required a national agenda, not even a local agenda. I mean ... it would have had to have been a national priority.

Clearly, once these graduates left their racially diverse high schools, desegregation and greater racial equality were no longer national priorities. In fact, dismantling school desegregation became a much higher priority. Meanwhile, there sat the class of 1980, more prepared for racial integration than any group before them—but with no place to go.

In essence, this diverse group of graduates told us that school desegregation was not easy, but it was worth it. They said they wished they had the same exposure to people of different racial backgrounds in their adult lives as they had in school. Furthermore, echoing public opinion polls on these issues, many lamented that in the current policy context—when test scores matter more than diversity—their own children do not have the same exposure to the racial diversity that they had. We argue that there are some fairly simple ways policy makers could amend existing school choice and accountability laws to help support racially diverse schools.[10] But to do so would require some shift in policy makers' priorities.

Thus we believe it is important to place the fairly optimistic perspectives of these graduates in the context of a society that was in many ways founded and developed along racially segregated lines. From our older history of slavery and legalized segregation to our more recent history of separate and unequal suburban sprawl and the public policies that support it, the United States has a long record of racial inequality. The public schools that have managed to bring people from different racial and ethnic backgrounds together for even a short period of time have been swimming against the tide of our society. The graduates of these schools have not changed the world. In fact, many of them have (sometimes unwittingly) done their part as adults to perpetuate our segregated society. Still, in the sense of loss they feel about the racial diversity they once enjoyed in high school, there is hope that our segregated society is not the way it has to be.

---

1. All names have been changed to protect the identity of the people we interviewed.
2. Our study, titled *Understanding Race and Education*, was funded by the Spencer Foundation, the Joyce Foundation, and the Ford Foundation. We are grateful to these foundations for their support, but the views expressed herein are our own. For our study, we designated a school as "racially mixed" when no one racial or ethnic group constituted more than 75% of the student population.
3. See Gary Orfield and Chungmei Lee, Brown *at 50: King's Dream or Plessy's Nightmare?* (Cambridge, Mass.: Harvard Civil Rights Project, January 2004); Gary Orfield, *Schools More Separate: Consequences of a Decade of Resegregation* (Cambridge, Mass.: Harvard Civil Rights Project, 2001); and "Resegregation in American Schools: A Civil Rights Alert," Harvard Civil Rights Project, Cambridge, Mass., 2002. These documents and other information related to desegregation can be found on the Web at www.civilrightsproject.harvard.edu.
4. Orfield, op. cit.; Erica Frankenberg and Chungmei Lee, *Race in American Public Schools: Rapidly Resegregating School Districts* (Cambridge, Mass.: Harvard Civil Rights Project, 2002); "Resegregation in American Schools"; and David Rusk, "Trends in School Segregation," in Century Foundation Task Force on the Common School, ed., *Divided We Fall: Coming Together Through School Choice* (New York: Century Foundation Press, 2002), pp. 61-85.
5. After 1974, when the U.S. Supreme Court ruled in *Milliken* v. *Bradley* that court-ordered urban/suburban school desegregation was possible only when plaintiffs could prove that suburban districts had helped to create the racial segregation in the cities, the potential impact of school desegregation on poor urban school districts was highly limited. But for the students who were living through school desegregation during the late 1970s, things were better, more hopeful, and certainly calmer than they had once been.
6. See Amy Stuart Wells and Robert L. Crain, "Perpetuation Theory and the Long-Term Effects of School Desegregation," *Review of Educational Research*, vol. 64, 1994, pp. 531-55.
7. For prior research on how the burden of busing was placed on students of color, see Derrick Bell, *And We Are Not Saved: The Elusive Quest for Racial Justice* (New York: Basic Books, 1987).
8. For prior research on the role of tracking in racially mixed schools, see Jeannie Oakes and Amy Stuart Wells, *Beyond the Technicalities of School Reform: Policy Lessons from Detracking Schools* (Los Angeles: UCLA Graduate School of Education & Information Studies, Policy Monograph, 1996).
9. For prior research on the importance of "colorblindness" in desegregated schools, see Janet Ward Schofield, *Black and White in School* (New York: Teachers College Press, 1989).
10. Amy Stuart Wells et al., *How Desegregation Changed Us: The Effects of Racially Mixed Schools on Students and Society* (New York: Teachers College, Columbia University, 2004).

AMY STUART WELLS is a professor of sociology of education at Teachers College, Columbia University, N.Y. JENNIFER JELLISON HOLME is a postdoctoral fellow at the University of California, Los Angeles. ANITA TIJERINA REVILLA is a graduate student at the University of California, Los Angeles, and an Irvine Visiting Scholar in gender/feminist studies and Chicano studies at Pitzer College, Claremont, Calif. AWO KORANTEMAA ATANDA recently received her doctorate from Teachers College and is a senior survey specialist at Mathematica Policy Research, Inc., Princeton, N.J. This article is drawn from a larger report titled How Desegregation Changed Us: The Effects of Racially Mixed Schools on Students and Society (Teachers College, 2004), available at www.tc.edu/newsbureau/features/wells033004.htm. The article and report are based on *In Search of Brown* (Harvard University Press, forthcoming)..

From *Phi Delta Kappan,* May 2004, pp. 670-679. Copyright © 2004 by Phi Delta Kappa International. Reprinted by permission of the publisher and author.

Minding the Gap
Addressing differences in student and school performance

by JENNIFER L. HOCHSCHILD

ABIGAIL THERNSTROM, a member of the Massachusetts State Board of Education, and Stephan Thernstrom, Winthrop professor of history at Harvard, have written an impassioned, informed, curiously uneven book about one of our country's most complex and important social problems: inequalities in what students learn at school. They frame the problem as a "racial gap" and focus on the disparities between test scores of non-Hispanic whites and Asian Americans, on the one hand, and blacks and Hispanics on the other. I shall ask later whether this is the best formulation, but let us start with their chosen perspective.

The problem the Thernstroms point to is now both well-known and widely agonized over, but it always warrants another examination. They lay it out clearly: African Americans, and to a lesser extent Latinos, do not learn as much in their passage through elementary and secondary school, at least as measured by test scores, as do Anglos and Asians. The average gap in test scores narrowed during the 1970s and 1980s, then widened in the 1990s; more than 50 percent (and in one case more than 70 percent) of black and Hispanic twelfth graders score "below basic" on national standardized achievement tests in most subjects, compared with roughly a quarter of Anglos and Asians. This failure to learn makes the former groups less able to graduate from college, less likely to attain or keep high-paying jobs, and less fully engaged in all aspects of American society. It is a "heartbreaking picture."

Although the Thernstroms appropriately emphasize the breadth and depth of the test-score gap, they also want to insist that it can be bridged. To do so, they believe, one must understand what causes it; here, too, their argument is not new but warrants careful attention. In their view, the educational gap for African Americans is no longer caused by direct racial discrimination but rather by a "cultural inheritance" that is itself "the product of a very long history of racial oppression." Black parents read less to their young children than white parents do, and black children are more disruptive in school than white children from the earliest grades, spend a "dismaying" amount of time watching television, and generally live in a culture that does not easily "connect . . . black students to the world of academic achievement."

> "Sixty percent of Americans would rather have their child be active in extracurricular activities than get A grades."

Hispanic students mostly suffer from the recency of their families' immigration, because many grow up in families and communities in which English is not the default language and because many immigrant parents urge their children to get jobs rather than stay in school. In an important analysis, however, the Thernstroms point out that the children of native-born Latino parents do move toward closing the test-score gap with Anglos—so the Thernstroms' main solution in their case is, implicitly, time (and English immersion), rather than any active intervention by public or private agencies.

The Thernstroms note that Asian-American students, in contrast, benefit enormously from their groups' cultures. (The authors recognize that there is no single "Asian culture," but perforce fall back on monolithic language and data that aggregate all Asians.) "In large part, Asian students typically do well in school because their parents insist upon it, and they feel obliged to comply with their parents' wishes." This finding, the Thernstroms assert, is "grounds for optimism" because "parental pressure to work extraordinarily hard in school . . . is a culturally transferable trait." Before turning to this implied solution to the test-score gap, however, let me note that the Thernstroms do not investigate Anglo culture; readers are given no help, therefore, in interpreting the fact that 60 percent of Americans would rather have their child "make average grades and be active in extracurricular activities" than "get A grades" (according to a 1996 survey by Phi Delta Kappa, the professional association for educators). More generally, we are left to assume that white parents endorse high achievement more than do black or Hispanic parents, but less than Asian parents. This is a plausible argument, but it is not self-evidently true and a direct discussion would have been valuable.

In any case, the Thernstroms move on to provide reasons for rejecting most liberal solutions to the test-score gap, such as more funding for urban public-school systems, smaller classes, more black and Hispanic teachers, or maintenance of federal programs targeted at disadvantaged students. Instead they endorse small, semi-independent schools that face the cultural challenge head on—especially the several dozen KIPP (Knowledge Is Power Program) charter schools now operating in a few cities. In KIPP schools, which remain within the public-school system but have considerably more autonomy (and a little less funding) than regular public schools, teaching is very carefully organized, controlled, and monitored ("every teacher's . . . blackboard . . . looks the same") and the only extracurricular activity is music.

These schools (or, very occasionally, classrooms in a regular public school) hold teachers, parents, and students to an extraordinarily high standard of achievement through written contracts, extra hours and weeks of schooling, strict order and discipline, and relentless attention to achievement. They also promote cultural change through pep talks, posters, and what appears to be continuous student chanting: "The day we visited Amistad, the kids were chanting . . . North Star has almost the identical chant. . . ." Or "at KIPP students chant rules in unison…" and " 'Why are you here?' a teacher asks in a 'call-response' chant that students run through in the morning circle." And so on. The justification for all of this is that "we are fighting a battle involving skills and values," according to one of the Thernstroms' exemplary school leaders. "We are not afraid to set social norms."

THE THERNSTROMS SHOW that the students in their model schools and classrooms score well on state tests. And their descriptions are moving and inspiring, just as their descriptions of horrible teachers in regular public schools are depressing and infuriating. I would rather have my children in a KIPP school, chanting, identical blackboards, and all, than in a lot of schools in America's largest cities (where a majority of black and Latino children live). But can an effort to expand these "little islands of true heroism" really solve the problem that the Thernstroms laid out so elegantly in the first chapter of *No Excuses?*

In principle, yes. As they point out, it requires no new funds or changes in the governance structure of schooling for all parents, teachers, and principals to simply decide that henceforth they will tolerate no disruption and will demand academic excellence from all students. But that is unlikely to happen, to put it mildly. Thus we need a more careful examination of the nature of the test-score gap, its causes, and the available solutions, before signing on to their program.

For one thing, the racial gap is at least partly a class gap. The Thernstroms concur, but before and after an elegant analysis of the role of social and economic standing in the achievement gap, they drop the point. By their reckoning, a third of the test-score gap is due to differences in family background. But their measures of family background pay no attention to levels of wealth (which is vastly more unequally distributed than income, and which has been shown to have an impact on schooling achievement); to an assessment of the education of *both* parents (rather than just of the parent with the higher level of schooling); or to other variables that could plausibly raise the explanatory power of class to, say, half of the gap. Class does matter, a lot: data from the *Digest of Education Statistics, 2001*, show that the test-score gap in math between 17-year-old students whose parents completed college and those whose parents did not complete high school is now greater than the comparable test-score gap between Anglos and African Americans. In addition, the social and economic status of one's schoolmates matters a great deal. Middle-class children achieve more than poor children do when both are in schools with mostly poor classmates. However, middle-class children in poor schools achieve less than do middle-class children in mostly middle-class schools—sometimes, in fact, they fare worse than poor children do in mostly middle-class schools.

The Thernstroms' solution to the achievement gap might remain the same even if they focused on class rather than, or in interaction with, race and ethnicity. After all, plenty of scholars argue that poor Americans lack the right culture for "connect[ing] . . . to the world of academic achievement." But perhaps new solutions would become available with this new lens on the problem. Attention to class disparities, for example, would allow many districts to "desegregate" high- and low-achieving students in a way that the Thernstroms insist is not possible with regard to racial desegregation. (They take school-district boundaries as given, rather than seeing them for what they are, a constitutionally malleable creation by a state.)

Or perhaps the racial gap is at least partly a state-policy gap. The *Digest of Education Statistics* also shows that if we compare eighth graders in central cities to those in the "urban fringe and large towns," the average national disparity in reading scores is 12 points. But in Connecticut, New York, and Minnesota, the disparity is double that, whereas in California, Florida, and Delaware it is half that or less. If states are acting so differently that children in some big cities are less harmed by their urban residence than are children in other big cities in different states, appropriate policy recommendations for closing the test-score gap would look very different from those offered by the Thernstroms.

Even if we accept that a large part of the reason for the achievement gap really is cultural, the Thernstroms' solution is insufficient. *Pace* their single statement to the contrary, the evidence has been strong and consistent for four decades that children's classmates have an enormous impact on their commitment to learning, on the environment in which they learn, and on the outcomes of their schooling. Culture matters. If black students need to absorb achievement-oriented values, or Hispanic students need to become acclimated to American values, or poor children need to learn middle-class values, then putting them in a classroom with students who already have those values (or at least, whose parents and teachers do) is the *most* effective way to reduce the test-score gap across the nation as a whole. That conclusion implies as much racial desegregation (across district lines if necessary), economic mixing, and ethnic or linguistic mixing as possible. (After all, once boys and girls started sitting in the same classrooms, they became more like each other in goals and outlooks—for better and for worse.)

> True mixing of students would also call on suburbanites to shed their own excuses for their racial and economic isolation.

Such a policy choice would no doubt be difficult and controversial, but it is no more difficult than struggling to find enough "heroes" to create the schools needed to transform the lives of millions of underachieving students. Such a policy would also call on middle-class, predominantly white, suburbanites to shed their own excuses for their racial and economic isolation.

The Thernstroms avoid this challenge by proposing that all schools containing underachieving African-American and Hispanic children be turned into charter schools. That solution would have the pseudo-advantage of letting affluent white suburbanites off the hook. It would also have the real advantage of enabling energetic, idealistic, imaginative citizens to try their hand at improving the terrible conditions in which too many children waste their days.

But a massive switch to charter schools is unrealistic as the central policy solution. To begin, manage, and invigorate a school for years on end, especially in a community with few resources, ingrained mistrust of neighbors and authorities, and deep needs, is very difficult. The charter schools that already exist show why this reform is not a panacea. Some are superb, some are hopelessly misman-aged or cynically corrupt, some are hoped-for profit centers for private corporations, and most produce about the same test results as the public schools near them. Our nation cannot rely on solving the problems of public education by retreating from the public arena.

Abigail Thernstrom and Stephan Thernstrom deserve praise for their passion for racial equality, their powerful prose, and their fascinating arguments. That their policy proposal seems more a counsel of despair than a solution is as much a commentary on the complexities of race, class, and American public schooling as it is a shortcoming of their book. Let us hope for more heroes in our children's classrooms—along with public policies that will truly leave no child behind. †

Jennifer L. Hochschild is Jayne professor of government and a member of the African and African American studies department; she is currently on leave as a Radcliffe Institute fellow for the 2003-2004 academic year. She is coauthor, with Nathan Scovronick, of *The American Dream and the Public Schools* (Oxford, 2003).

From *Harvard Magazine*, March/April 2004, pp. 24-28. Copyright © 2004 by Jennifer Hochschild. Reprinted by permission of the author.

Civic Education in Schools: The Right Time is Now

In schools across the nation, educators are developing new ways to teach students that citizenship is a rich experience that involves responsibilities as well as rights.

by Joyce Baldwin

The Roadrunners, a student group from the Skinner Middle School in northwest Denver, were concerned about pedestrian safety near their school, so they decided to study traffic patterns in the area. The youngsters drew up maps, recorded traffic incidents, polled hundreds of students and met with police and community leaders. The data were so well developed and the student voices so persuasive that the city installed a four-way stop sign at an intersection declared unsafe by the youngsters.

This is only one example of how schools across the country are encouraging youth to voice their opinions responsibly while learning firsthand how our system of democratic government works. Educators from Maine to California are encouraging students to grapple with public issues and tie them to academic lessons, so that the youngsters will become informed, active citizens.

Development of these model programs may mean that after years of being on the "endangered" list, civic education will not join the ranks of the dinosaurs after all. Instead of trailing off into extinction, the traditional social studies classes with students learning facts and more facts may be evolving into a dynamic new style of "civic engagement."

But how is the idea of civic engagement being translated into the day-to-day curriculum of schools around the country? The answer is, differently, in different places. In Hudson, Massachusetts, for example, second graders learned about seeing-eye dogs, therapy dogs and bomb-sniffing dogs. Then they organized a "Barkery" and made dog biscuits to raise funds for animal surgery at a local shelter. While making and selling the biscuits, the children practiced reading, measuring, math, communication and cooperation skills. In Washington, D.C., high school students, who were studying issues involved with labor and justice, applied their lessons in the community. When they discovered that a fast-food restaurant was paying its tomato pickers less than fair wages, the students boycotted the restaurant and organized a protest. In Modesto, California, students in Fairview Elementary School, most of whom are Hispanic, studied, discussed, debated and then voted on whether or not a five-year policy of requiring students to wear uniforms should be continued. The results were 458 students in favor of discontinuing the policy and 162 in favor of continuing it. The parent vote was 167 in favor of keeping the uniform policy and 139 against it. The staff vote was about evenly split. The School Safety Committee, which is made up of students, parents and staff representatives, met in late June to resolve the question and decided to discontinue the uniform policy since there was not sufficient sentiment in favor of it. However, the committee recognized that parents and staff were concerned about dress standards, so the group will develop a set of "expectations" for the kind of clothes students should wear. In the fall, the school is planning a "Rock the Vote" concert to encourage Latino parents to register to vote, so that they will practice and model this civic responsibility for their children.

The YOUNGER generation is increasingly prompted to help others and to become INVOLVED politically to support causes they believe in.

Teachers and administrators in these and other schools with similar programs report that the experiences the youngsters have in the community are reflected in a revitalized interest in academics. Grades and test scores improve as students grasp the link between what they learn in the classroom and how they can apply their skills and knowledge in the real world. Seeing this connection spurs even some of the most disaffected youngsters to achieve academically. What's more, the youngsters gain a deeper appreciation of how they can participate in the democratic process.

The Right Time

These vignettes of students engaged in civic learning are juxtaposed against alarming statistics that indicate youngsters are disconnected from civic and political institutions, perhaps in part because of a decline in civic education courses in U.S. schools. (See, *Does A Downturn in Civic Education Signal a Disconnect to Democracy?*) Yet, it is also clear that these same youngsters care deeply about helping to create a better world. Members of the younger generation are increasingly prompted to volunteer to help others and are also becoming involved politically to support causes in which they believe.

The North Carolina Civic Education Consortium (www.civics.org) recently released results of the first statewide survey of the civic skills, knowledge, behavior, opportunities and attitudes of teenagers and adults. The survey, which was supported by Carnegie Corporation, the Smith Richardson Foundation and the Z. Smith Reynolds Foundation, found that "North Carolina youth have a high level of confidence in their civic engagement skills, but their levels of political involvement and knowledge of government are low." Only 9 percent of teens surveyed knew the names of the two U.S. senators from their state and only 26 percent have ever sent a letter to a newspaper. By contrast, 73 percent of teens surveyed have recently volunteered to do community service, 49 percent have boycotted a product when they disapproved of a company practice and 32 percent have signed a petition circulated on the Internet. The strongest indicator of civic interest and participation was family income level, with youth from high-income homes more likely to report civic involvement than youth from low-income homes.

This unique set of parallel circumstances—a decline in civic education coupled with an upswing in youth interest in community involvement—may indicate that this is the time for renewal in civic education.

"Young people today are engaged in their communities, doing real work that leads to concrete results," says Cynthia Gibson, Carnegie Corporation program officer in the Strengthening U.S. Democracy program. "That fact, coupled with the decline in civic education, may offer unprecedented opportunities to strengthen our nation's educational system and provide these youngsters with opportunities to learn firsthand how to participate in a democ-

Does A Downturn in Civic Education Signal a Disconnect to Democracy?

Young people today are less informed about civic matters than youngsters were a generation or two ago. Students attending high school now often take only one government course, compared to a range of courses in civics, democracy and government that were available in the 1960s and earlier. The profile of civics and social studies education in elementary school students is also dismal: during the decade beginning with 1988, there was a reported decline of 49 percent of fourth graders who had a social studies lesson each day.

A multitude of factors have led to this decline, including emphasis on high-stakes testing, cut-backs that affect extra-curricular programs in which students can learn civic skills and teachers' concerns that discussing controversial subjects may result in negative reviews or even legal action.

In view of the sharp downturn in civics education, it is perhaps not surprising that young adults are becoming increasingly disconnected from civic and political institutions. One manifestation of this disconnection is that only about 13 percent of eligible young people cast ballots in the last presidential election. A recent National Youth Survey conducted by CIRCLE revealed that only half of the 1,500 young people polled believe that voting is important, and only 46 percent think they can make a difference in solving community problems.

The lack of interest in politics is especially alarming since there are 43 million people under the age of 30 who are eligible to vote, a full one-quarter of the electorate. A clue as to why these voters are turned off may be found in a recent non-scientific Youth Challenge Quiz conducted online (http://www.carnegie.org/sub/pubs/youthsurvey.html) by Carnegie corporation. Young people ages 15-24 were invited to participate in the quiz. One of the questions asked, "Why don't more young people vote or get involved in politics?" Of the nearly 2,000 respondents, the main answer was that they did not have enough information about issues and candidates. Other sources, such as the Center for Voting and Democracy (www.fairvote.org), report data indicating that young people say they'd be more inclined to participate in the U.S. electoral system if more candidates addressed issues of concern to younger citizens.

There are, however, signs that recent world events may be prompting young people to grapple with problems in our democracy. Data from UCLA's Higher Education Research Institute shows that the 2000 presidential election and events of September 11th, 2001, have reignited youths' interest in politics: 32.9 percent of college freshman surveyed said that keeping up with politics was either a very important or essential life goal, a jump up from 28.1 percent in 2000.

racy in a caring and responsible way—one that involves respect for and involvement with both the civic and political processes and institutions of a healthy democracy. We need to work with our schools to provide young citizens with the tools and knowledge to do just that."

Gibson is co-author with Peter Levine of *The Civic Mission of Schools*, a joint project of Carnegie Corporation of New York and CIRCLE (the Center for Information & Research on Civic Learning & Engagement; www.civicyouth.org), which is based at the University of Maryland. The report, which grew out of meetings with 55 of the nation's top education experts, recommends renewing civic education and political engagement with "real life" learning opportunities, not simply reviving the traditional civics class.

"Instead of stressing the deficits of young people, we need to help them get involved in a deeper, richer civic engagement, which is the focus of our report," Gibson explains.

Building a Bridge

Scholars and practitioners stress the need to develop an amalgam of education and service activities outside the classroom. Establishing a bridge between the two worlds, it is thought, will prompt youth to become engaged and energized participants in the democratic process.

"There is a level of service that is simply about doing good deeds. But if service is going to have implications for civic engagement, it has to go more deeply into the political and social dynamics that surround it," says Sheldon H. Berman, superintendent of the Hudson School District in Hudson, Massachusetts. "A service project should combine research, service, and report implications. It should also combine reading in an area, so that it is a study of an issue that has service as a field component of that study."

Learning simple and important SOCIAL skills is part of a commitment in the Hudson schools to help youngsters learn to build a COMMUNITY and express mutual respect.

National Attention

On May 1, 2003, the national spotlight was focused on the need to study the issue of civic education at "We the People," a daylong White House Forum on American History, Civics and Service. Leslie Lenkowsky, chief executive officer of the Corporation for National and Community Service (www.nationalservice.org), says that the forum represented "an effort to build on the outpouring of patriotic sentiments that we've seen since September 11th, 2001, and transform that into a real spirit of patriotic action. By that I mean, essentially, a kind of active citizenship that President Bush spoke about in his inaugural address. It is one thing for people to sing 'God Bless America,' for everybody to display the flag and for people to say they support our American troops, but we also need to do the things in our own lives that are essential to being an engaged citizen." The forum was hosted by the U.S. Department of Education, the Corporation for National and Community Service, the National Endowment for the Humanities and the USA Freedom Corps.

The need for studying history and civics is emphasized by "The American History and Civics Education Act of 2003," a bill introduced in March by senators Lamar Alexander (R-TN) and Harry Reid (D-NV). The bipartisan act is designed to allow teachers to attend two-week summer academies to learn more about American history and civics. In May 2003, Senator Alexander and Senator Bill Frist (R-TN) announced a Department of Education grant program that will award about $100 million to schools that submit successful applications for three-year projects in civics and American history.

Putting Civic Education into Action

There are a number of creative and innovative ways that civic engagement is being approached in the nation's schools. Among them:

- Peace Games (www.peacegames.org), an in-school violence prevention program started in 1992, develops curriculum about peacemaking as civic engagement and works with elementary schools to improve communication, cooperation, conflict resolution and engagement. The nonprofit organization helped youngsters cope with the trauma of September 11th, through the creation of community service-learning projects. Some of the students chose to assemble Peacemaker Care Packages with messages of peace and gave them to firefighters, police, emergency workers and other peacemakers.

- The ten-year-old nonprofit Earth Force (www.earthforce.org) helps young people take on projects that make lasting improvements to their environment and the community. The group works with about 35,000 young people and 1,500 educators in after-school and summer programs as well as in other educational settings in school districts across the country. One recent undertaking involved the Walnut Creek Middle School in Erie, Pennsylvania, where students in Judy Jobes' science class have been working for a few years to study the quality of water in their local creek and to educate the public about the importance of reducing pollution in their water. The class, which calls itself Walnut Creek S.E.W.E.R. (Saving Erie's Water & Environmental Resources), has had many initiatives to educate the community about cleaner water, including a billboard and brochures, such as *Your Lawn & Pesticides: What Goes Around, Comes Around*. They have also worked with local officials to increase street sweeping, which reduces runoff into the water.

- In the summer of 2003, Virginia high school students spent two weeks attending the inaugural High School Leaders Program, sponsored by the Virginia Citizenship Institute and the University of Richmond. The July institute provided an array of opportunities for interaction and debate among the students about public challenges facing their state; students also met with many elected officials including those serving their state in Congress.

- The First Amendment Schools (FAS) Project (www.firstamendmentschools.org) uses the five freedoms of speech, religion, press, assembly and petition to the government as a lens to help youngsters become responsible citizens and leaders. "Those five freedoms have been the instrument for advancing democracy and justice for greater numbers of people throughout our history. They are inalienable rights and the basic tools of democratic citizenship. We see that as a starting point for helping young people understand how to be active and effective citizens," says Charles Haynes, senior scholar of the Freedom Forum First Amendment Center, which together with the Association for Supervision and Curriculum Development (ASCD) created the FAS Project.

The group has awarded three-year grants to eleven elementary, middle and high schools to help them become laboratories for democracy and freedom. A reporter recently visited two of these schools to see how they are combining their classroom lessons with active citizenry.

Gentle Beginnings

The kindergarten classes in Hudson, Massachusetts, begin each day with a community meeting. As the "star" for a day late in April, Emma Nathan took attendance, asked how many of her classmates wanted milk and began passing a koosh ball, which has soft rubber spikes that give it a noticeable resemblance to a small, round porcupine. As the ball was tossed, each child greeted a classmate, making eye contact with the other child and saying "Good morning, Tim" and "Good morning, Amanda," until everyone had been included. Learning these simple and important social skills is part of a commitment in the Hudson schools to help youngsters learn to build a community and to express mutual respect for each other. These skills are the underpinning of a rich civic engagement that the children also begin to experience in kindergarten and continue throughout their school years.

As the morning progressed in Catherine Waugh's kindergarten class, the children took pride in putting the final touches on a quilt project that they had been working on for some time. With the help of Emma's mother, the youngsters carefully added "tying-off" knots to their quilt, which was made as a gift for a mother and child living in a Hudson homeless shelter. Each year every kindergartner designs and makes one square of their classroom quilt. Teachers encourage the children to express in their quilts something they would like to share about themselves with a less fortunate child. When the quilt is assembled, each child takes home the quilt and a journal, so that they and their parents can write a note in the journal about the project. When the journal is completed, the class presents the quilt to a mother and her child or to the director of the shelter. The journal shows how much the students care and how much they have learned in this hands-on civic education lesson.

"I'm glad I helped someone keep warm," wrote one child. Another expressed the thought that "This makes me want to help more people."

Kindergarten lessons of social responsibility are reinforced throughout the school year. For example, when the students learn about the letter "K," each time a youngster performs an act of "K"indness, a heart is added to a classroom poster proclaiming "100 Acts of Kindness." Later in the year and further along in the alphabet, other kindergartners performed 100 Acts of "R"esponsibility," such as pushing a chair under a table or throwing away scrap paper.

And so civic education begins in the Hudson school district (www.hudson.k12.ma.us). In a gentle way, students begin to gain social skills and to understand the connection their little classroom community has with the greater community in Hudson, which is an industrial town about 30 miles west of Boston.

A K-12 Emphasis

Lessons learned in the early school years echo again and again in middle school and throughout the high school years, helping Hudson students become empathetic, respectful citizens with a desire to be of service to their community.

Speaking of the importance of Hudson's comprehensive civic engagement curriculum, Charles Haynes of the Freedom Forum's First Amendment Center says, "Our view is that elementary schools are key because civic habits of the heart begin at a very early age." There are nearly 2,800 students in the Hudson school district. One-third of the student population is Portuguese-speaking; many emigrated from Brazil. Twelve percent of the students receive free lunches, yet despite their lower socioeconomic level, residents of Hudson recently ratified a $43 million budget to build a new high school slated to open in the fall of 2003. The school's architectural design features open spaces to accommodate "cluster" groups, communities within the school that will form the basis for democratizing the school and enhancing the student voice in determining day-to-day policies.

Teachers are eager to share what is happening in their Hudson classrooms. Patty Lima's second grade in the J.L. Mulready School read *The Mitten Tree* by Candace Christiansen (Fulcrum Publishing, 1997) and then worked on "Helping Hands Stay Warm," a project that encouraged students to do chores for their families to earn money for children's mittens and gloves that were donated to the Hudson Food Pantry. While studying adjectives, the children collected boxes of cereal, studied the advertising to find adjectives and then donated the cereal to the food pantry. Among other projects, Laura Mullen's second graders collected pledges from sponsors who contributed a small sum for each book a child read; the class raised more than $400 to buy a water buffalo, chickens and a pig for a family in another country.

Mullen echoed the words of other teachers in the district, saying, "Community Service-Learning is one of the things I really have a passion for because it is so important for our children."

Everywhere in Hudson, teachers and students together seem to have found inventive ways to develop lessons of civic education while improving academic accomplishments. SAT scores, attendance rates and enrollment in advanced placement classes have increased, while elementary class size has decreased to about 19 students in each class.

At the high school, a group of six students traveled to the Patanal wetlands in Brazil where they learned environmental research skills and conducted baseline research about the wildlife in the area. The trip, which was conducted in partnership with Earth Watch, taught the teens how to conduct an animal and plant census, how to analyze predator-prey relationships and how to begin preserving the wetlands. Students kept a daily journal and took turns sending reports back to their Hudson web site. The students were the second group to travel to South America, and the skills they learned are being put to use by the environmental class. Teacher Frank Gilliatt has been working with students for five years to develop a trail along the Assabet River, which runs behind the high school and used to be inaccessible. "As soon as the students get their hands dirty, they feel a partial ownership of the trail and are incredibly protective of it," Gilliatt says.

The mission of César Chávez High School is "to DEVELOP young people who will make the country a better place by INFLUENCING the public policies that affect their communities."

A required interdisciplinary Civics-English course that engages all ninth graders in exploring the rights and responsibilities of citizens begins the year with students learning about government and then segues into a study of what circumstances gave rise to the Holocaust. By spring, the students are energized for the community service-learning component of the course, with proposals ranging from conducting workshops in elementary schools, to organizing fund raisers, working at a nonprofit day care center and volunteering at a nursing home. A key question that is the focus of the course throughout the year is: "What is the individual's responsibility to create a just society?"

So what begins as a simple ritual of passing a koosh ball culminates in experiences that ripple throughout the community and emphasize the idea that citizenship is predicated on recognizing an individual's responsibilities as a citizen as well as his or her rights. "Kids come out of the Hudson school experience with an understanding of the common good," says Berman. "They understand what it means to be a responsible member of a community. They know better how to treat each other and work together effectively, they have an ethical and moral compass that we have helped them develop and some of the civic skills and competencies to make a difference."

A Laundry Becomes a Remarkable School

As a fourteen-year old Mexican immigrant, Irasema Salcido worked in the fields of California, picking strawberries on weekends for three of her teenage years. Now, years later, as founder and principal of the César Chávez Public Charter High School for Public Policy (www.cesarchavezhs.org) in Washington, D.C., she knows what it takes to help teenagers achieve.

The César Chávez student population is a diverse group of 250 students, with about 25 percent recent arrivals to the U.S. Many of the students are from El Salvador, one emigrated from Cameroon and two from Bosnia.

Salcido has recruited a staff of what she considers to be "the best teachers in the entire world," and is proud to have attracted 25 full-time, experienced teachers, some of whom graduated from Ivy League colleges and to include a lawyer, research scientist, poet and an artist on the staff.

Housed in a former laundry and with few amenities, César Chávez's mission is "to develop young people who will make the country a better place by influencing the public policies that affect their communities." School facilities are below average in many respects. Makeshift dividers separate areas into classrooms, so discussions from one area of a partitioned room intrude on another class. There are only a few computers, no science labs, and no gym or playground for physical education. "Our students don't get any exercise in school," says Kate McGreevy, director of development and community outreach, "even though many of them are out of shape and might have health problems."

While acknowledging the lack of facilities, the students are proud of the strengths of their school. After taking a Foundations in Public Policy course in the ninth grade, tenth graders select an issue that is relevant to their community, form a relationship with a local group and develop and put into action a plan that addresses that issue. The following year students partner with policymaking organizations and meet with government leaders. The students apply for a fellowship with a public policy organization and spend three weeks with the group. Meagan Labriola, public policy director at César Chávez says, "It's real work experience, not filing and answering phones. That means taking a student to planning meetings and hearings or to attend meetings on Capitol Hill."

The high school experience in the public policy arena culminates in a senior policy thesis that involves research and analysis of a problem and challenges the students to become experts who can propose solutions.

A school government and constitution were recently established and instituted. One of the first forays by the stu-

What is it Like to be a Student at César Chávez?

Carnegie corporation of New York interviews Carmella Royster, 16, who is going into her senior year at César Chávez Public Charter High School for Public Policy in Washington, D.C.

cc: Were you an involved student when you came to César Chávez?

Carmella: When I cam here in my sophomore year, I thought it would be a joy ride, like a regular public school. I talked too much in class and "pounced" on everybody. I was not dedicated at all to my education; I wasn't focused and was immature. In my other school I was failing a couple of classes.

cc: What's different about César Chávez?

Carmella: Here you have to do work; you can't get around it. When you don't turn in homework, you have detention, so your homework has to be done. If you don't, it's like a chain reaction and you don't do well on tests. You have no choice but to focus on self-improvement and maturing. You don't want to be a "get-by" student at César Chávez.

cc: What public policy experiences have you had?

Carmella: I had a National Parks Conservation Association (NPCA) internship for three weeks at the beginning of my junior year. We studied about national parks and I visited the Franklin D. Roosevelt Park, DuPont Circle (which a lot of people don't realize is a park), the Lincoln Memorial, the Vietnam Memorial and Harper's Ferry in Virginia. Then I taught first grade students at a nearby school about the importance of protecting parks. I also asked people at the Farragut North Metro Station area to sign postcard petitions asking the president to increase the budget for national parks.

cc: What else?

Carmella: I lobbied on the Hill three times, with NPCA, with common cause about national service and with bread for the World, talking about welfare reform. I also went with other students to lobby for a national memorial for César Chávez.

cc: What other things are happening?

Carmella: I was granted a fellowship with Eleanor Holmes Norton (D-DC) in her constituent services office. My politics and citizenship class brought the mayor to our school, and we started reading the newspaper every day and watching the news morning, noon and night. We also talked with people who are part of the board of education and the city council. When Rod Paige, the Secretary of Education, came to our school, I got up to ask him five questions. He called me a leader.

cc: What are you considering as a career?

Carmella: Communications or law. I want more. I'm hungry for education, and I want to explore the world.

cc: What would you like to add?

Carmella: César Chávez has shed a new light on education for me and has taught me public policy skills and prepared me to college and the work force. People look at schools in D.C. and teenagers and think we're not doing anything. But just come to our school and see the changes that we're making in our community and for ourselves academically. My goal is to be a successful adult and make my mark in the world and to give back what I've learned, so that everyone can gain from it.

---

dents in shaping school policy has been to reevaluate a rule that prohibits cell phones in the school. After a period of study and debate, the governing body, which meets every two weeks and comprises eight students and eight adults, submitted a revised policy to the principal and dean, who can veto a proposal. The administrators approved the new policy, which allows students to have cell phones in the school, but only if they are turned off. If students violate the regulation, their cell phone privileges are revoked.

Having the Courage

César Chávez opened in 1998 and at the end of that first year, two-thirds of the students were held back. Salcido wondered: "What am I doing?" She knew that some other schools routinely pass youngsters to the next grade, whether or not they have adequately mastered required work. "We couldn't continue making the same mistake. We were the *last* stop for them," says Salcido, who earned a masters degree from Harvard University. "I'm glad I had the courage to stick to my principles; it really shaped the way the school is today." When it came time for the first graduating class to prepare their theses, the staff pondered whether they should assign a 15-20 page thesis or allow students to write just a five-page paper. Once again, the decision was made to hold students accountable to high standards.

From the outset, strict discipline was an essential element of the school program. Late to class five times? Your grade is reduced one level. Late eight times and you fail the course. "Drugs, or weapons, you're out," Salcido says. "Fight and you get a twenty-five day suspension."

Despite the strict routine, a visitor saw clear signs that there was a caring, relationship between students and principal, between students and their teachers. A sign on a board in Salcido's office, written in blue marker and displayed proudly, proclaims "Class of 2003. We love you, Mrs. Salcido."

It is also clear that many of the students are articulate and forthright in talking about their newfound world at César Chávez. (See: *What is it Like to be a Student at César Chávez?*) During a lunchtime meeting students shared their thoughts about some of the issues that were uppermost in their minds

- "Children die every day because of child abuse and neglect," Cherry Wooten, a senior, said emphatically. "I've read *horrible* stories about parents who put their child in a dog cage without food or water, and the parents were not convicted." Cherry will present her thesis to her class, including recommendations for change in D.C. law to ensure that at least minimum punishment levels are in place for convicted child abuse offenders.

- Preventing teenage pregnancy was a high priority for Jajaira Mejia, a junior who is a teen mother of seven-month old Diana. "At first I was shy to share my opinions, " Jajaira said. "but now I have a public service announcement on the Internet about teenage pregnancy. I don't want other girls to make the same mistakes I made."

- Josue Cruz, a freshman, spoke enthusiastically about a school trip to Quebec where students stayed with host families. "It was way more than just fun, being in a different country and realizing the world is bigger than it seems."

Other public service projects at the school include helping a food bank keep its shelves stocked, organizing a D.C.-wide Earth Day event, and conducting a fund-raiser to purchase energy-conserving light bulbs, green plants and other items to create a "green space" in the school.

The first César Chávez class graduated in 2002, with 100% of the students going on to college including Brown University, American University, and George Mason University. In 2003, all students in the senior class were again accepted to college, one to Columbia University. Speaking of the pride she felt at seeing the students collect their diplomas, Salcido says that the experience was so moving—and so hard-won—that, "I thought I was watching a movie." She's sure that all her students are now firmly on track to become truly engaged and successful citizens.

Making a Difference

As *The Civic Mission of Schools* urges, both the Massachusetts school district and the D.C. public charter high school "infuse a civic mission throughout the curriculum . . . so that the students are able to 'live what they learn' about civic engagement and democracy." The experts whose input shaped the report recommend "conducting more research that helps to define and develop standardized indicators of civic engagement, especially those that expand the meaning of citizenship and take a broader view beyond voting, volunteering, and knowing facts about the government." Evaluation of the innovative ways in which civic education is changing in these schools and others throughout our country will yield valuable data to help states shape their education policies.

The Hudson schools and César Chávez are different in many ways, one a suburban school district, the other an urban high school drawing students from all parts of its city. The two academic institutions have developed different iterations of school-based civic education, yet they share a number of characteristics. In both Hudson and César Chávez, for example, all students—including those who might otherwise be disaffected—have ongoing opportunities to be engaged in the civic life of their communities, to begin to appreciate how classroom lessons are inextricably linked to their civic experiences and to learn how to voice their opinions and listen to the thoughts of others.

Civic engagement programs in the Hudson and Washington, D.C. schools help young people begin to understand how lessons learned in the classroom, in the Patanal of Brazil and in local governing groups in their communities resonate in their lives. Through civic engagement securely anchored to academics, the youngsters begin to gain a rich understanding of our democratic life and learn the skills needed to contribute to our nation in a meaningful way. As Carnegie Corporation president Vartan Gregorian has said, "When young people learn that they can make a real difference in their communities, civic lessons of the heart will become integral to their lives, and hopefully the youngsters will become active, caring citizens, who understand that the future of our democracy is truly in their hands."

A former teacher, Joyce Baldwin now enjoys reporting on significant educational issues. Baldwin also writes on health and medical topics for many publications and is author of two biographies for young adult readers.

From *Carnegie Reporter*, Fall 2003, pp. 13-21. Copyright © 2003 by Carnegie Corporation of New York. Reprinted by permission.

UNIT 7
Serving Special Needs and Concerns

Unit Selections

34. **Partnering with Families and Communities**, Joyce L. Epstein and Karen Clark Salinas
35. **Popular Culture in the Classroom**, Dale Allender
36. **Living and Teaching on the Edge of a Pop Culture World**, Robert Gardner
37. **At the Crossroads of Expertise: The Risky Business of Teaching Popular Culture**, Meg Callahan and Bronwen E. Low
38. **Healthier Students, Better Learners**, Beth Pateman
39. **The Arithmetic Gap**, Tom Loveless and John Coughlan

Key Points to Consider

- What can schools do to encourage students to read during the summer months? What can teachers do to encourage reading for pleasure throughout the school year?

- Describe life in an American suburban high school. What concerns do you have about student experience of this setting? If possible, use your own experiences as a guide.

DUSHKIN ONLINE Links: www.dushkin.com/online/
These sites are annotated in the World Wide Web pages.

Constructivism: From Philosophy to Practice
http://www.stemnet.nf.ca/~elmurphy/emurphy/cle.html

National Association for Gifted Children
http://www.nagc.org/home00.htm

National Information Center for Children and Youth With Disabilities (NICHCY)
http://www.nichcy.org/index.html

People who educate serve many special needs and concerns of their students. This effort requires a special commitment to students on the part of their teachers. We celebrate this effort, and each year we seek to address special types of general concern.

People learn under many different sets of circumstances, which involve a variety of educational concerns both within schools and in alternative learning contexts. Each year we include in this section of this volume articles on a variety of special topics that we believe our readers will find interesting and relevant.

The journal literature thematically varies from year to year. Issues on which several good articles may have been published in one year may not be covered well in other years in the professional and trade publications. Likewise, some issues are covered in depth every year, such as articles on social class or education and school choice.

There is a variety in this year's special topics as a wide range of educational concerns have been selected for consideration. First, the issue of developing partnerships between schools and families and the communities in which they are located is examined. We then have articles on how popular culture impacts middle school and high school students' studies in schools. This is followed by an article on student health, what sorts of things teachers need to teach about health to help their students become better learners. This is followed by an article on the arithmetic achievement gap between American students compared with students from other countries as well as comparisons of American students' mathematical achievement scores across recent decades.

There are well and long-recognized reasons to build good relationships between schools and the families which they serve. The students of a school or school system can benefit both academically and in other ways if partnerships between schools and communities can be encouraged. The authors of this article speak of building a professional learning community where students as well as their families are involved in learning together at home and in the community. The authors of the article report on the findings of the National Network of Partnerships schools. The activities of some of these schools are reported to provide us with some insights as to how to build closer ties among educators, families, and communities to encourage higher levels of student achievement. Various ways in which parents and teachers can cooperate to encourage student learning are shared.

The authors of the essays on the use of popular culture phenomena in teaching secondary English language arts provide perspectives on how they use students' expertise of popular culture to make connections with standard literature curricula. Dale Allender believes that the use of popular cultural themes from contemporary music and films to teach secondary school language arts has both affective and academic value for students. Robert Gardner discusses what it feels like to "live on the edge" of popular culture but not to be interior to it; he describes how he tries to tap into his students' knowledge of popular music and films to relate their knowledge to the standard English language arts curriculum. Meg Callahan and Bronwen E. Low argue that incorporating some forms of popular culture in the language arts classroom enables teachers and students to share their expertise. They discuss the ways that constructivist pedagogy can lead to dynamic interchange of thought on literacy and musical themes among students and teachers. Several interesting suggestions on how to use popular culture in media literacy are offered. It is interesting to see how the authors of these articles use popular cultures as a catalyst for creative, imaginative, and complex thought in media and language arts classes.

Next, Beth Pateman presents an article on how health relates to learning in schools. She describes effort at skills-based and standards-based approaches to teaching students to take care of themselves on the premise that there is a link between a student's health and his learning. She quotes that "healthy students make better learners." She cites work in this area sponsored by the Council of Chief State School Officers and the Association of State and Territorial Health Officials. The author describes the characteristics of effective health education programs in schools.

Tom Loveless and John Coughlan review the allegations of an "arithmetic gap" among American students of different generations. They use mathematics scores from the periodic National Assessment of Educational Progress.

Since first issued in 1973, this ongoing anthology has sought to provide discussion of special social or curriculum issues affecting the teaching/learning conditions in schools. Fundamental forces at work in our culture during the past several years have greatly affected millions of students. The social, cultural, and economic pressures on families have produced several special problems of great concern to teachers. Serving special needs and concerns requires greater degrees of individualization of instruction and greater attention paid to the development and maintenance of healthier self-concepts by students.

Article 34

Partnering with Families and Communities

A well-organized program of family and community partnerships yields many benefits for schools and their students.

Joyce L. Epstein and Karen Clark Salinas

What is the difference between a professional learning community and a school learning community? A *professional learning community* emphasizes the teamwork of principals, teachers, and staff to identify school goals, improve curriculum and instruction, reduce teachers' isolation, assess student progress, and increase the effectiveness of school programs. Professional teamwork is important and can greatly improve teaching, instruction, and professional relationships in a school, but it falls short of producing a true community of learners. In contrast, a *school learning community* includes educators, students, parents, and community partners who work together to improve the school and enhance students' learning opportunities.

One component of a school learning community is an organized program of school, family, and community partnerships with activities linked to school goals. Research and fieldwork show that such programs improve schools, strengthen families, invigorate community support, and increase student achievement and success (Epstein, 2001; Henderson & Mapp, 2002; Sheldon, 2003).

PIPE DREAM OR POSSIBILITY?

Is it a pipe dream to think that every school can become a true learning community, or is it really possible? During the past eight years, more than 1,000 schools, districts, and state departments of education in the National Network of Partnership Schools at Johns Hopkins University have worked with researchers to develop and implement programs of school, family, and community partnerships. Their efforts have produced not only many research publications but also research-based materials that elementary, middle, and high schools can use to customize and continually improve their programs of family and community involvement (Epstein et al., 2002).

RESEARCH-BASED APPROACHES

A well-organized partnership program starts with an Action Team for Partnerships. Made up of teachers, administrators, parents, and community partners, the Action Team is linked to the school council or school improvement team. With a clear focus on promoting student success, the team writes annual plans for family and community involvement, implements and evaluates activities, and integrates the activities conducted by other groups and individual teachers into a comprehensive partnership program for the school.

Annual action plans use a research-based framework of six types of involvement—parenting, communicating, volunteering, learning at home, decision making, and collaborating with the community—to focus partnerships on school improvement goals (see fig. 1, p. XX). By implementing activities for all six types of involvement, schools can help parents become involved at school and at home in various ways that meet student needs and family schedules. Input from participants helps schools address challenges and improve plans, activities, and outreach so that all families can be productive partners in their children's school success.

STORIES FROM THE FIELD

To understand how research on partnerships is applied in practice and to learn from educators and families about challenges that must be addressed to involve all families, each year the National Network of Partnership Schools collects what are called *promising partnership practices* (Salinas & Jansorn, 2003). The following examples illustrate how schools in urban, suburban, and rural locations are working to create effective programs of family and community involvement to strengthen their learning communities.

Welcoming All Families

A school learning community welcomes *all* families. Many schools serve a diverse range of students,

177

including new immigrants and refugees. The parents of such students, like all parents, want their children to succeed in school. These children, like all students, do better when their parents and teachers are partners. In a welcoming school, educators appreciate differences and involve all families in many ways throughout the school year.

Like many schools in the National Network of Partnership Schools, Madison Junior High in Naperville, Illinois, fosters a welcoming environment by implementing activities for all six types of family involvement. Last year, the school held evening discussions about adolescence to help parents share effective parenting strategies and network with one another on important topics; published newsletters; held "Thursday Things," a weekly activity for sending information home; created a database of volunteers; hosted honor roll breakfasts; conducted family literacy nights; built connections with business partners; and celebrated Dad's Day. All activities were linked to goals for students in the school improvement plan and help foster an active learning community.

Roosevelt Elementary School in St. Paul, Minnesota, organized the Second Cup of Coffee program—a monthly morning activity during which parents have the opportunity to meet with teachers, administrators, and other parents and discuss such school activities as testing, homework, and reading programs. Translators encouraged parents with diverse linguistic and cultural backgrounds to attend these and other school activities.

Early Childhood Center #17 in Buffalo, New York, conducted its Diversity Celebration program to help students, teachers, and families learn about and appreciate more than eight cultural groups represented in their learning community. Families and community volunteers contributed cultural items and worked with students on costumes, skits, poems, songs, and dances. The activities helped students develop language skills and other talents and involved diverse families in their children's learning.

Focusing on Achievement

A school learning community puts a laserlike focus on student learning and success. Schools in the National Network of Partnership Schools have implemented many family and community involvement activities to support and extend students' reading, writing, math, and goal-setting skills. The home, school, and community connections make school subjects more meaningful for students.

Reading. Many schools engage parents and community partners by offering workshop sessions on reading, by organizing reading volunteers, and by helping parents strengthen students' reading skills and encourage reading for pleasure at home (Baker & Moss, 2001; Sheldon & Epstein, in press-a). For example, Clara E. Westropp School in Cleveland, Ohio, conducted monthly family reading nights. The school librarian identified age-appropriate books for students from kindergarten through grade 4. Parents came to school with their children, selected books from the library, asked teachers questions about reading, and learned strategies to increase children's reading at home.

All students in grades 1-3 participated in the Book Check program at Ladysmith Elementary School in Ladysmith, Wisconsin. Parents, teachers, retired teachers, and high school students performing community service volunteered to listen to children retell the stories they had read and to discuss plots, settings, and characters. The students took tests on the books they had read and then moved on to new reading. The program expanded from a pilot project to a whole-school activity, creating an active reading community.

Many schools in the National Network of Partnership Schools conduct reading-partner programs once a week, twice a month, or on other schedules with a variety of volunteers, including parents, senior citizens, and community groups. Others hold special reading events. For example, Dr. Lydia T. Wright School in Buffalo, New York, ran a reading marathon for 26 days to focus the entire community on reading. This event involved parents, grandparents, and others in the community—for example, police officers, firefighters, local authors of books for children, the mayor, judges, local celebrities, and older students—in reading activities.

The Lea Conmigo (Read with Me) program, conducted by Families in Schools in Los Angeles, California, provided books to more than 23,000 students and families in an effort to improve the early literacy skills of preschool and kindergarten children. Teachers introduced the program to parents, many of whom did not speak English. Parents received English and Spanish books to take home and learned ways to encourage their children's reading. Data show that students improved their reading skills and parents increased the time they read with their children.

Writing. Partnerships for writing take many forms, including workshops on the writing process, activities that engage parents in writing, presentations by local authors, and celebrations of student writing before family and community audiences. At Highlands Elementary School in Naperville, Illinois, a writing workshop series helped more than 120 parents learn about the school's writing process, state writing tests, and ways to support student writing at home. All sessions were videotaped for parents who could not attend. Arminta Street Elementary School in North Hollywood, California, turned a classroom into the Arminta Café That Celebrates Literacy, serving coffee, tea, and cookies to parents who listened to students read their writing aloud. Other schools have students share their stories, poems, journals, and artwork with their parents. At Discovery School #98 in Buffalo, New York, students discussed their portfolios with family members or neighbors who came to class. Visitors were given a list of questions to ask to keep the discussion moving.

Many schools take other innovative approaches. Teachers from Loreto Elementary School in Los Angeles attended a district workshop on Parents as Authors and then worked with their students' parents on Thursday mornings for

FIGURE 1 Six Types of Involvement

- *Parenting.* Assist families with parenting skills, family support, understanding child and adolescent development, and setting home conditions to support learning at each age and grade level. Assist schools in understanding families' backgrounds, cultures, and goals for children.
- *Communicating.* Communicate with families about school programs and student progress. Create two-way communication channels between school and home.
- *Volunteering.* Improve recruitment, training, activities, and schedules to involve families as volunteers and as audiences at the school or in other locations. Enable educators to work with volunteers who support students and the school.
- *Learning at Home.* Involve families with their children in academic learning at home, including homework, goal setting, and other curriculum-related activities. Encourage teachers to design homework that enables students to share and discuss interesting tasks.
- *Decision Making.* Include families as participants in school decisions, governance, and advocacy activities through school councils or improvement teams, committees, and parent organizations.
- *Collaborating with the Community.* Coordinate resources and services for families, students, and the school with community groups, including businesses, agencies, cultural and civic organizations, and colleges or universities. Enable all to contribute service to the community.

Source: Epstein et al., 2002.

---

three months. Many new immigrant parents created books and videos about their lives and experiences, wrote poems about their children, and then presented their work to their children. The activity expanded when 5th grade teachers met with their students' families to create family books as gifts for the 5th grade graduates. In this way, the school's learning community grew to include parent-authors who had had little or no prior schooling in the United States.

Math. Family involvement in math may encompass events for parents and students, community connections, information sessions for parents on math curriculum and assessments, and homework support (Sheldon & Epstein, in press-b). In Cuyahoga Falls, Ohio, more than 600 people wanted to attend Woodridge Primary School's Math Night program, making it necessary for the school to conduct the program twice. For Math Night, the school invited families to learn about the new Ohio state math standards. The Action Team for Partnerships, in cooperation with parents, teachers, and community partners, provided dinner, conducted teacher-led math sessions on ways to help students with math at home, distributed take-home bags of math materials and information on state standards, handed out coupons from local businesses, and even held a math-related raffle.

Math also became a real-world activity at Kennedy Junior High in Lisle, Illinois. In an estimation project called Beat Pete, a math class followed Pete, a local moving man, to estimate the weight and cost of a moving job. The program provided students with bus transportation, printed materials to prepare for the estimation task, and prizes for best estimates.

> *In a welcoming school, educators involve all families in many ways.*

Thurmont Middle School in Thurmont, Maryland, conducted a highly focused workshop series for parents and students to help students prepare for the state's Functional Math Test. At monthly meetings, parents and students worked together under teachers' guidance and received math homework materials. Students who failed a practice math test were invited with their parents to additional sessions. More than 80 percent of the 6th graders passed the required math test, exceeding the school's goal by more than 10 percent and surpassing the percentage of passing 7th graders, who had not taken the workshops. The teachers enjoyed working with one another as well as with parents and students to reach an important school goal as they strengthened their math learning community.

Because most parents cannot frequently come to the school building to see what their children are learning, new designs for homework hold promise for engaging all parents in weekly discussions with their children about schoolwork. For example, an interactive homework process from the National Network of Partnership Schools called Teachers Involve Parents in Schoolwork (TIPS) helps elementary and middle school teachers design and assign homework that enables all students to share what they are learning with a family member (Epstein, Salinas, & Van Voorhis, 2001; Van Voorhis & Epstein, 2002). Homework is part of a full program of school, family, and community partnerships and extends the learning community to include student learning outside school (Epstein, 2001; Van Voorhis, 2003).

Planning for college and work. In school learning communities, educators, parents, and community partners help students focus on their plans for college and careers and on the education requirements they must fulfill to meet their goals. For example, at Glenmary School in Peace River, Alberta, Canada, high school students, parents, and faculty were involved in Career Portfolio Night. Eleventh graders researched a career of interest, interviewed a professional in their selected field, and created a personal career path and portfolio about that career. By involving families in this class assignment, the students' career portfolio displays, presentations, and evaluations became a shared learning experience and created new contacts for students with many potential future employers. This age-appropriate activity reflects research findings that demonstrate the importance of parent-student discussions throughout high school about education and future plans.

The Mother-Daughter College Preparation Program was started in District B in Los Angeles to help 5th grade Latinas and their mothers think about postsecondary education. In 2003, more than 160 mothers and daughters made college visits to California State University at Northridge. The program serves 17 schools and approximately 425 mother-daughter teams, and participation continues to grow. Due to its popularity, Families in Schools and District F expanded the Mother-Daughter College Preparation Program to form an extension known as Going On To (GOT) College. The GOT College program guides boys, girls, and family members to visit local colleges and to plan their middle and high school programs to enable students to qualify for college. By introducing postsecondary pathways early in students' education careers, families and students can plan more effectively for their futures—both educationally and financially.

Collaborating with the Community

A school learning community works with many partners to increase students' learning opportunities and experiences. Activities to enrich students' skills and talents may be conducted during lunch, after school, and at other times by school, family, and community partners (Sanders, 2001; Sanders & Harvey, 2002).

Teachers in the middle grades at Good Shepherd School in Peace River, Alberta, asked community instructors in tai chi, tae kwon do, and hip-hop dance to volunteer their time to conduct fitness classes for students during the lunch hour. This program, known as Try It at Lunch, enrolled many students, increasing interest in the community programs.

FamiliesFORWARD, working in Cincinnati, Ohio, conducted the Gifts We Share program to help students and families in high-poverty schools give of themselves, meet their neighbors, and improve students' writing and reading skills. Students wrote letters to invite senior citizens to become pen pals and to interact in other ways. Parents helped students coordinate several events, including a dinner to honor the seniors. The seniors, too, shared their talents and participated as guest readers, oral historians, and volunteers at school. The project extended the demographics of the learning community by including senior citizen neighbors.

Studies indicate that enriched learning activities help students do better in school, but not all families have extra resources for such activities. At East Taunton Elementary School in Taunton, Massachusetts, business partners provided part of the costs of buses and entrance fees for students and families to visit museums and attend cultural programs. Many community partners are more willing to help when they know that their investments contribute to student learning and success in school.

In school learning communities, educators, parents, and community partners help students focus on their plans for college and careers.

Allen and Lathrop Elementary Schools in Canton, Ohio, organized the Mercy Pals program to support two-way community service. Local medical center volunteers provided students and families with health care information and medical testing, gave presentations on careers and hobbies, led science activities, and supplied nutritious treats to sustain students during achievement testing. In return, students conducted community service activities for patients and hospital staff, created art displays, and performed at hospital celebrations.

STRENGTHENING SCHOOL LEARNING COMMUNITIES

Schools have a vested interest in becoming true learning communities. They are now accountable for *all* students' learning. The No Child Left Behind Act (NCLB) requires schools, districts, and states to develop academic programs that will increase students' proficiency in reading, math, and science. To learn at high levels, all students need the guidance and support of their teachers, families, and others in the community.

NCLB also requires schools, districts, and states to develop programs to communicate with all families about their children's education and to involve them in ways that help boost student achievement and success. The federal legislation, related state and district policies, school goals, family and student expectations, and useful research on partnerships are converging to encourage all schools to establish active and effective learning communities.

Most schools conduct at least a few activities to involve families in their children's education, but most do not have well-organized, goal-linked, and sustainable partnership programs. The schools featured here differ from most schools in two important ways. Organizationally, educators, parents, and other partners are working together to systematically strengthen and maintain their family and community involvement programs over time. Interpersonally, these partners recognize that they all have roles to play in helping students succeed in school—and that, together with students, they *are* the school's learning community.

REFERENCES

Baker, P. J., & Moss, R. K. (2001). Creating a community of readers. In S. Redding & L. G. Thomas (Eds.), *The community of the school* (pp. 319-333). Chicago: Academic Development Institute.

Epstein, J. L. (2001). *School family, and community, partnerships: Preparing educators and improving schools.* Boulder, CO: Westview Press.

Epstein, J. L., Salinas, K. C., & Van Voorhis, F. L. (2001). *Teachers Involve Parents in Schoolwork (TIPS) manuals and prototype activities for the elementary and middle grades.* Baltimore: Center on School, Family, and Community Partnerships, Johns Hopkins University.

Epstein, J. L., Sanders, M. G., Simon, B. S., Salinas, K. C., Jansorn, N. R., & Van Voorhis, F. L. (2002). *School family, and community partnerships: Your handbook for action* (2nd ed.). Thousand Oaks, CA: Corwin.

Henderson, A. T., & Mapp, K. L. (2002). *A new wave of evidence: The impact of school, family, and community connections on student achievement.* Austin, TX: Southwest Educational Development Laboratory.

Salinas, K. C., & Jansorn, N. R. (2003). *Promising partnership practices 2003.* Baltimore: Center on School, Family, and Community Partnerships, Johns Hopkins University.

Sanders, M. G. (2001). A study of the role of "community" in comprehensive school, family, and community partnership programs. *The Elementary School Journal, 102,* 19-34.

Sanders, M. G., & Harvey, A. (2002). Beyond the school walls: A case study of principal leadership for school-community collaboration. *Teachers College Record, 104*(7), 1345-1368.

Sheldon, S. B. (2003). Linking school-family-community partnerships in urban elementary schools to student achievement on state tests. *Urban Review, 35*(2), 149-165.

Sheldon, S. B., & Epstein, J. L. (in press-a). School programs of family and community involvement to support children's reading and literacy development across the grades. In J. Flood & P. Anders (Eds.), *The literacy development of students in urban schools: Research and policy.* Newark, DE: International Reading Association.

Sheldon, S. B., & Epstein, J. L. (in press-b). Focus on math achievement: Effects of family and community involvement. *Journal of Educational Research.*

Van Voorhis, F. L. (2003). Interactive homework in middle school: Effects on family involvement and students' science achievement. *Journal of Educational Research, 96*(9), 323-339.

Van Voorhis, F. L., & Epstein, J. L. (2002). *Teachers Involve Parents in School-work: Interactive homework CD.* Baltimore: Center on School, Family, and Community Partnerships, Johns Hopkins University.

Authors' note: This work is supported by grants from the National Institute of Child Health and Human Development and the Institute of Education Sciences. The opinions expressed are the authors' and do not necessarily represent the positions of the funding agencies.

The National Network of Partnership Schools at Johns Hopkins University provides professional development training, tools, and materials on school, family, and community partnerships. The Web site (www.partnershipschools.org) features research briefs; annual collections of promising practices from schools, districts, and states; descriptions of award-winning partnership programs; and information on how to join the network.

Joyce L. Epstein (jepstein@csos.jhu.edu) is Director and **Karen Clark Salinas** (ksalinas@csos.jhu.edu) is Communications Director, Center on School, Family, and Community Partnerships and the National Network of Partnership Schools at Johns Hopkins University, 3003 N. Charles St., Ste. 200, Baltimore, MD 20218; (410) 516-8800.

Popular Culture in the Classroom

Dale Allender

Brrriiinngggg! "That was the warning bell, Riverside. You now have three minutes to get to your classroom." The sound of the bell, followed by a high school student's quick announcement, gives way to "Whoomp! There It Is!" a funky number students immediately know. Previously sleepy adolescent faces—bemoaning that their parents, teachers, and administrators won't heed research asserting that teens should sleep in, come to school midmorning, and stay later in the afternoon for class—are now dipping and grooving at lockers and dancing down the halls to class. By the time the final bell rings, the halls are largely cleared and most of the students at Riverside High School are seated in their first-period classes.

Of course students chatter and there is residual rhythmic movement from the music. But I recognized this use of contemporary popular music as a proactive, affirming strategy to create an atmosphere of attentiveness and readiness. I almost never saw hall monitors or security guards working to clear halls and get students into the classrooms of this urban school. As a student teacher, I appreciated how the strategy effortlessly directed students into my classroom, ready to learn, by combining traditional and innovative elements, such as bells and music, with quick pacing accented by a voice students could recognize.

I usually stood in the doorway to enjoy watching the students dance their way to class and took attendance at the door so that when the final bell rang we moved right into the lesson. The strategy was relational in that it put the students in a good mood, administrative in that it got them to class on time, and pedagogical because it prepared students to participate in the activities ahead. Hats off to the principal from my student-teaching days for incorporating this activity into the school day.

Don Leibold, an active NCTE member since he became a classroom teacher about ten years ago, was also a student teacher at that time. Occasionally, we team-taught a class. I was always struck by his encyclopedic recall of information related to contemporary musicians and sitcom characters and their real-life alter egos. Don wasn't simply a walking television trivia Web site, though. He used his knowledge to create analogies to characters in novels or short stories the class was reading or to design writing prompts for students.

I was not as adept at knowing the ins and outs of the sexual tension between Mulder and Scully of *The X-Files* or the names of the Fly Girls on *In Living Color*. At that time I was more amused by the information Don possessed and how the use of that information made his classroom interactions more fluid and productive. Students liked that he wrote for a zine, reviewed music for magazines and newspapers, watched a lot of television and movies, and read a lot of books. They could tease him about a line from Janet Jackson's film *Poetic Justice* or something corny from the sitcom *Mad about You*. I thought this was admirable class rapport, but I didn't understand the pedagogical value of it all until later.

One morning in the teachers lounge—a place we rarely visited any time other than early morning—Don shared with me an assignment that he was developing. Don's idea was to have groups of students choose a television network and watch its prime-time local and national news with the intent of timing and labeling each segment of the program (e.g., news, sports, weather, special features, commercials, theme music, small talk, and so forth). Later, as the assignment evolved, students graphed each section of the program and then analyzed the content of each segment as a stand-alone and in relation to other segments. For example, they looked at how much small talk bled into the news time, which stories led off, and when commercials appeared. They considered the tonal quality of news and weather and compared the intent of the tonal delivery of each. It will come as no surprise to educators more experienced than we were at that time (thinking that we were the first to create such an assignment) that there is frequently little actual news reported during the network news. Experienced teachers will also note that there is value in this project.

Don's activity had value as a process and as a product. He engaged students in close intertextual and intratextual reading and analysis. His students explored rudimentary steps of discourse, conversation, and content analysis. They explored structure, composition and, to a lesser extent, the relationship between aesthetics and dramatic effect. They read additional information, on the stories covered on the news and they wrote during and about their process. And they did this in collaborative groups. (Not bad for a student teacher!) Students successfully completing this lesson, engaging the various language arts integrated within, would likely do well on any standardized test.

Don inspired me with this activity in the same way that the Riverside administrator who incorporated music into the beginning of the day inspired me. I wanted to work with popular culture in my classroom for its affective and academic value. I put together a unit on American identity, pairing novels or short stories with selected films. I enjoyed the unit, and I think the students enjoyed it as well. However, even as a novice student teacher, I knew that I wasn't doing anything quite as cutting-edge or progressive as I would have liked.

After I left student teaching, I was assigned sections of ninth-grade English at my first teaching position. The curriculum guides at this grade level generally require students to read, and teachers to teach, such canonical texts as *The Odyssey, To Kill a Mockingbird*, and *Romeo and Juliet*. This canon is curricular and pedagogical because literary texts are often accompanied by or driven by a long-standing favorite or popular instructional unit. To digress a moment, consider how many of us still teach *Romeo and Juliet* alongside *West Side Story*. I subverted (or expanded) this canon in part by beginning the *Romeo and Juliet* unit with an exploration of the music of Marvin Gaye.

We listened to a number of songs and analyzed the lyrics for metaphor, use of clichés, and complexity. We listened to the relationships between the music and the lyrics. We settled on several broad themes situated in a historic and African American cultural context with the help of a short profile on Gaye written by Cornel West. Next, we screened Mira Nair's film starring Denzel Washington, *Mississippi Masala*, where an African American man from the South falls in love with a young East Indian woman from Uganda who is living in exile with her parents. We took the film through the same process of analysis, noting historic, personal, and inter/intracultural influences on expressions of love, romance, and relationships. We also compared and contrasted the content of Gaye's music with Nair's film. Finally, we turned to Shakespeare, decentered but not dethroned. Final projects for this unit included music compilations with accompanying liner notes and full bibliographic references. The final media project ensured that students acted as producers and consumers of media.

Some of the students asked why I focused on Marvin Gaye rather than a more contemporary musician, such as Tupac or Puff Daddy. I told them I wanted someone whom they would be able to recognize and groove to but who would also be considered a classic or master musician. In later units, I paired the song "Mask" by the Fugees with Langston Hughes's short story "Who's Passing for Who" and Paul Lawrence Dunbar's poem "We Wear the Mask." These texts served as entry points into James Weldon Johnson's *The Autobiography of an Ex-Colored Man*. I taught this text set as an alternative to Harper Lee's canonized novel. One goal of such a pairing of texts was for students to understand the social and psychological significance of the mask as a trope in African American and African diaspora literature by examining the use of the symbol in a variety of texts representing multiple genres from different eras.

My point is this: Popular culture has affective and academic value: It should be used in a variety of ways as one would use texts generally in a constructivist, cultural studies classroom concerned with student achievement and transformative learning. Even *Lizzie McGuire* offers the possibility for learning about syntax, structure, and soliloquy. The TV show unfolds from a linear narrative with classic adolescent conflict. It is accented by animated soliloquies as McGuire works through her conflict in an internal dialogue full of humor and reflection. The show is further nuanced with snapshot images highlighting dramatic moments. The half hour concludes with a series of actual and performed bloopers from the show. This is a complex delivery pattern ripe for generative exploration, inquiry, and application.

Dale Allender Associate Executive Director of NCTE and Director of NCTE-West. University of California, Berkeley dallender@ncte.org

Living and Teaching on the Edge of a Pop Culture World

Robert Gardner

To my students, I am nothing less than an anachronism.

I stopped watching television in 1996. I have never seen an episode of *Friends*, I have missed the entire reality TV craze, and—to the utter disbelief of my students—I have missed the last six years of *The Simpsons*.

On the radio, our local university station and Minnesota Public Radio are my two stations of choice. Commercial-free radio means rarely having—or wanting—to change the station. I think I heard a Britney Spears song once while chaperoning a dance. I learned of performer Ludacris only through a student presentation.

I get my news from the radio and newspapers. The Internet serves me for research purposes only. I have not seen any television coverage of the latest war in Iraq. I saw footage of the airliner striking the World Trade Center only because it was used in Michael Moore's *Bowling for Columbine*.

When my students make a reference to some of the sights and sounds of popular culture, as often as not I must ask them to explain it to me, especially if it's a relatively recent movie or song. (I do *read* about television shows, movies, and music as they appear in newspapers and magazines, but these sources usually just provide me with a cursory knowledge, a quick roster of names, notables, and gossip.)

My students begin the year in a state of perplexity when they learn how removed I am from what is a large part of the lives of many of them. I am barraged with the usual questions:

Do you even own a TV?

Yes. I rent four or five videos per year.

How do you know what's going on?

I read the newspaper and listen to the radio.

Have you heard of [the hot singers of the moment]?

Yes, I've heard of them, though I wouldn't be able to pick them out of a lineup or identify their music.

What do you do with your time?

This question is the clincher. It may seem simple enough, but the tone with which it is asked implies much more. The real meaning is clear: anyone who doesn't watch television must live an empty life since many students cannot fathom such an existence—a reality that tells me too much about some of their lives.

So, I explain how I use my time, first discussing how I was unable to do as much as I do now, with nearly as much freedom, before I gave up watching television. I remember, back when TV was a part of my life, creating a schedule around certain programs—my own "must-see TV." Now my time is more truly my own, not set to revolve around some network's schedule.

(Oh, by the way, how do I use my time? I grade papers and plan lessons, of course, but I've also found the time to become active in several organizations, I read more, and I have more time for friends and meaningful conversation.)

After all of the questions are answered, some of my students still shake their heads in wonder and think I'm a little strange, but every teacher must have some eccentricity. I'm happy to make this one mine.

Students quickly learn to use my lack of pop culture knowledge as a class reference point. I've even had classes spontaneously begin to yell "pop culture" any time a student let slip a movie title or celebrity name. It's a joke directed toward me, I understand, but it also makes students much more aware of their frames of reference during class discussions.

At times in a class discussion a student will brighten with an inspired insight and offer a comparison between the story at hand and a contemporary film. Often, the comment appears to be a meaningful connection that helps the student understand the fiction, and it generally receives nods of agreement from some classmates, but when the student sees that I fail to understand the reference, it creates a brief, awkward moment. A gap of understanding opens, and the student must decide if the gap is worth bridging. Is the problem that the teacher simply doesn't know the reference, or is it actually a larger problem, that the conversational shorthand of pop culture fails to be fully appropriate? The student must quickly evaluate the comparison and decide if it is truly meaningful and worth developing for the entire class to consider.

Sometimes what seems to be a significant parallel is actually just a tangential connection.

To avoid such breakdowns in discussion, students begin to try to find appropriate literary allusions, assuming this is the one way they can relate their thoughts. They end up pushing their own learning in the process—an unexpected but pleasant side effect of sharing my lack of familiarity with this aspect of their world. Because we have been able to address my obliviousness to their world with humor, they are more apt to accept this difference as another piece of the diversity of life.

Yet, even with this humor, I have come to realize that my example may influence some students to question their own pop-culture consumption. My goal is not to have students abdicate their television viewing and music-listening habits; indeed, my personal choices toward these media involved no consideration of the students' choices, and I don't proselytize about my habits. But if my preference causes some students to examine their own habits, then it serves a positive (though originally unintended) purpose.

And that is reason enough to continue to use popular culture in my classroom—in this decidedly "unpopular" manner.

Article 37

At the Crossroads of Expertise: The Risky Business of Teaching Popular Culture

Based on extensive work with high school teachers and students, two university professors argue that incorporating forms of popular culture into the classroom provides a meeting place where students and teachers can share their expertise. They support the argument with examples of activities and projects in two different settings.

Meg Callahan and Bronwen E. Low

> Our elementary knowledge of popular culture as adults and educators seems to lag behind the "real time" expertise and understanding of the youth and students we teach. So how are we as educators supposed to incorporate popular culture into critical media literacy practices when we are unsure that we are focusing on current and not outdated popular culture forms?
>
> —Alvermann, Moon and Hagood, *Popular Culture in the Classroom*

A central issue for teachers concerns what role they will play when they incorporate popular culture into the classroom. The fleeting nature of the "popular," its questionable content, and countercultural values make its introduction into the classroom risky. Even the youngest and most "hip" teachers may feel out of touch and hopelessly inexpert regarding youth and popular culture. Human nature should lead us to avoid putting ourselves in such vulnerable situations—and yet, the teachers we worked with embraced this vulnerability, albeit in different contexts and different ways. Rather than attempting to keep up with youth culture, teachers can draw on their expertise in lesson design, language, and questioning and rely on students to bring their expertise on the texts of popular culture.

What Can Teachers Bring to a Pedagogy of Popular Culture?

Within a constructivist model, where teaching and learning is a dynamic interchange between all classroom participants, students and teachers can become coinvestigators of culture. To better understand the possibilities of this idea, we have served as researchers and teaching partners with three different secondary school teachers in five different classes. Each of the, authors spent most of a semester in these classes, studying the pedagogy of popular culture and critical media literacy. We share stories from two of these classrooms to provide new ways of understanding and negotiating expertise, as well as to provide encouragement for taking risks.[1]

Meg teamed up with Jill, an English teacher at a small, alternative high school in a working-class suburb. Jill was piloting a senior English course focused on media literacy and, as it was her first time teaching the course, she relied on several familiar strategies to integrate popular culture into the classroom. Prime Time Writing became a key resource for spontaneously capitalizing on student knowledge. Jill placed a prompt on the blackboard each day so that students could begin responding in their journals as soon as class began. Prime Time Writing varied in its forms from lists to more involved reflections and was not collected regularly: This familiar practice served the media class well in that most class sessions built naturally and effectively on the students' writing and, thus, their knowledge and expertise. Jill used the writing to poll the class and draw out students' knowledge of what was popular, while challenging them to think more carefully about their contributions. Jill could get in touch with students' understandings of and experiences with popular culture:

> One of the best days I had, one day when I was absolutely flat, in terms of Prime Time, and I said, 'What's being marketed to you right now' and make lists, and then they made incredible lists and I really enjoyed going through that with them and so, sometimes I just need to let the Prime Time be a time when they tell me what's going on in the world that I'm completely oblivious to.

Jill prepared for class meticulously, searching for resources and agonizing over how to support students' learning; She embraced this openness to spontaneous student input out of desperation on a "flat" day and, upon reflection, realized it was an important asset in dealing with popular culture and media. Even the students commented in interviews on the importance of Prime Time Writing for the class discussions. Said one student, "I like . . . with the Prime Times when we would like discuss them. . . . I liked when we did them and then we like talked about it 'cause you get everyone's [opinions]." Most of the students Meg interviewed felt that Prime Time Writing represented an effective way of drawing out students' opinions and expertise and that this was a worthwhile and motivating use of time. Some students mentioned that the prompts became tedious—especially on days when Jill did not take time to discuss them—which reminds us that even good activities should be used in moderation.

Jill also drew on other strategies in constructing the media literacy class. Students often entered class to find that they were to study vocabulary words using handouts. Nothing revolutionary here. In fact, Meg had hesitated in supporting such a traditional exercise in this more progressive curriculum. Yet Jill chose vocabulary—like *ubiquitous, subliminal,* and *aesthetic*—that became tools for exploring popular media. Somewhat surprisingly, several students identified this as an important element of the class. As one student reported, "The media literacy vocabulary words that we had to use—those were—I think that was the best for me. Like I learned the most from that." The key to the success of this seemingly mundane exercise was how effectively the class was built around these concepts and how the words were continually used to describe and deconstruct popular and mass media. Many of these words, especially *ubiquitous* and *subliminal,* were tossed around this class of senioritis-ridden students almost daily. The vocabulary may have provided them a language to speak about the myriad texts they lived within.

> **Through discussing the controversial nature of some of the language of hip-hop culture, Rob and Bronwen discovered that the students held a particular theory of language in which words could lose their historical baggage and be reinvented for new purposes.**

Bronwen worked with an English teacher at an urban arts school who had his own set of strategies for working with popular culture in the classroom. Rob felt that in the past he had missed occasions to engage with the hip-hop culture of the students. He wondered "how many times were there opportunities to gain access . . . but because I lacked either the knowledge or the language or the understanding—I missed the opportunity, you know." A creative writing teacher and published haiku poet, Rob felt that the oral poetry that shaped the lives of many of his students was an untapped resource. To gain access, he invited a university researcher who had done work on the educational implications of rap music and slam poetry and who provided teaching support as well as CDs and videos of rap music and slam poetry. Rob also invited local spoken word poets to class.

Rob was comfortable relinquishing the role of expert. During a discussion with one group of students about the nuances and politics of language in popular culture and, in particular, about the prevalence of terms in rap and youth culture such as *bitch* and *nigga,* Rob admitted to his students some of the challenges he was facing as a cultural outsider:

> I'm the minority here . . . by virtue of my age…basically I'm a minority because of my culture and to have this conversation . . . yeah—it's a difficult thing. Some of the stuff is hard to hear and worse than that, some of it's hard to understand, you know. I'm trying to get it and I think that's a good point in that. But how often out there are the roles reversed?

Through discussing the controversial nature of some of the language of hip-hop culture, Rob and Bronwen discovered that the students held a particular theory of language in which words could lose their historical baggage and be reinvented for new purposes. In dropping the n-word's suffix *er* for an *a*, for instance, the students felt that they could transform the racist pejorative into an expression of camaraderie within particular communities of African American youth. Rob's struggle to understand—both morally and semantically—the language his students use and the music and lyrics they listen to was part of what made the experience worthwhile. Roles were reversed, and the students were explaining culture to their teacher. This reversal required the teacher's willingness to relinquish some control. Rob elaborated in an interview:

> I wish I could tell you I knew what I was doing and although I'm not entirely lost I'm pretty lost most of the time. But here's my feeling about that. . . . Not knowing exactly what one is doing and certainly not knowing where one is going are not necessarily bad things you know…. It's sort of like that game you played as a kid where somebody blindfolded you, spun in three circles and said pin the tail on the donkey and you knew the donkey was out there somewhere and you had faith in the fact that if you tried long enough you'd get the tail in the right direction.

Willingness to feel lost, to allow and even cultivate experiences of "not knowing," is a testament to Rob's confidence that grappling with some of the messiness of youth culture is working in "the right direction." It demonstrates his commitment to "become a better communicator to those I serve." While Rob might describe himself as "pretty lost most of the time," he is in fact a skilled and experienced English teacher who can employ what he already knows about teaching poetry to use in relation to hip-hop. For instance, he had students do frequent freewriting exercises (like Jill's Prime Time Writing) after watching or listening to spoken word performances, using some of his favorite prompts, including "Men die every day for what they miss in poetry" (a paraphrase of William Carlos Williams) and "Poetry heals the wounds inflicted by reason" (Novalis). (Both phrases were the basis for one student's poem presented at the competitive slam.)

> By creating documentary films, students expressed their tacit expertise with media forms and genres.

What Can Students Bring to a Pedagogy of Popular Culture?

While Jill created opportunities for student sharing through the Prime Time Writing and discussions, she also found that students shared their expertise through production of media texts. By creating documentary films, students expressed their tacit expertise with media forms and genres. Because it was important for students to own the project, Jill and Meg allowed students a great deal of freedom in the choice of topics.

Meg and Jill asked students to create "a documentary with a message," and students interpreted these directions in unexpected ways. It was only through reflection afterwards that students revealed how their knowledge of popular media shaped their choices. For example, Matthew and Jim created a video documentary about mice attacks. Jill and Meg were confused and annoyed that the boys had used the documentary project to create something so seemingly inane, especially as the model documentaries they had shared engaged important political and social messages. Yet the boys took their project seriously and took a great deal of pride in it. When Meg asked about the origins of the project, Jim informed her that it had been inspired by the television program *When Animals Attack*. The two boys had carefully created a spoof of this genre and, upon reflection, Jill and Meg began to see how students benefited by "hands-on" expression of their expertise. Jim described himself as a lazy student, but he and his partner devised creative ways to use their simple handheld camera to simulate footage of an attack from a mouse's-eye view and to make their footage of mice seem ominous. Jim explained, "I just never realized the amount of work and effort that goes into ads and things like that—what they use to get our attention."

Most projects demonstrated that the students had extensive, though usually tacit, knowledge of popular media genres and techniques. Jim's story exemplifies the lessons learned as students took control of the media as insiders. While most students resisted the political and social topics that Jill and Meg had encouraged, choice allowed them to pursue their interests while learning important lessons about production processes.

It was clear from the beginning of Rob and Bronwen's spoken word project that the students were the authorities. After hearing about the project, one African American male student announced to Rob that there "was a lot going on in school that teachers don't know about" and decided to record some of these hallway artifacts for group discussions. During the first class, another African American student, Morris, mentioned the word "ciphering." When Bronwen asked for a definition, Morris said that he and others would perform one after class: a group freestyle (or improvised rhyming oral poem) in which the youths would rap from one to the next over an instrumental backbeat they played on the class CD player.

Not only do students bring insider knowledge of youth culture, but they also bring a passion for and investment in its texts and practices. A pedagogy of popular culture takes such passion and investment seriously. As one student in the spoken word project explained of his interest in this curriculum: "Someone was finally paying attention to me—it's not people don't talk about it as much—like you don't hear a lot of people try to understand you—instead you hear people try to downplay it and like and ignore, you."

While students' pleasure in popular culture forms offers important grounds for bringing them into the classroom, their inclusion can also create ambivalence about analysis. Two students in the spoken word project had expressed their frustration over some of the class discussions. In an interview one student explained, "I don't like to put labels on things— ... to me it's just music is music." The other student added, "it sort of takes away from it you know what I mean ... if you know like how something works it just ... like you show a magic trick and then it doesn't." An important aspect of the pleasure of popular culture is that it exists outside of school and that its "magic" is experienced rather than dissected.

Benefits of Bringing Together Expertise of Teachers and Students

So, why bring popular culture into the classroom if both students and teachers might find their identities and pleasures made vulnerable? Why interrupt the comfortable structures and hierarchies of the classroom? Because popular culture can become a site where the intersection of student and teacher expertise results in genuine dialogue, a dialogue that holds potential for literacy learning that goes beyond a recitation script. While not all of Jill's and Rob's classes reached this potential, there were many instances of exchanges and insights that resulted from intersecting expertise.

> While most students resisted the political and social topics that Jill and Meg had encouraged, choice allowed them to pursue their interests while learning important lessons about production processes.

Students in Jill's class were all white, middle and working-class seniors, and Meg and Jill were constantly challenging the limits of their life experiences in speaking about media and culture. Jill called on students' knowledge through skillful questioning. For example, having returned from a day off, Jill heard from a substitute teacher that the students had made somewhat racist comments while watching the documentary *Hoop Dreams*. Disturbed by this report, Jill used the subsequent class period as an opportunity to reflect on how popular culture and media shape impressions of "the other":

> I finally ended up asking them in their Prime Time to write down the circumstances in which they know people of another race...like write the person's name down and then what's your relationship to them—are they really close friends—somebody who would come over and spend the night at your house, or do you know them because you've been in class with them, but you don't really know anything about their lives beyond that.... What's your relationship... and it became very apparent that most of their impressions were from the media... and I said, OK, so what does that mean? And they had this great conversation about how everything they know may have been shaped by people who were trying to shape their impressions. That what they—often what they know firsthand runs entirely against what they see in the media and it was a great discussion where I never voiced an opinion and I loved it. It was an "aha" moment where they were telling me back as if didn't know it, but I was trying to get them to understand. I was thrilled. So it was the best moment, and it was utterly unplanned, it really was.

Although Jill emphasizes that this lesson was unplanned, her skillful questioning created the opportunity for students to interrupt the comfortable positions they had taken regarding African. Americans. By challenging these viewpoints, Jill not only addressed a serious social issue, but she also provided students with a strategy for making available for scrutiny their tacit awareness of media messages.

Not only do students bring insider knowledge of youth culture, but they also bring a passion for and investment in its texts and practices.

One male student in Jill's class expressed his casual acceptance of advertising's representation of the good life: the beer, the fast car, and the girl. Jill recounts her subsequent response:

> And I said, "oh, beer, that's a product, fast car, that's a product, girl, that's a human being. How interesting." Well, you know, we had a great discussion suddenly about that. By that time [Lara and Kris and Kitty} and some other people could voice how they reacted to that and the boys were trying to kind of shout us down ... I mean they were trying to dismiss us as feminists ... but they couldn't quite do it and there were male voices saying, "you know, they've got a point."

Jill's reframing of a common media tactic allowed the students to recognize potentially damaging cultural messages embedded in advertisements. Although such discussions could be heated and upsetting for teacher and students alike, they represented the cultural explorations that Jill and Meg hoped could open up genuine learning for the students. Students became invested in the life of the class and said that they appreciated hearing the opinions of their classmates, however they may have differed.

By challenging these viewpoints, Jill not only addressed a serious social issue, but she also provided students with a strategy for making available for scrutiny their tacit awareness of media messages.

Giving students authority had unexpected results in Rob's class. In the spoken word poetry unit, at the close of the first class, one African American student, Jared, announced, "I think we [the students] should all just teach this class"—a statement that seems to undermine the teacher's contributions and so confirms the anxiety over expertise expressed in Alvermann, Moon, and Hagood. In an interview, Bronwen asked another student, Adam, about this comment and about being placed in a position of authority in school and wondered whether or not he felt he had learned anything from working with the teacher and researcher. Adam recalled a class conversation about the creation and spread of slang. Some students had discussed their neighborhoods and the fact that they could identify the street someone lived on by their idiom. Rob and Bronwen had been amazed by this; they repeatedly questioned the students as to how and why this process might happen and what it taught us about linguistic innovation and transformation in contemporary culture. Adam said that he had never considered that "some other people they really don't have no idea of these words or why we say them, where they originated from" and realized that "it's like it will take a lot of practice to know this ... I didn't never think of that you know." Not only did Adam realize that he possessed specialized knowledge, but in conversation he also suggested that this knowledge was made more interesting to him and others as they were questioned about it: "Most people really don't put too much effort into it until we started getting into the thought process of it.... I don't know ... just the questions that you asked, did they think about it differently ... I think it really affected them."

Through class discussions, these language practices were made strange and thus, in Adam's words, "fascinating." The students' everyday language practices and neighborhoods emerged as worthy subjects of curricular inquiry, of the close attention offered by analytic questioning and discussion.

As in Jill's media literacy class, Bronwen and Rob offered students a new vocabulary for talking about familiar content. Most of the students in the spoken word project were not familiar with the term *spoken word*, which grouped together practices such as freestyle and rap, nor had most of them heard of slam poetry, a genre that, according to one student, also combined many seemingly disparate interests: "Yeah I write but I don't like this and ahhh ... yeah I rap, I flow ... and some other people, like I read poetry but now it's like all that comes together with slam poetry. It's all one and by that it made the whole class become one."

This project also asked students to be active producers of culture. In the poetry slam that concluded the unit, students performed before their peers the poems they had written. This gave them the opportunity to express their intimate, even visceral, knowledge of popular culture as participants rather than outsiders.

A Catalyst for Complex Thinking

Often, popular culture is used as a "hook" or "attention grabber" in the classroom to draw students into the traditional elements of the English curriculum. Perhaps this is a more comfortable use of popular texts, in that it doesn't open up the students' pleasures to the scrutiny and dissection of academic analysis—it simply serves as a fun way to begin before moving on to more serious fare. Keeping the focus on traditional texts also keeps the teacher firmly in the role of expert. Yet Rob and Jill took their commitment to popular culture beyond this stage and, as a result, there were times when teachers and students felt vulnerable. Because of this risk taking, however, both groups seemed to be more engaged and invested in the life of the classroom. Although several of Jill's students thought a class focused on media literacy might be easier than a traditional English course, they admitted at the end of the semester that they had found the course to be both challenging and relevant:

Marty: I thought it would be easy ... [but it was] not easy. It feels like it's almost sometimes, it feels like you're using a different part of your brain. Like I don't know how—it's weird to explain, but it makes you think about stuff you usually would never think about.

Sheryl: I knew before like half the stuff we learned in the class, but never really thought about it, which I found kind of mind boggling, in a way.

Julie: It makes you think. Like you discuss what life is really about, and what's really happening, going on, what you don't see, what you don't normally think about. It just gets you to think, basically.

Bronwen and Meg both concluded from their research that many students identified the use of popular culture in the classroom as a catalyst for complex thinking. Perhaps this is because popular culture provides a site where students can experience competence at the same time that teachers provide appropriate challenges through careful support, reframing, and questioning. These conditions can engage the kinds of self-motivation (Ryan and Deci) required for critical thinking. After all, we cannot force students to think critically; we can only invite them to do so. And we invite them as scholars of the now, as thinkers armed with an intimate, if sometimes tacit, knowledge of the dynamics and transformations of contemporary culture. In the exchanges of expertise and "not knowing" between teachers and students lies the vital lesson that the most interesting ideas are always up for questioning, negotiation, and reconsideration.

The students' everyday language practices and neighborhoods emerged as worthy subjects of curricular inquiry, of the close attention offered by analytic questioning and discussion.

Note

1. Teacher and student names are pseudonyms. The teachers have provided informed consent and have encouraged us to tell their stories; we changed their names to further protect the anonymity of their students: For more information on methodology, please contact the authors.

Works Cited

Alvermann, Donna E., Jennifer S. Moon, and Margaret C. Hagood. *Popular Culture in the Classroom: Teaching and Researching Critical Media Literacy.* Newark: Internatl. Reading Assn. and Natl. Reading Conf., 1999.

Ryan, Richard M., and Edward L. Deci. "Self-Determination Theory and the Facilitation of Intrinsic Motivation, Social Development, and Well-Being." *American Psychologist* 55.1 (2000): 68-78.

Meg Callahan is assistant professor at the Margaret Warner Graduate School of Education and Human Development, University of Rochester. She teaches English methods courses, and her research focuses on the integration of critical media, literacy in high school English. *email:* meg.callahan@rochester.edu. **Bronwen E. Low** is also assistant professor at the Margaret Warner Graduate School of Education and Human Development. She researches the challenges and possibilities popular youth cultures pose for education and teaches courses on adolescence, language, and literacy. *email:* bronwen.low@rochester.edu.

Article 38

Healthier Students, Better Learners

The Health Education Assessment Project helps teachers provide the skills-based, standards-based health instruction that students need.

By Beth Pateman

When we think back on health classes from our school days, many of us have only vague memories. We may recall some discussion of food groups, a film about puberty, or a lecture on dental hygiene conducted when the weather was too rainy to go outside for physical education. Few of us remember our K-12 health education experiences as being relevant to our lives outside the classroom.

Fortunately, that picture is changing. Asserting that "healthy students make better learners, and better learners make healthy communities," the Council of Chief State School Officers (CCSSO) and the Association of State and Territorial Health Officials (ASTHO) (2002) have summarized compelling research evidence that students' health significantly affects their school achievement. Even if their schools have the most outstanding academic curriculum and instruction, students who are ill or injured, hungry or depressed, abusing drugs or experiencing violence, are unlikely to learn as well as they should (Kolbe, 2002).

Effective health education programs have a vital role to play in enhancing students' health and thus in raising academic achievement. Kolbe's 2002 review of the research found that modern school health programs can improve students' health knowledge, attitudes, skills, and behaviors and enhance social and academic outcomes. How do these modern health programs differ from those that most of us remember from our school days? Thanks to growing knowledge about how to prevent unhealthy and unsafe behaviors among young people, today's exemplary health education combines *skills-based* and *standards-based* approaches.

Focus on Skills

The Centers for Disease Control and Prevention have identified six types of behavior that cause the most serious health problems in the United States among people over 5 years old: alcohol and other drug use, high-risk sexual behaviors, tobacco use, poor dietary choices, physical inactivity, and behaviors that result in intentional or unintentional injury. Stressing the importance of education efforts, the Centers state that

> these behaviors usually are established during youth; persist into adulthood; are interrelated; and are preventable. In addition to causing serious health problems, these behaviors contribute to many of the educational and social problems that confront the nation, including failure to complete high school, unemployment, and crime. (n.d.)

Effective health education programs have a vital role to play in enhancing students' health and thus in raising academic achievement.

In response to the Centers' focus on these major health-risk behaviors, education researchers have worked to identify educational approaches that positively affect health-related behaviors among young people. Many research studies have established the effectiveness of skills-based school health education in promoting healthy be-

Health Education Standards

- *Standard 1: Students will comprehend concepts related to health promotion and disease prevention.* For example, students will be able to identify what good health is, recognize health problems, and be aware of ways in which lifestyle, the environment, and public policies can promote health.
- *Standard 2: Students will demonstrate the ability to access valid health information and health-promoting products and services.* For example, students will be able to evaluate advertisements, options for health insurance and treatment, and food labels.
- *Standard 3: Students will demonstrate the ability to practice health-enhancing behaviors and reduce health risks.* For example, students will know how to identify responsible and harmful behaviors, develop strategies for good health, and manage stress.
- *Standard 4: Students will analyze the influence of culture, media, technology, and other factors on health.* For example, students will be able to describe and analyze how cultural background and messages from the media, technology, and friends influence health choices.
- *Standard 5: Students will demonstrate the ability to use interpersonal communication skills to enhance health.* For example, students will learn refusal and negotiation skills and conflict resolution strategies.
- *Standard 6: Students will demonstrate the ability to use goal-setting and decision-making skills to enhance health.* For example, students will set reasonable and attainable goals—such as losing a given amount of weight or increasing physical activity—and develop positive decision-making skills.
- *Standard 7: Students will demonstrate the ability to advocate for personal, family, and community health.* For example, students will identify community resources, accurately communicate health information and ideas, and work cooperatively to promote health.

Source: Joint Committee on National Health Education Standards. (1995).

havior and academic achievement (ASTHO & Society of State Directors of Health, Physical Education, and Recreation, 2002; Collins et al., 2002; Kirby, 2001). Lohrmann and Wooley (1998) determined that effective programs

- Focus on helping young people develop and practice personal and social skills, such as communication and decision making, to deal effectively with health-risk situations;
- Provide healthy alternatives to specific high-risk behaviors;
- Use interactive approaches that engage students;
- Are research-based and theory-driven;
- Address social and media influences on student behaviors;
- Strengthen individual and group norms that support healthy behavior;
- Are of sufficient duration to enable students to gain the knowledge and skills that they need; and
- Include teacher preparation and support.

New Standards for a Skills-Based Approach

In 1995, the American Cancer Society sponsored the development of national health education standards that use a skills-based approach to learning (Joint committee on National Health Education Standards, 1995). The standards, summarized below, advocate health literacy that enhances individuals' capacities to obtain, interpret, and understand basic health information and services and their competence to use such information and services in health-enhancing ways (Summerfield, 1995).

Together with the Centers for Disease Control and Prevention's priority health-risk behaviors, the national health education standards provide an important new framework for moving from an information-based school health curriculum to a skills-based curriculum. Skills-based health education engages students and provides a safe environment for students to practice working through health-risk situations that they are likely to encounter as adolescents.

An information-based approach to tobacco use prevention might require students to memorize facts about the health consequences of tobacco use, such as lung cancer, heart disease, and emphysema. In contrast, a skills-based approach ensures that students demonstrate the ability to locate valid information on the effects of tobacco use. Students learn and practice a variety of skills: For example, they use analysis to identify the influences of family, peers, and media on decisions about tobacco use and they use interpersonal communication skills to refuse tobacco use.

The skills-based approach outlined in the national health education standards helps students answer questions and address issues that are important in their lives. For example, young children need to learn how to make friends and deal with bullies. Older children need to practice a variety of strategies to resist pressures to engage in risky health behaviors while maintaining friendships. Early adolescents need to learn how to obtain reliable, straightforward information about the physical, emotional, and social changes of puberty. High school students need to learn to weigh their health-related decisions in terms of their life plans and goals. All students need to learn how to respond to stress, deal with strong feelings in health-enhancing ways, and build a reliable support group of peers and adults.

> ## Sample Performance Task: Advocacy for Mental Health
>
> **Student Challenge**
>
> Your challenge is to select and examine a mental health problem, such as anxiety, depression, eating disorders, suicide ideation, bipolar disorder, or schizophrenia. Your tasks are to
> • Locate and analyze valid information sources to determine the causes and symptoms of the problem.
> • Explore treatment options and health-enhancing ways of managing the problem.
> • Recommend helpful tips for talking with friends or family members who might be experiencing the problem.
> • Provide a list of helpful community resources.
> • Design a computer-generated brochure or presentation targeted to high school students that includes a summary of your information on causes, symptoms, and management/treatment; tips for talking with others; and a list of community resources.
>
> **Assessment Criteria for a Great Presentation**
>
> Your work will be assessed using the following criteria. You will be required to
> • Provide accurate and in-depth information and draw conclusions about relationships between behaviors and health.
> • Cite your information sources accurately and explain why your sources are appropriate.
> • Provide specific recommendations for health-enhancing ways of managing stress and ways of talking with others about the problem.
> • Demonstrate awareness of your target audience (high school students) and persuade others to make healthy choices.
>
> Additional criteria may be determined by class members.

The Health Education Assessment Project

Standards-based health education requires a new approach to planning, assessment, and instruction. Although many educators are excited about the prospect of standards-based teaching in health education, they may lack a clear picture of what standards-based performance would look like in their classrooms. To address this need, the Council of Chief State School Officers' State Collaborative on Assessment and Student Standards initiated the Health Education Assessment Project in 1993 (see www.ccsso.org/scass).

The Health Education Assessment Project develops standards-based health resources through a collaborative process. Funding for the project comes from the Centers for Disease Control and Prevention and the membership fees of 24 state and local education agencies. During its first decade, the project has built a foundation for a health education assessment system, created an assessment framework, developed and tested a pool of assessment items, and provided professional development and supporting materials to help teachers implement the assessment system and framework.

> A skills-based approach to tobacco use prevention ensures that students demonstrate the ability to locate valid information on the effects of tobacco use.

The project helps educators translate theory into practice. It provides educators with a wide range of assessment items developed in a variety of formats, including selected response, constructed response, and performance tasks (see the sample below). The project provides teacher and student rubrics for assessing performance and examples of student papers for scoring practice. Perhaps the greatest benefit to educators has been the hands-on professional development opportunities to practice aligning standards, assessment, and instruction for their own classrooms (CCSSO, 2003).

Classrooms in which students are evaluated by health education standards and criteria are substantially different from classrooms in which many teachers have taught and been taught. Teachers need hands-on preparation and experience with planning, implementing, and evaluating curriculum and instruction aligned with standards and assessment. The Health Education Assessment Project can improve the health of students by providing teachers with the tools they need to meet the important health needs of today's youth.

Beth Pateman is an associate professor at the Institute for Teacher Education, University of Hawaii at Manoa, Honolulu, HI 96822; (808) 956-3885; mpateman@hawaii.edu.

References

Association of State and Territorial Health Officials & Society of State Directors of Health, Physical Education, and Recreation. (2002). *Making the connection: Health and student achievement* (CDROM). Washington, DC: Authors.

Centers for Disease Control and Prevention, Division of Adolescent and School Health. (n.d.). *Health topics* [Online]. Available: www.cdc.gov/nccdphp/dash/risk.htm

Collins, J., Robin, L., Wooley, S., Fenley, D., Hunt, P., Taylor, J., Haber, D., & Kolbe, L. (2002). Programs that work: CDC's guide to effective programs that reduce health risk behavior of youth. *Journal of School Health, 72*(3), 93-99.

Council of Chief State School Officers. (2003). *Improving teaching and learning through the CCSSO-SCASS Health Education Assessment Project*. Washington, DC: Author.

ANNUAL EDITIONS

Council of Chief State School Officers & Association of State and Territorial Health Officials. (2002). *Why support a coordinated approach to school health?* Washington, DC: Authors.

Joint Committee on National Health Education Standards. (1995). *National health education standards: Achieving health literacy.* Reston, VA: Association for the Advancement of Health Education.

Kirby, D. (2001). *Emerging answers: Research findings on programs to reduce teen pregnancy.* Washington, DC: The National Campaign to Prevent Teen Pregnancy.

Kolbe, L. J. (2002). Education reform and the goals of modern school health programs. *The State Education Standard, 3*(4), 4-11.

Lohrmann, D. K., & Wooley, S. F. (1998). Comprehensive school health education. In E. Marx & S. F. Wooley (Eds.), *Health is academic: A guide to coordinated school health programs* (pp. 43-66). New York: Teachers College Press.

Summerfield, L. M. (1995). *National standards for health education* (ERIC Digest No. ED 387 483). Washington, DC: ERIC Clearinghouse on Teaching and Teacher Education. Available: www.ericfacility.net/databases/ERIC_Digests/ed387483.html

---

From *Educational Leadership,* December 2003/January 2004, pp. 70-74. Reprinted by permission of the Association for Supervision and Curriculum Development. Copyright © 2003 by ASCD. All rights reserved. The Association for Supervision and Curriculum Development is a worldwide community of educators advocating sound policies and sharing best practices to achieve the success of each learner. To learn more, visit ASCD at www.ascd.org

The Arithmetic Gap

Can U.S. students add, subtract, multiply, and divide better than previous generations? Does it matter?

By Tom Loveless and John Coughlan

In the mid-1990s, U.S. students' mediocre performance on the TIMSS, an international assessment of mathematical ability, captured public attention. But more recently, researchers have pointed to causes for optimism. Scores on the main math test of the National Assessment of Educational Progress (NAEP) have risen steadily in the past decade. From 1990 to 2003, 8th graders picked up 15 scale score points and 4th graders increased their results by a whopping 22 scale score points, which is equal to almost two years of knowledge or 0.69 standard deviation units (National Center for Education Statistics [NCES], 2003).

These data suggest that the United States' future in math achievement looks bright. Should Singaporean kids, at the top of the tables in the most recent TIMSS, be casting nervous glances over their shoulders as the up-and-coming U.S. students rapidly narrow the gap?

The Trend NAEP

Unfortunately, these encouraging results from the main NAEP mask a significant deficiency in U.S. students' mathematics performance: computation skills. When it comes to students' ability to add, subtract, multiply, and divide using whole numbers, fractions, and decimals and to accurately compute percentages, the picture is not so rosy.

The main NAEP test items are based on the curriculum frameworks developed by the National Assessment Governing Board (NAGB). Because these frameworks are based on curriculum standards developed within the field, the content of the main NAEP evolves to match changing instructional practices. This limits the ability of the main NAEP to measure change reliably over time.

In contrast, the long-term trend NAEP, an entirely different assessment, has used the same testing instruments since its first administration. This stability enables comparisons of student performance over time. In addition, the mathematics trend NAEP has retained a greater emphasis on computation than the evolving main NAEP.

Last given in 1999, the trend NAEP shows more modest overall gains than the main NAEP (see fig. 1). In the 1990s, 9-year-olds gained 2 scale score points; 13-year-olds gained 6 points, and 17-year-olds gained 3 points. The most glaring discrepancy between the two tests is with the youngest students—the 9-year-olds. When the gains are expressed as standard deviations of the 1990 tests—a metric used by statisticians to compare gains on different scales—the main NAEP indicates gains that are more than 10 times larger than gains on the trend NAEP (0.69 compared to 0.06).

Does the varying emphasis on computation in the two tests explain the contrasting results? To explore this question, we conducted a problem-by-problem analysis of trend NAEP results in the past 20 years.

Basic Skills Achievement

A wall of jargon confronts interested parents, policymakers, and citizens who want to know whether students can add whole numbers or make sense of fractions. Computation results are hidden in the subcategory of "Number sense, properties, and operations," which includes problems requiring 4th graders to "choose a number sentence," 8th graders to "translate words into numbers," and 12th graders to "apply numerical reasoning" (NAGB, 2001). As valuable as these skills are, we must also determine whether students can compute correct answers after they have chosen number sentences, translated words into numbers, and applied numerical reasoning.

We took trend NAEP results from the past two decades and scrutinized them problem-by-problem to find those that tested students' basic computation skills. We cast aside problems requiring 13-year-olds to "identify an even number" or "identify a number sentence." To be included in one of our arithmetic clusters, a problem had to test addition, subtraction, multiplication, or division of whole numbers for 9-year-olds and the same operations with whole numbers, fractions, decimals, and percentages for 13- and 17-year-olds—all without a calculator. Given the small number of test items in any one cluster, the data we obtained are not definitive. But some consistent patterns do emerge.

As Figure 2 shows, the results are little cause for celebration. After overall steady increases in the 1980s, the gains slowed, leveled off, and even reversed in the 1990s. Older students' performance on problems involving fractions was particularly disappointing. In 1982, 67 percent of 17-year-olds answered questions dealing with fractions correctly. By 1990, 76 percent answered correctly—considerable progress in less than a decade. By 1999, however, the bottom had fallen out—only 56 percent of 17-year-olds answered correctly. Although this is the most dramatic swing among our skill clusters, evidence of a decline in computation skills abounds. Only in the skill of computing with percentages, which rose for both 13- and 17-year-olds, were there gains in the 1990s.

Why Does Arithmetic Matter?

Even if students can't compute very well, should we be concerned? We often hear statements reflecting apathy about students' declining arithmetic skills:

> My 9-year-old may not be able to divide 56 by 7 in his head, or figure out that 8 is one-third of 24, but the little guy has his own Web site and programs TiVo for me when I'm away at work. Besides, I was never a "math person," and I turned out OK.

Concern over the recent decline in arithmetic skills among U.S. students is not merely the province of a group of cranky mathematicians. Basic skills are important for three reasons.

Computation skills are necessary to advance in mathematics and the sciences. Learning mathematics is an incremental process. Eighth graders who cannot do basic arithmetic with ease, who cannot find the right answer quickly and confidently without a calculator, will be hampered in their efforts to learn algebra and geometry in high school. Without some proficiency in algebra, students will have little grasp of calculus, physics, or chemistry and little chance of succeeding in college mathematics and science courses.

Computation skills are an increasingly important predictor of adult earnings. Learning basic computation skills is not just for our future brain surgeons and rocket scientists. In Murnane, Willett, and Levy's discussion of their landmark study on cognitive skills as a predictor of future earnings, they observe that a high school senior's mastery of skills taught in American schools no later than the 8th grade is an increasingly important determinant of subsequent wages. (1995, p. 264)

Computation skills promote equity in math achievement. Declining arithmetic achievement in the United States also raises concern about racial equity. The achievement gap in computation skills between black and white students narrowed in the 1980s but began to widen in the 1990s (Lee, 2002). From 1990 to 1999, for instance, white 9-year-olds' performance on division problems dropped one-tenth of a percentage point, whereas their black counterparts' performance fell by 6 percentage points. Thirteen-year-old white students fell 2.1 percentage points on fractions compared with a drop of 4 percentage points for black students. Most eye-opening is 17-year-olds' tumble in fractions. White students' performance fell nearly 18 percentage points, whereas that of black 17-year-olds decreased by 33.6 percentage points.

How Did This Happen?

Although these data are the best we have on a national level, they are hardly robust enough to make a declarative statement of causality. However, we suspect three major factors for this decline, all interrelated: the poor preparation of elementary and middle school math teachers; an increasing reliance on calculators in the classroom from a young age; and math "reform" standards and curriculums that gained favor in the early 1990s.

Poor teacher preparation. Recent survey data from the TIMSS suggests that U.S. math teachers are less prepared in their subject area than their more successful counterparts abroad: 78 percent of Singaporean students and 89 percent of Flemish Belgian 8th graders have teachers who majored in math, compared with only 41 percent of U.S. 8th graders. U.S. math teachers majored in education more than teachers in any other country (Loveless, 2001a; TIMSS, 2003). Richard Askey (1999), a math professor at the University of Wisconsin, notes the deficiencies in math education courses taken by elementary and middle school teachers. He derides time-wasting workshops and calls for an overhaul of professional development and a greater emphasis on deepening teachers' understanding of elementary mathematics.

Use of calculators in elementary school classrooms. On the NAEP, 4th graders who say that they use calculators every day on classwork have significantly lower math scores than students who never use them. The relationship reverses at 8th grade. Of course, correlation is not proof of causality. Generally speaking, research shows neither a positive nor a negative effect of calculator use on students' computation skills (Ellington, 2003), but most of the calculator studies have involved middle and high school students. Very few have focused on the elementary grades or on the long-term impact of calculators on students who are first learning arithmetic. Even less is known about whether calculators help or hinder students who are struggling to catch up with their peers in mathematics.

Reformist math standards and curriculum. The National Council of Teachers of Mathematics (NCTM) came up with the NCTM Standards in 1989. The 24 drafters of the Standards included faculty from teacher education schools and universities, as well as two K-12 teachers—but not a single mathematician. The vague standards suggest that K-4 students should devote more attention to "operation sense" and "cooperative work" while spending less time doing long division and using pencil and paper to compute fractions. An emphasis on using calculators at all ages runs through the entire document (Klein, 2002; Loveless, 1998; NCTM, 1989).

The publication of the standards coincided neatly with then-President George H. W. Bush's call for national standards at a meeting of state governors in 1989. The NCTM guidelines became a model for U.S. national standards. With the support of National Science Foundation grants, curriculums aligned with the NCTM standards spread throughout state departments of education, school districts, and education schools and universities (Loveless, 2003).

The spread of NCTM-based curriculums met considerable resistance from parents, teachers, and mathematicians who believed that the less demanding programs were shortchanging their children and students. After considerable effort on the part of the national organization Mathematically Correct and other like-minded groups of parents and mathematicians, the state of California replaced its NCTM-based state standards with a more rigorous set of expectations for K–12 students. Similar protests took place in Massachusetts. The U.S. Department of Education's 1999 list of 10 recommended textbooks—all created with NCTM standards in mind—prompted an open letter addressed to Secretary of Education Richard Riley decrying the recommendations. More than 200 prominent mathematicians and policymakers signed the letter (Klein, 2002).

Supporters of the NCTM standards often couch the basic debate in terms of "conceptual understanding" and promoting higher-order thinking versus "basic skills" and the monotony of memorizing multiplication tables (Loveless, 2001b). Berkeley mathematician Hung-Hsi Wu lambastes this "bogus dichotomy," noting that "conceptual advances are invariably built on the bedrock of technique" (1999, p. 14). Would Einstein have come up with the theory of relativity if he couldn't compute with fractions?

Basic Proficiency for All Students

Critics deride an emphasis on basic skills as a return to the "drill-and-kill" drudgery of the past. We are not advocating a return to the past, but rather a better preparation for the future.

No one wants students to become robotic human calculators who blindly follow the rules of computation to arrive at correct answers. We would simply like all students to learn how to add, subtract, multiply, and divide using whole numbers, fractions, and decimals—and accurately compute percentages—by the end of 8th grade. Only by mastering these skills will students have the opportunity to learn higher-level mathematics. If U.S. students are proficient in basic arithmetic, they and the nation will be much better off.

References

Askey, R. (1999, Fall). Knowing and teaching elementary mathematics. *American Educator*, 1-8.

Ellington, A. J. (2003). A meta-analysis of the effects of calculators on students' achievement and attitude levels in pre-college mathematics classes. *Journal for Research in Mathematics Education*, 34(5), 433-463.

Klein, D. (2002). A brief history of American K-12 mathematics education in the 20th century. In J. Royer (Ed.), *Mathematical cognition: A volume in current perspectives on cognition, learning, and instruction*. Greenwich, CT: Information Age Publishing.

Lee, J. (2002). Racial and ethnic achievement gap trends: Reversing the progress toward equity? *Educational Researcher*, 31(1).

Loveless, T. (1998). The use and misuse of research in education reform. In D. Ravitch (Ed.), *Brookings papers on education policy 1998*. Washington, DC: Brookings Institution Press.

Loveless, T. (2001a). *The 2001 Brown Center report on American education*. Washington, DC: Brookings Institution Press.

Loveless, T. (Ed.). (2001b). *The great curriculum debate: How should we teach reading and math?* Washington, DC: Brookings Institution Press.

Loveless, T. (2003). The regulation of teachers and teaching. In M. T. Hallinan, A. Gamoran, W. Kubitschek, & T. Loveless (Eds.), *Stability and change in American education: Structure, processes, and outcomes*. Clinton Corners, NY: Eliot Werner Publications.

Murnane, R. J., Willet, J. B., & Levy, F. (1995). The growing importance of cognitive skills in wage determination. *The Review of Economics and Statistics*, 77(2), 251-266.

National Assessment Governing Board. (2001). *Mathematics framework for 2005* (prepublication ed.). Available: www.nagb.org/pubs/2005framework.doc

National Center for Education Statistics. (2003). *Mathematics 2003 major results*. Available: www.nces.ed.gov/nationsreportcard/mathematics/results2003

National Council of Teachers of Mathematics. (1989). *Curriculum and evaluation standards for school mathematics*. Reston, VA: Author. Available: http://standards.nctm.org/previous/CurrEvStds/index.htm

Trends in International Mathematics and Science Study. (2003). Available: timss.bc.edu/timss2003.html

Wu, H. H. (1999, Fall). Basic skills versus conceptual understanding: A bogus dichotomy in mathematics education. *American Educator*, 14-19, 50-52.

Tom Loveless is Director of the Brown Center on Education Policy, The Brookings Institution, Washington, DC; tloveless@brookings.edu.

John Coughlan was Senior Research Assistant at the Brown Center on Education Policy; he now resides in Belgium and works for the European Union.

UNIT 8
The Profession of Teaching Today

Unit Selections

40. **The Search for Highly Qualified Teachers**, Barnett Berry, Mandy Hoke, and Eric Hirsch
41. **The Other Side of Highly Qualified Teachers**, Wade A. Carpenter
42. **The Marriage of Liberal Arts Departments and Schools of Education**, Sidney Trubowitz

Key Points to Consider

- What is "expertise" in teaching? Be specific and use examples.

- Describe the learning needs of new teachers in terms of curriculum, instruction, assessment, management, school culture, and the larger community. How important is maintaining order?

- How would a teacher education program that is based on the premise of developing novice teachers as "transformative" urban educators place student teachers in urban classrooms?

- Why do teachers leave the profession? What can be done to solve schools' staffing problems?

Links: www.dushkin.com/online/
These sites are annotated in the World Wide Web pages.

Canada's SchoolNet Staff Room
http://www.schoolnet.ca/home/e/

Teachers Helping Teachers
http://www.pacificnet.net/~mandel/

The Teachers' Network
http://www.teachers.net

Teaching with Electronic Technology
http://www.wam.umd.edu/~mlhall/teaching.html

The task of helping teachers to grow in their levels of expertise in the classroom falls heavily on those educators who provide professional staff development training in the schools. Meaningful staff development training is extremely important. Several professional concerns are very real in the early career development of teachers. Level of job security or tenure is still an issue, as are the concerns of first-year teachers and teacher educators. How teachers interact with students is a concern to all conscientious, thoughtful teachers.

We continue the dialogue over what makes a teacher "good." There are numerous external pressures on the teaching profession today from a variety of public interest groups. The profession continues to develop its knowledge base on effective teaching through ethnographic and empirical inquiry about classroom practice and teachers' behavior in elementary and secondary classrooms across the nation. Concern continues about how best to teach to enhance insightful, reflective student interaction with the content of instruction. We continue to consider alternative visions of literacy and the roles of teachers in fostering a desire for learning within their students.

All of us who live the life of a teacher are aware of those features that we associate with the concept of a good teacher. In addition, we do well to remember that the teacher/student relationship is both a tacit and an explicit one—one in which teachers' attitude and emotional outreach are as important as students' response to our instructional effort. The teacher/student bond in the teaching/learning process cannot be overemphasized. We must maintain an emotional link in the teacher/student relationship that will compel students to want to accept instruction and attain optimal learning. What, then, constitutes those most defensible standards for assessing good teaching?

The past decade has yielded much in-depth research on the various levels of expertise in the practice of teaching. We know much more now about specific teaching competencies and how they are acquired. Expert teachers do differ from novices and experienced teachers in terms of their capacity to exhibit accurate, integrated, and holistic perceptions and analyses of what goes on when students try to learn in classroom settings. We can now pinpoint some of these qualitative differences.

As the knowledge base of our professional practice continues to expand, we will be able to certify with greater precision what constitutes acceptable ranges of teacher performance based on more clearly defined procedures of practice, as we have, for example, in medicine and dentistry. Medicine is, after all, a practical art as well as a science—and so is teaching. The analogy in terms of setting standards of professional practice is a strong one. Yet the emotional pressure on teachers that theirs is also a performing art, and that clear standards of practice can be applied to that art, is a bitter pill to swallow for many. Hence, the intense reaction of many teachers against external competency testing and any rigorous classroom observation standards. The writing, however, is on the wall: The profession cannot hide behind the tradition that teaching is a special art, unlike all others, which cannot be subjected to objective observational standards, aesthetic critique, or to a standard knowledge base. The public demands the same levels of demonstrable professional standards of practice as are demanded of those in the medical arts.

Likewise, we have identified certain approaches to working with students in the classroom that have been effective. Classroom practices such as cooperative learning strategies have won widespread support for inclusion in the knowledge base on teaching. The knowledge base of the social psychology of life in classrooms has been significantly expanded by collaborative research between classroom teachers and various specialists in psychology and teacher education. This has been accomplished by using anthropological field research techniques to ground theory of classroom practice into demonstrable phenomenological perspectives. Many issues have been raised—and answers found—by basic ethnographic field observations, interviews, and anecdotal record-keeping techniques to understand more precisely how teachers and students interact in the classroom. A rich dialectic is developing among teachers regarding the description of ideal classroom environments. The methodological insight from this research into the day-to-day realities of life in schools is transforming what we know about teaching as a professional activity and how to best advance our knowledge of effective teaching strategies.

Creative, insightful persons who become teachers will usually find ways to network their interests and concerns with other teachers and will make their own opportunities for creative teaching in spite of external assessment procedures. They acknowledge that the science of teaching involves the observation and measurement of teaching behaviors but that the art of teaching involves the humanistic dimensions of instructional activities, an alertness to the details of what is taught, and equal alertness to how students receive it. Creative, insightful teachers guide class processes and formulate questions according to their perceptions of how students are responding to the material.

To build their aspirations, as well as their self-confidence, teachers must be motivated to an even greater effort for professional growth in the midst of these fundamental revisions. Teachers need support, appreciation, and respect. Simply criticizing them while refusing to alter social and economic conditions that affect the quality of their work will not solve their problems, nor will it lead to excellence in education. Not only must teachers work to improve their public image and the public's confidence in them, but the public must confront its own misunderstandings of the level of commitment required to achieve teacher excellence. Teachers need to know that the public cares about and respects them enough to fund their professional improvement in a primary recognition that they are an all-important force in the life of this nation. The articles in this unit consider the quality of education and the status of the teaching profession today.

The Search for Highly Qualified Teachers

At the same time that NCLB has given states a mandate to staff their classrooms with "highly qualified teachers," the federal government is pushing a dangerously narrow definition of the knowledge and skills that today's teachers need.

BY BARNETT BERRY, MANDY HOKE, AND ERIC HIRSCH

OVER THE last decade, policy makers and business leaders have come to realize what parents have always known—teachers make the most difference in student achievement. Thanks to new statistical and analytical methods used by a wide range of researchers, the evidence is mounting that teacher quality accounts for the lion's share of variance in student test scores.[1] However, while consensus is growing among school reformers that teachers are the most important school-related determinant of student achievement, there is not much more than ephemeral agreement on what we mean by "teaching quality" or what steps we must take to see that every student has access to high-quality teachers.[2]

Much has been written about the ideological divide between those who view teaching as highly complex work, requiring professionals with formal, specialized preparation, and those who view it as routine work that most reasonably smart people could do (and would do more readily if "misguided" government or professional regulations did not limit entry into the field).[3] The former view is well represented in the research of Linda Darling-Hammond of Stanford University and the oft-cited reports of the National Commission on Teaching and America's Future (NCTAF). NCTAF's reform framework emphasizes teacher education, state licensing, professional accountability, and compensation as the primary means to strengthen teacher quality. These positions are based on evidence that good teachers must have a host of subject-matter and technical knowledge, including the knowledge and skills needed to help every member of an increasingly diverse student population reach much higher academic standards.[4]

The latter view is best reflected in the statements by Chester Finn and the reports from the Thomas B. Fordham Foundation, which recommend a number of market-based initiatives designed to countermand traditional teacher education practices. For example, the foundation advocates for policies designed to loosen, if not eliminate, existing requirements for those entering the field of education. In their place, Finn would institute short-cut alternative certification programs that he and his followers believe will improve the quality and quantity of the teacher supply.[5] The foundation's positions are based on a number of studies that link teachers' scores on aptitude and subject-matter tests to student achievement scores, as well as on the assumption that the teaching profession has—and will continue to have—a very weak knowledge base. The foundation's perspective is that new teachers can easily learn on the job anything they need to know about *how* to teach.

> Consensus is growing among school reformers that teachers are the most important school-related determinant of student achievement.

With the reauthorization of the Elementary and Secondary Education Act, more popularly known as the No Child Left Behind (NCLB) Act, what was once a largely academic debate has now become a national controversy with long-term consequences for the public school systems of every state. NCLB's mandate that every teacher of a core academic subject be "highly qualified" by the end of the 2005-06 school year poses unprecedented challenges for state education policy leaders and for practitioners. In the hands of highly capable leaders, this mandate also offers unprecedented opportunities to reshape teacher preparation in ways that will finally produce the gains in student achievement that reformers have long sought.

NCLB's "highly qualified teacher" provisions are now familiar to most education watchers. The law states that highly qualified teachers must "hold at least a bachelor's degree from a four-year institution; hold full state certification; and demonstrate competence in their subject area." In addition, the law requires state departments of education to publicly report what they are doing to improve teacher quality along with how their efforts are progressing, including identifying the distribution of "highly qualified" teachers across low- and high-poverty schools.

Given that states lack the capacity to adequately fund public education and that many poor, rural, and small school districts struggle to compete in the "highly qualified" teacher labor market, we believe the federal government should assume a greater role in supporting and improving the teacher development system. Much has been said about the long—and often sordid— history of state policy makers who have not been willing to enforce the teaching standards that they established, the well-documented practice of school administrators misassigning teachers, and the fact that poor students and those of color are more likely to be taught by unqualified teachers.[6] NCLB *could* be a welcome federal intervention that could help to eliminate a long-neglected barrier to higher levels of achievement. Already, the law has local school administrators focused on teacher standards to an unprecedented degree, and its core provisions could become the tools we need to build a more uniform and consistently enforced teacher licensure and assessment system.

Unfortunately, ongoing research by the Southeast Center for Teaching Quality (SECTQ) on the implementation of NCLB suggests that the teacher-quality blueprint embedded in the law is largely being ignored—severely limiting the possibility that all students will have access to caring, competent, and qualified teachers in the next decade. SECTQ is involved in a multistate policy research project investigating the impact on underperforming schools of the teacher-quality mandates and opportunities in NCLB. Among the preliminary findings: the recent actions, and in some cases inactions, of the federal government have often led to confusion and uncertainty as to how state and local policy makers ought to proceed to ensure that each student has a "highly qualified" teacher.

DEFINING THE TERM

Although NCLB acknowledges that teachers need both subject-matter and pedagogical knowledge in order to be considered "highly qualified," the current leadership of the U.S. Department of Education (ED) has chosen to emphasize the former and give little weight to the latter. Last July, Secretary of Education Rod Paige released his *Second Annual Report on Teacher Quality*—intended to document the progress states have made toward meeting the challenges of NCLB's "highly qualified teacher" provisions.[7] Much like the secretary's first report, this one focuses on raising academic standards for teachers while simultaneously lowering barriers to those trying to enter the profession. Based on the Fordham Foundation's teacher-quality framework, ED's rule making and recent investments seek to improve teacher quality by simply requiring teachers to pass standardized subject-matter tests and allowing teachers to become licensed by entering alternative certification programs that require no preservice training.

The secretary's report largely ignores much of the knowledge and many of the skills that are critical to administrators and teachers working in high-challenge schools. In its research on schools in the Southeast, SECTQ found that educators need more knowledge of and support for working with an increasingly diverse population of students—especially English-language learners. Subject-matter knowledge is necessary, but clearly not sufficient. The current strategy to implement NCLB drives school administrators to require teachers to pass multiple-choice subject-matter tests that provide little insight into teachers' ability to teach the content to a diverse student population. Similarly, many teachers are required to take additional university-based subject-matter courses that may not include teaching strategies that have demonstrated success in improving the learning of diverse student populations.

The research literature on teacher quality—taken as a whole—sends a strong message to policy makers and practitioners that teachers need to know their subject matter and how to teach it. The demands on our public schools clearly require all teachers to know a great deal about how humans learn and how to manage the complexity of the learning process.[8] Today this means knowing how to manage classrooms, develop standards-based lessons, assess student work fairly and appropriately, work with special-needs students and English-language learners, and use technology to bring curriculum to life for the many students who lack motivation. These skills can be readily learned through effective teacher education, induction, and professional development experiences, and new research shows that teachers who are better prepared to meet such varied challenges are more likely to remain in teaching.[9]

WHAT'S WRONG?

Rather than using NCLB as an opportunity to help states truly raise standards for teachers, ED does not require or even encourage states to revamp their teacher-certification systems. In its pursuit of a narrow teacher-quality agenda, ED—as demonstrated in the secretary's report—ignores a vast array of credible research on teacher education and certification. This fact is especially unsettling in light of NCLB's emphasis on using only "scientifically based research" to judge policies and programs designed to improve teacher quality and student achievement.

> The research literature on teacher quality sends a strong message to policy makers and practitioners that teachers need to know their subject matter and *how* to teach it.

The SECTQ research has revealed that, in the absence of a comprehensive vision of teacher development, most states are simply tweaking license definitions in order to maximize the number of teachers that they can designate as highly qualified. Without the resources to develop more appropriate and more sophisticated measures of teacher and teaching quality, states will rely on the rather narrow subject-matter tests already in place to gauge whether or not teachers are highly qualified.

Of even greater concern are the requirements for alternative routes to teacher certification. Guidance issued by ED allows "teachers" participating in an alternative route program—often with just a few weeks of training—to be deemed highly qualified, as long as they are making satisfactory progress toward full certification as prescribed by the state.[10] This means that a novice teacher who has had just a few weeks of training and has no track record of success would be placed in the same category as an accomplished teacher—such as those certified by the National Board for Professional Teaching Standards. The result is a definition worthy of George Orwell's *1984*—now *highly qualified* actually means, at best, *minimally qualified*. What is most disheartening about the federal guidelines is that no other profession would consider practitioners to be "highly qualified" until they had demonstrated that they possessed and could apply the knowledge required to serve the best interest of their clients.

In the SECTQ case studies, we heard a consistent chorus from administrators that relying primarily on alternative certification to solve the teacher-quality problem "will not cut it." As one local human resource administrator from Alabama noted, "Nine out of 10 people we have hired on alternative routes are dismal failures. We hired one person who had a great science background but did not have one class in how to teach. He had no clue."

Yet ED has suggested that a single, machine-graded test now being developed by the American Board for Certification of Teacher Excellence (ABCTE) can serve as the sole proxy for teacher preparation and licensure.[11] Such certification would waive the need for prospective teachers to have specialized knowledge of students, to be familiar with community and cultural contexts, or to undergo internships in which they can learn their craft under the guidance of accomplished veterans.

The Education Trust has claimed that there is "essentially a conspiracy of silence about teacher quality in which the U.S. Department of Education is complicit."[12] In a scathing 2003 report, the Education Trust asserted that ED has been "dragging its heels" on defining more clearly what a "highly qualified" teacher is and how districts and states can more equitably distribute them. The Education Trust called for ED to "send clear, unequivocal signals that highly qualified means just that."[13]

WHAT CAN BE DONE?

Given current teacher shortages and the limits of what any newly minted teacher can be expected to accomplish in our hardest-to-staff schools, no one can question the need to recruit and retain "highly qualified" teachers. But so long as federal guidelines choose to define teacher quality solely by subject-matter competence, we will continue to experience a flood of new teachers who may know their subjects but not much else about teaching and learning. These ill-prepared teachers will flow into (and out of) our most challenged schools, and the students in these schools—who desperately need expert teaching—will continue to be victimized. So what must we do?

1. *The teaching profession needs to be opened up to those other than traditional college-aged students from traditional university-based preparation programs.* Alternative-route programs do not have to sacrifice quality for quantity. In fact, there are many good alternative-route programs that provide candidates with intensive preparation before they begin teaching and then offer them extensive mentoring once they enter the classroom. For example, the Academy for Urban School Leadership in Chicago contracts with the local school district to provide participants with a $30,000 living stipend, a no-cost MAT degree, and a state certificate. This highly selective program (12.5% acceptance rate) prepares teachers through a 10-month residency in a high-performing urban school, one week of observation and guided practice in a high-need public school, and one week at the academy working on teaching at a different grade level. Candidates are trained by classroom mentors and take specially designed courses in teaching methods. Their preparation is standards-based, and their mentors are compensated for the time spent mentoring and attending professional development. After graduation, the academy provides new teachers with five years of follow-up professional development and support, including bimonthly meetings, observation and feedback, continuing training, and support for career development.

2. *More investments need to be made in school systems and universities that recruit and prepare teachers specifically for urban and rural hard-to-staff schools.* Several foundations, including the Carnegie Corporation of New York, the Kauffman Foundation, and the Osborne Foundation, have launched a series of teacher education initiatives that recognize the need for special preparation for teaching in hard-to-staff schools. A model worth emulating is Center X, the highly effective teacher education program at UCLA. Center X attracts and prepares academically able students to offer high-quality teaching to California's racially, culturally, and linguistically diverse children who attend urban schools. In the first year of this two-year, post-baccalaureate program, students with majors in an academic discipline take a full course load and do student teaching. In the second year, participants complete a residency in which they are paid to work as teaching assistants in a school, while completing coursework and compiling a teaching portfolio. An ongoing assessment of the program reveals that only 10% of its graduates leave teaching after three years, compared to over 50% in most other urban schools.

3. *Multiple and more complete measures of teachers' knowledge of students, teaching, and community need to be created.* These new assessments could be coupled with ABCTE's exam, which focuses almost solely on subject-matter competence. The National Council for Accreditation of Teacher Education (NCATE) and ETS are revising the PRAXIS teacher tests to be consistent with NCATE's content and teaching standards for all new teachers graduating from its approved programs. Meanwhile, the Interstate New Teacher Assessment and Support

Consortium (INTASC) has been developing a Test of Teaching Knowledge—a constructed response, paper-and-pencil test that will assess beginning teachers' understanding of child development, of the theories of teaching and learning, and of the role of students' backgrounds in the learning process, as well as other knowledge and skills essential to effective teaching. These tests, while far more expensive to administer than multiple-choice tests, capture the complexities of good teaching and learning. A good prototype for effective teacher assessment can be found in Connecticut, where a portfolio review system that provides rich information about novices has been successful at weeding out weak candidates and developing strong ones. The system costs about $800 per candidate, but the state's policy makers see it as a cost-effective tool that results in lower teacher turnover and higher student achievement.[14]

4. *School districts and universities must be more inventive in making use of accomplished teachers to prepare and support teacher candidates in alternative-route and new-teacher-induction programs.* If a school cannot hire enough genuinely "highly qualified" teachers, then it should be restructured to allow more time for a cadre of accomplished teachers to supervise the work of all underqualified personnel, in addition to their regular teaching load. This will mean redesigning schools into much smaller learning communities and investing more in developing teachers as leaders as well as instructors.

5. *Teacher salaries and working conditions need to be improved.* Secretary Paige's report is stunningly silent on the need to raise teachers' salaries. How can one even contemplate the phrase "highly qualified teachers" without considering the need to raise teacher pay—when today's "inflation-adjusted" average teacher salary is only 7% higher than it was three decades ago?[15] National opinion polls consistently report that the public believes teacher salaries are just not high enough and that they are willing to pay more in taxes to reward high-quality teachers and teaching.[16]

Recent analyses of working conditions in high-poverty schools reveal that teachers in these schools are far more dissatisfied than their counterparts in low-poverty schools with weak administrative support, a lack of influence in decision making, a lack of time to do their work, and classroom intrusions.[17] Teachers are more likely to remain in demanding jobs when they are successful, and there is growing research that shows that professional supports and redesigned schools are important for creating more effective teachers and teaching.[18]

However, under NCLB's scatter-gun approach to accountability, the fear of teaching in a school that fails to make its Adequate Yearly Progress goal (as did 87% of the schools in Florida this year) may very well serve as a major barrier to recruiting and retaining high-quality teachers in the schools that need them most. Existing research has demonstrated how negative school labels discourage qualified and experienced teachers from working in underperforming schools.[19] These underperforming schools are more likely to have grim working conditions, including grossly inadequate time to work with and learn from expert colleagues. States and districts should take a cue from Gov. Mike Easley of North Carolina, who is now leading an effort to systematically assess and report on the working conditions of the state's teachers.

WHAT IS HOLDING US BACK?

The discord over how to define and develop "highly qualified" teachers has less to do with research evidence than with funding and politics. Each of our proposed actions will cost a great deal more money than we currently spend on the teaching profession. Of equal significance, perhaps, is the reality that the professionalized teaching force we envision threatens public education's traditional top-down authority structure.

Teachers who know both their subject matter and how to teach it to diverse learners and who are given the supports and incentives to work in our hardest-to-staff schools will not only change children's lives but will demand the kind of autonomy and collective responsibility common in other professions. Increasing the ranks of these more professionalized teachers will transform the current bureaucratic system of public schooling, with its centralized mandates, prescriptive curriculum, and excessive testing regimes that narrow opportunities to learn for our most disadvantaged students.

We recognize that some advocates view accountability tests that impose uniform standards of achievement, such as those required by NCLB, as engines of social justice that will force schools to meet the needs of all students. We agree on the urgent need to hold schools accountable for the success of every child, but tests alone will not raise achievement to high levels. Our schools must be staffed by teachers who have the increasingly sophisticated skills as well as the cultural competence necessary to make learning meaningful for every student.

We believe the authors of NCLB envisioned a law that would improve the quality of America's teaching force to unprecedented levels. It will be truly unfortunate if the implementers of the law continue to ignore the full range of skills and knowledge teachers need to be "highly qualified" and choose instead to pursue a narrow ideological agenda that is certain to weaken, not strengthen, our public schools.

NOTES

1. Ronald F. Ferguson, "Paying for Public Education: New Evidence on How and Why Money Matters," *Harvard Journal on Legislation,* vol. 28, 1991, pp. 465-98; Daniel D. Goldhaber and Dominic J. Brewer, "Evaluating the Effect of Teacher Degree Level on Educational Performance," in William J. Fowler, ed., *Developments in School Finance* (Washington, D.C.: National Center for Education Statistics, U.S. Department of Education, 1996), pp. 197-210; Eric A. Hanushek, *School Resources and Achievement in Maryland* (Baltimore: Maryland State Department of Education, 1996); Richard J. Murnane, "Understanding the Sources of Teaching Competence: Choices, Skills, and the Limits of Training," *Teachers College Record,* vol. 84, 1983, pp. 564-89; and William L. Sanders and June C. Rivers, *Cumulative and Residual Effects of Teachers on Future Student Academic Achievement* (Knoxville: Value-Added Research and Assessment Center, University of Tennessee, 1996).

2. Jeff Archer, "Research: Focusing in on Teachers," *Education Week,* 3 April 2002, pp. 36-39.

3. Marilyn Cochran-Smith and Mary K. Fries, "Sticks, Stones, and Ideology: The Discourse of Reform in Teacher Education," *Educational Researcher,* November 2001, pp. 3-13.

4. Lee Shulman, "Knowledge and Teaching: Foundations of the New Reform," *Harvard Educational Review,* February 1987, pp. 1-22; John D. Bransford, Ann L. Brown, and Rodney R. Cocking, eds., *How People Learn: Brain, Mind, Experience, and School* (Washington, D.C.: National Academy Press, 1999); and Megan L. Franke et al., "Understanding Teachers' Self-Sustaining, Generative Change in the Context of Professional Development," *Teaching and Teacher Education,* January 1998, pp. 67-80.

5. Chester Finn, Marci Kanstoroom, and Michael Petrilli, *The Quest for Better Teachers: Grading the States* (Washington, D.C.: Thomas Fordham Foundation, 1999).

6. *What Matters Most: Teaching for America's Future* (New York: National Commission on Teaching and America's Future, 1996); Richard M. Ingersoll, *Out-of-Field Teaching, Educational Inequality, and the Organization of Schools: An Exploratory Analysis* (Seattle: Center for the Study of Teaching and Policy, R-02-1, January 2002); Patrick M. Shields et al., *The Status of the Teaching Profession 2001* (Santa Cruz, Calif.: Center for the Future of Teaching and Learning, 2001).

7. *Meeting the Highly Qualified Teachers Challenge: The Secretary's Second Annual Report on Teacher Quality* (Washington, D.C.: Office of Postsecondary Education, U.S. Department of Education, July 2003).

8. Bransford, Brown, and Cocking, op. cit.; Linda Darling-Hammond and Peter Youngs, "Defining 'Highly Qualified Teachers': What Does 'Scientifically Based Research' Tell Us?," *Educational Researcher,* December 2002, pp.13-25; and Lee S. Shulman, "Taking Learning Seriously," *Change,* July/August 1999, pp. 10-17.

9. *No Dream Denied: A Pledge to America's Children* (New York: National Commission on Teaching and America's Future, 2003).

10. *Improving Teacher Quality State Grants: Title II, Part A, Non-Regulatory Guidance* (Washington, D.C.: U.S. Department of Education, 2002).

11. Julie Blair, "Essays on New Teachers' Test to Be Graded by Computers," *Education Week,* 3 September 2003, p. 11.

12. *In Need of Improvement: Ten Ways the U.S. Department of Education Has Failed to Live Up To Its Teacher Quality Commitments* (Washington D.C.: Education Trust, 2003).

13. Ibid, p. 7.

14. Suzanne Wilson, Linda Darling-Hammond, and Barnett Berry, *A Case of Successful Teaching Policy: Connecticut's Long-Term Efforts to Improve Teaching and Learning* (Seattle: Center for the Study of Teaching and Policy, 2000).

15. F. Howard Nelson, Rachel Drown, and Jewell C. Gould, *Survey and Analysis of Teacher Salary Trends 2001* (Washington, D.C.: American Federation of Teachers, 2002).

16. *Demanding Quality Public Education in Tough Economic Times: What Voters Want from Elected Leaders* (Washington, D.C.: Public Education Network and Education Week, February 2003).

17. Richard M. Ingersoll, "Teacher Turnover and Teacher Shortages: An Organizational Analysis," *American Educational Research Journal,* Fall 2001, pp. 499-534.

18. Anthony S. Bryk and Barbara L. Schneider, *Trust in Schools: A Core Resource for Improvement* (New York: Russell Sage Foundation, 2002).

19. Charles Clotfelter et al., "Do School Accountability Systems Make it More Difficult for Low-Performing Schools to Attract and Retain High-Quality Teachers?," *Journal of Policy Analysis and Management,* Spring 2004, in press.

BARNETT BERRY is the executive director of the Southeast Center for Teaching Quality, Inc., Chapel Hill, N.C, where MANDY HOKE is a policy associate and ERIC HIRSCH is the senior director for Policy and Partnerships.

From *Phi Delta Kappan,* May 2004, pp. 684-689. Copyright © 2004 by Phi Delta Kappa International. Reprinted by permission of the publisher and author.

The Other Side of Highly Qualified Teachers

by Wade A. Carpenter

One of the recurring abuses of classical and tutorial education was…er, uh … "overfamiliarity" between teacher and student.[1] So we modern, progressive Americans have overwhelmingly put our children into public schools. In doing so, we've taken our children out of the hands of pedophiles and put them into the hands of politicians. So this is an *improvement?*

For teachers and schools and schoolchildren, the politics of education is a no-win situation. My favorite writer on the left, Joel Spring, has put his finger on one of the most basic problems of public education: Public schools serve public purposes.[2] That mission makes them political, so the interests of the children and teachers are at best secondary. Given that there are hundreds, perhaps thousands, maybe even 270 million purposes for public education, schools and the people in them are completely vulnerable to attack by politicians. Consequently, we will spend countless hours and dollars responding to every demand of every parvenu who can raise money for advertising time. So let's say, just for argument, that some statistical and pedagogical miracle actually elevates 100 percent of our kids to grade level by 2012. Immediately, somebody will point out that too many kids are overweight. Then, if educators get that problem solved, it will be dental hygiene. Next, crime, or they can't talk to foreigners, or read a road map (and fully 48 percent will never, ever ask directions!), or tell a hickory tree from an oak or…. Get the idea? Since teachers and schools and kids will *always* fail at *something*, educators might as well understand that they will be an endless source of exploitable issues. Then we should also remember the business-community axiom that "If you say something ten times, it becomes true" and that astute politicians can afford to say anything they want just about as often as they want. In contrast to the educator, for the demagogue it's a no-lose situation.

So what's the latest illustration of my point? Obviously, No Child Left Behind. Things are even worse than the contributors to this issue report, especially in teacher education. Here the problem arises from the administration's decision to leave the definition of the term "highly qualified teacher" up to the states. Like the "disaggregation of data" requirements that Lowell Rose and the others discuss, the "highly qualified" notion itself was a splendid idea, an encouraging response to long-standing complaints about out-of-field teaching, including some published in **educational HORIZONS**.[3] State control is another eminently defensible idea that can be debated by intelligent people of good will. The problem is that teachers and teacher educators, like our children, are defaulting into the hands of the politicians. They and their administrative minions are deciding the criteria for "highly qualified teacher" for at least three reasons: (a) professors have uneven credibility and teachers have little real empowerment; (b) the public neither knows nor cares about what makes a highly qualified teacher; and most important, (c) most people couldn't care less about their children's education, but they are very concerned with their children's success. Educators have, I'm afraid, completely misread the public on that one, and the politicians have gotten it right. Success is of interest to everyone, but education is of interest only to the educated.

A couple of weeks ago education professors in Georgia were notified that the Professional Standards Commission will establish a test-out option for teacher certification.[4] Similar to the practice in Texas, Idaho, and several other states, anyone with a college degree will be able to take the PRAXIS tests and become a teacher in-field.[5] Even more dismaying is the proposal to allow anyone with master's degrees in anything to become principals. The insult to teachers, the danger to kids, and the threat to teacher preparation are chilling. As of this writing (December 17, 2003), it appears to be a "done deal."

We were appalled, but as always, there are different ways of depicting this:

1. It may bring new blood and new ideas into the public schools. This, of course, is a nice way of saying that it may break the dominion of left-leaning, warm-and-fuzzy education professors on the teaching force. Although I would not be opposed to breaking up such a monopoly, I am not convinced that one exists. Certainly there are a lot of "lefties"

in the professoriate, and a lot of advocates of "soft" pedagogy, but to say the least, their influence on actual teaching practice is dubious.[6] Furthermore, the proposal completely nullifies the past decade's substantial improvements in many ed schools, and that will hurt children.
2. It may close down those schools of education that have been turning far too many semi-literates out into the schools. The downside here is that *improving* teacher education is probably a better idea. While I am not convinced that well-educated educators will solve all the world's problems, I'm pretty sure that less-well-educated teachers will not.
3. It may encourage people with "serious" majors to become teachers, thereby raising the level of content knowledge in the teaching force. Additionally, it can be seen as getting warm bodies into the classrooms. Georgia is said to have a terrible teacher shortage. The problem with this line of reasoning, both the silver lining and the dark side, is that there is no general teacher shortage in the state. Oh, certainly there are holes here and there (not enough science teachers in Dahlonega or special ed teachers in Waycross, etc.), but *there is no general teacher shortage*. What exists is a shortage of people willing to teach in Georgia schools. There are thousands upon thousands of fully trained and certified teachers who will not teach in Georgia schools, and nationally there are hundreds of thousands of fully certified people who have walked away from what school teaching has become in the hands of the politicians. This is a crucial distinction, since if the problem really were a teacher shortage, the solution would be precisely what the authorities are doing—recruiting warm bodies. If, however, the problem is a shortage of teachers willing to teach, the solution is to make conditions in the schools better.[7]
4. It's better than the current policy requiring only high school diplomas for substitutes ... including *long-term* substitutes. Then again, maybe it really isn't necessary. After all, *anybody* can teach, right? And think of all the money we could save just by going down to the corner for day-laborers. Speaking of which:
5. It may ease budget pressures on reelection-conscious legislators and budget-strapped administrators. As far as they are concerned, there is no downside to this argument. Teachers and children, however, might not be so enthusiastic. And as far as teacher educators are concerned, the actions of those state agencies amount to a stab in the back. As any salesperson knows, putting one's entire reliance on one customer or client is usually bad business. The states' actions have now shown clearly and brutally that government is a bad business partner, and that teacher educators have been naive to have entrusted their jobs—much less children's futures—to them.

Can we fight back with the argument that "the research" supports teacher education courses? I'm not sanguine, since

1. Much of the research on both sides is methodologically suspect: the opponents of teacher education can provide just about as much "documentation" to support their claims as the proponents can, and most of it on both sides is open to accusations of self-interest.
2. Even the research that has been done well still depends on what questions the researchers asked and how they asked them. Any researcher who cannot frame questions to favor his or her own point of view should not have been granted the doctorate.
3. Only a tiny fraction of the public would be able to understand technically respectable research. And even if by some unhappy chance the data were overwhelmingly and undeniably to go against the researcher's position, the rhetoric of the report can still nullify the outcome of the research. For instance: a measly rise from one percent effectiveness to two percent can be reported as "a whopping 100 percent improvement." Likewise, "The research suggests ..." actually means nothing more than "I found at least one article that agrees with me," but the public doesn't know that. Et cetera, et cetera. So politicians can selectively and skillfully use what passes as "research" and spout their nostrums ten times—virtually no one will ever know the difference. To put it nicely: the problem with democracy is that although it is the most responsive form of government, it is also the most embarrassing. Finally,
4. Only a tinier fraction of the public cares what the research says. American anti-intellectualism is proverbial, and analyzed ad nauseum by commentators from H. L. Mencken to Richard Hofstadter.[8]

On a more positive note, I suspect that regardless of the research, we can establish the need for teacher education in the public's mind by slightly redefining the argument: Does a teacher (singular) need teacher education? No, of course not. We've all known excellent teachers without a shred of formal pedagogical preparation, and, alas, we've all known fully certified idiots.

On the other hand, do teachers (plural) need teacher education to teach well in the schools the politicians have created? Damn right they do. The ironic thing is, we don't even need research to document that, since the politicians' own rhetoric about how rotten the schools are, combined with the well-earned distrust and contempt they have brought upon themselves over countless generations, has already hoisted them on their own petards. Character counts, but an absence of character is even easier to count.

So now, let's look on the bright side of the dark side: states that are allowing test-out options for teacher certification have, whether they know it or not, deregulated teacher preparation. Now we are free to do right by our students and their students. For too long we have turned out highly certified teachers. Now we maybe we can turn out highly qualified ones. The ed schools will, I hope, take different approaches, each building on its own strengths. As long as they prepare their students to pass the states' stupid tests, the students can get certified. True, ed schools are no longer protected by the politicians, but then again, they are no longer answerable to them, either. And maybe teacher educators can now understand that politicians are not to be trusted. Not now, not ever. As Henry VIII's ex-chancellor Cardinal Wolsey said on his deathbed: "If I had serued God as dyligently as I haue don the kyng he wold not haue given me over in my gray heares."[9]

Wade A. Carpenter, Ph.D., is the chair of the education department at Berry College, Mount Berry, Georgia.

Notes

1. The standard work on classical pederasty is H. I. Marrou, *Education in Antiquity,* trans. George Lamb (Madison: University of Wisconsin Press, 1948; 1982), 26-35.
2. *American Education: An Introduction to Social and Political Aspects,* 5th ed. (New York: Longman, 1991), 4.
3. E.g., Richard M. Ingersoll,"Deprofessionalizing the Teaching Profession: The Problem of Out-of-Field Teaching," *Educational Horizons* 80 (1): 28-31; Gregory Kent Stanley,"Faith without Works? Twenty-five Years of Undervaluing Content Area Knowledge," *Educational Horizons* 80 (1): 24-27.
4. For the full text of the proposal, and a response to it by the deans and chairs of Georgia ed schools, see "Certification Redesign" and "Who Will Teach Georgia's Children?" Georgia Association of Independent Colleges of Teacher Education WebCenter, <http://www.gaicte.org/>.
5. Michelle Galley,"Texas Ponders Easing Route to Secondary Teaching," *Education Week,* December 3, 2003: 16; AACTE Education Policy Clearinghouse, <http://www.edpolicy.org>. Accessed December 12, 2003. Descriptions of alternative certification programs in other states litter the Internet. For a good start, see the ERIC System's *Becoming a Teacher.* ERIC InfoCard #2, http://www.ericsp.org/pages/become/alternativeRts.html.
6. See Larry Cuban, *How Teachers Taught: Constancy and Change in American Classrooms, 1890-1990,* 2nd ed. (New York: Teachers College Press, 1993). The critiques of ed schools' content and effectiveness are, of course, beyond numbering, and range wildly in quality. Perhaps the most recent is discussed by Bess Keller, "Education Courses Faulted as Intellectually Thin," *Education Week,* November 12, 2003: 8.
7. For an excellent discussion of this issue, see "TalkBack Live: A Highly Qualified Teacher for Every Classroom: Teacher Recruitment and Retention." *Education Week on the Web.* December 9, 2003, <http://www.edweek.org/ew/tb/tblive/transcript_12-09-2003.htm>.
8. Mencken's famous quote,"Nobody ever went broke underestimating the taste of the American public," can be found, with many others apropos to this column, at <http://www.quotationspage.com/quotes/H._L._Mencken/>; Richard Hofstadter, *Anti-Intellectualism in American Life* (New York: Knopf, 1972).
9. From George Cavendish's *The Life and Death of Cardinal Wolsey,* 178-179, <http://www.ibrary.utoronto.ca/utel/ret/cavendish/cavendish.html>.

From *Educatioonal Horizons,* Winter 2004, pp. 103-107. Copyright © 2004 by Wade A. Carpenter. Reprinted by permission of the author.

Article 42

The Marriage of Liberal Arts Departments and Schools of Education

by Sidney Trubowitz

There is a growing momentum in academia for liberal arts departments to become involved with schools of education in the preparation of teachers and efforts to improve schools. This drive has been accelerated by reports indicating substandard performance by students in all areas but particularly in mathematics and science. It is reinforced when we find that school systems lack full complements of certified teachers in these areas. There is general agreement that cooperation between the different academic communities would be helpful. However, if such efforts are to be productive, universities implementing such partnerships should be aware of the problems that will inevitably occur.

A major difficulty comes from the stereotypical view that each group has of the other. For example, liberal arts professors accuse education faculty of ignoring content and focusing on ideas like critical thinking and hands-on learning. E. D. Hirsch capsulizes the criticism when he says,"[O]ne cannot think critically without knowledge of facts, and many aspects of reading don't lend themselves to hands-on learning especially after first grade" (*New York Times*, Op Ed. page, November 4, 1999). Education faculty counter by pointing to the inanity of teaching isolated facts and refer to the classic first chapter of Charles Dickens's *Hard Times* and Mr. Gradgrind's pronouncements:

Now, what I want is, Facts. Teach these boys and girls nothing but Facts. Facts alone are wanted in life. Plant nothing else, and root out everything else. You can only form the minds of reasoning animals upon Facts: nothing else will ever be of any service to them.

So long as each group maintains a rigid perception of the other's view and fails to see that process and facts are not separate domains but rather exist in mutual support, difficulties in collaboration will prevail. For example, professors of education may define research differently than liberal arts professors. Their educational research may result from extensive observation in classrooms, exploring such ideas as children's use of metaphor, their responses to different kinds of questions, and their use of materials. Many liberal arts professors, on the other hand, view research as involving experimentation, the establishment of control groups, and other elements of what might be accomplished in a laboratory setting.

Difficulties emerge also from opposite ideas regarding what represents rigorous scholarship. Some liberal arts professors value only publications replete with scholarly references and even go so far as to deprecate material written in plain language. Case studies, analyses of experience, and reports of action research are regarded less than highly. This attitude, joined by a questioning of the appropriateness of professional-preparation units on a university campus, can lead to the idea that education faculty are "soft" in their thinking. The result is that in initial contacts, some professors of education find themselves in the position of having to prove themselves.

Although schools of education may occupy the bottom rung of the prestige ladder, it is not unusual for other forms of hierarchical thinking to be the case on college campuses: science professors look down on social science faculty, physics professors deem themselves superior to chemistry instructors, and so the pecking order operates. If individuals and groups are to work with each other in a collaborative fashion, attitudes generated by this kind of thinking need to change.

Other problems arise when there is no shared view on how to develop curriculum. For some the task of curriculum implementation is simple. Find a textbook or curriculum bulletin, order materials, and provide the teacher with a guide about what to say or do. This lack of awareness of what constitutes meaningful curriculum development is illustrated by the comment of a well-meaning professor who told a group of teachers that when they didn't know something, he'd be willing to fill in the gaps in their grasp of information. It was his belief that children's learning comes simply from mastery of content.

We have seen over and over how, after a brief flurry of enthusiasm, curricula developed by eminent professors join a long list of discarded innovations. A vivid example is the New Math. Authorities in the field believed that instruction would improve if teachers simply learned and applied particular techniques. Little consideration was given to the inevitable wide range of teacher reaction; the problems faced by parents in dealing with the New Math; the effects of administrative behavior on teacher relationships; and the innumerable other ways in which the school's social system would be impacted. If liberal arts academicians and education professors are to work together on teacher preparation and school improvement, there needs to develop some commonality of view about how to effect change.

Connected to this problem is the fact that many professors lack familiarity with schools. They talk glibly about developing programs and materials that can be transported from school to school like a vaccine to cure or prevent illness. They do not understand that each school is different and that prescribed, mechanical approaches unmodified by knowledge of a school's culture, personnel, student body, and community are unlikely to be productive. The problem of unfamiliarity with schools is compounded when professors from varied disciplines assume they have sufficient knowledge of educational institutions since as students they all have had twelve years of schooling.

Narrowness of experience sometimes leads to a superficial understanding of school operation. In our own effort to establish a campus school at Queens College, some professors mouthed phrases without pausing to give them meaning. For example, one stated, echoing the feelings of others, "The principal runs the school." There was no discussion of what it means to be principal of a campus school; what is the role of college faculty, teaching staff, and parents in decision-making; or how decisions are to be made. On another occasion glib approval was given to the idea of parental involvement without stopping to discuss what in real terms was meant by the phrase. In still another instance professors stressed the need for a literacy committee to establish a curriculum appropriate for the pre-kindergarten and kindergarten classes, the grades with which our campus school was beginning. The only stated goal for such a committee was to identify a program, a textbook to teach literacy, or both. Again there was no sharing of ideas regarding the meaning of literacy, no exploration of how published materials support its development, and no consideration given to what constitutes a broad-based approach to the development of literacy. Attempts to raise questions were dismissed with the retort that the school needed to have a curriculum, as though a body of printed material separate from a discussion of implementation would suffice. Lack of mutual understanding led to a surface approach to the development of sound educational practice.

Another source of misunderstanding comes from different views of how children learn. Lecturing is the most common method of instruction on the university level. By telling, some professors presume that absorption will take place. They anticipate that students come with a readiness to learn and that pupil interest and involvement matches their own; thus, they tend to see students as vessels to fill with knowledge rather than as active participants in learning. The problems for children in profiting from this approach become even more pronounced with younger children, for whom play is the important work and for whom hands-on experience is the way to learning.

Despite predictable problems, cooperation and collaboration between liberal arts departments and schools of education can result in great benefit to schools. But in addition to recognizing the inevitability of problems, there should be an identification of appropriate roles for individuals and representatives of different disciplines. For example, what is the appropriate role for a Ph.D. in chemistry or mathematics in working with kindergarten children? How can the resources represented in the different disciplines be integrated into programs for teacher preparation, curriculum development, and school improvement? What needs to be considered in selecting professors to work in schools: familiarity with student socio-economic class background; comfort level with age group; knowledge of school culture?

There should also be ongoing assessment of the collaborative process, not only as it relates to how professors from different specialties interact but as to how university personnel from varied disciplines work with public school faculty. It is not surprising that people coming from a range of backgrounds will bring different perceptions to projects on which they may be working together. This situation calls upon the participants to develop sensitivity to the point of view of others.

We cannot bridge the gap between liberal arts departments and schools of education by talk alone. Years of separate thinking will not yield to an exchange of words. At Queens College a few professors have hurdled departmental barriers to co-teach courses. In one case, a professor of education and a member of the history department agreed to collaborate on teaching a course about using literature to teach history. Their planning together, their reading the same books from the class bibliography on literature for adolescents, and their joint visits to schools allowed them to learn about each other's worlds. The two professors maintained an ongoing dialogue and illustrated their cooperative approach by regularly exchanging views as part of class discussions. In the course, students learned about history and also how to think like historians. The two professors began to share a common language and to develop a better understanding of how to bring history to children.

If professors from liberal arts departments and schools of education are to become productive partners in attempts to improve education, they need to move past negative perceptions of each other, to open themselves to different ideas, to go beyond jargon, to find opportunities to co-teach courses, and together to increase their familiarity with schools and how children learn.

Sidney Trubowitz is a professor emeritus at Queens College in New York City.

From *Educational Horizons,* Winter 2004, pp. 114-117. Copyright © 2004 by Sidney Trubowitz. Reprinted by permission of the author.

UNIT 9

For Vision and Hope: Alternative Visions of Reality

Unit Selections

43. **Building a Community of Hope**, Thomas J. Sergiovanni
44. **Mission and Vision in Education**, Edward G. Rozycki
45. **Education in America: The Next 25 Years**, Irving H. Buchen
46. **An Emerging Culture**, Christopher Bamford and Eric Utne

Key Points to Consider

- What might be the shape of school curricula by the year 2020?

- What changes in society are most likely to affect educational change?

- How can schools prepare students to live and work in an uncertain future? What knowledge bases are most important? What skills are most important?

- What should be the philosophical ideals for American schools in the twenty-first century?

Links: www.dushkin.com/online/
These sites are annotated in the World Wide Web pages.

Goals 2000: A Progress Report
http://www.ed.gov/pubs/goals/progrpt/index.html

Mighty Media
http://www.mightymedia.com

Online Internet Institute
http://www.oii.org

There are competing visions as to how persons should develop and learn. Yet there is great hope in this competition among alternative dreams and specific curriculum paths which we may choose to traverse. In this, all conscientious persons are asked to consider carefully how we may make more livable futures for ourselves and others. This is really an eternal challenge for us all. We will often disagree and debate our differences as we struggle toward what we become as persons and as cultures.

Which education philosophy is most appropriate for our schools? This is a complex question, and we will, as a free people, come up with alternative visions of what it will be. Let us explore what might be possible as more students go on the Internet and the wonder of the cyberspace revolution opens to teachers and students. What challenges can we expect in using the technology of the cyberspace revolution in our schools? What blessings can we hope for? What sorts of changes need to occur in how people go to schools as well as in what they do when they get there?

The breakthroughs that are developing in new learning and communications technologies are really quite impressive. They will definitely affect how human beings learn in the very near-term future. While we look forward with considerable optimism and confidence to these educational developments, there are still many controversial issues to be debated in the early years of the twenty-first century; the "school choice" issue is one. Some very interesting new proposals for new forms of schooling, both in public schools and private schools, are under development. We can expect to see at least a few of these proposals actually tried.

Some of the demographic changes and challenges involving young people in the United States are staggering. Ten percent of all American teenage girls will become pregnant each year, the highest rate in the developed world. At least 100,000 American elementary school children get drunk once a week. Incidence of venereal disease has tripled among adolescents in the United States since 1995. The actual school dropout rate in the United States stands at 30 percent.

The student populations of North America reflect vital social and cultural forces at work to destroy our progress. In the United States, a massive secondary school dropout problem has been developing steadily through the past decade. The next decade will reveal how public school systems will address this and other unresolved problems brought about by dramatic upheavals in demographics. In the immediate future, we will be able to see if emergency or alternative certification measures adopted by states affect achievement of the objectives of our reforms.

At any given moment in a people's history, several alternative future directions are open to them. North American educational systems have been subjected to one wave after another of recommendations for programmatic change. Is it any wonder that change is a sensitive watchword for persons in teacher education on this continent? What specific directions it will take in the immediate future depend on which recommendations of the reform agenda are implemented, which agencies of government (local, state/provincial, and federal) will pay for the very high costs of reform, and which shifts in perceived national educational priorities by the public will occur that will affect fundamental realignments of our educational goals.

Basic changes in society's career patterns should also be considered. It is estimated that in the United States the average nonagricultural worker now makes a major job change about five times in his or her career. The schools will surely be affected, indirectly or directly, by this major social phenomenon. Changes in the social structure due to divorce, unemployment, and job retraining efforts will also have an impact. Educational systems are integral parts of the broader social systems that created them; if the larger social system experiences fundamental change, this is reflected in the educational system.

In the area of information science and computer technologies applicable for use in educational systems, the development of new products is so rapid that we cannot predict what technological capacities may be available to schools 20 years from now. We are in a period of human history when knowledgeable people can control far greater information (and have immediate access to it) than at any previous time. As new information-command systems evolve, this phenomenon will become more and more meaningful to all of us.

The future of education will be determined by the current debate concerning what constitutes a just, national response to human needs in a period of technological change. The history of technological change in all human societies since the beginning of industrial development clearly demonstrates that major advances in technology and breakthroughs in the basic sciences lead to more rapid rates of social change. Society is on the verge of discoveries that will lead to the creation of entirely new technologies in the dawning years of the twenty-first century. All of the social, economic, and educational institutions globally will be affected by these scientific breakthroughs. The basic issue is not whether schools can remain aloof from the needs of industry or the economic demands of society but how they can emphasize the noblest ideals of free persons in the face of inevitable technological and economic changes. Another concern is how to let go of predetermined visions of the future that limit our possibilities as free people. The schools, of course, will be called upon to face these issues. We need the most enlightened, insightful, and compassionate teachers ever educated by North American universities to prepare the youth of the future in a manner that will humanize the high-tech world in which they live.

All of the essays in this unit can be related to discussions on the goals of education, the future of education, or curriculum development.

Building a Community of Hope

Hopeful school communities clearly articulate their articles of faith and then create realistic structures to translate faith into action.

Thomas J. Sergiovanni

Archimedes once said, "Give me a lever long enough ... and I shall move the world." In many schools, the lever that can make difficult situations manageable and challenging goals attainable is *hope*. Placing hope at the core of our school community provides encouragement and promotes clear thinking and informed action, giving us the leverage we need to close the achievement gap and solve other intractable problems.

The evidence suggests that hope can be a powerful force. We know that sick people who belong to groups that provide encouragement, prayer, or other forms of support get healthier and stay healthier than do sick people who lack the benefit of this hopeful support. According to Roset,

> Medical researchers find that a sense of hopefulness, from an increased sense of control, is connected with biological changes that enhance physical, as well as mental, health. (1999, p. 7)

But too often, hope is overlooked or misunderstood. Modern management theory tells us that the only results that count are those you can see and compute—not those you can feel. According to this theory, we must be objective; look at hard evidence before we dare to believe, think, or judge; and in other ways blindly face reality. "If it can't be measured," the saying goes, "it can't be managed."

Why tie our hands and discourage our hearts when we know that hope can make a difference? Educators can be both hopeful and realistic as long as the possibilities for change remain open. Being realistic differs from facing reality in important ways. Facing reality means accepting the inevitability of a situation or circumstance; being realistic means calculating the odds with an eye toward optimism.

Hope and Wishful Thinking

Hoping is often confused with wishing. But hope is grounded in realism, not in wishful thinking. Menninger, Mayman, and Pruyser write about *realistic hope*, which they define as

> the attempt to understand the concrete conditions of reality, to see one's own role in it realistically, and to engage in such efforts of thoughtful action as might be expected to bring about the hoped-for change. (1963, p. 385)

The activating effect of hope makes the difference (see fig. 1). Some education communities engage in wishful thinking but take no deliberate action to make their wishes come true. Hopeful education communities, in contrast, take action to turn their hopes into reality.

Hope and Faith

Hope and faith go together. Faith comes from commitment to a cause and strong belief in a set of ideas.

> Hope is so closely linked to faith that the two tend to blend into one.... No matter what we put our faith in, when faith goes, hope goes with it. In some ways, hope is faith—faith with our eyes on possibilities for the future. (Smedes, 1998, p. 21)

Leaders of hopeful school communities recognize the potential in people and in situations.

This quotation brings us closer to an understanding of how hope works to help schools become effective learning communities. Organizations often communicate faith as a set of assumptions. By publicly articulating and endorsing our key assumptions, we make them come alive

FIGURE 1 Wishful Leaders/Hopeful Leaders

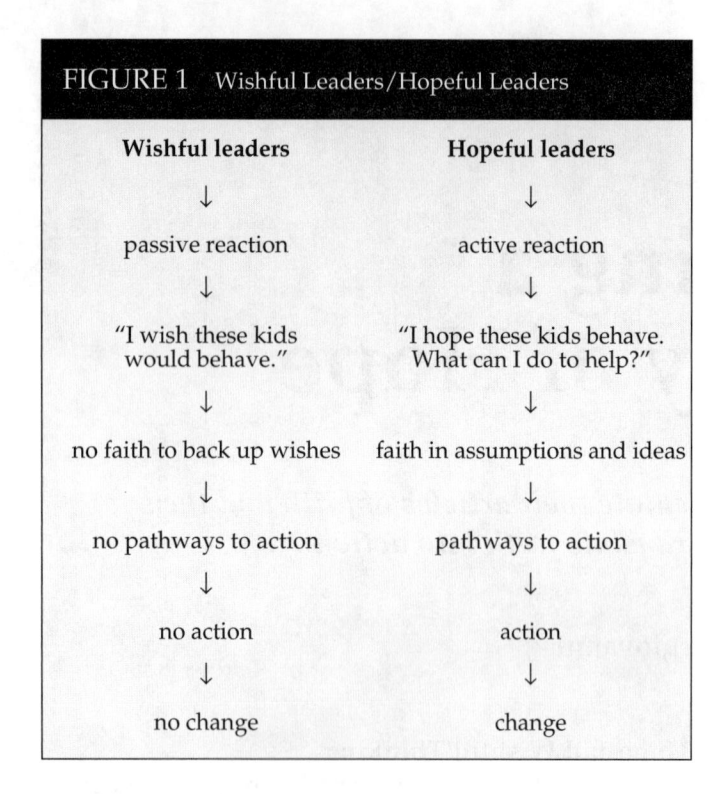

Wishful leaders	Hopeful leaders
↓	↓
passive reaction	active reaction
↓	↓
"I wish these kids would behave."	"I hope these kids behave. What can I do to help?"
↓	↓
no faith to back up wishes	faith in assumptions and ideas
↓	↓
no pathways to action	pathways to action
↓	↓
no action	action
↓	↓
no change	change

and give them the power to stir others to action. We might have faith, for example, that

- All students can succeed if given appropriate support.
- Under the right conditions, both students and teachers will take responsibility for their own learning.
- Schools can transform themselves into caring learning communities.
- Given the opportunity and the training, all parents can be effective partners in the education of their children.
- Under the right circumstances, all teachers can become leaders if the issues are important to them.

These assumptions suggest pathways that bring faith and action together. For example, our faith that all students can succeed will remain wishful thinking unless we transform it into hope by providing the necessary support to ensure that all students *do* succeed.

School leaders have an important responsibility here. They need to guide the school community in developing and articulating its articles of faith, thereby creating a powerful force of ideas. These ideas provide the basis for becoming a community of hope, and they fuel the school's efforts to transform hope into reality. Developing a community of hope elevates the work of leadership to the level of moral action.

Schools Built Around Hope

The following examples show how faith fuels hope and how hope can transform a school.

A Framework for Hope

In 1995, test scores at Wyandotte High School in Kansas City, Kansas, were among the lowest in the state, threatening the school's accreditation. "Even at their worst, other schools in the district could always guarantee that they were 'at least better than Wyandotte'" (Stewart, 2004, p. 75).

Instead of closing the school, the district made a last-ditch effort to improve it. Wyandotte administrators were hopeful that the school could succeed, but they recognized that their hope needed to be embedded in ideas that they trusted. A framework of reform called First Things First, developed by the Institute for Research and Reform in Education and adopted districtwide in Kansas City, provided the key to building a new community of hope at Wyandotte. School staff committed to this framework, which identified seven crucial conditions for school improvement (Institute for Research and Reform in Education, n.d.).

Four features specifically applied to students. The school would

- Provide continuity of care by forming Small Learning Communities that keep the same group of professionals and students together for extended periods during the day and across multiple school years.
- Set high, clear, and fair standards for academics and conduct that clearly define what all students will know and be able to do by graduation and at key points along the way.
- Reduce student-adult ratios to 15:1 or lower during core instructional periods, primarily by redistributing the professional staff.
- Provide enriched and diverse opportunities for students to learn, perform, and be recognized.

Three features specifically applied to teachers and administrators. The school would

- Equip, empower, and expect all teaching staff to implement standards-based instruction that actively engages all students in learning by giving teaching teams the authority to make instructional decisions, creating opportunities for continual staff learning, and specifying clear expectations about what good teaching and learning look like.
- Give Small Learning Communities the flexibility to quickly redirect resources (time, money, people, and space) to meet emerging needs.
- Ensure collective responsibility for student outcomes by providing collective incentives and consequences for teaching teams based on improvements in district performance.

As the Wyandotte staff worked toward faithful implementation of the First Things First framework, staff members increasingly committed to aligning their practice with the framework. Each of the school's eight Small

Learning Communities pairs a team of 10 teachers with a group of 150-200 students, who remain together throughout their high school experience. Mutual commitment to and belief in the framework have created a greater sense of community among school staff members. Teacher study groups have emerged, and peer coaching has become an established practice, further helping to develop a collaborative culture.

In a sense, moving from an ordinary school to a community of hope is a kind of psychological magic.

Ample evidence exists that the Wyandotte of today has been remarkably successful in improving student learning as measured by a variety of tests and other indicators. Perhaps most telling, however, is that "families used to stand in line to have their child transferred from Wyandotte. Now families are asking to transfer their child to Wyandotte" (Stewart, 2004, p. 82).

Pathways to Success

Samuel Gompers Elementary School in Detroit, Michigan, houses approximately 350 students in an economically distressed urban neighborhood.[1] More than 90 percent of the students live at the poverty level. Students come to Gompers with basic needs for food, clothing, shelter, and security. Many have never visited a dentist or received their basic health immunizations before coming to school. Yet the school espouses an ambitious goal: to ensure "that our students have the skills to become contributing members of a global society." To achieve that goal,

> Our school will successfully educate all students in a clean, safe, and healthy learning environment. We will meet the needs of the whole child through the developmental pathways: cognitive-intellectual, physical, social-interactive, speech and language, moral, and psycho-emotional. (Samuel Gompers Elementary School, 2000, p. 9)

The developmental pathways that provide the structure to turn Gompers's hopes into reality are components of the Comer process—officially known as the School Development Program. This approach to school improvement rejects the belief that low-income parents cannot adequately prepare children for school and that low-income children cannot perform well in school. Instead, the Comer process assumes that teachers, principals, and other members of the school community are willing and able to ensure that students succeed. It also assumes that schools are concerned with the whole child—that fulfilling students' needs and providing a supportive climate create the essential conditions for academic learning (Comer, 1980).

In 1993, Gompers Elementary School committed to the assumptions underlying the Comer process. The staff put its faith into action through Corner's developmental pathways, which provide a research-based strategy for improvement.

- The *cognitive-intellectual pathway* emphasizes the ability to understand and use information and the ability to understand and change the environment. The school pursues this core pathway through hands-on teaching and learning, metacognitive learning, academic clubs, and after-school tutoring. One out of every three students received tutoring during the 2001-2002 school year. Students who fall behind attend a required Summer Learning Academy.

- The *physical pathway* stresses that each student will receive proper nutrition, be physically fit, and enjoy good health. Gompers ensures that its students have warm and clean clothes to wear. Groups such as the local post office and the National Association of Women Business Owners have supplied almost all students with new coats each winter (McDonald, 2003). The hum of a washing machine and dryer in the school is nearly continuous. Students are given "safe route" maps to follow in getting to school and back home again. Breakfast is served to all students in their classrooms.

- The *social-interactive pathway* emphasizes students' ability to be empathetic, to communicate in relationships, and to interact with others who differ from them. The school provides a full complement of sports, extracurricular clubs, peer mentoring, cross-age reading parties, and other opportunities that encourage cooperative learning.

- The *speech and language pathway* emphasizes building communication skills across the curriculum. The school also addresses this pathway through a daily morning assembly, a variety of school productions, and speech and language workshops. The school invites parents with 2- and 3-year-old children to attend workshops designed to help them support their children's growing language skills.

- The *moral pathway* emphasizes respect for the rights and needs of others and addresses additional character development issues. For example, a weekly "Efficacy" class for 3rd, 4th, and 5th graders helps students make choices that respect the rights and interests of others.

- The *psycho-emotional pathway* addresses self-esteem issues and the ability to express emotion while respecting others. In an enriched co-curricular program, the school provides both intervention programs—such as anger management and living with ADHD—and enrichment programs, such as dance, art, and drama.

Hope at Gompers does not occur by accident; the school staff nurtures hope through a carefully planned, sustained school improvement effort. The developmental pathways outlined by the Comer process provide practical and successful means to address problems and improve conditions. Faith in the assumptions underlying the pathways gives Gompers staff members hope.

And their hope has become a reality. Gompers students have consistently improved their Metropolitan Achievement Test scores. In 2000, Gompers ranked 221 of 2,013 Michigan schools on the Michigan Educational Assessment, earning the highest scores in the state among schools in its size category (School Development Program, 2001). Test scores aside, the school earned the U.S. Department of Education's 1996 National Title I School Recognition Award for outstanding progress in compensatory education and was listed in 1995 as one of the 10 best schools in Detroit. The Department of Education selected Gompers as a Blue Ribbon School in 2000-2001.

From Hope to Action

Other schools have high hopes, too, but are not succeeding because they have no systematic process for transforming hope into action. As Snyder and colleagues (1991) write,

> Individuals with high hope possess goals, find pathways to these goals, navigate around obstacles, and develop agency to reach their goals.

The process of turning hope into reality requires that we answer the following questions:

- What are our goals? (What do we hope for?)
- What are our pathways? (What routes will we take to realize our hopes?)
- What obstacles do we face?
- How committed are we to actually doing something to realize our hopes?
- Is efficacy present in sufficient strength? (Do we believe strongly enough that we can make a difference?)
- If our school's efficacy is low, how can we strengthen it?

Educators can be both hopeful and realistic as long as the possibilities for change remain open.

The question of efficacy is crucial. The jury is still out on which view of human nature will prevail—optimistic or pessimistic. But I believe that leaders of hopeful school communities recognize the potential in people and in situations. To these hopeful leaders,

> what people can achieve, or aspire to, is just as surely part of human nature, just as surely summoned by the human condition, as are more negative traits and dimensions. (Selznick, 2002, p. 70)

In a sense, moving from an ordinary school to a community of hope is a kind of psychological magic. But we can make this magic happen by identifying and committing to our key articles of faith, by establishing structures that translate our hopes into action, and by providing the context for both the school and the individual members of the school community to realize their potential.

Note

10. Except where otherwise noted, the Gompers story is drawn from the school's 2000-2001 Blue Ribbon Program Application.

References

Comer, J. P. (1980). School power: *Implications of an intervention program*. New York: Free Press.

Institute for Research and Reform in Education. (n.d.). *First things first: An introduction*. Philadelphia: Author. Available: www.irre.org/pdf_ffiles/FTF_Intro.pdf

McDonald, M. (2003, Jan. 22). School succeeds with some help from its friends. *The Detroit News* [Online]. Available: www.detnews.com/2003/detroit/0301/29/s04-64852.htm

Menninger, K., Mayman, M., & Pruyser, P. (1963). *The vital balance: The life process in mental health and illness*. New York: Penguin Books.

Roset, S. M. (1999). *Exploring hope: Implications for educational leaders*. Master of Education Thesis, Department of Educational Administration, University of Saskatchewan, Canada.

Samuel Gompers Elementary School. (2000). *2000-2001 Blue Ribbon Schools Program application*. Detroit, MI: Author.

School Development Program. (2001). Selected achievement by SDP schools [Online]. Available: http://info.med.yale.edu/comer/about/achievements.html

Selznick, P. (2002). On a communitarian faith. *The Responsive Community, 12*(3), 67-74.

Smedes, L. (1998). *Standing on the promises: Keeping hope alive for a tomorrow we cannot control*. Nashville, TN: Thomas Nelson.

Snyder, C. R., Harris, C., Anderson, J. R., Holleran, S. A., Irving, L. M., Sigmon, S. T., et al. (1991). The will and the ways: Development and validation of an individual-differences measure of hope. *Journal of Personality and Social Psychology, 60*(4), 570-585.

Stewart, M. (2004). An urban high school emerges from chaos. In *Breaking ranks II Strategies for leading high school reform* (pp. 75-82). Reston, VA: National Association of Secondary School Principals.

Thomas J. Sergiovanni is Lillian Radford Professor of Education at Trinity University, San Antonio, Texas; tsergiov@trinity.edu. His forthcoming book, *Strengthening the Heartbeat: Leading and Learning Together* (Jossey-Bass, fall 2004) discusses in more detail how hope, trust, and other virtues can help build effective learning communities.

Mission and Vision in Education

by Edward G. Rozycki

> Happy talk, keep talking happy talk,
> Talk about things you'd like to do,
> You gotta have a dream, if you don't have a dream,
> How you gonna have a dream come true?
>
> —Rodgers and Hammerstein, *South Pacific*

Junk Food

Like all sweet things, happy talk risks being addictive. Our educational institutions, responding to public pressure for the upbeat and the heart-warming, have become intellectually obese with happy talk: sweet slogans that enervate clear definition of goals, that obscure inquiry into their achievability, and that have provoked the "fad diets" of standardized testing, teacher accountability, and lockstep curriculum.

A recent vogue has been to introduce another layer of happy talk on top of the timeworn expatiation on missions and goals: statements of vision. Theoretically, we might say that vision statements justify leadership claims on resources. A non-academic might ask, "Just what do you do to earn your salary?" "Provide vision," comes the answer. Absent critical examination, however, there may be precious little difference between vision and delusion, if by "statements of vision" we mean verbal concatenations mistaken for causal analyses.

As generally conceived, vision statements provide the impetus for missions. And mission statements provide the targets for goal statements. We might find the relationships easy to understand with this simple illustration:

Vision statement: We'll have pie in the sky by and by.
Mission statement: We'll bake something that flies.
Goal statement: We'll make some dough.

Unfortunately, as the history of American education so vividly attests, once this goal has been reached, the missionaries absent themselves from the educational scene with alacrity. The point here is not to ridicule visions or missions, but to suggest they be tempered with a sense of proportion, a knowledge of resources available, and cool evaluation of the likelihood of success. Above all else, it is important to stop sacrificing the Good to pursuit of a Vision of the Best.

Mission and Vision Statements: The GIGO Effect

Much criticism has it that teachers are ill prepared in college for the reality of their jobs in schools. Little attention has been paid, however, to how teachers are subjected, once they have been hired, to group-think processes of indoctrination, usually called "staff development." Staff development works not infrequently to increase their credulity, stultify their normal critical abilities, and undermine their capacity for reasoned judgment. Much staff development in education is dedicated to examining mission and vision statements.

Here is a mission statement from an affluent school district just outside Philadelphia: *Empower each student to succeed in life and contribute to society.* There is perhaps no more certain indicator of the depth to which our society has been secularized than in the mission statements of those who arrogate to themselves heretofore Divine attributes of Omnipotence and Omniscience. Imagine educators in a middle or high school knowing that they have empowered their students to succeed in life—or perhaps that is merely hyperbole for teaching the students to be literate and minimally mathematical. Are we, then, to imagine that educators are so ego-deficient that someone must routinely, grandiosely, recast their humble yet important achievements of basic schooling as feats of historical significance?

Another nearby community has its schools profess: *The mission of the X School District is to ensure that every student is inspired and prepared to be a passionate lifelong learner and a productive, invested participant in the local and global communities.* (Can one even say this aloud without hyperventilating?) Weeks of faculty time are spent cooking this mission down into supposedly operational goals. On the surface, the issue is this: how are teachers to bring the mission into their day-to-day pursuits? Instruction time is forgone as teachers meet to pursue this will-o'-the-wisp. In their committees they find out that the surface is only to be polished: hardly ever scratched. Insightful or possibly critical questions are deflected during the group-think process by the school's resident lickspittle, who cajoles those assembled into "preserving a collegial atmosphere" and "keeping everyone on task"—an insinuation that probing inquiry is "out of place" or "not quite professional." Whatever scatter-brained confabulations the staff generates are taken as answers, solemnly recorded and duly acceptable to local, state, and regional accrediting agencies. As they say in the computer-programming world, GIGO—garbage in, garbage out.

Such activity wastes time, spirit, and intellect—ask any educator (in private)—because the mission statement is never subjected to careful scrutiny prior to attempts to "operationalize" it: "Our vision is yadda, yadda. Our mission, therefore, is blah, blah, blah. What does this mean for your classroom?" "For me it means glug, glug, glug!" "Excellent! We'll definitely meet our accreditation requirements now."

Mission and Vision Statements: Organizational Sporks

Unless you have dealt with preschoolers, you may not have encountered a Spork. Sporks are plastic spoons with a few dull tines molded into their tips so they can work somewhat like forks to pick up food. Sporks are for novices—those too inexperienced to handle spoon and fork expertly on their own. We also give children Sporks if we do not trust them to use them as we want, e.g., as eating utensils rather than as swords for dueling or shovels for digging, or whatever fertile imagination may dream up. Sporks are safe. But they are hardly precision instruments.

The primary use of mission or vision statements is as dull utensils of publicity and persuasion: they are slogans intended to motivate people to selected ends and to obscure the real differences of opinion normally found in school communities. Clever staff-development processes invite all members of the school community to "contribute" to the formulation of mission statements but leave the authority for interpreting those vague residues of concern in the hands of the few. That's why probing questions are discouraged. When authority and control of resources are the real issues, educators are invited to keep talkin' happy talk.

Educator Dementation

I work with doctoral students in education. Most of them are principals, superintendents, or other school administrators. They are intelligent, dedicated, hard-working people. But they are so involved in the political environment of the schools that they confuse the language appropriate to such an environment with that necessary to delineate a research problem carefully. They imagine that visions, missions, and goals automatically relate as causes and effects. They believe that ideas which are articulable are variables which are measurable; that voices which are ignored are voices of assent.

When I talk to my students about non-educational matters, I notice that they have not lost their capacity for careful judgment; they have a clear sense of costs and benefits and of the likelihood of achieving them. They have a normally developed conception of cause and effect. And they know how to deliberate on ethical issues as well as anyone. But when the discussion wanders into the field of education, their common sense suddenly shrivels: they treat their general knowledge, their life's wisdom, as nothing. That, I believe, is the consequence of the indoctrination they have received as educators. That is what is wrong with the pre-service training of teachers, not some lack of technical expertise or content-area knowledge. In-service staff development—in particular, the perpetual blather about visions, missions, and goals—just reinforces their intellectual, psychological, and moral lobotomy.

Assessing Visions and Missions

So I train my students to ask questions. I assure them it is legitimate to subject the dogmas and slogans of their profession to the same kind of scrutiny that they do other concerns of life. In particular, I teach them to consistently formulate two kinds of questions: critical questions, and criteria questions.

Critical questions worry the causal assumptions of a vision or mission statement. They may also look to uncover alternatives to the means-ends relationships alluded to. Criteria questions ask how we identify items mentioned in a mission or vision.

For example, let's examine the mission mentioned earlier:

The Mission of the X School District is to ensure that every student is inspired and prepared to be a passionate lifelong learner and a productive, invested participant in the local and global communities.

Critical questions are:

1. How does what happens to students during the time they are in X School District cause them to be lifelong learners? Are there later important influences? How can we ensure that outcome?
2. Need they be passionate about it?
3. Is inspiration necessary or sufficient to have that effect?
4. How does what happens to students during the time they are in X School District cause them to be productive participants in either the local or global community? Are there later important influences?
5. Need it be both local and global communities?
6. Will we not be satisfied if they are not "invested"?

Criteria questions hammer away at two points: what are the criteria for identifying important terms, and how will we know at any given time that those criteria have been met? Some examples are:

7. What are the criteria for being a lifelong learner? How can we tell whether an eighth-grader will meet those criteria at age forty-five, or if he will be "passionate" about it?
8. Does a successful, compulsive gambler count as a passionate lifelong learner?
9. What do we mean by a "productive, invested participant"?
10. What kind of participation counts as being in the local, or global, community?

My students who undertake analyses of vision or mission statements find this activity easy, once they get over the shock that I am inviting them to think along these lines. They burst out frequently in gleeful laughter yet insist that they will never have the opportunity to ask such questions on the job.

I ask them, "Why is that, do you suppose?"

I get many variations on the same answer: "You ask questions like that and they'll take you for a troublemaker."

Then I get down to the moral of the lesson: Be assertive. Tell your potential critics that you are coming at the vision and mission statements from a research and implementation perspective. If they will not or cannot answer your critical and criteria questions, then all the visioning and missioning in the world will not amount to anything more than wishful thinking and wasted time.

Edward G. Rozycki is a twenty-five-year veteran of the school district of Philadelphia. He is an associate professor of education at Widener University, Widener, Pennsylvania.

From *Educational Horizons*, Winter 2004, pp. 94-98. Copyright © 2004 by Edward G. Rozycki. Reprinted by permission of the author.

Article 45

Education in America:
The Next 25 Years

by Irving H. Buchen

The driving force in education in the next 25 years will be choice, fueled by changing roles for teachers, administrators, students, and entire communities.

Many people in the United States are unhappy with public education. Teachers complain about being battered and intimidated, educational administrators find themselves and their contributions unappreciated, school boards are increasingly criticized for micromanaging, parents are beset by a whole new set of alternative schooling choices, and students are being tested to death.

In spite of stresses and strains on the educational system, there is more to celebrate than to lament, especially over the long term. In short, education has a future—indeed, a significant and interesting one. If we could leap ahead 25 years to view the current educational scene, we would see four factors driving educational change: decentralization and educational options; performance evaluation and success measurement; changes in leadership and leadership roles; and reconfigurations in learning spaces, places, and times.

School Choices

Although competition arrived late in the history of education, it rapidly changed virtually everything. By offering a wide range of possibilities rather than a single focus, competition has given education a new lease on life.

Traditionally, education offered three choices: public, private, and parochial schooling. Public education dominated, and for good reason: It educated the poor and middle classes, prepared them for work or college, acculturated wave after wave of new immigrants, and provided significant employment for many professionals. Private and parochial schools continue to appeal to middle- and upper-middle-class families disenchanted with public education; homogeneous and traditional, their future is rooted in the attitudes of the past.

The variety of educational choices has dramatically increased. Home schools, for instance, enrolled an estimated 850,000 students in the United States in 1999, according to the National Center for Education Statistics, and support for this method of instruction continues to increase. Charter schools enrolled nearly 580,000 students, according to Center for Education Reform 2001 statistics. Run by different private groups in a variety of ways, charter schools receive public financial support from their home district.

Because high schools with large numbers of students can be unmanageable, school district administrators have restructured many into a series of schools within a school, each with a core of teachers serving between 100 and 150 students. Students and teachers in each smaller school know and relate to each other. Although restructuring does not alter class size, it reduces student–teacher ratio.

> Private educational management companies have intensified the competitive environment of education. Often invited to take over failing schools, many of these companies are publicly owned, have stockholders, and are committed to making a profit.

Private educational management companies have intensified the competitive environment of education. Often invited to take over failing schools, many of these companies are publicly owned, have stockholders, and are committed to making a profit. Although evidence for their success is mixed, they are a permanent fixture on the

Article 45. Education in America: The Next 25 Years

MACHINE TEACHERS

Machines—computers and/or other technology—can and probably will replace teachers in the future because they can provide solid and competent instruction. However, three major obstacles continue to keep technology out of the classroom for the immediate future:

- **Economics:**

Education's insulation from economic and market forces has done it an enormous disservice. Economic incentives have yielded powerful, sophisticated, and flexible teaching and learning technologies, changing how we learn and acquire knowledge. Education should be at the center of these innovations, but its isolation has kept it from benefiting from technology to the fullest possible extent.

- **Teacher fears:**

Technology is ubiquitous, invasive, and substitutive, and most teachers know it. So they ignore technology. Nothing matches the variety and subtlety of human activity, they say; no one enlivens and inspires students better than a teacher. Teachers' objections and fears of technology are profound, the number of converts few, and the prospects for new perspectives dim.

- **Critiquing technophiles:**

Education cannot reaffirm its traditional position or stake its future role without asking substantive questions (What problem does this technology solve? What new problems does it create?) that challenge the technology community and incorporating these questions into teaching. Challenging and critiquing technophiles will result in the best of both worlds, where education asks the questions and technology performs the tasks. If this partnership falters or fails, there is little doubt that technology will fill the vacuum and appear as both educator and performer.

Creating technologically savvy teachers as well as machines to serve as teachers depends on examining these obstacles. Whether the change will be gradual, accelerated, or radical depends on how fast we overcome them.

—*Irving H. Buchen*

---

educational scene and add significantly to the range of available choices.

Private companies such as William Bennett's "K12" education program offer online curricula through electronic schools, so students can complete and graduate from a basic high-school program online. Electronic offerings also provide advanced placement, language, and special studies courses that normally attract few students. They are a boon to small rural districts and serve as a key underpinning for home schooling.

In short, education in 2025 will be totally decentralized, offering parents, students, adult learners, and citizens in general a dazzling menu of choices. Many people will opt for an amalgam of different educational sources that may be altered as desired. Whatever the selection, students and their parents—not schools—will drive educational choice.

Measuring Success

Major shifts will occur in the ways educational success is measured; some of these shifts are discernible now. Teachers were once evaluated on how they organized lesson plans, gained student interest, and involved the entire class in discussion. Now the focus is student achievement, usually measured by class performance on high-stakes mandated tests. Data now dominates the current educational scene, and its importance will intensify in the future.

Because allocating funds is increasingly tied to student performance, school district comptrollers often divert substantial appropriations to designing, administering, and evaluating tests, compromising instruction as a result. Many teachers, therefore, are "teaching to the test"—which would not be bad if, as one superintendent wryly observed, there was a really good test to teach to. School officials assign teams of extra teachers, tutors, and specialists to schools with low scores or failing grades, sometimes stripping the curriculum down to only tested subjects. Some schools in competitive environments advertise their test scores to attract students, further accelerating the process of constant testing. Parents have been known to request test scores of schools within a district to decide where they should send their kids.

In Florida and other states, students in schools that fail basic skills tests twice consecutively are offered financial vouchers to use in whatever school they wish. Preliminary research shows that voucher programs help drive improved student performance. Vouchers also drive choice and decentralization and significantly drain enrollment from "mainstream" schools.

A number of state governments have taken over failing schools, placing them under receivership or turning them over to private management companies. Philadelphia's school district was turned over to a private management company, Edison Schools Inc., because of poor student performance. In New York City, private management companies operate some 30 schools. Perhaps the most embarrassing consequence of this is a cynical reversal of graduation requirements in many states and schools that tie graduation to test scores. Many schools have postponed implementing requirements, lowered minimum scores, or revised graduation tests for students failing to achieve minimum scores but who were already scheduled to graduate, accepted to college, or had jobs.

The Principal's Changing Role

According to the U.S. Department of Labor, the school administration profession faces a shortage of 40,000 principals by 2005. That has been intensified by the reduction of school superintendents' terms of office to an all-time low of two to three years. Part of the difficulty of attracting administrators is that a principal's salary is not much higher than the highest paid teachers in a district; and when longer hours and more days of work are taken into account, the difference is often minuscule. As an indication of education increasingly becoming subject to business market forces, there is the trend toward hiring MBAs rather than education MAs, and even changing the title of superintendent to CEO. In fact, New York City split the top job into academic and business components. Los Angeles followed suit with an additional twist: Signaling the extent to which superintendency is increasingly political, the head of the Los Angeles school district hired a former governor of Colorado (Roy Romer) as school superintendent. But like the decentralization of schools, leadership is no longer solely of one type. The variety of leaders mirrors school choice.

Recently, the National Association of Elementary School Principals (NAESP) published a 96-page document calling for principals to be instructional leaders and to lead the charge on behalf of student achievement. To many outside the field, that might seem an odd request. Haven't principals always done that? Actually, they seldom did because of bureaucratic, financial, and security tasks heaped on their plates.

NAESP called for appointing assistant principals to provide relief and free principals to become instructional leaders. Whether school boards with tight or reduced budgets are willing or able to increase administrative staff at a time when teaching staff is stretched has yet to be determined. But if they do, a whole new corps of principals will emerge who are far more visionary, aggressive, and knowledgeable about school reform and improvement. They will resemble their business counterparts more than principals of the past do.

Do We Really Need Principals?

Although clearly there are principals who are effective leaders no matter how burdened they are, a significant new form of management is appearing. At Chicago's McCosh School, for example, the principal and her team of teacher-managers run the school. The principal still reports to the superintendent and the board, but once she has her marching orders and budget, she and her team take it from there. How effective has that arrangement been? McCosh has the best test scores in the district, and the morale of teachers, students, and parents is high.

This arrangement has an advantage over even the most exemplary performance of a number of assertive principals: There are no subject matter or competency gaps between administration and instruction. The typical principal struggles with the handicap of being outside the classroom, perhaps for many years, and leading teachers in all subjects without possessing the credibility of pedagogical competence. But a management team of certified teachers already possesses subject matter competence. Harvard University education professor Richard Elmore calls this *distributed leadership* and sees it as the future of site-based management. It creates a democratized structure in which the traditional vertical management structure has been leveled to horizontal collective action.

Perhaps the most dramatic and radical version of distributed leadership is where the responsibility for running the school is in the hands of teacher-leaders and learning teams consisting of teachers, tutors, technical advisers, counselors, parents, and students. There are no principals at all. The teacher-leader oversees the team following the principle of author Robert K. Greenleaf: *primus inter pares*—first among equals. Being first is not fixed but rotates based on situation needs.

But perhaps the most futuristic aspect of this new development, setting it apart from other developments and standing perhaps the best chance of becoming a significant part of education in 2025, is its attention to both *external* and *internal integration*. Externally, distributed leadership unites school, parents, students, and the community. Internally, through its basic collaborative governance structure, distributed leadership aligns and combines administration, instruction, and evaluation.

Parents' New Roles

Parents are taking on more assertive roles, moving well beyond the stereotype of running bake sales. For example, parents in South Pasadena, California, serve as teacher aides and tutors. Their major task, however, is to raise substantial amounts of money annually to supplement the budget. They have successfully built and stocked a computer lab, turned the library into a state-of-the-art electronic information and resource center, and created an extensive budget for teacher professional development.

In this and other ways, parents have become leaders involved in significant and often unique school reform. One of the most promising examples is a proposal by the Parents Center for Education Reform for students to lead teacher and parent conferences. Under this arrangement, students would set the agenda and facilitate discussion about their own performance. The fact that this initiative arose from a parents' group rather than from the public education mainstream dramatizes the extent to which parents have assumed a greater leadership role. The U.S. Department of Education officially recognizes and facilitates parental leadership through its Partnership for Family Involvement in Education.

The National Network of Partnership Schools based at Johns Hopkins University focuses on a comprehensive and aggressive plan of parent-teacher-student involvement and interaction. It features a program for teachers to generate homework assignments that require family participation. Teachers and parents use holidays and summer vacations to develop skills, anticipate academic problems, and develop solutions. All these and other efforts improve communication not only between schools and families, but also within families.

Linking Business To Education

Driven by a desire for a well-trained and motivated workforce as well as a sense of social responsibility, many CEOs have forged partnerships with schools. For example, Florida-based Paradigm Learning, which develops corporate board games, developed a high-school game called "Strive to Drive." The game takes students through all the steps of choosing, buying, financing, maintaining, and paying for a car; the game significantly and rapidly improved reading, math, and planning skills in the process. Tutor Inc., an online tutoring service, developed a partnership with the Boys Choir of Harlem, buying laptop computers for choir members to stay on top of assignments while traveling and providing access to the company's computer tutors to keep them current and on target.

The most important leadership contribution of business executives is that they are forming direct relationships with educational administrators, including sharing and exchanging different ways of effective management. Thus, the Public Education and Business Coalition received a grant to train some 100 principals in the Denver area. What business leaders discovered is that educators read and hearken only to other educators writing about education—they know little or nothing about the business world, the effect of increasing competition, the difficulty of balancing quality control with productivity—in short, precisely what education is newly encountering.

The Pearl River School in Rockland, New York, uses a continuous improvement business model to set incremental goals for students, raising achievement every year since 1989. The number of students graduating from Pearl River with the academically rigorous state regents' diploma has jumped from 32% to 86%.

A few business CEOs are sharing libraries, research resources, and attendance at executive conferences with education CEOs. There is a strong likelihood that such business CEOs may become school superintendents in the future. If so, then education may increasingly be defined or perceived as a business.

Business leaders have created a number of organizations to support school reform, such as the Business Coalition for Educational Reform, the National Association for Partners in Education, the National Employer Leadership Council, and the School-to-Work Learning Center. Looking only to education for education leadership impoverishes the resources and sources of change.

New Learning Spaces

Seldom, if ever, do parents or citizens who already have raised and schooled their kids revisit schools. If they did, they would find many things have remained the same but some things have changed dramatically. Technological changes would top the list, but these are perhaps predictable compared with the reconfiguration of learning places, spaces, and times.

The size, holdings, and sheer physical variety of a fairly new high school are overwhelming. Built to accommodate a small town of thousands of students, a new school is surrounded by many practice and playing fields—perhaps even a football stadium—as well as extensive parking spaces for daily student use as well as for athletic events. Inside is a modern gymnasium equipped with seats for 2,000 students and a huge auditorium with seats for 3,000 and state-of-the-art theater equipment. The library, equally enormous but generally underused, is completely computerized with relatively few real books in sight.

When demographics (especially in the suburbs) indicate a significant increase in the school-age population, municipal planners quickly draw up plans to build new school-cities. Of course, expenses for building a new school are higher than they were for building the last school, not only because of increased costs of construction and materials, but also because some communities try to outdo others by constructing bigger and more splendid high schools. Yet research studies suggest that schools can be too big and impersonal.

Extending the School Day

Once again, economics rears its ugly head when discussion of extending the school day, lengthening the school year, or reducing class size begins. In the face of severe budget cuts, many communities are naturally unwilling to extend the school calendar or reduce class size. The obvious solution is technology.

Technology can reduce class size to one student. School days can be extended easily and laptop computers mean education can continue during vacations and trips. A total tested electronic curriculum already exists. It has been used by high schools that do not have enough students to take certain advanced or specialized courses, foreign languages, or advanced placement courses. Electronic instruction has bailed out many rural schools with too few students to permit face-to-face teaching at acceptable costs. Electronics already has helped many high schools reconfigure themselves into smaller schools—within schools—by providing them with their own electronic curriculum, including specialization in arts, sciences, business, and communications. Moreover, the availability of such electronic courses has spread as a number of states bind together in electronic consortia, making their curricula available virtually without cost.

ANNUAL EDITIONS

RESOURCES FOR DISTANCE LEARNING

The following Web sites offer information on distance-learning opportunities for students:

Distance Learning Exchange (www.dle.state.pa.us) is a free Web-based clearinghouse of distance learning and Internet project opportunities. It includes a directory listing individuals or groups who provide distance-learning activities.

Jefferson County, Colorado, Public School District (jeffcoweb.jeffco.k12.co.us) offers online courses nationwide. Students participate in numerous group interactions in real time with other students, teachers, and mentors.

Laurel Springs School (www.laurelsprings.com) integrates home schooling, independent study, distance learning, and virtual schooling into a personalized educational experience.

The Internet Academy (www.iacademy.org) provides learning opportunities meeting state standards for students anywhere.

The Babbage Net School (www.babbagenetschool.com) is a virtual high school offering courses taught in a highly interactive classroom by certified teachers.

Issues to consider when selecting an online program include the parent organization's credentials, qualifications of the teaching staff, assignment and assessment of student work, course structure and administration, and whether the college of your choice will recognize courses.

Sources: U.S. Distance Learning Association, 8 Winter Street, Suite 508, Boston, Massachusetts 02108. Web site www.usdla.org.
Distance Learning Resource Network, 2020 North Central Avenue, Suite 660, Phoenix, Arizona 85004. Web site www.dlrn.org.

Accepting technology as a legitimate and equal teaching partner will make this happen.

Student-Led Learning And Schools

Every school district placing an ad for administrators or teachers claims to have student-centered schools. Usually that means allowing students to express their views at great length, but ultimately ignoring them. Student-led schools are something else. Allowing students to conduct teacher-parent conferences is an example of a genuine learning and mastering experience for all involved, especially for the student. But many student-led schools go far beyond that.

In large part, what drives student learning is just that—student learning. The learning focus is not on different subjects but on comprehensive projects, including community-based ones. Because that requires knowledge of many subjects, an academic progression develops not unlike the system of apprenticeship. Using dialogue, mentors steer students to an initial plan to test the project. The process is subject to an incredible number of revisions. Gradually, the dominant mentor moves to the periphery as the student moves toward the center. The gradual exchange of positions signals the beginning of mastery. Only then does student leadership appear, earned through sweat equity and the accumulation of a knowledge and research base. Initially, the mentor talks and the student listens; eventually, the student talks and the mentor listens.

Such arrangements do not occur only at the high-school level or only with exceptional students. At Rover Elementary School in Tempe, Arizona, former principal Sandra McClelland explored the future of education with various organizational theorists, not just by reading materials about education. The result is not just a student-centered but a student-driven school. Student leadership teams have replaced the student council to make basic structural and political decisions. A collaborative group of teachers, students, and administrators implements the school's vision and goals. Team learning is the dominant mode; older students mentor younger ones. There is a concerted search for financial supplements and greater independence from state funds; toward that end, teachers are given, are in control of, and are accountable for their classroom budget. Finally, a formal pedagogical partnership has been formed with Southwest Airlines: The school shares its effective and collaborative teaching strategies, Southwest its team management training. Clearly, Rover is a futures lab.

What to Expect from Education in 2025

Here are some of the most likely essential features of education by 2025.

- Education will be intensely decentralized, offering a significant number of choices to teachers, parents, and students.
- Increasingly, school and learning will be related to time rather than to place, available everywhere that there is connectivity 24 hours a day all year.
- Space and place for learning will exist for the community and no longer be reserved for the young.
- Increasingly, learners will become autonomous, almost totally free agents; nevertheless, they must earn their independence through mastery of prescribed knowledge bases.
- Cost controls and supplemental financing will steadily take hold as municipalities divert fed-

eral, state, and local funds away from education to other social crises such as health care and the aged. Education has at most only another 10 or 15 years as the favored focus of funding and attention.
- Increasingly, teachers will be at the center of administration, instruction, and evaluation; in some programs, they may replace principals.
- Horizontal collaboration among teachers, students, and parents—rather than vertical hierarchies—will characterize school governance. A commonality of vision and purpose will be arrived at and implemented collectively.
- Parents will become indispensable to effective learning. Very busy parents may hire parent surrogates as substitutes.
- Initially, business practices will only benefit education; eventually, educational innovations will provide models for business.
- Increasingly, minorities will take over educating minorities, mostly through charter schools. They will accomplish more through chosen rather than *de facto* segregation, and, in the process, save a whole generation of urban kids.

Irving H. Buchen is a business and education consultant. He serves on the doctoral faculty of the online Capella University and as senior research associate for EdVisions Cooperative and the Center for School Renewal in Minnesota. His address is 8650 Kilkenny Court, Fort Myers, Florida 33912. E-mail ibuchen@msn.com.

Originally published in the January/February 2003 issue of *The Futurist*, pp. 44-50. Copyright © 2003 World Future Society, 7910 Woodmont Avenue, Suite 450, Bethesda, MD 20814. Telephone: 301/656-8274; Fax: 301/951-0394; http://www.wfs.org. Used with permission from the World Future Society.

An Emerging Culture

RUDOLF STEINER'S CONTINUING IMPACT IN THE WORLD

by Christopher Bamford and Eric Utne

Beginning at the end of the 19th century, a relatively unknown Austrian philosopher and teacher began to sow the seeds of what he hoped would blossom into a new culture. The seeds were his ideas, which he sowed through extensive writings, lectures, and countless private consultations. The seeds germinated and took root in the hearts and minds of his students, among whom were individuals who would later become some of the best known and most influential figures of the 20th century. Since the teacher's death in 1925, a quiet but steadily growing movement, unknown and unseen by most people, has been spreading over the world, bringing practical solutions to the problems of our global, technological civilization. The seeds are now coming to flower in the form of thousands of projects infused with human values. The teacher, called by some "the best kept secret of the 20th century," was Rudolf Steiner.

Steiner, a truly "Renaissance man," developed a way of thinking that he applied to different aspects of what it means to be human. Over a period of 40 years, he formulated and taught a path of inner development or spiritual research he called "anthroposophy." From what he learned, he gave practical indications for nearly every field of human endeavor. Art, architecture, drama, science, medicine, economics, religion, care of the dying, social organization—there is almost no field he did not touch.

"My meeting with Rudolf Steiner led me to occupy myself with him from that time forth and to remain always aware of his significance. We both felt the same obligation to lead man once again to true inner culture. I have rejoiced at the achievements his great personality and his profound humanity have brought about in the world."

Albert Schweitzer

Today, wherever there is a human need you'll find groups of people working out of Steiner's ideas. There are an estimated ten thousand initiatives worldwide—the movement is a hotbed of entrepreneurial activity, social and political activism, artistic expression, scientific research, and community building. In this report we limit our investigation to a tiny, representative sampling of these initiatives, primarily from North America.

Waldorf Schools

EDUCATION FOR THE HEAD, HANDS, AND HEART

Waldorf education is probably the most widespread and mature of Steiner's many plantings. There are more than 150 Waldorf schools in North America and over 900 worldwide, double the number just a decade ago, making it possibly the fastest growing educational movement in the world. Steiner's interest in education was lifelong. As a young man, he earned a living as a tutor, starting at 14 helping fellow students. Then, from the age of 23 to 29, he lived in Vienna with the family of Ladislaus and Pauline Specht, undertaking the education of their four sons, one of whom, Otto, was hydrocephalic. At the age of 10, Otto could hardly read or write. His parents were uncertain whether he could be educated at all. Steiner took responsibility for him. Believing that, despite appearances, the boy had great intellectual capacities, Steiner saw his task as slowly waking the boy up and bringing him into his body. To do this, he knew he first had to gain the child's love. On this basis, he was able to awaken his dormant faculties. He was so successful that Otto went on to become a doctor.

Waldorf students create their own "main lesson books" for each subject.

For Steiner, Otto was a learning experience. As he says in his *Autobiography*: "The educational methods I had to adopt gave

Article 46. An Emerging Culture

Lao Tsu (604-531 BC) Tao Te Ching, Chapter 42

*The Tao begot one.
One begot two.
Two begot three.
And three begot
the ten thousand
things.*

Dear Reader,

Over the last 30 years I've encountered Rudolf Steiner's ideas in a number of different venues: as an active parent of four Waldorf-educated boys; as a natural foods merchant distributing Biodynamic® foods (grown according to Steiner's indications); as a truth seeker, struggling unsuccessfully to understand Steiner's dense and, for me, impenetrable writings; as a former architecture student intrigued by Steiner's contributions to 20th-century art and architecture; and, more recently, as the seventh and then eighth grade class teacher at City of Lakes Waldorf School in Minneapolis.

Despite all this exposure to the manifestations of his philosophy, I didn't begin to fathom Steiner's own thinking until several years ago when I began reading his writings in earnest. His language suffered from translation, was often time- and culture-bound, and frequently filled with archaic and new-agey references. Yet, as I kept at it, his ideas soon became more accessible and increasingly meaningful to me. After I "graduated" with my class in June 2002, I decided to meet some actual people whose lives had been touched by Steiner's ideas. Last summer, my 17-year-old son Oliver and I traveled 2,500 miles around Europe, visiting centers of Steinerian activity. In Järna, Sweden, we participated in an international youth conference for some 200 Waldorf-educated 16- to 30-year-olds from every race and 40 countries. In Dornach, Switzerland, we met the leadership of the worldwide General Anthroposophic Society, founded by Steiner. In other places we met people who have been involved in various aspects of Steiner's work for two or three generations. Since returning, I've been taking similar people-meeting excursions to the East and West Coasts.

What I've found is fascinating and heartening to me, and I wanted to share it with you. So I went to see the folks at the Rudolf Steiner Foundation and asked them to underwrite the costs of researching, writing, and publishing a special section on the continuing legacy of Rudolf Steiner. They turned around and raised the funds from private donors. My co-author of this section is Christopher Bamford, who has written widely on a variety of topics, including the recently published *What Is Anthroposophy?* (Anthroposophic Press, Great Barrington, Massachusetts) and "An Endless Trace: The Passionate Pursuit of Wisdom in the West" (Codhill Press, New York).

As you read the section I think you'll agree that the people influenced by Steiner's ideas are at least as interesting as the ideas themselves. Like the rest of society, they are a diverse lot. Some are well-scrubbed and impressively accomplished, like the actresses Jennifer Aniston and Julianna Margulies, and American Express president and CEO Kenneth Chenault, all of whom are Waldorf educated. Others, like me, are rather wacky, basically inept, unreconstructed idealists and malcontents. But then, I never had a Waldorf education!

The people involved in Steiner's ideas that I find most compelling are working within the framework of communities, in Waldorf schools, Biodynamic® farms, anthroposophical medical clinics, Camphill Villages for the handicapped, early childhood and elder-care centers, and artistic collaboratives. They're not isolated and alienated, stuck in institutions inhospitable to their values. They're developing the social skills necessary to form real, viable communities. If they study anthroposophy, Steiner's nonreligious path to self-knowledge, they're struggling to learn what we all sign on for in this human life—they're learning how to love.

There are an estimated ten thousand initiatives around the world that trace their lineage to Steiner and his ideas. These initiatives add up to an insurgent movement today that just may be the seedbed of a new, more just and humane emerging culture—the alternative that so many of us have been searching for all our lives. I believe these people, the heirs to Rudolf Steiner's legacy, are building, in our midst, a truly viable template for a greener and kinder world.

—Eric Utne

---

me insight into the way that the human soul and spirit are connected with the body. It became my training in physiology and psychology. I came to realize that education and teaching must become an art, and must be based upon true knowledge of the human being."

As with everything Steiner did, his curriculum for Waldorf education began with a question. In 1919, in the chaos following the First World War, Emil Molt, director of the Waldorf Astoria Cigarette Company, asked Steiner to help with the creation of a school for his workers. Four months later, the first Independent Waldorf School opened in Stuttgart, Germany. From that spontaneous beginning arose the now worldwide Waldorf School Movement.

Waldorf Education: It's All in the Curriculum

Whenever he visited a Waldorf school, Rudolf Steiner's first question to the students was always, "Do you love your teacher?" Similarly, he would ask the teachers, "Do you love your students?" The class teacher accompanies the children from first grade through eighth grade, i.e., from childhood into the beginning of adolescence. Children and teacher grow together. Making and doing, creating beauty, and working with one's hands—knitting, crocheting, painting, drawing, and woodworking—are an integral part of the educational and developmental process. Besides teaching manual dexterity and training eye-hand coordination, the work with color, form, and different materials develops an aesthetic sense, which permeates all other activities. Coordinated physical movement, learning through the body, accompanies all stages of development. The practice of Eurythmy—Steiner's art of movement, which makes speech and music visible through action and gesture—allows the child to develop a sense of harmony and balance. Rhythm is an important component of all these activities. Rhythm (order or pattern in time) permeates the entire school day, as well as the school year, which unfolds around celebrating festivals drawn from different religions and cultures.

"I loved school. I hated being sick because I didn't want to miss anything. I felt teachers cared about me so much, it gave me confidence. Now I feel there's nothing I can't do."

Jessica Winer '80,
artist

The curriculum is based upon an understanding of the developing child. From birth through ages six or seven, children absorb the world through their senses and respond primarily through imitation. As they enter the primary school years, they are centered more in feeling and imagination. Then, as they continue their journey into the middle school, rational, abstract thinking begins to emerge. The curriculum respects this developmental process and gives it substance. Based on the idea that "ontogeny recapitulates phylogeny," that a developing child goes through the phases of human cultural evolution, children at different ages study what is appropriate to their development. Thus they learn reading by first "becoming" the letters, through physical gesture. In their "main lesson" books that are their textbooks, crayoned pictures of mountains and trees metamorphose into the letters M and T, and form drawings of circles and polygons become numbers.

Most Waldorf kids actually like school and develop a real love of learning.

Movement, music, and language (including foreign languages) begin in first grade. They hear fables and stories of the holy ones of different cultures. They learn to knit and crochet and play the recorder. Leaving the "paradise" of the first two grades, they encounter the sacred teachings of their culture. For example, in North America, the stories of the Old Testament are taught. In Japan, ancient Shinto stories are told. Farming, gardening, house building, measurement, and grammar now enter the curriculum. They memorize poems and begin to play stringed instruments.

With the fourth grade comes mythology, embroidery, zoology, geography, and geometric drawing. Mathematics and languages become more complex; art becomes more representational. In the fifth grade, history enters; they recite poems, begin botany, learn to knit with four needles, and start woodworking. And thus it continues, each grade providing more wonders.

Rather than pursuing several subjects at a time, the Waldorf curriculum unfolds in main lesson blocks of three or four weeks. The students create their own texts, or "main lesson books" for each subject. This enables students to live deeply into the subject. In this age of distraction, Waldorf children learn to be able to concentrate and focus.

Students learn the alphabet by first discovering the forms of the letters in nature

With high school, the mood changes in harmony with the tremendous developmental changes occurring at this time. Students no longer havea class teacher, but specialists in different fields who teach the various blocks and encourage dialog and discussion. Exact observation and reflection are prized. The aim is to engage students in the present and build on the confidence and ability to think for oneself that developed in the lower grades.

Waldorf Schools in North America

Waldorf education in America developed almost imperceptibly. The first school was founded in New York in 1928 and, over the next 20 years, only six more schools were founded. But something had germinated and slowly began to spread. Looking back, the growth was steady. The number of schools more or less doubled every decade. The reasons for this success are not hard to find. Waldorf schools appeals to parents seeking a truly holistic, child-centered, loving, artistic, practical, and wonder-filled education.

An Example: The Green Meadow Waldorf School

The Green Meadow Waldorf School in Spring Valley, New York, founded in 1950, is one of the oldest Waldorf schools in North America. As you approach the wooded suburban enclave you realize that this is a different kind of school. The several buildings are clustered around a courtyard, forming a little campus, which in turn is surrounded by mature oaks and white ash. Gardens, large climbing logs and stones, and sculpture abound. Each building has its own character and form, yet the entire assemblage works as a whole. The colors are warm and natural, not bright. There's no graffiti. The roofs are shingled and gently sloped. Many of the walls are set at softer, more oblique angles. Even many of the windows have their rectangular shapes softened with another edge, making them five- or six-sided instead of just four-sided.

There is something peaceful in the air. The impression intensifies as you enter. Warmth pervades the space. Your senses begin to dance. Beauty, color, and natural flowing forms surround you. Children's paintings adorn the walls. Muffled sounds filter through the classroom walls and doors as you walk down a corridor. You can hear musical instruments, singing, children reciting a poem, the calm voice of a class teacher. And the smells! Bread baking in the kindergarten, fragrant plants and nontoxic paints. When you enter a classroom, the impression is confirmed—this is what a school ought to be. The children are happy, they are learning, they seem to love their teachers and each other.

"My parents... felt that the Waldorf school would be a far more open environment for African Americans.... I think the end result of Waldorf education is to raise our consciousness.... It taught me how to think for myself, to be responsible for my decisions. Second, it made me a good listener, sensitive to the needs of others. And third, it helped (me) establish meaningful beliefs."

Kenneth Chenault,
President & CEO,
American Express Corporation,
Waldorf alumnus

The Green Meadow School is home to a veritable United Nations of religious diversity. Of the 388 students (K–12) in Green Meadow, more than 60 are of Jewish descent, approximately 25 are the children of members of the nearby Jerrahi Islamic Mosque, and the rest come from Protestant, Catholic, Buddhist, agnostic, atheistic, and who-knows-what other religious traditions. Waldorf schools are sometimes assumed to be Eurocentric because of their European origins, yet the curriculum turns out to have universal appeal, adapting well in cultures as diverse as the *favelas* (slums) of Sao Paolo, Brazil, the black settlements of South Africa, rural Egypt and urban Israel, Eastern Europe, India, Southeast Asia, Australia, Japan, and the Pine Ridge Lakota Indian reservation in South Dakota.

Waldorf Graduates

Parents considering Waldorf want to know "What will become of my child?" According to Harm Paschen from the University of Bielefeld, Germany, studies of European Waldorf high school grads show that Waldorf graduates do very well indeed. Kids who go to Waldorf schools are as likely, or more likely, to attend college as students from public and other private schools. And after college, they are more likely to be employed than non-Waldorf grads. They are disproportionately well represented in teaching, the arts, business, medicine, and the social services professions. Similar research with North American grads is clearly needed.

On a recent college visit, Donna Badrig, associate director of undergraduate admissions for Columbia University, told one student, "We love Waldorf kids. We reject some students with 1600s on their SATs and accept others based on other factors, like the creative ability Waldorf students demonstrate." Similar enthusiasm for Waldorf grads was heard from admissions officers at Wesleyan University. City of Lakes Waldorf School (K–8) and Watershed High School (a new Waldorf charter school), both in Minneapolis, have seen their students go to such colleges at Sarah Lawrence, Juilliard, Wellesley, Hampshire, Wesleyan, and MIT, among others. But not all Waldorf grads go to college after high school. Many take a break from study to travel or do volunteer work before getting a job or going on to higher education.

Waldorf education is possibly the fastest growing educational movement in the world.

From our own observations, Waldorf students seem to share certain common characteristics. They are often independent and self-confident self-starters. They have genuine optimism for the future. They also tend to be highly ethical and are compassionately intelligent. They keep their sense of wonder about learning and the interdisciplinary sense that everything is connected. They seem to have a very healthy measure of what author Daniel Goleman calls "emotional intelligence," a much more reliable predictor of "success" in life, by any definition, than IQ or SAT scores. Generally speaking, they are both artistic and practical. They seem to know intuitively how to do many things.

Waldorf grad Paul Asaro, an architect, says: "I still draw upon the problem-solving skills that were nurtured... during my adolescent years." Other graduates stress independent thinking, imagination, and the relationships they developed and enjoyed with faculty and fellow students. "That's what's so wonderful about Waldorf education," says actress Julianna Margulies. "You're exposed to all these different ideas, but you're never given one view of it. You're encouraged to think as an individual." Rachel Blackmer, a veterinarian, writes: "Waldorf education is learning in its purest form. It is learning to think, to feel, and to act appropriately and with conscience." Mosemare Boyd, president and CEO, American Women Presidents, adds: "At Waldorf, we were taught to see things from the perspective of others. We saw that doing things together... was always more fun.... We learned to love learning."

Behind the Scenes

According to the Association of Waldorf Schools of North America (AWSNA), in the United States there are currently 56 full member Waldorf Schools, 15 sponsored Waldorf Schools (on their way to full membership), 69 developing Waldorf Schools, and 29 Waldorf Initiatives affiliated with AWSNA. Besides this there are a number of Waldorf-inspired or Waldorf method charter schools, as well as other Waldorf-related initiatives in the public schools.

"A Steiner education teaches you to think differently from the herd. I've found that independent ideas can be very valuable in the investment world."

David Nadel '87,
managing director,
Bear Stearns

Trained, qualified Waldorf teachers are much sought after. In North America each year, schools hire a combined total of between 300 and 400 new teachers, yet the various teacher-training centers graduate less than half that number. Many of the teachers are parents making a mid-life career change, perhaps seeking new challenges or a way to contribute to society. Robert Amis, who sold a successful equipment leasing company and took early retirement at 46, found himself accepting an offer to become a class teacher at City of Lakes Waldorf School in Minneapolis. "It's the hardest work I've ever done," he says. "I feel like I'm in a crucible, much the same as my students; and we're all wondering what changes are being wrought."

Side by Side, a leadership development program of Sunbridge College, trains 17-to 23-year-old youth who then facilitate weeklong arts and environmental overnight camps for underserved children ages 8 to 12 in New York and Los Angeles.

There are five full teacher-training centers: Rudolf Steiner College in Sacramento, California; Waldorf Institute of Southern California in Northridge, California; Center for Anthroposophy/Antioch Graduate School in Keene, New Hampshire; Sunbridge College in Spring Valley, New York; and Rudolf Steiner Center in Toronto, Ontario. In addition, there are two sponsored centers, one in Eugene, Oregon, and one in Detroit; and five developing centers—in Duncan, British Columbia; Sausalito, California; Honolulu; Chicago; and Seattle. And the Rudolf Steiner Institute, a summer school for adults and children, presently located at Thomas College in Waterville, Maine, provides a strong introduction to Waldorf education.

Waldorf in the Public Schools

According to George Hoffeker, former principal of the Yuba River Charter School in Nevada City, California, "Waldorf methods are so exciting and enlivening for all children that they shouldn't be reserved just for those who can afford it." Mary Goral, a professor at St. Mary College in Milwaukee and director of its early childhood education program, echoes this sentiment. She says, "I truly believe that what is needed in public schools is something much more like Waldorf, something that engages the whole child—body, soul, and spirit."

The first move in this direction began in September 1991 when the Milwaukee Urban Waldorf School opened—with 350 students, more that 90 percent of them African American—as part of the Milwaukee Public School System. Robert Peterkin, then superintendent of schools, had seen the need for a healthy education to serve the special needs of children in educationally deprived areas. Public school leaders, Waldorf educators, public school teachers, and scholars all worked together to found a school that would bring the integrated artistic, intellectual, and developmental Waldorf curriculum into the heart of an American city. Under the direction of Ann Pratt, an experienced Waldorf teacher, the experiment pioneered the development of an intensive teacher-training program for public school teachers. The result: reading scores increased and attendance stabilized. The school became a safe, quiet, well-ordered, attractive place to learn. A visitor recounted a telling anecdote. Waiting to see the principal, the visitor found himself seated opposite a student who was also waiting. According to the visitor, the student was, "threateningly large and had clearly committed some infraction. But there he sat outside the principal's office, quiet and self-composed, knitting."

Some publicly funded Waldorf schools are currently in transition. The Milwaukee experiment is still regrouping since losing founding principal Dorothy St. Charles to promotion. St. Charles' departure, combined with the school's move to "the worst zip code in Milwaukee," led to the loss of half its certified Waldorf teachers. The school, under the leadership of new principal Cheryl Colbert, is working with Cardinal Strich College to develop a teacher-training program to fill the need for certified Waldorf teachers. And the Sacramento school district, which operates a Waldorf-method magnet school, and the Twin Ridges Elementary School District of North San Juan, California, which operates seven Waldorf-inspired charter schools, including the first charter school in the United States to use Waldorf methods—the Yuba River Charter School—are in the midst of a court battle. The plaintiff's suit asserts that Waldorf education is religious in nature and that the two school districts are therefore in violation of the U.S. and California constitutional separation of church and state. The district court dismissed the suit, but on appeal, the circuit court gave the case new life, sending it back to district court.

"Society tells you that there is only one way to do things. Steiner students learn to create their own initiative and to be can-do thinkers."

Deborah Winer '79,
playwright

Opponents of Waldorf education, which is based on Steiner's insights into child development, equate the curriculum with anthroposophy, which they claim to be a religion. Waldorf advocates respond that Rudolf Steiner's anthroposophy is determinedly nonreligious and isn't taught in Waldorf schools anyway. The Waldorf curriculum stands on its own, they say, no matter what else Steiner taught or believed. "Anthroposophy is a founding philosophy, not a curriculum," says John Miller, a teacher at Watershed High School in Minneapolis. "Look at John Dewey, the educational reformer. Did anyone accuse his followers of teaching 'Deweyism'? No, because they just used a methodology he developed."

Critics also point to Steiner's early involvement in the Theosophical Society and to his more controversial views, such as his references to the lost continent of Atlantis. Several racist-sounding comments are often quoted to paint him as a racist. Waldorf's defenders say they reject racism out of hand. They say that Steiner was a person very much of his times, that his comments were made at the turn of the century, taken out of context, and are completely at odds with the vast preponderance of his statements having anything to do with race. They point out that many of Steiner's most reputable contemporaries shared beliefs with him that may appear today to be suspect or downright silly (Mahatma Gandhi was a member of the Theosophical Society, and Albert Einstein believed that Atlantis was a historical reality).

Despite the controversy, Waldorf-inspired charter schools are popping up all over the country. It is difficult to say just how many charter schools there are. Conservative estimates put the number at about 20 and growing. Though some fear a watering down of Steiner's principles, Donald Bufano, chairman of AWSNA, says, "Parents, and especially children at Waldorf or Waldorf-methods schools can enjoy the benefits of the education without commitment to its foundations just as one can enjoy Biodynamic® food or anthroposophic medicine whether or not they know how they work or where they come from."

Early Childhood Initiatives

The Waldorf approach to education is not limited to school-age kids. Recent students have pointed repeatedly to the critical importance of the nurturing children receive in early childhood, when infants and children are especially at risk. The combination of the breakdown of the family, the need for two working parents, and the growing number of single-parent families has left caregivers, whether at home or in daycare, uncertain how to care for children. Activities that were once natural and instinctive, like what to eat and how to bring up a baby, must now be learned consciously.

"Children," says Cynthia Aldinger, "are like sponges. They drink in everything and everyone around them." It is not only a question of the physical surroundings. What we say and do around a child, even how we think, is critical. A grassroots organization growing out of the Waldorf Early Childhood Association, Life Ways is devoted to the deinstitutionalization of child care. Founded in 1998, Life Ways provides courses and training in parenting and child care and is expanding to establish child care homes, centers, and parenting programs throughout North America.

A related effort is Sophia's Hearth in Keene, New Hampshire. Taking its name from the ancient goddess of wisdom, Sophia's Hearth works with "the art of becoming a family." As founder Susan Weber puts it, "Our work supports families in creating an atmosphere of loving warmth, joy, and respect for their infants and young children, while at the same time nurturing each parent."

The Caldwell Early Life Center at Rudolf Steiner College acts as a center for these and similar initiatives. Only two years old, but with a prestigious advisory board including naturalist Jane Goodall, well-known authors and researchers Jane Healy and Joseph Chilton Pearce, and education and child advocate Sally Bickford, it is halfway through raising the $2.5 million needed to complete a building to house its activities. These will cover the full range of early childhood needs, from working to reduce stress and isolation for families in ethnically and economically diverse neighborhoods to the creation of a demonstration daycare component.

Another Example: The Wolakota Waldorf School

In the early 1990s a group of Lakota Sioux educators began to look for a better education for their children and discovered Waldorf education. They found that it paralleled their own wisdom traditions in many ways. Their hope was to create not only a school but also eventually a model community. In 1993 they created the Wolakota Waldorf Society as a nonprofit organization.

The Wolakota School is located on 80 acres of the Pine Ridge Reservation, near Oglala Lakota College, in Shannon County, South Dakota, the poorest county in the United States. Pine Ridge, the site of the Wounded Knee massacre, has been home to many famous Native American leaders, including Black Elk, Chief Red Cloud, and Fool Crow. The school serves 24 Lakota children. Among Waldorf schools it is unique, depending entirely on donations. There are only two teachers, Susan Bunting and Chris Young, who do everything from cooking breakfast and lunch to transporting children. If funds and space can be found, Edwin Around Him, Sr., will be hired next year as the school's third teacher. This year Edwin teaches Lakota and operates the van, when it's working.

Sponsored by Rudolf Steiner Foundation and Utne Magazine

From *Utne Reader*, May/June 2003, pp. 1-14. © 2003 by Eric Utne and Christopher Bamford. Reprinted by permission of the authors.

Test Your Knowledge Form

We encourage you to photocopy and use this page as a tool to assess how the articles in *Annual Editions* expand on the information in your textbook. By reflecting on the articles you will gain enhanced text information. You can also access this useful form on a product's book support Web site at *http://www.dushkin.com/online/*.

NAME: DATE:

TITLE AND NUMBER OF ARTICLE:

BRIEFLY STATE THE MAIN IDEA OF THIS ARTICLE:

LIST THREE IMPORTANT FACTS THAT THE AUTHOR USES TO SUPPORT THE MAIN IDEA:

WHAT INFORMATION OR IDEAS DISCUSSED IN THIS ARTICLE ARE ALSO DISCUSSED IN YOUR TEXTBOOK OR OTHER READINGS THAT YOU HAVE DONE? LIST THE TEXTBOOK CHAPTERS AND PAGE NUMBERS:

LIST ANY EXAMPLES OF BIAS OR FAULTY REASONING THAT YOU FOUND IN THE ARTICLE:

LIST ANY NEW TERMS/CONCEPTS THAT WERE DISCUSSED IN THE ARTICLE, AND WRITE A SHORT DEFINITION:

We Want Your Advice

ANNUAL EDITIONS revisions depend on two major opinion sources: one is our Advisory Board, listed in the front of this volume, which works with us in scanning the thousands of articles published in the public press each year; the other is you—the person actually using the book. Please help us and the users of the next edition by completing the prepaid article rating form on this page and returning it to us. Thank you for your help!

ANNUAL EDITIONS: Education 05/06

ARTICLE RATING FORM

Here is an opportunity for you to have direct input into the next revision of this volume.
We would like you to rate each of the articles listed below, using the following scale:

1. **Excellent: should definitely be retained**
2. **Above average: should probably be retained**
3. **Below average: should probably be deleted**
4. **Poor: should definitely be deleted**

Your ratings will play a vital part in the next revision.
Please mail this prepaid form to us as soon as possible.
Thanks for your help!

RATING	ARTICLE	RATING	ARTICLE
	1. Public Schools; Public Will		28. True Blue
	2. Game Theory, Teen-Style		29. A Profile of Bullying
	3. Coming of Age in Consumerdom		30. An Unfinished Journey: The Legacy of *Brown* and the Narrowing Of the Achievement Gap
	4. Generational Pull		
	5. When I Was Young		31. Against the Tide: Desegregated High Schools and Their 1980 Graduates
	6. Is America Raising Unhealthy Kids?		
	7. The 36th Annual Phi Delta Kappa/Gallup Poll of the Public Attitudes Toward the Public Schools		32. Minding the Gap
			33. Civic Education in Schools: The Right Time is Now
	8. No Child Left Behind: The Mathematics of Guaranteed Failure		34. Partnering with Families and Communities
			35. Popular Culture in the Classroom
	9. Test Today, Privatize Tomorrow: Using Accountability to 'Reform' Public Schools to Death		36. Living and Teaching on the Edge of a Pop Culture World
	10. Leadership That Sparks Learning		37. At the Crossroads of Expertise: The Risky Business of Teaching Popular Culture
	11. Meeting Challenges in Urban Schools		
	12. Transforming High Schools		38. Healthier Students, Better Learners
	13. Reinventing America's Schools		39. The Arithmetic Gap
	14. A Balanced School Accountability Model: An Alternative to High-Stakes Testing		40. The Search for Highly Qualified Teachers
			41. The Other Side of Highly Qualified Teachers
	15. Turning Accountability on Its Head: Supporting Inspired Teaching in Today's Classrooms		42. The Marriage of Liberal Arts Departments and Schools of Education
	16. Accountability with a Kicker: Observations on the Florida A+ Accountability Plan		43. Building a Community of Hope
			44. Mission and Vision in Education
	17. No Flower Shall Wither; or, Horticulture in the Kingdom of the Frogs		45. Education in America: The Next 25 Years
			46. An Emerging Culture
	18. The Power of Testing		
	19. Why Students Think They Understand—When They Don't		
	20. The Homework Wars		
	21. Studying Education: Classroom Research and Cargo Cults		
	22. Practicing Democracy in High School		
	23. Values: The Implicit Curriculum		
	24. The Missing Virtue: Lessons From Dodge Ball & Aristotle		
	25. Heading Off Disruptive Behavior		
	26. How Disruptive Students Escalate Hostility and Disorder—and How Teachers Can Avoid It		
	27. Good Behavior Needs to Be Taught: How a Social Skills Curriculum Works		

(Continued on next page)

ANNUAL EDITIONS: EDUCATION 05/06

BUSINESS REPLY MAIL
FIRST CLASS MAIL PERMIT NO. 551 DUBUQUE IA

POSTAGE WILL BE PAID BY ADDRESEE

McGraw-Hill/Dushkin
2460 KERPER BLVD
DUBUQUE, IA 52001-9902

NO POSTAGE
NECESSARY
IF MAILED
IN THE
UNITED STATES

ABOUT YOU

Name   Date

Are you a teacher? ☐   A student? ☐
Your school's name

Department

Address   City   State

School telephone #

YOUR COMMENTS ARE IMPORTANT TO US!

Please fill in the following information:
For which course did you use this book?

Did you use a text with this ANNUAL EDITION?   ☐ yes   ☐ no
What was the title of the text?

What are your general reactions to the *Annual Editions* concept?

Have you read any pertinent articles recently that you think should be included in the next edition? Explain.

Are there any articles that you feel should be replaced in the next edition? Why?

Are there any World Wide Web sites that you feel should be included in the next edition? Please annotate.

May we contact you for editorial input?   ☐ yes   ☐ no
May we quote your comments?   ☐ yes   ☐ no